The Substance of Style

The Substance of Style

Perspectives on the American Arts and Crafts Movement

EDITED BY

Bert Denker

Henry Francis du Pont Winterthur Museum
WINTERTHUR, DELAWARE

Distributed by University Press of New England
HANOVER AND LONDON

Copy Editor: Onie Rollins
Production Editor: Susan Randolph

Library of Congress Cataloging-in-Publication Data

The substance of style : perspectives on the American arts and crafts
    movement / edited by Bert Denker.
        Papers from the 1990 Winterthur Conference.
        ISBN 0-912724-33-1
        1. Arts and crafts movement—United States.   I. Denker, Bert R.,
    1946–   .   II. Winterthur Conference (1990)
    NK1141.S8   1996
    745′.0973—dc20   95-20617
                                                                 CIP

Contents

Introduction

Bert Denker

Surprise was a common reaction when I proposed the topic "The Sub-stance of Style: Perspectives on the American Arts and Crafts Move-ment" for the 1990 Winterthur conference. While many researchers had come to Winterthur to study seventeenth-, eighteenth-, and early nineteenth-century decorative and fine arts, few were aware of the exceptional library collections of primary documentation for the later arts and crafts movement. As co-chair (with Cheryl Robertson), I envi-sioned the conference as an opportunity to highlight important library holdings such as the Gustav Stickley United Crafts enterprise business papers and photographs and the Rose Valley community archives. In addition, I wanted to emphasize the institution's commitment to the study of American material culture after 1860. The publication of these papers contributes to the realization of those goals, and I am indebted to the conference participants for their hard work, scholarship, and friendship and to Onie Rollins and Susan Randolph for their indispens-able assistance with the editing and production of this volume.

By 1990 the arts and crafts movement in America was a subject of increased interest. Building on exhibitions and catalogues that included Wendy Kaplan, *"The Art That Is Life": The Arts and Crafts Movement in America, 1875–1920* (Boston: Museum of Fine Arts, 1987) and Robert Judson Clark, ed., *The Arts and Crafts Movement in America, 1876–1916* (Princeton: Princeton University Press, 1972) as well as impressive regional studies such as Coy Ludwig, *The Arts and Crafts Movement in New York State, 1890s–1920s* (Hamilton, N.Y.: Gallery Association of New York State, 1983), scholars were exploring the broad boundaries of the movement. Winterthur's conference provided a forum for this research.

Several major themes emerged from the proposals for papers, defining the sessions of the conference and, now, this publication. To introduce the background and intellectual underpinnings of the arts and crafts movement and discuss style and ideology in national and international contexts, Nicola Gordon Bowe explores "The Search for Vernacular Expression: The Arts and Crafts Movements in America and Ireland." Her essay convincingly documents foreign influence on the American movement beyond the well-known English figures of John Ruskin, William Morris, and Christopher Dresser. "The Influence of C. R. Ashbee and His Guild of Handicraft on American Silver, Other Metalwork, and Jewelry," by W. Scott Braznell, examines the successes and failures of the revival of the medieval handicraft guild system in England and how American craft practices and marketing were affected.

Kathleen Eagen Johnson describes other European aspects of the movement in "Frans Hals to Windmills: The Arts and Crafts Fascination with the Culture of the Low Countries," while the essays by Melanie Herzog, "Aesthetics and Meanings: The Arts and Crafts Movement and the Revival of American Indian Basketry," and Lonn Taylor, "Arts and Crafts in the Santa Fe Style," reveal the importance of native American design and craft practices in the movement. Finally, "'One Who Has Seen More and Knows More': The Design Critic and the Arts and Crafts," by Beverly K. Brandt, traces the dialogue between craftsmen and critics, especially as it took place within the Society of Arts and Crafts, Boston.

The popularity of the mission style in arts and crafts products was fueled by the ability of large manufacturers to provide the marketplace with a wide array of consumer goods at attractive prices. Although the individual craftspersons, shops, and guilds may have been more in tune ideologically with the arts and crafts movement, American businessmen were quick to capitalize on the commercial aspects of the new aesthetic. This interaction between design and industry is investigated by Anna Tobin D'Ambrosio in "'The Distinction of Being Different': Joseph P. McHugh and the American Arts and Crafts Movement," which portrays McHugh as the quintessential entrepreneur, the self-proclaimed originator of American mission-style furniture. Donald A. Davidoff's contribution, "Maturity of Design and Commercial Success: A Critical Reassessment of the Work of L. and J. G. Stickley and Peter Hansen," examines another of the most influential and successful manufacturing firms as well as the impact of a single designer on its products. "The Bradley and Hubbard Manufacturing Company and the Merchandising of the Arts and Crafts Movement in America," by Richard Stamm, studies an established American manufacturer of metal goods that produced a wide range of household items; the company's role in the movement hinged on its dissemination of style rather than its philosophy. In contrast, Neville Thompson's "Louise Brigham: Developer of Box Furniture" discusses an individual's influence and her complete devotion to the principles and philosophy of the movement.

In addressing the redefinition of crafts techniques, Marcia Gail Anderson writes of the local guild approach to craft in "The Handicraft Guild of Minneapolis: A Model of the Arts and Crafts Movement." Michael L. James demonstrates in "Charles Rohlfs and 'The Dignity of Labor' " that the ideals of the English arts and crafts movement were carried into practice in American manufactories, and David B. Driscoll compares an American visionary to William Morris in "Henry Chapman Mercer: Technology, Aesthetics, and Arts and Crafts Ideals." Many traditional craftsmen in the United States found their markets dwindling as products were manufactured inexpensively by large companies. Ellen M. Snyder-Grenier illustrates Cornelius Kelley's adaptation to the new era in "Cornelius Kelley of Deerfield, Massachusetts: The Impact of Change on a Rural Blacksmith."

The essays that address the unification of the fine and decorative arts demonstrate that the dialogue among painters, sculptors, muralists, potters, ceramic decorators, and cabinetmakers contributed to a breakdown of old barriers. Ellen Paul Denker's "The Grammar of Nature: Arts and Crafts China Painting" chronicles the struggle of ceramic decorators to define themselves as artists. "American Tonalism and Rookwood Pottery," by Anita J. Ellis, draws on the author's extensive research into this preeminent American art pottery and investigates its artists' and designers' responses to contemporary trends in landscape painting. David Adams's contribution, "Frederick S. Lamb's Opalescent Vision of 'A Broader Art': The Reunion of Art and Craft in Public Murals," studies the revolution in stained glass window design and production and its role in Lamb's career as a public muralist. The decoration of furniture was popular in the British arts and crafts, and Catherine L. Futter examines the American response in " 'Color in the House': Painted Furniture of the American Arts and Crafts Movement."

One of the enduring legacies of the movement, that of community visions, is interpreted in the concluding essays of this publication. At the turn of the century, a broad range of community options, from planned suburbia to religious and social reform settlements, was available. Cleota Reed describes the synergy of businessmen and women and educators in "'Near the Yates': Craft, Machine, and Ideology in Arts and Crafts Syracuse, 1900–1910." In "The Monastic Ideal in Rural Massachusetts: Edward Pearson Pressey and New Clairvaux," Jeannine Falino details this utopian arts and crafts community that, like others, provided a focus for the philosophical idealism and reform craftsmanship of the movement. Bryn Athyn, Pennsylvania, home to a group of high-church Swedenborgians, employed craft as a means to a religious end and is discussed in "The Bryn Athyn Cathedral Project: Craft, Community, and Faith," by Shelley K. Nickles. The suburban ideal, a still-viable dream of millions of Americans, is defined in Mary Corbin Sies's "George W. Maher's Planning and Architecture in Kenilworth, Illinois: An Inquiry into the Ideology of Arts and Crafts Design." Entrepreneurial spirit also drove Edward G. Lewis, who founded arts and crafts communities in University City, Missouri, and Atascadero, California. The final contribution, "Midwest to California: The Planned Arts and Crafts Community," by Karen J. Weitze, analyzes capitalist and socialist impulses in the reformation of American communities.

Although these papers represent but a sampling of emerging scholarly research on the arts and crafts movement in America, they do clearly demonstrate a willingness to seek the truth in the details of individuals and their ideals and accomplishments. Broad historical movements and their consideration in the past or present frequently obscure the messiness of reality. It is as natural for the social reformer as for the historian to direct and organize ideas and events, but nothing pleases me more than the acknowledgment of disorder and conflict in achievement. That affirmation will always provide a new perspective on "the substance of style."

The Search for Vernacular Expression
The Arts and Crafts Movements in America and Ireland

Nicola Gordon Bowe

Embodied in the arts and crafts movement is the idealistic search for an aesthetically and morally satisfactory environment.[1] Even if the basic ideology remains more or less constant, this search varies in conception, execution, and realization. Some factors involved include the galvanization and organization of labor; leadership; patronage; the education, motivation, and skills of craftsmen and women; and the availability and relevance of reconciling local materials, retail and market outlets, and exhibition facilities as well as economic, national, and ethnic differences. The expression of style frequently seems to be less important than contextual integrity and the "honest" use of materials.

The search for vernacular expression was an intrinsic part of the national romantic spirit that prevailed by the end of the nineteenth century. This spirit had been fueled by visionary and revolutionary writers, poets, political leaders, archaeologists, and utopian socialists throughout the century. When Gustav Stickley's magazine, *The Craftsman*, featured articles on the Franciscans in California, medieval guilds

---

[1] As incorporated by Gustav Stickley into the subtitle of his monthly magazine, *The Craftsman*, inaugurated in 1901, "In the Interest of Better Art, Better Work, and a Better and More Reasonable Way of Living."

and their revival, American Indian folk art and song, and even African
American music—in his eclectic pursuit of "a national art based on
sound aesthetic and economic principles"—and when Oscar Lovell
Triggs at the same time, among the products of "art and labour" in
the Chicago Industrial Art League's salesroom, stressed the inclusion
of Indian goods "all of genuine native manufacture,"[2] the two were
emulating Thomas Carlyle, John Ruskin, and William Morris in the
wake of the Massachusetts transcendentalists such as Ralph Waldo Emerson and Henry David Thoreau.

In California, Charles Lummis's exemplary collection of Native
American artifacts in his Southwest Museum (opened 1914, although
its association was founded in 1903) revealed the romantic pioneering
spirit expressed in his home, El Alisal (begun in 1895). As Robert
Winter has noted in a discussion on why southern Californians were
so interested in the Spanish/Mexican past, "Lummis was . . . a Romantic seeking the resurrection of a past that never really existed."[3] It is
ironic in the context of this article that El Alisal bears a marked resemblance to those Irish peasant dwellings that the Labourers' Act of 1906
sought to replace with model cottages. Similarly, Clyde Browne's Abbey San Encino (begun in 1909, completed in 1925) celebrated an
eclectic fusion of Mexican, mission, arroyo boulder, and Morris idi-
oms, just as Morris and his colleagues had sought to preserve and
extend English native skills and traditions. Browne's incorporation of
fanciful contemporary expressions of the Californian past (such as the
Judson Studios' stained glass roundel of a Franciscan teaching an Indian to print on a Kelmscott-inspired handpress) into the dressed boul-
ders of his architectural gem finds echoes in the Hiberno-Romanesque
revival Honan Chapel (1913–17) in Cork, Ireland, a punched ashlar

    [2] Gustav Stickley, Foreword, *The Craftsman* 1, no. 1 (October 1901): ii. "The
Industrial Art League," *House Beautiful* (February 1902), reprinted in Oscar Lovell
Triggs, *Chapters in the History of the Arts and Crafts Movement* (Chicago: Bohemia
Guild of the Industrial Art League, 1902), p. 195.
    [3] Robert W. Winter, "The Arroyo Culture," in *California Design, 1910*, ed. Timo-
thy J. Andersen, Eudorah M. Moore, and Robert W. Winter (Salt Lake City, Utah:
Peregrine Smith, 1980), p. 16. For a later, small-scale Californian boulder/mission
interpretation of an Irish theme, Blarney Castle (ca. 1925) in Tujunga, see David Geb-
hard and Robert W. Winter, *Architecture in Los Angeles* (Layton, Utah: Gibbs Smith,
1985), p. 333.

paraphrase studded with Celto-Byzantine stained glass, enamels, and embroidery.

Endeavors to preserve, protect, record, or incorporate ancient or disappearing structures and techniques reworked in a modern idiom could result in arts and crafts follies like the above Californian ones or in Henry Chapman Mercer's three recycled masterpieces: his purpose-built concretions of Fonthill, his Moravian Pottery and Tile Works, and the Museum of Tools of the Nation Maker, reflecting the local folk decoration of Pennsylvania German settlers. Such collections, often initially dismissed as "junk collecting" by nostalgic hoarders or archaeological scavengers in America and Europe, now form the bases of national museums and anthropological studies, providing a vital source for contemporary craftspersons and artists as well as a link with a preindustrial past from which we feel increasingly alienated.

For some nations, the rediscovery, collection, and careful investigation of folk arts and crafts had a further significance. They provided an elemental link with a rustic, precolonial, nonimperialist past and a refreshingly simple design vocabulary of political expediency and uncomplicated popular appeal. In Finland, Norway, Poland, Russia, Hungary, and Ireland, for example—all struggling for political and cultural independence at the turn of this century—the expression of style through appropriate forms, images, and materials assumed a particular urgency, erupting in revolution and national upheaval.[4]

The Celtic dimension, whether Irish or Scottish, was perceived in various guises during the period, depending on political and cultural persuasions. When Oscar Wilde swept America in 1882 with his Ruskin-inspired lectures, among his most fervent admirers was Alice Pike Barney. Her 1902 mission-style house, furnished with Cincinnati art-carving–class furniture, Tiffany glass, and tiles from the Moravian Pottery and Tile Works, became a cultural center in Washington, D.C., where she also established a neighborhood settlement house. Although Wilde's fickle brand of aestheticism was nurtured in Ireland by his parents' intellectual involvement in the earlier years of the nationalist movement, it was only during his American tour "that he rediscovered himself as an Irishman." His eccentric lectures "The House Beautiful"

---

[4] See Nicola Gordon Bowe, ed., *Art and the National Dream: The Search for Vernacular Expression in Turn-of-the-Century Design* (Dublin: Irish Academic Press, 1993).

and "The Decorative Arts" constituted the most determined and sustained attack upon materialistic vulgarity that America had seen.[5]

Against the immense industrial wealth of the United States ("far richer per capita than England"), where Morris had lamented the inevitability of his artwork's appeal to the idle rich, the American protagonists of an arts and crafts ideology sought to "substitute the luxury of taste for the luxury of costliness" through "co-operation and constructive socialism"; and to replace the jumbled "coarse, crude, gilt and gaudy displays of wealth" of American "parvenu" and English "bourgeois" taste with the handcraft of simple, self-sufficient, and harmonious endeavor. Altruism was invoked as a remedy for conspicuous consumption. For the many who responded—especially women, often of elevated backgrounds—such style as they sought might relate to the ethnic mix of the workforce they recruited but more likely to the ideals of utility, simplicity, and beauty/enthusiasm versus apathy rather than to the "vagaries of fashion." An object could be in the name or period of Paul Revere in Boston, be based on a Swiss chalet, adobe hut, Californian Franciscan mission, or of Japanese or art nouveau inspiration anywhere on the North American continent, but as long as the ideology was sound and the materials revealed and defined their intended form and function, the goal was reached. For devotees, this involved seeking "harmony with nature and a retreat from the reality of an economy of exploitation." "In spite of [the arts and crafts movement's] great contribution to the practical in the applied arts," it "was first and foremost a spiritual crusade and had the weaknesses as well as the strengths of a religious revival."[6]

Sources (and outlets) for the philosophy were the often short-lived art magazines, exhibitions, applied-art museums and schools, workshops, classes, and industries that proliferated on both sides of the Atlantic and had a common root in the international art industrial expositions between 1880 and 1914. As Alan Crawford has pointed

[5] Richard Ellmann, *Oscar Wilde* (London: Hamish Hamilton, 1988), pp. 185, 195.
[6] On the quoted philosophies, see Elbert Hubbard, *The Roycroft Shop—A History* (East Aurora, N.Y.: Roycroft Press, 1908), p. 4; Stickley, Foreword, pp. i, ii; Elbert Hubbard, *The Book of the Roycrofters* (East Aurora, N.Y.: Roycroft Press, 1907), p. 12. Gustav Stickley, "Textiles Old and New," *The Craftsman* 1, no. 4 (January 1902). Winter, "Arroyo Culture," p. 16. Robert W. Winter, "Arts and Crafts as a Social Movement," *Princeton University Art Museum Record* 34, no. 2 (1975): 36–40.

out, however, original arts and crafts associations formed part of an axiomatic visual style with common fundamental qualities but no strictly definable design features.[7]

During the course of the movement in Ireland, artists/craftworkers alternated between inspiration from the styles of the two outstanding periods in the country's artistic heritage: early Christian Romanesque and eighteenth-century Georgian. A romantic symbolist mythological iconography comes a close third. This disparity of stylistic influence posed a dilemma when the design was weak and the concept unclear, but the work of two founding members of the Arts and Crafts Society of Ireland (ACSI), Sir Edward Sulevan (bookbinder, scholar, and collector) and Edmond Johnson (jeweler and silversmith) was only strengthened by their knowledge and imaginative synthesis of these two periods in a modern idiom.[8]

Nobody understood the complexities of Irish-American attitudes better than Sir Horace Plunkett, rural reformer and founder of the Irish cooperative movement. In 1889, after ten years in the United States, the idealistic but shrewd Irish aristocrat returned to Ireland to "design and effect a comprehensive scheme for the regeneration of country life based on the twin pillars of cooperation and education"—this in a land torn by sectarian and political conflict and scarred by famine, educational and industrial poverty, and emigration. His Irish Agricultural Organization Society, founded in 1894, and its journal, *Irish Homestead* (1895), regarded agriculture as an industry, a business, and a way of life whose enlightened organization could positively transform the life of the community, so long officially neglected by British rule. With the Gaelic League (founded in 1893), the Sinn Fein party (founded in 1905), and the literary and arts revivals, Plunkett's work was widely considered the best hope for Ireland's realistic future. George "AE" Russell, artist, poet, agrarian reformer, and key Irish arts and crafts figure, saw that "the problem of creating an organic life in Ireland, a harmony of our people, a union of their efforts for the common good and for the manifestation of whatever beauty, majesty,

[7] Alan Crawford, paper delivered at the symposium "The Arts and Crafts Movement in America," Museum of Fine Arts, Boston, April 11, 1987.

[8] See Nicola Gordon Bowe, "The Arts and Crafts Movement in Ireland," *Antiques* 142, no. 6 (December 1992): 864–75.

and spirituality is in us, must be one we ourselves must solve for ourselves." Plunkett shared contemporary concerns "that if Irish traditions, language, art, music, and culture are allowed to disappear, it will mean the disappearance of the race" and insisted that education be nationalized. Thus, in 1901 he inaugurated educational competitions among rural cooperatives. His many lively schemes included his trusteeship of countrywide libraries funded by the Carnegie U.K. Trust. Theodore Roosevelt, his enthusiastic supporter since 1895, wrote, "I wish you were an American and in the senate or my cabinet . . . You take an interest in just the problems which I regard as vital, and you approach them in what seems to me the only sane and healthy way." Roosevelt continued, "We Americans owe much to Ireland and to Plunkett in the task we have been trying to do in the United States."[9]

The Gaelic League, to which a number of early Irish art industries owed their inception, was well publicized in America in its campaign to revive native Irish language, literature, folk, and music traditions. Its spirit was evoked by the best-known apostle of the Irish revival, the poet W.B. Yeats. An enraptured disciple of Morris in London, he was seen as leading the "handful of men and women who . . . dare to face this age of steam and steel with the vision of the soul." In 1901, the year before he encouraged his sisters to join Evelyn Gleeson, nationalist, suffragist, painter, and carpet designer, in returning to Ireland to set up the Dun Emer Guild—an idealistic Morrisian venture of Celtic inspiration and one of the most successful Irish arts and crafts workshops—he made an evocative appeal. He urged Irish writers, painters, and craftsmen "to move hearts in every cottage" by giving visual expression to the "wild beauty" of their landscape and its legends, to "re-create the ancient arts . . . as they were understood when they moved a whole people and not a few people who have grown up in a leisured class and made this understanding their business." Yeats's renown in

[9]Theodore Roosevelt to Horace Plunkett, 1906, quoted in Trevor West, *Horace Plunkett, Cooperation and Politics* (Washington, D.C.: Catholic University Press, 1986), p. 133. Roosevelt, about Plunkett, 1909, in West, *Horace Plunkett,* p. 134. Plunkett's second book, *The Rural Life Problem of the United States* (New York: Macmillan, 1910), set his philosophy in an America context. For more on Plunkett, see West, *Horace Plunkett,* p. 3. Horace Plunkett, *Ireland in the New Century* (London: John Murray, 1904), p. 150. *Sinn Fein* means "we ourselves," the original motto of the 1882 Irish Industries Exhibition. George Russell, *The National Being—A Design for Developing Ireland* (Dublin: Maunsel, 1916), p. 172.

America and the support of the Yeats family's patron, New York lawyer, bibliophile, and collector John Quinn, undoubtedly helped the sale and exhibition of his sisters' work for their subsequent Cuala Industries (1908–40), whether in embroidered textiles, handpainted wooden items, or hand printing and binding.[10] Yeats's interest in traditional forms was expressed through Thor Ballylee, the Norman tower house in County Galway, which was restored and furnished for him in 1916 by the outstanding revivalist architect, William A. Scott.

The profound involvement of Yeats and Russell in hermetic religion, magic, and occult philosophy inspired two American women who spent a number of formative and deeply committed years in Ireland. In 1901 Pamela Coleman Smith's involvement with the Celtic revival led to her theater designs; her collaboration with Yeats on hand-colored graphics for *A Broad Sheet* (1901–2), her publishing and illustration of *Green Sheaf* magazine (1903–4); her creation of greeting cards, hand printed by Elizabeth Yeats, and one of twenty-four embroidered banners, *St. Brigid* (1902–4), worked in silk and wool on linen by Lily Yeats for Lough Rea Cathedral, Galway, at the Dun Emer Guild. Stickley embraced the "wild fancy" of Smith's 1907 exhibition at Alfred Stieglitz's first painting show in his pioneering New York Photo-Secession Gallery and published her liberating thoughts and her "Fairy Faith and Pictured Music." Ella Young, another zealous spiritualist, Celtic nationalist, and actress, transferred her involvement with the Irish cause to that of the Mexican Indians after her politics forced her to emigrate in 1925. She also documented the arts and crafts metalwork and jewelry of the St. Louis-born but Dublin-based Mia Cranwill, which illustrated lines from ancient and contemporary symbolic myth and poetry. In America, Cranwill's enameled monstrance, sanctuary lamp (fig. 1), candlesticks, cope clasp, and ornamental mounts framing Joseph Tierney's illuminated cards for Saint Patrick's Church in San

[10] On Yeats, see Eugenia Brooks Frothingham, "An Irish Poet and His Work," *The Critic* 44 (January 1904): 26–31. William Butler Yeats, "Ireland and the Arts," *United Irishman*, August 3, 1904. "Quinn arranged for a display and sale in the fall [1905] of the sisters' goods at the Irish Industrial Exhibition in New York and achieved good sales by badgering his friends and acquaintances. He also advised his American friends to visit Dun Emer when they traveled abroad" (William Murphy, *Prodigal Father—The Life of John Butler Yeats, 1839–1922* [Ithaca, N.Y.: Cornell University Press, 1978], p. 287).

[11] *Green Sheaf* was published in London and New York. On Yeats, see Gustav Stickley, "Als Ik Kan," *The Craftsman* 9 (March 1907): 768–71. Pamela Coleman Smith, "A Protest Against Fear," *The Craftsman* 9 (March 1907): 728; Pamela Coleman Smith,

Francisco are major expressions of the latter period of the Irish movement.[11]

In 1893, the year before the ACSI was founded, Irish industries had first featured prominently at the Chicago World's Columbian Exposition, mainly due to the energy and fund-raising efforts of the well-connected Lady Aberdeen (Vicereine in Ireland in 1886 and 1905–15). Her inclusion of Irish lace, crochet, needlework, and rural handcrafts in the Women's Home Industries section at the 1886 Edinburgh International Exhibition of Industry, Science, and Art had led her to establish the Irish Industries Association. By 1891 its countrywide activities were expanded by sales depots in London and Dublin; a charitable fund; and philanthropic, educational, and critical reorganization. With financial surety from influential friends such as Andrew Carnegie, Marshall Field, and Gordon Selfridge (author of the Ruskin-inspired *Romance of Commerce* [1918]), and the backing of the Chicago press, Lady Aberdeen's Irish village at the exhibition netted £50,000 worth of sales, enough to fund a team of girls and establish an Irish Industries depot in Chicago. The venture successfully revealed the quality, extent, and possibilities of Ireland's craft industries against a setting of reconstructed Irish historical monuments and artifacts, featuring Lady Aberdeen (fig. 2) spinning at her wheel, in contrived "Celtic" dress and paradoxical emulation of the virtues of authentic native domestic craftsmanship.[12]

Lady Aberdeen's election of the enlightened town planner and civic-housing theorist, John Nolen of Cambridge, Massachusetts, to join Patrick Geddes and, later, Raymond Unwin in advising on Dublin's urban development as it battled with strikes, slums, and high-density tenement dwellings, was further proof of her American experience. Similarly, her scheme of anti-tuberculosis Christmas Health and Wealth stamps in 1909, designed by Elizabeth Yeats, was based on a successful American Red Cross Christmas stamp initiative in Delaware in 1907 and 1908, for which Howard Pyle had provided the stamp

---

"Should the Art Student Think?" *The Craftsman* 9 (March 1907): 728; 14 (1908): 417–19. *The Craftsman* 23 (1912): 20–34. Ella Young, "An Artist in Metal," *Dublin* 1, no. 6 (January 1924): 549–51. Young's autobiography, *Flowering Dusk* (New York and Toronto: Longmans, Green, 1945), features her photographic portrait by Ansel Adams. Tierney became a member of the Society of Arts and Crafts, Boston, in 1926.

[12] The entire exhibit of Dublin jeweler and silversmith Edmond Johnson's work was purchased by the University of Chicago for its collection.

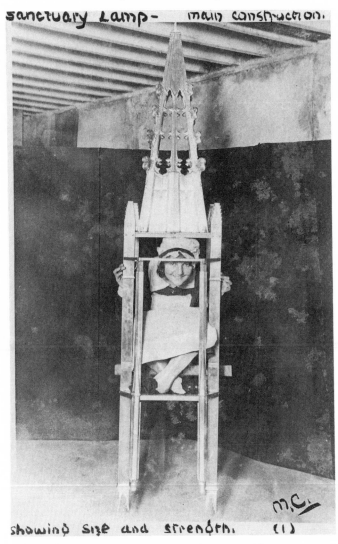

Fig. 1. Mia Cranwill, sanctuary lamp, Dublin, 1927–31. Bronze with enamels; H. 7′, W. 20″, D. 20″. (Saint Patrick's Church, San Francisco.)

Fig. 2. Lady Aberdeen at the 1893 Chicago World's Columbian Exposition. (Lady Pentland.)

design. By 1911 Lady Aberdeen's Women's National Health Association of Ireland (1907) had influential supporting committees in New
York and Detroit. Her journal, *Sláinte* (Health, in Irish) recorded international, particularly American, advances in health, hygiene, and
housing. In 1916 she wrote effective fund-seeking articles in the *Yale
Review* and *Outlook* on giving "the children of Ireland a better chance
for life, health and happiness."

Lady Aberdeen's was not the only Irish village in Chicago; another, also set in a multicultural context, demonstrated the output of
the famine-relief Donegal Industrial Fund, set up in 1883 by Mrs.
Ernest Hart, editor of the English *House Beautiful* and the wife of an
eminent English physician and collector of Japanese art. The fund's
hand-spun, dyed, woven, and knitted goods and acclaimed "Kells Embroidery" (called after the early Christian illuminated manuscript the
Book of Kells, first reproduced in 1845) had already led to a commission
for Celtic-inspired curtains from Louis C. Tiffany's and Candace
Wheeler's Associated Artists of New York in 1886.[13]

Donegal became synonymous with the Irish industry best known
in America when in 1898 the enlightened Scots carpet manufacturer,
Alexander Morton, and the Congested Districts Board set up a series
of carpet factories using local, skilled, low-paid labor to produce hand-
tufted carpets. Designs were adapted from "Turkey" rugs and carpets
or to suit clients' specifications and occasionally were based on works
of a well-known artist, such as C. F. A. Voysey, but always "with broad
effects and well blended coloring" that brought them "into complete
harmony with the CRAFTSMAN scheme of furnishing." Stickley
stocked and ordered the carpets in his New York Craftsman Workshops
and featured an account of them in the third issue of *The Craftsman*
as exemplifying "honesty of material, beautiful color and fine qualities
of design." The huge carpets were a feature of the early exhibitions of
the ACSI until 1910, when the formation of the Guild of Art Workers
led to individual craftsman displays rather than those of collective industries. While manifestly of an arts and crafts aesthetic, it was their
manufacture, quality, and ethos rather than specifically "Celtic" design

[13] Priscilla Leonard, "The Christmas Stamp in America," *Outlook* (October 3,
1908), reprinted in *Sláinte* 1, no. 1 (November, 1909): 198–99. Lady Aberdeen, "Help-
ing Ireland to Help Herself," *Outlook* (March 29, 1916): 761–66; Paul Larmour, *The
Arts and Crafts Movement in Ireland* (Belfast: Friars Bush Press, 1993), p. 26.

that represented a major achievement in the Irish art industries movement. The same is true of the smaller and shorter-lived Abbey Leix carpet industry, which nonetheless provided carpets for the ill-fated *Titanic*.

Because Ireland was not a separate political entity in 1904, she could not have a national pavilion at the Louisiana Purchase International Exposition in St. Louis. The recently formed, progressive Department of Agriculture and Technical Instruction set up an Irish Exhibit Company to arrange an ambitious "village" that featured Irish and Irish-American historic loan collections; the department's promotion of home and cottage industries, education, and arts and crafts; a medley of facsimile historic monuments from outstanding periods of architecture in Ireland; and an industrial hall, "Norman-Irish in style and decoration."[14] Of note in the Artistic Handicraft section were the Liverpool Della Robbia Art Pottery's Irish clay pieces with Celtic decoration; the Keswick and Guild of Handicraft–inspired art metalwork from Fivemiletown, County Tyrone; Oswald Reeves's Alexander Fisher–inspired enamel work; Turkey-based rugs from Abbey Leix and Kildare; and a range of books, rugs, embroidery, tapestry, and fans from the Dun Emer Guild.

The Dun Emer Guild work was of mixed inspiration: Lily Yeats had spent from 1886 to 1894 in May Morris's London embroidery shop, and her sister Elizabeth taught art in London until she took a course at the London Women's Printing Society rather than paint furniture, as she had intended. Gleeson's main influences were Alexander Millar, a Morris disciple and carpet designer for Templeton's of London and Glasgow; her father's philanthropic Athlone Woolen Mills; the London women's Pioneer Club; and a Yeatsian utopian socialist dream of a new Ireland. Her early designs evoke a typically eclectic mix of Navajo, fifteenth-century Flemish, Celtic zoomorphic, and the pan-mythological, always adhering to fundamental arts and crafts principles of production. Her colors were intended to evoke the Irish landscape. Designs for much of Yeats's work (fig. 3) were provided by her sister, brother Jack, and his wife, Mary Cottenham. When not the

[14]Gustav Stickley, *Craftsman Fabrics and Needlework from the Craftsman Workshops* (1905; reprint, Madison, Wis.: Razmataz Press, 1989), pp. 96–97. "A New Irish Industry," *The Craftsman* 1 (December 1901): 34–39. *Irish Industrial Exhibition, World's Fair, St. Louis, 1904* (Dublin: D.A.T.I., 1904), p. 12.

Fig. 3. Lily Yeats (*second from right*) in the embroidery workshop at Dun Emer, Dundrum, County Dublin, Ireland, 1905. (Anne Yeats.)

distinctively graphic images of the latter two, the designs show parallels with the textiles of the Glasgow and Hungarian schools and the internationally prevalent style as seen in shops like Liberty's, where they were exhibited.

Although Elizabeth Yeats modeled her Dun Emer Press on the Doves, Kelmscott, and Chiswick presses, with advice from Emery Walker, Sydney Cockerell, and W. B. Yeats, she stated in her first prospectus that the press had "been founded in the hope of reviving" the "beautiful craft" and art of book printing, "little practised since the 18th century in Ireland." She deliberately chose "a good 18th century fount of type," clear and easy to read, and paper "made of linen rags and without bleaching chemicals." In doing so, she achieved "a distinctive quality which commercial imitators on both sides of the Atlantic failed to capture." In 1903 Yeats wrote to her from New York, discussing "the work of other presses . . . in particular the publications of the Roycrofters at East Aurora, New York" as possible models. Several special Dun Emer bindings produced circa 1904 by Norah Fitzpatrick show a marked similarity to those of the Roycrofters in their limp suede and vellum with yapp edges and silk ties, while Fitzpatrick's finely tooled leather bindings resemble those of her American contemporary, Ellen Gates Starr, who had studied under T. J. Cobden-Sanderson at the Doves Bindery.

Unfortunately the rug inspired by the swirling water on the Atlantic sea voyage from St. Louis, conceived by the honorary secretary and organizer of the Irish arts and crafts exhibit, T. W. Rolleston, was only realized on his return home. Rolleston was a perceptive critic in the national search for style and form in the early years of this century: "Study the arts of the past, above all those of your own land, but remember that you do not live in the times of Brian Boru, but of Mr. Edison. Recollect that the decorative artist has primarily to decorate objects of utility. See that they are fit to be used and that the decorative never interferes with the object."[15]

Rolleston refuted the common perception of the Celtic style in art: "The true Celtic art was of a simple . . . and refined character. There is no trace of interlacing in [its] beautifully modulated curves . . . All the traditional forms of art have been so jostled together and blurred in our minds by . . . museums, books and travel . . . that their purity and distinction are lost beyond recall. The age of tradition and authority is past . . . and the central art of the time will be done by workers of strong artistic personality who will work to please themselves . . . and not to assert . . . whatever . . . may have come to them from the past . . . Be rough if you must, but be strong. Above all things, be *yourself* . . . Don't imitate; don't conceal the qualities of your material."[16]

Sophia St. John Whitty, one of several skilled lady woodcarvers, echoed Rolleston's views: "Because people have been content to copy the work of their neighbours, they have lost the intimate touch of realism. That is the life-spring of true art, and only by going back to learn the nature-history of our own lands will national art be possible again."[17]

The ACSI's fourth exhibition, in 1910, showed considerable improvement, largely due to restructured art schools and several art indus-

[15] On E. Yeats, see Liam Miller, *The Dun Emer Press, Later the Cuala Press* (Dublin: Dolmen Press, 1973), p. 32. W. B. Yeats is quoted in Miller, *Dun Emer Press*, p. 35. C. H. Rolleston, *Portrait of an Irishman* (London: Methuen, 1939), p. 8.

[16] T. W. Rolleston, "Art Work at Irish Exhibitions," *Journal and Proceedings of the Arts and Crafts Society of Ireland* (Dublin, 1906), pp. 278–87.

[17] S. J. Whitty, "The Development of National Art," *Journal and Proceedings of the Arts and Crafts Society of Ireland* (Dublin, 1906), p. 277.

tries, mostly initiated and sustained by women with design backgrounds. Notable were Mary Montgomery's Fivemiletown Art Metal Industry, Florence Vere O'Brien's Limerick Lace and Clare Embroidery (with clear affinities to the Deerfield Society of Blue and White Needlework), Gleeson's Dun Emer Guild, the Yeats sisters' Cuala Industries, St. John Whitty's Bray Art Woodcarvers and Furniture Industry, Lady Mayo's Naas Co-operative Home Industries and Royal Irish School of Art Needlework, and Sarah Purser's stained glass cooperative, An Túr Gloine (tower of glass). The versatile sculptress Beatrice Elvery also exhibiting with Cuala and An Túr, was judged, along with the metalwork and stained glass classes at the Dublin Metropolitan Art School, to strike the note of skilled, imaginative, native expression so avidly sought.

The Irish revivalists encouraged those skills historically associated with Irish art patronage: sculpture, plasterwork, needlework, metalwork, carved wood, jewelry. Stained glass, although with no long historical precedent, was seen to incorporate the ancient skills of metalwork, jewelry, enameling, and architecture at a time when the native craft had fallen to particularly low levels because of increasing foreign competition. Curiously, jewelry tended to be incidental—white metals, semiprecious or nonprecious stones, and enamels favored—partly due to lack of enlightened, moneyed patronage and to an innate conservatism in all but revivalist clothing. Three-dimensional design of scale or function tended to be weak, as were most graphics and ceramics, none being a priority on the educational syllabus. The most original ceramicists, Elvery, Rosamond Praeger, and Kathleen Cox, used clay sculpturally rather than functionally. James Hicks, a consummate cabinetmaker and craftsman, seemed unable to go beyond superb Sheraton and Chippendale revival pieces: "The Irish craftsman is content if he can graft his modern shoot upon the goodly tree of Hepplewhite or Sheraton, and is well pleased if his marquetrie approaches theirs in its delicacy of execution. While the severe simplicity of plain oak or stained wood cupboards would seem to have little charm for his Celtic imagination, he has not yet found a method of expression that is . . . in harmony with it."[18] Perhaps the most successful furniture expression, albeit short-lived and conservative, was the Kilkenny Art Wood-

[18]Hicks is quoted in *The Studio* 19 (1900): 127. Only John Vinycomb, Joseph Campbell, and Wilhelmina Geddes, outstanding individual exhibitors, were educated in the northern Ireland system.

workers, whose simple, explicit crafting from local timber and labor finds echoes of Voysey, Liberty, Roycroft, and Stickley. The lack of a supportive industrial framework, so crucial to the success of the American movement, was a major handicap in the association of art with life—the major creed on both sides of the Atlantic.

Another weakness in Ireland was the lack of individual architectural commitment to an arts and crafts ideology, despite contributions from private philanthropic companies. In 1894 Lord Mayo, the founder of the ACSI, had approached the Royal Institute of Architects of Ireland for positive support, but only William Scott, first professor of the National (then Royal) University's School of Architecture, and Richard Caulfeild Orpen, editor of the association's *Journal* (1909–22), responded. Between 1899 and 1929, Scott was able to successfully amalgamate Irish Romanesque and Byzantine with Voysey in his sensitive treatment of churches and buildings for prominent Celtic revival patrons, such as the Kilkenny furniture and woolen industries' model farm village for the bookbinder Otway Cuffe. R. M. Butler, architect and editor of *Irish Builder* from 1899 to 1929, wrote that he "opposed the idea of devising a 'purely national style'" since "styles were never invented but represented a natural growth, arising 'from the natural habits and aspirations of the people.'" Between 1912 and 1915, "his articles . . . on modern architecture, Norman Shaw and American architecture were enthusiastic in tone and demonstrated a lively and scholarly interest in the work of the day." But rich patrons tended to employ English architects or support work based on the early English style, except for churches and monuments, which fared better in the latter half of the nineteenth century, in the earlier phase of the more archaeologically informed Celtic revival. In February 1910, a paper entitled "Some Lessons from America," read to the Royal Institute of Architects of Ireland in Dublin, was confined to McKim, Mead, and White, a far cry from the work of a 1907 member, the Dublin architect Louis du Puget Millar, who moved to Pasadena in 1909 after two years in practice in Los Angeles. His shingled Cheesewright house (1909) "recalls the hooded eaves and thatched roofs found throughout the English Cotswolds."[19]

---

[19]Only the short-lived *Irish Architect and Craftsman* (1911–14) attempted regular reports on the society. On Butler, see Sean Rothery, "Some Irish Writers on Architecture in the Early Twentieth Century," in *150 Years of Architecture in Ireland*, ed. John Araby (Dublin: R.I.A.I., 1989), p. 63. On Millar, see Winter, "Arroyo Culture," p. 12.

In April 1908, *The Craftsman* stressed the cooperative and remunerative nature of the Dun Emer Industries, whose young, female,
"saved peasants" could avoid emigration while making beautiful things
by hand from original designs using the finest native, natural materials.
That year, Gleeson lectured to the Society of Arts and Crafts, Boston.

There are interesting parallels and differences between the Boston
and Dublin societies, founded in 1897 and 1894 respectively, which
were consciously modeled on their English archetype. Where the much
larger and wealthier, but apolitical, Boston turned to Morris, C. R.
Ashbee, and its own colonial revival, Dublin was torn between its roots
in the English movement, recognition of the golden age of eighteenth-
century Irish Georgian craftsmanship, and nationalist calls for a "modern" interpretation of a native Irish style. To the latter, Irish Romanesque and early Christian decorative art seemed the obvious
response, despite accusations of "slavish reversion to ancient forms."
Unlike the English and Boston movements, the Dublin work tended
to avoid "childlike assumptions" in favor of a symbolist approach.[20]
Both the Boston and Dublin societies were led by Brahmin philanthropists and educators of artistic persuasion rather than practice. The roles
of Sarah Wyman Whitman (1842–1904) and Sarah Purser (1848–
1943) may be cited.

Whitman's book covers and paintings and Purser's paintings are a
stronger aesthetic testament than their respective stained glass to the
major role each played in her city's cultural revival. Affluent, broadly
educated, and well connected, they were pioneers in a traditionally
male-oriented trade. Through their social contacts, dedication, and
close involvement with every stage of the craft in their city workshops,
they each ensured that stained glass became an important part of Boston
and Dublin arts and crafts expression. While Whitman followed John
La Farge and Purser espoused Christopher Whall, it was Purser's re-
cruits from the Dublin Art School whose contribution to twentieth-
century stained glass is outstanding. The character, skill, and beauty

[20] On the Boston society, see Beverly Brandt, " 'Mutually Helpful Relations': Archi-
tects, Craftsmen, and the Society of Arts and Crafts, Boston, 1897–1911" (Ph.D. diss.,
Boston University, 1984). On interpretations, the only specifically Irish reference I have
found in the society's records is that of the Carrig-Rohane Cooperative Hand-Carved
Frame Shop in Boston, started by Herman Dudley Murphy in 1903; see also P. Oswald
Reeves, "Irish Arts and Crafts," *Studio* 72, no. 295 (October 1917): 17, 18.

of their windows and panels are due to their being primarily painters and first-rate draftsmen fully versed in arts and crafts principles.

Charles Connick, the stained glass movement's principal spokesman in America, who opened his Boston studio in 1912, championed the half dozen An Túr artists' work in establishing "stained glass craft as a sincere expression of Christian art in terms that are universal and at the same time distinctly Irish . . . untouched by the commercial blight." Of Wilhelmina Geddes's 1918 Ottawa War Memorial, he wrote, "Nowhere in modern glass is there a more striking example of a courageous adventure in the medium. This devotee of the craft stood before it recently with a feeling of personal gratitude for the spiritual beauty, the poetry and youthful audacity that are wrought into that goodly fabric of glass, lead and iron."[21]

Harry Clarke, as well known in America for his book illustrations (notably Edgar Allen Poe's *Tales of Mystery and Imagination* [1919]) as his glass, was considered unparalleled in his "mastery of technique" and "application of it to the ends of exceeding beauty, significance, and wondrousness," manifesting a modern spirit and "strong individual character" while being "Celtic to a degree."[22] He was also the only artist to fuse a daring but traditionally based consummate skill and vivid imaginative inventiveness with business acumen (fig. 4). In the late 1920s Connick obtained major commissions for Clarke and An Túr in America. He acted as adviser and agent in 1925 when George Booth, the newspaper magnate, philanthropist, and patron of the Detroit Society of Arts and Crafts, purchased a stained glass panel from An Túr. The panel, *St. Patrick Lighting the Paschal Fire*, by Michael Healy (fig. 5), was designed for the Cranbrook Academy of Art library. In the mid 1930s Healy also made four graphically etched panels on blue glass for the philanthropic Chicago cattle baron, Arthur Leonard, well known for his early patronage of the arts and crafts silversmith Robert Jarvie.

In 1916 an earlier link had been forged with the Detroit society through the plays of Lord Dunsany, a nephew of Sir Horace Plunkett,

[21] Charles J. Connick, *Adventures in Light and Color* (New York: G. Harrap, 1937), p. 334. Charles Connick, "Modern Glass—A Review," *International Studio* 80, no. 329 (October 1924): 46.
[22] Reeves, "Irish Arts and Crafts," p. 22.

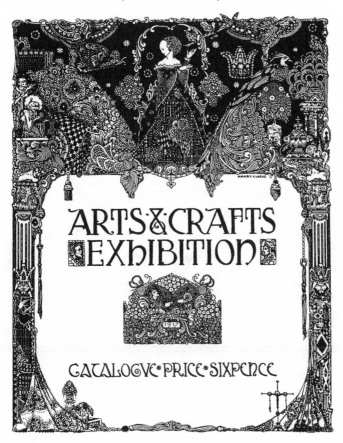

Fig. 4. Harry Clarke, cover design, Dublin, 1917. Pen and ink; H. 8½", W. 7". (Society for Design and Craftwork, Dublin.)

when Samuel Hume directed an avant-garde production on Booth's estate of Dunsany's *Tents of the Arabs* as part of the newly established arts and crafts little theater's first season. Hume also staged the play for the Society of Arts and Crafts, Boston, in 1916.

In his foreword to the catalogue of the seventh and last exhibition of the original ACSI, in 1925, the enamelist Reeves concluded that, with the birth of a new state, any "distinctive national style in the arts"

Fig. 5. Michael Healy, *Saint Patrick Lighting the Paschal Fire*, Dublin, ca. 1925. Stained glass; H. 30½", W. 31½". (Cranbrook Art Museum, Bloomfield Hills, Mich.)

could only depend "upon a determined vital striving on the part of a people to achieve in their actual lives their settled ideal of human dignity," not on an adopted Celtic idiom. "The style that may distinguish the future work of Ireland no man can foretell."[23]

[23] P. Oswald Reeves, Foreword, *Seventh Exhibition of the Arts and Crafts Society of Ireland* (Dublin, 1917), p. 19.

The Influence of C. R. Ashbee and His Guild of Handicraft on American Silver, Other Metalwork, and Jewelry

W. Scott Braznell

By the first decade of the twentieth century, American silver, other metalwork, and jewelry were revealing the reform influence of the English arts and crafts movement. England's guiding star leading this shift was Charles Robert Ashbee (1863–1942). An architect and designer—and in the words of his biographer Alan Crawford, "romantic socialist"—Ashbee provided the example that inspired changes in these crafts in America as well as in Britain and throughout Europe. As Crawford has observed, it is easy to see why Ashbee appealed to the arts and crafts public in America, but it is not easy to distinguish Ashbee's contribution from that of British arts and crafts as a whole. James Benjamin built on the work of Crawford and other Ashbee scholars in his study of Ashbee's American activities and connections. This

The author is most indebted to Alan Crawford, whose biography of Ashbee inspired this further assessment of Ashbee's influence. Crawford's kind assistance and that of Marcia Anderson, Felicity Ashbee, James E. Benjamin, Rosalie Berberian, Margaret Caldwell, Constance R. Caplan, Annette Carruthers, David Hanks, David Hart, Alice Johnson, Frank Johnson, Catherine Kurland, Thomas S. Michie, Diana J. Strazdes, Jeffrey Williams, Lori Zabar, and Ghenete Zelleke, helped the research for this essay. The author also thanks his wife, Patricia E. Kane, for her encouragement and guidance.

essay now seeks to augment the information on the influence Ashbee and his Guild of Handicraft had on American metalworkers and jewelers, including those Americans known to have trained or visited at the guild as well as those not known to have studied with Ashbee but whose work evinces Ashbee's influence.[1]

In 1886 Ashbee took up residency at London's Toynbee Hall, the pioneer university settlement house established in 1884. There he organized evening classes where men and boys from the slums studied the writings of John Ruskin. These classes stimulated the pupils to undertake practical work and became the foundation of the Guild and School of Handicraft that Ashbee founded in 1888. Viewing factory training as a disadvantage and preferring to introduce unskilled men and boys to handicraft, Ashbee's revolutionary concept was that training in art and design be conducted alongside actual production, a dramatic departure from contemporary practice.

Ashbee sought to regenerate lost traditions associated with preindustrial production and the bonds of comradeship that humanized the workshop. His goal was to have the guild develop as a self-sufficient, self-governing body of independent craftsmen with design and production as a collaborative process whereby the men would be responsible for the product throughout every stage of development. Lectures and classes, an in-house library, access to museum objects chosen for knowledge and inspiration, and a metropolitan sales outlet for the products were integral to the guild as were group activities including theatricals, songfests, swim meets, cricket, bicycling, and gardening.

After rapid expansion, the guild moved in 1891 to larger quarters at Essex House in London, but while Ashbee's experiment continued to flourish he envisioned an escape from the evils of the city and the opportunity for a simpler life in a rural setting. In the summer of 1902

[1] Alan Crawford, *C. R. Ashbee* (New Haven: Yale University Press, 1985), pp. 403–20. James E. Benjamin, "C. R. Ashbee in America, an Englishman's Observations on the Arts and Crafts Movement, Architecture and Culture, 1896–1916" (Master's thesis, Cornell University, 1989); Fiona MacCarthy, *The Simple Life* (London: Lund Humphries, 1981). For more on Ashbee, see W. Scott Braznell, contributor to Wendy Kaplan, *"The Art That Is Life": The Arts and Crafts Movement in America, 1875–1920* (Boston: Museum of Fine Arts, 1987) (hereafter cited as Braznell, metals or jewelry entries); W. Scott Braznell, "Metalsmithing and Jewelrymaking, 1900–1920," in *The Ideal Home*, ed. Janet Kardon (New York: Harry N. Abrams, 1993), pp. 55–63.

the guild—some 150 men, women, and children—relocated in the medieval town of Chipping Campden. After two years Ashbee successfully established the Campden School of Arts and Crafts as a counterpart to the guild's endeavors. The output of the guild's eight workshops ranged from furniture to printed books. Although the work was meant principally to be the product of good fellowship, aesthetic excellence was the driving force. From its remote location, however, the guild was unable to compete profitably with the cheaper renditions of its innovative designs marketed by Liberty and Company and others. Bankruptcy brought about the guild's liquidation and formal end in 1908, but some guildsmen stayed on and, in a revised and less-formal association, continued the Guild of Handicraft under a trust until 1919. A core of craftsmen remained in the metal workshops, and a succeeding generation continues silversmithing today.[2]

Metalwork and jewelry were the major and best-known crafts of the guild. Guildsman John Pearson produced the first metalwork, which consisted of large copper dishes and brass bowls with repoussé decoration. Ashbee's initial metalwork designs probably were made during the summer of 1889, predating the guild's first work in silver and electroplated wares by a year. Beginning experiments with precious metals by Ashbee and the guild were apparently cast, such as a salt cellar with onyx bowl from about 1893, composed with spheres, repeated whirling patterns, and openwork pedestal support. The wrought silverware begun at the guild in the early 1890s generated a momentous departure from the flawless finish and highly ornamented machine-produced wares of the day by presenting a hammer-texture finish communicating human endeavor. Other salient features of the guild's revolutionary metalwares include punched and cast beading, saw-piercing, and notable innovations such as the use of applied semiprecious cabochons, colored enamels, and extruded wire for supports, handles, and finials. Found objects, such as Turkish cigarette mouthpieces of carved ivory used as knife and fork handles, occasionally played a part in Ashbee's designs.[3]

[2] Annette Carruthers and Frank Johnson, *The Guild of Handicraft, 1888–1988* (Cheltenham, Eng.: Cheltenham Art Gallery and Museums, 1988), pp. 12, 16; Clive Fewins, "Silversmiths' Time Capsule," *Financial Times*, May 21, 22, 1994.
[3] On early metalwork, see Aymer Vallance, "The Furnishing and Decoration of the House," *Art Journal* 54 (1892): 373–74, figs. 2, 4; Crawford, *Ashbee*, pls. 12, 157. Ashbee's design vocabulary is discussed in Crawford, *Ashbee*, pp. 318, 321, pl. 160. On

Ashbee deplored the use of jewelry to display wealth—particularly the late nineteenth-century fashion for wearing diamonds with minimal settings in an allover display—and was a pioneer in returning artistic emphasis to jewelry through the use of colored semiprecious stones enhanced by imaginative and occasionally narrative settings. Jewelry making by Ashbee and the guild began in 1890, with a clasp created for Ashbee's mother, and developed rapidly. Whirling petals or leaves with beading surrounding a cabochon are characteristic of Ashbee's jewelry designs.[4] Guild of Handicraft jewelry at the turn of the century was distinctive for its lack of machine-regularized finish. Naturalistic motifs such as flower blossoms and insects—especially butterflies or moths—subtle color play, chains with pendant drops, and random-shape pearls are among Ashbee's jewelry mannerisms.

The impact of the guild's production on a generation of designers and craftsmen was widespread, reaching America not only through direct contact but also through American craftsmen's contact with producers abroad inspired by the guild's example. The Guild of Handicraft was the model for the founding of the Austrian Wiener Werkstätte, and its ensuing metalwork and jewelry designs are stylistically indebted to the guild. Ashbee also influenced designs in Germany—notably those by Peter Behrens. The devices of ornamental cabochons and openwork pedestal supports were adopted by the Danish silversmith Georg Jensen.[5]

---

wrought silverware, see Lionel Lambourne, *Utopian Craftsmen* (New York: Van Nostrand Reinhold Co., 1980), fig. 162; Mabel Cox, "The Arts and Crafts Exhibition, London, 1906," *House and Garden* 9 (May 1906): 214. On guild work, see Crawford, *Ashbee*, pl. 161. C. R. Ashbee, "On Table Service," *Art Journal* 60 (1898): 337; C. R. Ashbee, "A Little Talk on the Setting of Stones," *Art Journal* 56 (1894): 183, no. 7.

[4] See the diamond fashion in Margaret Flower, *Victorian Jewelry* (New York: A. S. Barnes, 1967), p. 217, fig. 95. Crawford, *Ashbee*, pl. 174. Ashbee, "Little Talk," p. 182, no. 3.

[5] See Crawford, *Ashbee*, chap. 15, and a list of exhibitions where Ashbee showed, p. 460 n. 8. Compare a 1906 Werkstätte bowl in the Christie's Monaco catalogue, "Arts Décoratifs du Vingtième Siècle" (December 8, 1985), p. 11, to Ashbee's design for salts from about 1900 in Hugh Honour, *Goldsmiths and Silversmiths* (London: Weidenfeld and Nicolson, 1971), p. 293; compare Behrens's 1908 electrical heater in Herwin Schaefer, *Nineteenth-Century Modern* (New York: Praeger Publishers, 1970), fig. 281, to Ashbee's picture frame in Dora J. Janson, *From Slave to Siren* (Durham, N.C.: Duke University Museum of Art, 1971), fig. 179; compare Jensen's 1912 bowl design in Honour, *Goldsmiths and Silversmiths*, p. 295, with Ashbee's cup in the Christie's London catalogue, "The Modern Movement" (November 8, 1984), pp. 40–41; Jensen established his shop in 1904, and his early silverware incorporating cabochons is well known.

The fundamental means by which Americans were inspired by Ashbee and his guild include Ashbee's writings and American lectures; the championing of the guild by influential writers; exhibitions of the guild's work; first-hand acquaintance as visitors to the guild; and actual crafts practice at the guild. Ashbee's extended United States lecture tours in 1896, 1900–1901, 1908–9, and 1915–16 brought Americans into direct contact with his teachings and dominating personality. Chicago and Boston, where Ashbee visited and lectured in 1896, not only founded America's first arts and crafts societies the following year but also developed as the nation's two leading centers for arts and crafts movement metalwork and jewelry.

Most Americans probably learned of Ashbee and the guild's production through domestic and foreign periodicals such as *House Beautiful* and *International Studio*. Their coverage of crafts exhibitions illustrated guild metalwares and jewelry, and their articles played a crucial role in disseminating the ideals on craft and life that Ashbee continuously set down in books and articles. As early as January 1897 the newly founded *House Beautiful* carried George R. Twose's laudatory review of Ashbee's 1894 publication, *A Few Chapters on Workshop Reconstruction and Citizenship*, and urged readers to become acquainted with Ashbee's higher ideals of citizenship and views on the "commercial article" made not to use but to sell. Oscar Lovell Triggs also drew upon that publication in his 1902 book, *Chapters in the History of the Arts and Crafts Movement*, where he proposed that factories be replaced with workshops that combined studio and school and molded men as well as goods. In 1902 the Guild of Handicraft was championed in a report on British arts and crafts by Rho Fisk Zueblin for *The Chautauquan*. In 1903 Horace Traubel commented in *The Artsman*: "Ashbee so far is not much known on this side of the Atlantic. But he deserves suffrage and will get it. Not only for his shop, which is germinal, but for his written speech, which strikes fire way up where men dream and way down where men root." Frederick A. Whiting, secretary of the Society of Arts and Crafts, Boston, recommended Ashbee's writings to a correspondent in Iowa in 1910.[6]

[6] Horace Traubel, "Arts and Craft to Date," *The Artsman* 1 (November 1903): 61; see especially "The Guild of Handicraft: A Visit to Essex House," *International Studio* 3 (November 1897): 27–36; Aymer Vallance, "Modern British Jewellery and Fans," *The Studio* 12 (1902): 43–44, 64–65, 67–68; "British Decorative Art in 1899," *International Studio* 9 (November 1899): 104–31; James Smithies, "On the Practice of Repoussé

Influential displays of guild metalwork and jewelry began in 1897 in Chicago and Boston and continued to 1916 in New York City. The Easter exhibit of arts and crafts held by Hull-House in 1897 is the earliest documented exhibit of guild jewelry and metalwares in America. The same year Boston's first exhibition of the arts and crafts included seven examples of beaten copper work loaned by Gorham Manufacturing Company from the London Arts and Crafts Exhibition Society. There is little doubt that guild work was among them.[7]

Jane Addams, after visiting Ashbee, was the first American to found a cooperative organization that would produce American metal-work and jewelry (fig. 1). She went to Toynbee Hall in the spring of 1888 and a year later established Hull-House, where the Chicago Arts and Crafts Society was later founded. *House Beautiful* noted, "If [the Chicago Arts and Crafts Society] shall result in the ultimate foundation of a practical workshop and school, similar to Essex House in England, it would be an odd coincidence, as the latter is an outgrowth of Toynbee Hall, the original inspiration of Hull House."[8] Indeed, such proved to be the case when the Hull-House Labor Museum—which was really a school—opened in 1900.

Work," *House Beautiful* 5 (February 1899): 119–25; ten issues of *House Beautiful* between June 1909 and August 1910 carried Ashbee's articles: "Art and Crafts in England" and "Man and the Machine." For a list of Ashbee's published writings, see Crawford, *Ashbee,* pp. 484–86. C. R. Ashbee, *A Few Chapters on Workshop Reconstruction and Citizenship* (London: E. Arnold, 1894); George R. Twose, "Workshop Reconstruction by C. R. Ashbee: A Review," *House Beautiful* 1 (January 1897): 8–14; Oscar L. Triggs, *Chapters in the History of the Arts and Crafts Movement* (Chicago: Bohemia Guild of the Industrial Art League, 1902); Rho Fisk Zeublin, "The Arts and Crafts Movement: A Survey of the Arts and Crafts Movement in England," *Chautauquan* 36 (November 1902): 169–70; Frederick A. Whiting, "A Successful English Experiment," *Handicraft* 2 (April 1903): 139–58; roll 300, frame 647, Society of Arts and Crafts, Boston, Papers, Archives of American Art, Washington, D.C. (hereafter cited as SACB Papers).
    [7] *Hull-House Bulletin* 2, no. 5 (June 1897): 4; the following is a list of later American exhibitions at which Ashbee showed: 1897, Exhibition of the Arts and Crafts, Copley Hall, Boston [assumed]; 1898, Chicago Arts and Crafts Society, Art Institute of Chicago; 1899, Architectural Exhibition of the T-Square Club, Philadelphia, traveling to New York, Chicago, St. Louis, Detroit, Cleveland, and Pittsburgh; 1900, Architectural Exhibition of the T-Square Club, Philadelphia; Architectural League of New York; 1904, Louisiana Purchase International Exposition, St. Louis; 1907, National Society of Craftsmen, New York; 1908, Rhode Island School of Design, Providence; 1915, Society of Arts and Crafts, Boston; 1916, Little Gallery, New York. On the 1890 Boston exhibition, see roll 322, frame 204, SACB Papers.
    [8] "Notes," *House Beautiful* 3 (December 1897): 29.

Fig. 1. Isadore V. Friedman, compote, ca. 1910. Silver; H. 6¹⁵/₁₆″. Mark: HULL-HOUSE SHOPS/ HAND WROUGHT/ I [a pitcher enclosing] V and F/ STER- LING. (Private collection: Photo, Wit McKay.)

The preeminent complement of the Guild of Handicraft in America was the spin-off enterprise of the Society of Arts and Crafts, Boston—the Handicraft Shop, established in 1901. Initially the shop was closely attuned to Ashbee's example, and it rapidly emerged as a cooperative workshop for metalsmithing, jewelry, and enamels. English immigrant architect H. Langford Warren, a founder of Boston's Society of Arts and Crafts, visited Ashbee at Campden in September 1903. Two months later he became the society's new president and teamed with Whiting, who shared his esteem for Ashbee's guild. Before the year was out the ambitions of the two men were fulfilled when the Handicraft Shop—echoing the guild's departure from London—left Boston for suburban Wellesley Hills, with the idea of replacing the corrupting influence of the city with a more wholesome life afforded by the country. The shop's location was chosen for the convenience of its craftsmen—most of whom were commuters—but its accessibility to the trolley lines and railroad station may also have resulted from an awareness of the hardship caused by the remoteness of the guild in Campden.[9] Although the shop returned to Boston in 1907, it continued to exemplify Ashbee's aims as a cooperative workshop that combined the skills of designers and craftsmen with teaching.

Other American crafts practitioners and administrators followed Ashbee's lead in seeking a rural environment in which to practice. J. William Fosdick, treasurer of the New York City-based National Society of Craftsmen, was undoubtedly influenced by the Guild of Handicraft's provincial setting. Fosdick signed the visitors book at Chipping Campden on September 16, 1907, and the following June it was reported in *International Studio* that the summer quarters of the National Society of Craftsmen would be at Fosdick's country estate in the White Mountains of New Hampshire. The resulting crafts activity there also attracted Boston handicraft jeweler Edward Everett Oakes, who established a studio at Sugar Hill, where jewelry continues to be produced by a third generation of the Oakes family. It is apparent that Ashbee's designs and workshop organization guided Clara Pauline Barck, who founded Chicago's Kalo Shop in 1901. Following Barck's marriage in 1905 to George S. Welles, a self-taught amateur metalworker, the couple moved the shop to their home in suburban Park Ridge. Known as the Kalo Art-Craft Community, this workshop and school was complemented by a metropolitan retail outlet duplicating the guild's scheme.[10]

The Society of Arts and Crafts, Boston, continued to thrive, with metalsmiths, jewelers, and enamelers advancing the goals of its architect-member leadership through "mutually helpful relations." Patrons from the society's associate membership were encouraged to support craftsmen members through commissions, with the design of major

[9]On the Handicraft Shop, see Braznell, metals entries, nos. 134–35. For Warren's visit, see September 3, 1903, visitors book for the Guild of Handicraft, in the collection of the Guild of Handicraft Trust, Chipping Campden (hereafter cited as visitors book at Chipping Campden). On the shop's move, see roll 300, frame 378, SACB Papers; Margaretha Gebelein Leighton, *George Christian Gebelein* (Boston: Privately printed, 1976), p. 37.
[10]"Rural and Summer Colonies of the Arts and Crafts," *International Studio* 34 (June 1908): 151–52. Sharon S. Darling, *Chicago Metalsmiths* (Chicago: Chicago Historical Society, 1977), p. 45.

works given over to member architects.[11] In 1906—in a close parallel to the Guild of Handicraft—it achieved free admission for craftsmen members to the city's Museum of Fine Arts, classes held in a rented studio using loaned silversmithing tools, a reference library, and a salesroom that was financially self-sufficient. In 1907 the society's metalworkers organized to become the first of the society's guilds that bonded disparate social classes and reinforced member allegiance and morale. Although the society evolved as an organization politically removed from labor reform and almost exclusively devoted to design and taste, guild methods they chose to implement between 1903 and 1906 had a profound effect on the future practice of their nationwide membership of silversmiths and jewelers. From 1907 into the Great Depression of the 1930s, annual sales of the society's metalsmiths and jewelers typically made up more than half the receipts of its salesroom.

Warren also participated in the organization of the English immigrant silversmith Arthur J. Stone's shop, which echoed practices Ashbee instituted at the Guild of Handicraft. In 1901, at age fifty-four, Stone was able to fulfill a lifelong dream of escaping the factory system and establishing a shop of his own. Urged by Warren, Stone began to take on apprentices in 1906, to pass on his skills to future generations.[12] Like Ashbee, Stone directed and provided the designs for his rural-based shop and played a paternal role to his workmen, who shared in the profits. He also saw to their cultural development by maintaining a library in the shop and by sending them to museum exhibitions. Unlike Guild of Handicraft silver, however, Stone silver, which set a standard for New England handicraft silversmiths, displayed a rigorous level of craft technique learned through a traditional seven-year apprenticeship and years of experience. In a departure from the convention followed by the guild, the Stone shop silversmiths gained recognition through individual letter marks identifying their work.

Those who led America's large silver companies customarily made annual visits to Europe to acquaint themselves with ongoing developments in design and production. On such a trip, English-born William

[11] Beverly Brandt, " 'Mutually Helpful Relations': Architects, Craftsmen, and the Society of Arts and Crafts, Boston, 1897–1917" (Ph.D. diss., Boston University, 1985), pp. 191–202.

[12] Elenita C. Chickering, *Arthur J. Stone* (Boston: Boston Athenaeum, 1981), p. 7 n. 15.

C. Codman, chief designer of the Gorham Manufacturing Company, signed the Guild of Handicraft's London visitors book in June 1904. Codman was well aware of Ashbee. In a January 1901 meeting in the jewelers' department of Gorham's factory in Providence, Codman had tossed Ashbee some drawings saying, "These are our latest designs." Ashbee noted in his memoirs, "Among them was a copy of a little brooch made a year or two ago by Bill Hardiman at Essex House."[13] Gorham founded a special school within their factory in 1896 to undertake their ambitious art silver line, later named Martelé. This training, which allowed silversmiths to acquire manual skills necessary for forming and ornamenting wares from beginning to end, was analogous to Ashbee's guild.

The guild's special emphasis on education and its interdependence with a school drew the interest of influential American teacher-practitioners. Among the first signatures in the visitors book at Chipping Campden is that of Forest Emerson Mann, entered on July 4, 1903. After teaching arts and crafts at Chautauqua, New York, and at Dayton, Ohio, he organized students at Grand Rapids, Michigan, to found his Forest Craft Guild in 1907. A description of Mann's guild a year later as a cooperative shop where inexperienced men and women designed and made jewelry and wrought metal that was sold in a local salesroom documents an organization closely modeled after the Guild of Handicraft. Ashbee's frequent complaint of his designs being copied and corrupted by others for profit was not lost on Mann, who patented his designs for a belt clasp, stickpin, backcomb, hatpin, and a belt shield in 1907.[14]

Ernest A. Batchelder's leadership in American handicrafts was also influenced by his sojourn at Ashbee's guild. In February 1905 he wrote from Chipping Campden to Whiting, "Am at work in the Guild Shops and enjoy it thoroughly. . . . The workmen . . . are thoroughly skilled technically and have opportunities to exercise considerable judgement

[13] Ashbee Memoirs, January 1901, vol. 1, p. 284, Victoria and Albert Museum Library (hereafter cited as Ashbee Memoirs); see support for Ashbee's claim in Benjamin, "Ashbee," p. 83, fig. 7. Codman signed the guild's visitor book presumably used at its retail gallery in London; see June 22, 1904, in *Manuscripts, Chipping Campden, Visitors Book: April 8, 1903–July 1905*, which is in the Victoria and Albert Museum Library, London.

[14] On Mann, see Braznell, metals entries, no. 202; "Patent Department," *Jewelers' Circular* 56 (May 20, 1908): 82.

in working out designs." Later that year Batchelder began a five-year association with the newly founded Handicraft Guild of Minneapolis, which developed from his first-hand observation of Ashbee's organization. With students from nearly every state, the Minneapolis guild's year-round school program was combined with a salesroom where members sold work on commission. By 1907 a new building included a school of design, permanent exhibition areas, studios for resident craftsmen, salesroom, lecture hall, and the state's leading dealer in books on art. Crafts from the guild, comprised mostly of metalwares and jewelry, were seen in exhibitions around the country from 1906 until World War I. In addition to using repoussé for metalwork embellishment, the Handicraft Guild of Minneapolis also drew upon two devices particular to Ashbee's metalwork designs: saw-pierced ornament (see Anderson, "Handicraft Guild of Minneapolis," fig. 4) and cabochon stones. A cup made in 1914 by Batchelder's pupil and colleague, Douglas Donaldson, displays Ashbee design devices in its guild-cup form on a hexagonal base and its embellishment with colorful cabochon stones and enamels.[15]

Canadian-born craftsman and educator H. Stuart Michie was among Pratt Institute's early metalwork students in 1902 and subsequently made at least three visits to Ashbee's Guild of Handicraft.[16] After his first visit in March 1906, he began a year teaching design and metalwork at the Handicraft Guild of Minneapolis. In 1908 Michie enrolled as a special student at Ashbee's metalwork shop, and when he returned again in 1911 he was the principal of the school of the Worcester Art Museum, where metalworking classes were conducted.

Silversmith Theodore Hanford Pond, another prominent organizer of arts and crafts educational programs, would have been familiar with the Guild of Handicraft. From 1911 to 1913 he directed his Pond Applied Art Studios in Baltimore, where his system of apprenticeship

[15] See Batchelder's letter in roll 300, frames 478–79, SACB Papers; see saw-pierced ornament in Crawford, *Ashbee*, fig. 165; Minneapolis is discussed in Braznell, metals entries, no. 187; Marcia G. Anderson, "Art for Life's Sake: The Handicraft Guild of Minneapolis," in *Minnesota 1900: Art and Life on the Upper Mississippi, 1890–1915,* ed. Michael Conforti (Newark: University of Delaware Press, 1994), p. 159. The cup is discussed in Braznell, metals entries, no. 185.

[16] Thomas S. Michie, letter to author, June 25, 1990; see March 26, 1906, and August 14, 1911, visitors book at Chipping Campden.

"such as in vogue in England" was described in *Arts and Decoration.*
Pond's method of integrating design theory and practice and paying a
fair wage for the work produced corresponded to the Guild of Handicraft custom. Moreover, a silver box Pond produced echoes an example
of guild silversmithing.[17]

Ashbee scholar Fiona MacCarthy has stated that Americans were
particularly welcome at Chipping Campden, and leading metalsmiths
and jewelers were among them. Silversmith, jeweler, and enameler
Helen Keeling Mills, of New York City, signed the visitors book on
March 30, 1904, and her subsequent silversmithing reveals the guild's
influence. She employed colorful semiprecious stones in work she exhibited in 1907, and hammer-texture surfaces can be observed in her silver
at the National Cathedral in Washington. Eleanor D'Arcy Gaw, a Canadian designer who worked in Chicago and San Francisco, was a pupil of
the guild—probably about 1906. The well-known lamps from San Francisco's Dirk Van Erp Studio originated from a partnership that combined
Gaw's design talent and Van Erp's coppersmithing skill, a cooperative
effort that logically stemmed from Gaw's indoctrination at the Guild of
Handicraft. Norwich, Connecticut, native Frank Gardner Hale studied
at that city's distinguished art school, and he may have heard Ashbee's
talk to the art students there in October 1900. Indeed, Hale went to England in 1906 and spent a year studying silversmithing and enameling at
the Guild of Handicraft and then jewelry making with former guildsman
Frederick Partridge, in London. A Hale jeweled pendant published in
1916 closely resembles one of Ashbee's peacock pendants from about
1900. Hale did not lack for designs of his own but honors a favorite Ashbee
motif, the peacock, which was first seen in guild jewelry about 1899. The
skills of Cleveland's leading silversmith, enameler, and jeweler, Horace
E. Potter, were advanced by guild training; the visitors book at Chipping
Campden records his sojourn there on August 19, 1907. Ashbee signature stem-and-leaf supports are skillfully combined with Bacchus-like
masks on Potter's standing dish (fig. 2). Guild precedent often underlies
Potter Studio work, such as demitasse spoons with applied, enameled,
copper ornament resembling cabochons and vessels with exaggerated
saw-pierced handles. Ashbee's technique of designing metalwork with
other objects was repeated in Potter Studio wares such as brass bookends
embellished with Batchelder ceramic tiles, and in bowls by Rookwood

[17]Braznell, metals entries, no. 186.

Fig. 2. Potter Studio, standing dish, Cleveland, ca. 1910. Silver; H. 4″. Mark: POTTER STUDIO/ STERLING. (Collection of Stanley Skwarek.)

and other Ohio potteries with silver or pewter lids incorporating Chinese ivory or jade finials.[18] Mary Blakeslee visited the Guild of Handicraft and signed the visitors book on August 23, 1907. By November that year Cleveland's Rokesley Shop came into existence with Blakeslee as one of its founders.

[18] MacCarthy, *Simple Life*, p. 78 n. 21. On Mills, see *Exhibition of the Society of Arts and Crafts, Copley Hall* (Boston: Society of Arts and Crafts, 1907), pp. 17, 26, 43, 93; Frank E. Cleveland, "The Arts and Crafts," *Christian Art* 2 (November 1907): 78–80. For more on Gaw, see Braznell, metals entries, no. 137. Compare Ashbee's pendant in Flower, *Victorian Jewelry*, fig. 100d, to Hale's pendant in Florence N. Levy, ed., *American Art Annual* 13 (Washington, D.C.: American Federation of Arts, 1916), facing p. 45. On Potter wares, see Braznell, metals entries, no. 44; a Potter tea service, Yale University Art Gallery (1991.7.1); the other examples have been in the marketplace.

American visitors to Chipping Campden repeated Ashbee's prac-
tice of using colorful semiprecious cabochons in jewelry and metal-
wares, which particularly identify Ashbee influence rather than that of
English work in general. As early as 1897 Gabriel Mourey suggested that
Ashbee's work was the source of inspiration for contemporary French
work ornamented with cabochons. Early silver produced by the Kalo
Shop was also adorned with cabochons as was a belt buckle created by
George Fass at the art department of the School of Industrial Art of the
Pennsylvania Museum—now known as the Philadelphia College of Art
and Design—where Ashbee visited in 1896. A spectacular Rokesley silver
tea and coffee service incorporates moonstones in the Ashbee manner.
Californians Beatrice Rolfe and her daughters Bertha and Olivia, who
were the wife and children of Ashbee's friend and lecture-tour organizer,
Henry Winchester Rolfe, studied at Campden. Jewelry and silverplated
hollowware embellished with cabochons made by them about 1911 survive in a private collection.[19]

Madeline Yale Wynne championed the precedent set by Ashbee
in reaffirming jewelry's role as a vehicle for artistic adornment, and not
for displaying wealth, by exploiting modest materials, even pebbles in
their natural state, for their intrinsic properties. Wynne and her colleague at Hull-House, A. Fogliata, both made pendants or brooches
with unfaceted stones suspended on individual chains, a compositional
device Ashbee had introduced in the 1890s, not only in jewelry but in
overhead electric light fixtures as well. In 1906 Wynne described her
working methods for jewelry and silver tableware noting, "I consider
each effort by itself as regards color and form much as I would paint a
picture." Although Wynne was also a painter, her words recall a statement Ashbee had made twelve years earlier, "Every jewel you set must
have its colour scheme, every jewel must be treated as a painter would
treat his picture." The similarity of the two statements suggests an
awareness of Ashbee's writings.[20]

Evidence of his guildsmen's efforts was valued by Ashbee, and the

[19] Gabriel Mourey, "The Decorative Art Movement in Paris," *International Studio*
1 (April 1897): 122–23, 126. Darling, *Chicago Metalsmiths*, no. 56. *Bulletin of the
Pennsylvania Museum* 3 (October 1905): 75. On Rokesley, see Braznell, metals entries,
no. 133. Alan Crawford shared references and slides of the Rolfes' work.

[20] For Wynne, see Braznell, jewelry entries, no. 125; Ashbee, "Little Talk," p. 184.
Crawford, *Ashbee*, pl. 28, illustrates a light fixture.

hammer-texture silver finish he adopted launched a widely imitated motif for handwrought silver, particularly from Chicago, and subsequently gained popularity in mass-produced metalwares. The bold effects, even primitive quality, of a buckle and other copper and enamel pieces by Wynne recall the early experiments of Ashbee's guild. Like Ashbee, Wynne and other craftsmen of the Chicago Arts and Crafts Society were protesting against the machine-made article and valued the earnestness of their purpose more than the outcome of their efforts. Typical of Chicago's handicraft silver, the hammer-texture compote made by Isadore V. Friedman at Hull-House (see fig. 1) bears the struck marks "HAND WROUGHT," a proud and moralizing appellation that also enhanced its commercial value. Its composition follows guild models. The compote was a design replicated by Friedman and other silversmiths associated with the Kalo Shop. Its distinctive trumpet-form base is a routine feature of Clara Welles's designs that owes a debt to Ashbee, conspicuous in a silver and chrysoprase covered cup made by his Essex House guildsmen in 1900–1901. Other makers such as Chicago's Marshall Field and Co. Craft Shop capitalized on the fashion for hammered metal surfaces with silverware produced under assembly-line methods. What became a custom among handicraft metalsmiths was adopted by quantity producers such as the Roycrofters and mimicked by the large silver manufacturers, who offered mass-produced silver and silverplated flatware and hollowware whose hammer-beaten appearance was rendered through dies and the drop press. This texture was promoted as having the quality of fine craftsmanship, and it was also often linked to silverware for the colonial revival market. Examples include the International Silver Company's "Van Dyke" sterling flatware introduced in 1910 and silverplated hollowware by the Colonial Silver Company in 1924.[21]

[21] Mabel Key, "A Review of the Recent Exhibition of the Chicago Arts and Crafts Society," *House Beautiful* 6 (June 1899): 6–7; Braznell, jewelry entries, no. 125. Robert Bruce Kahler, "Art and Life: The Arts and Crafts Movement in Chicago, 1897–1915" (Ph.D. diss., Purdue University, 1986), pp. 124–25. See Ashbee cup, Yale University Art Gallery (1970.49.7); also see trumpet-form Kalo Shop candlesticks at Yale (1982.84.1a,b). For Marshall Field and Co. Craft Shop, see Darling, *Chicago Metalsmiths*, pp. 74–78; Eileen Boris, *Art and Labor* (Philadelphia: Temple University Press, 1986), p. 113. See Roycroft in Leslie Greene Bowman, *American Arts and Crafts: Virtue in Design* (Los Angeles: Los Angeles County Museum of Art in association with Bulfinch Press/Little, Brown, 1990), pp. 112–15; advertisements for "Van Dyke" flatware in *Jewelers' Circular* 62 (March 29, 1911): 23, and for Colonial Silver Co., in *Keystone* 51 (March 1924): 29.

Fig. 3. Elinor Klapp, brooch, Chicago, ca. 1899. From Madeline Yale Wynne, "What to Give," *House Beautiful* 7 (December 1899): 46.

Other American work published in the period exhibits an awareness of Ashbee's designs. A brooch (fig. 3) by Elinor Klapp, a jewelry designer based in Chicago and later New York, closely follows Ashbee's precedent: distinct whirling pattern and cabochon stones. Klapp and Ashbee both exhibited jewelry in the 1898 exhibition of the Chicago Arts and Crafts Society and at the Paris Exposition Universelle in 1900. Ashbee's recurrent pierced whirling motif was also employed in the pendant of a necklace by the Boston jeweler Margaret Rogers. A covered loving cup (fig. 4) in *Good Housekeeping* for December 1906, illustrated another Ashbee innovation: suspending a body from handles. Designed by Frances Barnum Smith and made in collaboration with two other Cleveland women—Jane Carson and Mildred Watkins— who were skilled in metalsmithing, enameling, and jewelry, the cup's configuration and embellishment with enamel, cabochons, and saw-pierced ornament all owe a debt to Guild of Handicraft silver. Carson made a European study tour in 1907. Her further acquaintance with

Fig. 4. Frances Barnum Smith (designer), Jane Carson, Mildred Watkins, covered loving cup. Silver, enamel, opals. From Claire M. Coburn, "The Art of the Silversmith," *Good Housekeeping* 43 (December 1906): 627.

Fig. 5. Marcus and Company, belt clasp, New York, ca. 1905. Silver, green enamel, pearls, chrysoprases; W. 3½". Mark: STERLING / MAR-CUS&CO. (Private collection: Photo, Wit McKay.)

Guild of Handicraft silver abroad seems likely and may account for her use of colored enamels, chrysoprase cabochons, and supporting spheres in a silver tennis trophy she made the following year.[22]

Silver and jewelry by Marcus and Company of New York relates closely to Guild of Handicraft work. A Marcus dish replicates the ingenious designs for dishes with wire handles and cabochon stones that Ashbee had introduced as early as the 1900 Paris exposition. The dull finish, materials, and punchwork bead border of a Marcus and Company belt clasp (fig. 5) show a close affinity to Guild of Handicraft work. The Marcus inkstand (fig. 6) repeats Ashbee's use of cabochons and wire for supports and leaf stems, while its dome-topped vertical mass recalls guild pepper casters. The growing body of Ashbee-like

---

[22] See a photograph of jewelry by Margaret Rogers annotated "26 Lime St. opal–olivines–sapphire–+ enamel," in archives, Society of Arts and Crafts, Boston, Boston Public Library; Claire M. Coburn, "The Art of the Silversmith," *Good Housekeeping* 43 (December 1906): 627; C. R. Ashbee, "Suggestions for the Improvement of Sporting Cups and Trophies," *International Studio* 10 (May 1900): 159. Cleveland Museum of Art (86.44) owns the tennis trophy.

Fig. 6. Marcus and Company, inkstand, New York, ca. 1905. Silver, jade, pearls; W. 8″. (Collection of Constance R. Caplan: Photo, Duane Sutter.)

work bearing Marcus and Company marks presupposes a Marcus crafts-man with firsthand experience at the Guild of Handicraft.[23]

Information is scant on jewelry and silver that Americans un-doubtedly acquired from the Guild of Handicraft. Ralph Radcliffe Whitehead, who founded his utopian Byrdcliffe Colony at Woodstock, New York, in 1903, was listed as the owner of Ashbee jewelry that was published in 1894. A photograph taken a decade later documents an

[23] See the Marcus dish in Braznell, metals entries, no. 47. C. R. Ashbee, *Modern English Silverwork* (London: B. T. Batsford, 1909); for wire as supports and leaf stems see plates 17, 20, 41, 46; for dome-topped vertical mass, see plate 38. For additional Marcus pieces see an inkwell in Janson, *From Slave to Siren*, fig. 179; a picture frame in the Christie's catalogue "Important American Furniture, Silver, Folk Art, and Decora-tive Arts" (June 4, 1988), lot 17; a dish is in the Sotheby's catalogue "Fine Americana" (June 23, 1993), lot 19; salt cellars are in a private collection.

Ashbee brooch worn by Whitehead's wife, Jane. Ashbee corresponded with Whiting about selling guild silverware through the Society of Arts and Crafts, Boston, but because of the high duty on foreign silverware, it seems that it was not routinely imported to America for resale. At least one American retailer, however, appears to have sold such silverware. Three examples of Ashbee's design for a two-handled footed dish ornamented with cabochon stones that bear the retail mark of Shreve, Crump, and Low Co., of Boston, compare so closely in dimensions, gauge, and soldering techniques to hallmarked Guild of Handicraft dishes as to leave little doubt that the Shreve dishes were part of the guild's production. The major difference is that the three-letter monograms on the Boston dishes are engraved, whereas the guild inscriptions were routinely pricked.[24]

Europe was at war when Ashbee sailed for America in March 1915. Failed utopian dreams and a decreasing momentum to the arts and crafts movement may have accounted for the decision of the council of Boston's Society of Arts and Crafts not to fund an Ashbee lecture. Nevertheless, invitations from the society went out to its members to attend an Ashbee lecture paid for by Arthur J. Stone, then widely acknowledged as the dean of American silversmiths. Ashbee's memoirs record many instances of the difficulties experienced by craftsmen and the need for reform in arts education. All this he noted during his visit. About the Handicraft Club of Baltimore he wrote, "I found Miss [Emily] Graves who was in charge of the shop and Mr. C[harles]. Y. Turner who is in charge of the [Maryland] Institute, both down hearted . . . The Handicraft Club has 150 non-professional members, 50 craftsmen members, and of the latter perhaps, barely 5 earn their livelihood at their work." Of his visit to Byrdcliffe he recalled, "Their great arts and crafts experiment—a really fine venture—has like so many of ours, petered out." Nearby in Milton-on-Hudson he called on the jewelers and metalsmiths of the young Elverhoj Colony in June 1915 and ob-

[24]On Whitehead, see Ashbee, "Little Talk," p. 183, no. 5; Crawford, *Ashbee,* plate 181. Importation is discussed in roll 300, frames 427, 439, SACB Papers. Ashbee incorrectly assumed the duty on the silverware to be 60 percent (the duty on jewelry) when it was 45 percent. For dish examples, see Catherine Kurland and Lori Zabar, *Reflections: Arts and Crafts Metalwork* (New York: Kurland-Zabar, 1990), pp. 6, 14, no. 3, fig. 1; Crawford, *Ashbee,* figs. 167–69, 200; *Rhode Island School of Design Museum Notes* (1989), p. 28.

served, "So far they do not seem to have struck our economic rock, and they maintain the life out of what they produce. . . . There was a good deal of stock and a nervousness as to making more."[25]

If the interest in Ashbee's ideals and the experiments he spawned was ebbing, his influence would nonetheless live on in the field of art education. In his 1916 book, *Industrial Arts Design*, William H. Varnum illustrated Ashbee's guild designs for a loop-handle dish and spoon embellished with cabochon stones, and no historical survey of design since that time seems complete without one of Ashbee's metalwork designs. In 1956 Nikolaus Pevsner summarized, "All the same, one thing is certain: the ideas of Morris and those of Ashbee, after thirty or sixty years, have lost nothing of their vitality and generative power, and on that account alone it seems justified to point out and emphasize their significance for the present."[26]

The Guild of Handicraft was a community whose influence significantly altered the appearance and fabrication methods of American silver, other metalwork, and jewelry while generating sweeping changes in the shop organization, training, locale, and social interaction of those who produced it. Its practices, adopted for both high-minded and commercial purposes—not necessarily with the same goals as Ashbee's—played a major role in defining America's arts and crafts movement. Ashbee and the guild inspired classes in metalwork and jewelry both here and abroad that laid the groundwork for formal educational programs that continue today. As the art critic Frederick W. Coburn wrote in 1915, "It has never been a great enterprise so far as numbers employed and volume of output go; but it has exerted an influence out of proportion to its size."[27]

[25] Ashbee Memoirs, vol. 4, pp. 107, 200, 204. For more on the lecture, see roll 300, frame 775; roll 316, frame 156, SACB Papers.
[26] Nikolaus Pevsner, "William Morris, C. R. Ashbee and the Twentieth Century," *Manchester Review* 7 (Winter 1956): 458. William H. Varnum, *Industrial Arts Design* (Peoria, Ill.: Manual Arts Press, 1916), fig. 440.
[27] Roll 322, frame 330, SACB Papers.

Frans Hals to Windmills
The Arts and Crafts Fascination with the Culture of the Low Countries

Kathleen Eagen Johnson

At the turn of the twentieth century, Americans employed Dutch symbols and stereotypes to articulate ideals associated with the arts and crafts movement. The fascination with the Low Countries (Belgium, Luxembourg, the Netherlands) expressed via material culture took three basic forms: objects imported from the Low Countries as well as those aping Dutch prototypes but made in the United States; artifacts employing Dutch motifs; and products that were marketed with little or no direct tie to Dutch styles by means of allusions to Dutch and Flemish history. Proponents of the American arts and crafts movement believed that the culture of the Low Countries embodied a rich tradition of art; quality workmanship; ideal folk life; middle-class patronage of the arts; an emphasis on the home as a simple, comfortable, clean, yet picturesque refuge; and a stable lifestyle achieved through the use of uncomplicated technology.

Americans drew on stereotypes of the Dutch that had evolved during the nineteenth century. The seventeenth-century burgher represented a kindred figure to the American businessman. In his passion

The author thanks the following scholars who have shared references: Bert Denker, Winterthur Library; Ellen Paul Denker, Wilmington, Del.; Cheryl Robertson, Milwaukee Art Museum; Kenneth R. Trapp, Oakland Museum; and Craig Williams, New York State Museum.

for commerce, the quintessential trader symbolized the significance and value of mercantile pursuits. Through his *Rise of the Dutch Republic*, John Lathrop Motley (1814–77) chronicled the heroic revolt of the Dutch middle class against the Spanish and the creation of a political system similar to that gained by Americans during their revolution. This history found a highly sympathetic audience in the United States. The burgher also represented the period considered the zenith of art in the Netherlands. He and his contemporaries were the patrons as well as the subjects of such artists as Frans Hals (ca. 1588–1666). Followers of the arts and crafts movement respected Dutch patronage of the arts, which was spearheaded by the merchant class.[1]

The protomodern lifestyle of the Calvinist, urban Dutch burgher and his family also held great appeal. The Dutch were first among Europeans to develop the concept of "home," a comfortable physical as well as psychological refuge. Americans were familiar with seventeenth-century Dutch homes as portrayed in genre paintings and appreciated these interiors that were filled with light and air, spotlessly clean, simply but richly furnished, and adorned with inspiring art. The household centered around the children, and even the wealthiest of wives undertook domestic chores. To the burgher and his family, business was paramount, and profits were expended on house and gardens.[2] The stereotypic view of the Dutch burgher mirrored the lifestyle of the American middle-class bungalow dweller.

How did this stereotype evolve? Americans had read popular histories of the Netherlands and were familiar with Dutch paintings either through printed reproductions or originals on display in museums. European and American artists rediscovered the genius of such old masters as Hals, Rembrandt van Rijn, and Sir Anthony Van Dyke. Americans had also inherited enormous reverence for Dutch and Flemish art and architecture as part of the British arts and crafts movement. With the advent of the Glorious Revolution of 1689, England and the Netherlands had shared the same monarchs, William of Orange, and

---

[1] John Lathrop Motley, *The Rise of the Dutch Republic*, 3 vols. (New York: Harper and Brothers, 1855); D. Dodge Thompson, "Frans Hals and American Art," *Antiques* 137, no. 5 (November 1989): 1170–83.

[2] Witold Rybczynski, *Home: A Short History of an Idea* (New York: Viking, 1986), pp. 59–62, 72.

Mary, daughter of James II. These rulers introduced a wave of Continental influence to Britain via Dutch baroque fine and decorative arts and architecture. American as well as British arts and crafts followers treasured this shared history.[3]

The fairy-tale land inhabited by the Dutch peasant was another viable allegory, a place where blonde-haired, blue-eyed farm folk strolled among tulip fields and canals. Provincial costumes included wooden sabots, lace caps, and wide breeches. Men, boys, and women smoked pipes incessantly. Their cozy, well-ordered cottages contained cupboard beds, gaily painted furniture, delftware, and gleaming copper and brass. These industrious people derived pleasure from hard work and lived in balance with nature. They constructed dikes to hold back the ever-threatening sea and employed that most simple and benign machine, the windmill. Some of them even called windmills home. Americans saw these people as the perfect "folk."

The peasant stereotype was based largely on travel experience and literature. Favorite tourist spots included Vollendam and the Isle of Marken, North Sea fishing villages where residents wore nineteenth-century provincial dress and lived in folk houses. American tourists assumed that seventeenth-century citizens of New Netherland had shared a similar existence.

A host of writers offered the armchair traveler a tour of the Low Countries via the printed word. One of the most memorable of these travelogues is *Holland Sketches*, for which Edward Penfield (1866–1925) provided haunting poster-style renderings and descriptive reminiscences (fig. 1). Many Americans shared his love of the Netherlands and dreamed that life in New Netherland had been as equally picturesque.[4]

Children's literature was a particularly potent vehicle for the dissemination of stereotypical views. Books describing the national traits of various peoples contributed to both the burgher and peasant stereotypes by focusing on the Dutch love of money, cleanliness, hard work, and, of course, smoking. Mary Mapes Dodge (1831–1905) added to

[3]Thompson, "Frans Hals," pp. 1172–73, 1174–75, 1176, 1178, 1180.
[4]Edward Penfield, *Holland Sketches* (New York: Charles Scribner's Sons, 1907), pp. 69–70; see also: William Elliot Griffis, *The American in Holland* (Boston: Houghton Mifflin, 1907); J. P. Mahaffy and J. E. Rogers, *Sketches from a Tour through Holland and Germany* (London: Macmillan, 1889); and Nico Jungman and Beatrix Jungman, *Holland* (London: Adam and Charles Black, 1904).

Fig. 1. A Marken interior. From Edward Penfield, *Holland Sketches* (New York: Charles Scribner's Sons, 1907), p. 101. (Gregory and Kathleen Eagen Johnson.)

this body of lore through *Hans Brinker; or, The Silver Skates*. The book presents positive images such as the brave peasant boy Hans, his plucky sister Gretel, and the lad who saves his village by standing for hours plugging up a leaking dike. Through Dodge and other authors of juvenile literature, appealing stereotypes proliferated.[5]

Washington Irving (1783–1859) created the third stereotype, that

[5]*Men of Different Countries* (Cooperstown, N.Y.: H. and E. Phinney, 1837), p. 12; *A Description of Various Nations* (Concord, N.H.: Rufus Merrill, 1843), p. 8; Mary

of the Dutch New Yorker who wore two faces. The first was that of the fat, phlegmatic buffoon who spent most of his time smoking, drinking, and trying to untangle himself from troublesome situations as described in Irving's first major work, *History of New-York*. The second falls into a sadder and more reflective vein. Rip Van Winkle, who appeared in *The Sketch Book*, epitomized the dreamer who had unwittingly lost his world to awaken in a much-changed new one. Irving, through his descriptive style of writing, created mythic and unforgettable characters.[6]

Irving's writings underwent a resurgence in popularity around 1900. Many new editions were enhanced by arts and crafts–style illustrations. E.W. Kemble (1861–1933) filled the art nouveau–style page borders of an edition of *History of New York* with tankards, clay pipes, and other Dutch touches. Will Bradley (1868–1962) produced *Rip Van Winkle* and *The Legend of Sleepy Hollow* with bold illustrations reflective of his fascination with eighteenth-century woodcuts. Dard Hunter (1883–1966) designed an edition of *Rip Van Winkle* for the Roycroft Shops. His title page and capital letters, also in a woodcut style, incorporate commonly found Dutch motifs. Maxfield Parrish (1870–1966) used a 1900 edition of the *History of New York* as a springboard for his own "other worldly" visions. The affable image of the Dutch New Yorker was further disseminated by the actor Joseph Jefferson (1829–1905), who made a career playing Rip Van Winkle through a series of international tours beginning in 1865. New Yorkers, and Americans in general, took a certain pleasure in Irving's tales, which had achieved the status of folklore.[7]

In the creation of these positive stereotypes, certain national traits and historical realities were softened, forgotten, or rejected. The Dutch had not always been considered a model ethnic group. The derisive connotation of the word *dutch* in English slang is reflective of the ill

---

Mapes Dodge, *Hans Brinker; or, The Silver Skates: A Story of Life in Holland* (1865; reprint, New York: Airmont, 1966), pp. 226–40, 101–4.

[6]Dietrich Knickerbocker [Washington Irving], *A History of New-York, from the Beginning of the World to the End of the Dutch Dynasty* (New York: Inskeep and Bradford, 1809); Washington Irving, *The Sketch-Book of Geoffrey Crayon, Gent.*, 2 vols. (London: John Murray, 1820).

[7]Dietrich Knickerbocker [Washington Irving], *History of New York*, 2 vols. (New York: G. P. Putnam's Sons, 1894); *Rip Van Winkle: From the Sketch Book of Washington Irving* (New York: R. H. Russell for Will Bradley, [1897]); Washington Irving, *Rip Van Winkle* (East Aurora, N.Y.: Roycroft Shop, 1905); Dietrich Knickerbocker [Washington Irving], *History of New York* (New York: R.H. Russell, 1900).

will shown by the English to their rival during the seventeenth century. Some usage reflects parsimoniousness, as in the case of the familiar "dutch treat." Other phrases suggest the love of alcohol ascribed to the Dutch, as in "dutch courage"—valor provided by liquor. The supposed cheerless Dutch disposition is referred to in "dutch consolation" and "dutch uncle," a stern critic. Travelers to New York also had many unkind things to say about the Dutch. During the 1740s Peter Kalm harped on the cold-hearted stinginess of the inhabitants of Albany, a trait attributed to the Dutch worldwide. Nearly one hundred years later Nathaniel Parker Willis sneered, "Albany looks so good from a distance, that you half forgive it for its hogs, offals, broken pavements, and other nuisances more Dutch than decent," a comment suggestive of a less-than-ideal tidy Dutch town. As the Dutch of Albany and surrounding backwaters were assimilated, such unpleasantries vanished and were replaced in New Yorkers' minds by visions of glorious ancestors or by comic images drawn from Irving's writings. Time passed, and flaws attributed to the Dutch were viewed in a different light: theirs was an ability to drive a hard bargain, not penuriousness; the tendency for overindulgence in food, drink, and tobacco was now viewed as a charming foible; and their collective disposition was not dour but even tempered.[8]

These stereotypes, with few exceptions, served as a vehicle for the promotion of antimodern, rather than progressive, ideals. Although the Netherlands and Belgium were home to such avant garde art movements as de stijl and symbolism, Dutch symbols and products generally reflected conservative values and styles in America. Exceptions included art nouveau–style pottery, created in Gouda and Arnhem and imported into the United States. At least one American firm, the Van Der Muelen and Wykstra Pottery of Dunkirk, New York, created wares in a similar style although the majority of its products were in the more traditional delftware style.[9]

[8]Willis is quoted in William Kennedy, *O Albany!* (New York: Viking, 1983), p. 57. On special terminology, see *The Compact Edition of the Oxford English Dictionary*, 2 vols. (New York: Oxford University Press, 1971), 1:729; Adolph B. Benson, ed., *Peter Kalm's Travels in North America, The English Version of 1770*, 2 vols. (New York: Dover, 1966), 1:344–46.

[9]Advertisement, *Crockery and Glass Journal* (January 2, 1908): 4; Coy L. Ludwig, *The Arts and Crafts Movement in New York State, 1890s–1920s* (Hamilton, N.Y.: Gallery Assoc. of New York State, 1983), p. 110.

The use of the term *dutch* vis-à-vis mission furniture is confusing. Is this allusion forward or backward looking? Oscar Onken's Shop of the Crafters catalogue contained sixteen plates of modern-style Dutch interior design, with such titles as *Suggestion for a Dining Room in Old Dutch* and *Suggestion for a Living Room in Flemish*. The text of the Charles P. Limbert Company catalogues also stressed a close association with then-current European trends in art furniture. When Alwyn T. Covell used the term *dutch* to refer to mission furniture of extremely heavy proportions in "The Real Place of Mission Furniture," what was the aim? Was the term an accepted "buzz word" for the massive mission furniture of the sort created by the Limbert Company of Grand Rapids, Michigan, and the Shop of the Crafters in Cincinnati? Both concerns stressed ties to northern European traditions of craftsmanship as well as modern styles in their trade catalogues. Could the term be an antimodern reference to substantial specimens of Dutch cabinetmaking like the *kas*? Was it chosen because the proportions and brass-studded leather upholstery of some mission chairs were reminiscent of the farthingale chair of the seventeenth century? W.F. Halstrick of Chicago advertised a mission armchair as "a *hand-made* reproduction of an Antique Dutch Chair finished in Flemish Oak, with cane or leather seat. Solidly built on true colonial lines." Aymar Embury II (1880–1966) remarked that "the better designed craftsman furniture is not dissimilar from the rudest and roughest of the homemade colonial" in *The Dutch Colonial House*. This allusion may well be a mixed metaphor, expressive of progressive as well as conservative ideals, symbolically as well as stylistically.[10]

By 1900 American culture held the artistic output and traditions of the Low Countries in extremely high regard. Artists and art critics from the mid nineteenth century onward venerated the golden-colored

[10] Aymar Embury II, *The Dutch Colonial House: Its Origin, Design, Modern Plan, and Construction* (New York: McBride, Nast, 1913), pp. 106–7; *Arts and Crafts Furniture: Shop of the Crafters at Cincinnati*, ed. Stephen Gray (New York: Turn of the Century Editions, 1983); *Charles P. Limbert, Cabinetmakers, Booklet No. 112* (reprint, New York: Turn of the Century Editions, 1981), p. 8. Alwyn T. Covell, "The Real Place of Mission Furniture," *Good Furniture* 6, no. 6 (March 1915): 360. Advertisement, *House Beautiful* 7 (November 1900): 706, quoted in Wendy Kaplan, *"The Art That Is Life": The Arts and Crafts Movement in America, 1875–1920* (Boston: Museum of Fine Arts, 1987), p. 356.

Fig. 2. Rookwood Pottery, vase, Grace
Young (decorator), Cincinnati, 1903. Buff
earthenware; H. 12″. (Don Treadway Antiques.)

canvases of the old masters. American arts and crafts followers had
inherited respect for the medieval period "art life" of the Low Countries
from William Morris and the Pre-Raphaelites. This reverence extended
to the work of Jan van Eyck and other "Flemish primitive" painters as
well as to the flourishing guild system, whose members established
standards of quality, oversaw the training of journeymen and apprentices, and conducted charitable activities. The creators and vendors of

American arts and crafts—style products drew upon the sterling reputation of Low Countries artists and artisans for design and marketing inspiration, and consumers responded readily. From Gustav Stickley's use of the slogan *Als ik kan* (as well as I can), borrowed from van Eyck via Morris, to the discourses on Dutch art history contained in furniture catalogues, American arts-and-crafters considered the employment of such references to be suggestive of artistic knowledge and taste.[11]

Indebtedness to Dutch and Flemish art was an ongoing theme expressed in profound and prosaic ways. As artists made study copies of and skilled visual allusions to the work of Hals and others in the area of "high art," decorators working at Rookwood Pottery also emulated the painterly style and subject matter of the old masters (fig. 2). The reproduction of the subject matter of Dutch canvases on vases and plaques reflected our culture's widespread recognition of works by Hals and van Dyke as inherently suitable for "art pottery." While on one plane the Metropolitan Museum of Art mounted a landmark exhibition of seventeenth-century Dutch painting and *The Craftsman* contained articles on the appreciation of Dutch art and the history of the Dutch guild system, similar allusions were made in the popular press. In 1910 William H. Goodyear wrote "What the Dutch School Stands for," with the audience of the *Ladies' Home Journal* in mind. A Limbert catalogue copywriter praised the "genuine artistic spirit" found among the Dutch factory workers employed there, "the fellow countrymen of Rembrant, Rubens, Van Dyke, and Frans Hals." Even the promoters of pyrography, the art of creating burned decorations on wood, traded on the fame of the old masters with the name Flemish Art Company.[12]

Arts and crafts followers attributed a high degree of craftsmanship

---

[11] Mary Ann Smith, *Gustav Stickley, The Craftsman* (Syracuse, N.Y.: Syracuse University Press, 1983), p. 31.

[12] Kirsten Hoving Keen, *American Art Pottery, 1875–1930* (Wilmington: Delaware Art Museum, 1978), p. 17, fig. 27; Edward Hagaman Hall, *The Hudson-Fulton Celebration 1909: The Fourth Annual Report of the Hudson-Fulton Celebration Commission to the Legislature of the State of New York*, 2 vols. (Albany: State of New York, 1910), 1:177–80; Louis Arthur Holman, "Rembrandt and His Etchings," *The Craftsman* 11, no. 1 (April 1906): 26–42; Irene Sargent, "German and Netherlander: Their Guilds and Art," *The Craftsman* 3, no. 4 (January 1903): 201–14; William H. Goodyear, "What the Dutch School Stands for," *Ladies' Home Journal* 27 (May 1910): 20–21; *Charles P. Limbert Company, Cabinetmakers, Booklet No. 100* (reprint, Watkins Glen, N.Y.: American Life Foundation, 1982), p. 4.

to the Dutch and saw in that culture a fusion of art and craft. For centuries the Dutch had enjoyed world renown for their artistry in delftware; this reputation was bolstered by the popularity of china collecting, reborn during the aesthetic period. Art pottery sprang forth from this renewed appreciation. Businesses such as the Holland Delft and Specialty Company imported specimens of delft art to the United States. At least two American potteries, Cook Pottery in Trenton, New Jersey, and the Van Der Muelen and Wykstra Pottery (in partnership 1906–9) emulated delftware in the form of white earthenware with freehand decoration in blue. Cook Pottery had begun to manufacture delftware in 1897. Gerrit Wykstra had trained in Delft as a ceramicist, immigrated to the Buffalo area in 1900, and continued to make wares in a delft style long after the Van Der Muelen and Wykstra Pottery partnership had dissolved. Other art potteries relied on conventional Dutch motifs. Roseville Pottery introduced its "Dutch," "Landscape," and "Holland" patterns in 1900, 1915, and 1930 respectively. Weller Pottery marketed lines decorated with Dutch girls and windmills under the names "Holland" and "Dresden," unveiled between 1907 and 1909, and, starting in 1904, the Owens Pottery Company created bucket-shape, blue-and-white wares with Dutch scenes that it termed *delft*. Dutch peasants, windmills, and sailing ships became part of the standard vocabulary of ornament.[13]

The superiority of Dutch artisans was also expressed through other media. Dirk Van Erp (1859–1933), an immigrant to San Francisco who had been born and trained as a coppersmith in Leewarden, used a windmill as part of his mark when he opened his own shop in 1908—a nod to his origins. To many, Van Erp epitomized the unmatched Dutch craftsman.[14]

---

[13] Advertisement, *Crockery and Glass Journal* (January 2, 1908): 4; Edwin AtLee Barber, *The Pottery and Porcelain of the United States* (1909; reprint, New York: Feingold and Lewis, 1976), pp. 485–86; the only known example of the Cook Pottery Company's delft survives in the collection of the New Jersey State Museum in the form of a jardiniere or ice jug (New Jersey State Museum catalogue sheet 83.53); Ludwig, *Arts and Crafts Movement*, p. 110; the New York State Museum owns examples of Van Der Muelen's delftware (unidentified clipping attached to New York State Museum catalogue sheets 52.9.5-.13); Ralph Kovel and Terry Kovel, *The Kovels' Collector's Guide to American Art Pottery* (New York: Crown Publishers, 1974), pp. 250, 252, 310, 157. Weller also used the name "Flemish ware" to refer to several patterns, none of which had an overt link to subject matter of the Low Countries; Kovel and Kovel, *Collector's Guide*, p. 310.

[14] Kaplan, "*Art That Is Life,*" pp. 275–76.

Mission furniture companies used Dutch artisanship as a marketing technique. The Limbert Company employed Dutch workers and played the connection to the hilt in advertising copy. Text praising the virtues of the Dutch craftsman and illustrations of busy factory laborers dressed in modern clothing but wearing sabots underscored the point.[15]

The Shop of the Crafters also marketed American arts and crafts–style furniture with a few Dutch allusions. It offered "Flemish oak" among finishes and furniture with "dutchy" decoration, such as hall seats and hat racks with tulip-shape cutouts, or Dutch names such as the "Van Dyke Clock," a model supposedly copied from an original in the artist's home but which resembles a standard mission tall-case clock. Furniture makers stressed a Dutch connection to suggest quality and refinement.[16]

The largely conservative proponents of the arts and crafts movement found what they considered to be a parallel and sympathetic society in seventeenth-century Holland. The turn of this century was a time of tumult in the political, social, and technological arenas, and Americans responded by fashioning their own world view. Theirs was a society driven by capitalism, conservatism, and Calvinism, where ethnic stereotypes held true and one could escape growing global pressures by lavishing attention to one's home environment.

Writer after writer turned to the Dutch as a model. Edmondo de Amici spoke for many when he outlined the admirable qualities of the Dutch, including good sense, tenacity, orderliness, and prudence. Sydney R. Jones wrote that the domestic art of the Netherlands was "essentially the expression of a nation urgently concerned with the material, matter-of-fact side of life, . . . it was corporeal rather than spiritual in aspect, reflective of the market-place, the fireside, and the home." William Laurel Harris recorded his views on Vreedryk Felypsen in *Good Furniture*. Felypsen, a carpenter, rose to a premier financial position in the province of New York as a result of his business acumen. A high level of craftsmanship present in New York was evidenced by Felypsen's house and decorative arts in general. Harris concluded: "As an illustrious hero and as an example of intelligence and virtue, it is well for us in modern America to study and imitate Felypsen

[15] *Limbert Booklet No. 112*, pp. 5–7; *Charles P. Limbert, Cabinetmakers, Booklet No. 119* (reprint, New York: Turn of the Century Editions, 1981), pp. 26–64.
[16] Gray, *Arts and Crafts*, pp. 10, 51, 63, 66.

. . . in many of our social, industrial, and artistic undertakings." This sort of heroic sentiment echos the reliance on Dutch motifs for the decoration of masculine furniture forms and retreats such as dens. The Dutch considered the partaking of tobacco and alcohol suitable leisure pastimes, as did many of their arts and crafts–period counterparts. The Shop of the Crafters created furniture with Dutch decoration for men: a shaving stand with Dutch girl painted on the door; a combination shoe box-valet with inset delftware tiles; and an "Old Holland" clock, the sort used in dens and smoking rooms, with decoration on its face in the form of two men—probably monks—drinking and conversing. A Quaker Shop catalogue, *The Den, and How to Furnish It*, featured a stein and plate rack ornamented by a scene of Dutch boys frolicking at leapfrog while girls look on (fig. 3). For display on such a rack, Clewell Studio offered "faithful reproductions of the original old Holland Steins of four hundred years ago" made of hammered copper with a porcelain lining. As outlined in a chapter on smoking rooms in Oliver Coleman's *Successful Houses*, a Dutch-style room should reflect the "sober and severe" nature of this people. The author earmarked such architectural features as high wainscoting topped by a shelf, rough plaster painted a rich yellow, a hooded and tiled fireplace, and built-in settles. Furniture included "chairs in Dutch shapes." The crowning accessories include steins, delftware plates, pewter mugs and flagons, pipe racks, rare prints, brass candlesticks and andirons, and hanging iron lamps.[17]

Interior design emulated the burgher's surroundings. The Holland Delft and Specialty Company boasted, "We furnish Dutch rooms" and

[17] Edmondo de Amici, *Holland and Its People* (New York: G. P. Putnam's Sons, 1885), pp. 13–14; Sydney R. Jones, *Old Houses in Holland* (London: The Studio, 1913), p. 4; William Laurel Harris, "Vreedryk Felypsen, His Mills, His Commerce, and the Furnishings of His Castle," *Good Furniture* 8, no. 3 (March 1917): 158. I am indebted to Cheryl Robertson for pointing out the connection between Dutch decoration and dens and for sharing related references; *The Den, and How to Furnish It as Suggested by the Quaker Shop* (Philadelphia, [ca. 1903]), p. 12; Kovel and Kovel, *Collector's Guide*, p. 16; Oliver Coleman, *Successful Houses* (Chicago: H. S. Stone, 1899), p. 80; Gray, *Arts and Crafts*, pp. 46, 58, 67. Similar decoration extended to private clubs. A stained glass window depicting Antony Van Corlear, trumpeter of New Amsterdam, who is surrounded by women with glass held high, was designed by Howard Pyle, executed by Louis Comfort Tiffany, and installed in Manhattan's Colonial Club around 1896. The window is now in the collection of the Delaware Art Museum, Wilmington.

Stein and Plate Rack No. 1201

With imported Dutch Panel. 44 inches Wide; 21 inches High

Price, ...$9 00

Fig. 3. Stein and plate rack no. 1201. From *The Den, and How to Furnish It as Suggested by the Quaker Shop* (Philadelphia, [ca. 1903]), p. 12. (Winterthur Library.)

offer "complete lines of Delft Art, Vases, Placques, Mantel Sets, Holland Art Pottery (new), Holland Green (new), Tiles, Tile Pictures, Paintings on Canvas, Water Colors, Modern and Old Brass, Dutch Silver, etc." Although aimed primarily at a British market, a special 1913 supplement to *The Studio* was devoted totally to "old houses in Holland" and their influence on home decoration. The most revealing inclusions are the advertisements that document a full array of Dutch-inspired products ranging from wallpapers to electrified chandeliers.[18]

[18]Advertisement, *Crockery and Glass Journal* (January 2, 1908): 4; Jones, *Old Houses*, pp. viii, ii.

Designers also drew on the seventeenth-century Low Countries furniture of oak and walnut as prototypes for a revival style referred to as "Flemish" or "Flanders." In the same issue of *The Studio*, a London concern offered reproduction furniture with twist-turned legs. "Flanders Furniture, Its New Popularity" appeared in magazines like *Suburban Life* (1910); in the same year Comepackt advertised "Flanders" style furniture. This sort of revival furniture appeared in *The Craftsman* and was one of several styles offered by the Limbert factory. The translation of the style to fit the needs of the modern family included some startling adaptations. Embury illustrated sets of baroque-style twin beds, one pair with twist-turned uprights and stretchers and caned headboards and footboards and the other with inverted baluster-turned members. Flemish-style furniture was another romantic link to the rich and comfortable interiors of the burgher's home of the seventeenth century.[19]

Interest in the Dutch coincided with a growing consumption of commercial cleaning products. Americans had taken the arts and crafts tenet stressing the value of dirt-free and dust-free surroundings to heart. Contemporary periodicals featured apt and appealing advertising trademarks often rendered in a poster style, including the Dutch boy representing the purity of white lead in house paint, Old Dutch Cleanser's "earnest Dutch matron with stick in hand 'chasing dirt' " (fig. 4), and the Dutch boy designed by Parrish for Colgate and Company. Penfield contributed a rendering of the facade of a Dutch urban house with housewife reading in the attic and husband ensconced on the stoop with pipe in hand for the January 1903 cover of *Good Housekeeping*. An editorial note points out that "the spick and span housekeeping of the Netherlands is proverbial." Identification of a well-ordered home with the Dutch was so strong that the designer of the *Larkin Housewives Cook Book* could not resist placing a Dutch woman on the cover, even though the Dutch are not well known for culinary pursuits. Cleanliness and orderliness had long held the position of a religion of sorts in the

[19] Advertisement in Jones, *Old Houses*, p. i; Flanders furniture is mentioned in Kaplan, "Art That Is Life," p. 356 n. 79; Comepackt advertisement, *Ladies' Home Journal* 27 (April 1910): 93; "The Value of Flowers in Interior Decoration," *Craftsman* 29, no. 4 (January 1916): 427; Flanders-style secretary-bookcase by Limbert illustrated in Kaplan, "Art That Is Life," p. 167; beds illustrated in Embury, *Dutch Colonial*, p. 100, figs. facing p. 98.

Fig. 4. From *Hints for Housewives, Old Dutch Cleanser* (Omaha, Nebr.: Cudahy Packing Co., [ca. 1900]). (Gregory and Kathleen Eagen Johnson.)

Netherlands, and Americans immediately identified with this national trait.[20]

The arts and crafts appreciation of folk culture translated into a reverence for the Dutch as model peasants. Although the late nineteenth century also witnessed the last wave of Dutch immigration to the United States, this time to the Midwest, "old Americans" did not fear the Dutch, in marked contrast to their xenophobic view of immigrants from southern and eastern Europe. Sentimental renderings of Dutch peasants graced a plethora of objects in their homes. Even Queen Wilhelmena I of the Netherlands assumed the role of the model peasant in M. Paul Berthon's 1901 poster-style portrait, an extremely popular print in America. The lithograph shows the queen wearing a lace cap, with tulips and windmill in the background. She transcends her royal status to represent Dutch womanhood.[21]

Peasants also appeared in marketing pieces. Stickley's Craftsman Shops employed the image of Dutch peasants using mission furniture in an early advertisement. The Limbert Company drew on such an association again and again. In one catalogue, a woman in an arts and crafts–style interior gazes out a window at a Dutch scene of canal and windmill (fig. 5). In an advertisement, a Dutch woman wearing provincial garb serves tea to a woman in contemporary dress. Both are at home with Limbert Company arts and crafts furniture.[22]

The tenet that designers look to regional, vernacular culture for inspirtion was also applied to colonial Dutch New York. Tracing its beginnings back to the shingle style of the late nineteenth century, the revival of the Dutch colonial-style house enjoyed national acceptance,

[20] See advertising brochure, *Hints for Housewives, Old Dutch Cleanser* (Omaha, Nebr.: Cudahy Packing Co., [ca. 1900]), p. 4; *Good Housekeeping* 36, no. 1 (January 1903): 63, cover; *Good Housekeeping* 47, no. 3 (September 1908); *Good Housekeeping* 47, no. 3 (September 1908); Coy Ludwig, *Maxfield Parrish* (New York: Watson-Guptill, 1973), p. 212; *Larkin Housewives Cook Book* (Buffalo, N.Y.: Larkin Co., 1915). According to Witold Rybczynski, the Dutch obsession with cleanliness in the seventeenth century was not associated with health and hygiene but rather denoted home "as a separate, special place." It is no accident that "the Dutch word for clean, *schoon*, also expresses beauty and purity" (Rybczynski, *Home*, pp. 65–66).

[21] Gray, *Arts and Crafts*, p. 46; Victor Arwas, *Berthon and Grasset* (London: Academy Edition, 1978), pp. 114–16.

[22] The advertisement for the Craftsman Workshops in *Boyd's Syracuse City Directory* (Syracuse, 1904) is illustrated in Ludwig, *Arts and Crafts Movement*, p. 63; *Limbert Booklet No. 112*, facing p. 64; *The Craftsman* 27, no. 2 (November 1914): 45a.

Fig. 5. From *Charles P. Limbert, Cabinetmakers, Booklet No. 112* (reprint, New York: Turn of the Century Editions, 1981), facing p. 64.

in part due to Embury's book. The form, with its overhanging gambrel roof, is reminiscent of eighteenth-century houses built in rural areas surrounding Manhattan, but the term *dutch colonial* is a bit of a misnomer, according to Embury. In America, the use of a gambrel, rather than a steeply pitched Gothic roofline, in areas of Dutch colonization is considered an English introduction. This "ethnically mongrel" style flourished in eighteenth-century Long Island and northern New Jersey, areas of mixed Dutch and English settlement. Embury saw the revival of this style as a suitable answer to Americans, many of whom desired long, low houses. Interior finishing could include the use of light colors in a colonial style or rough plaster, wainscoting, and exposed beams, which he termed *dutch*. "The most we can claim for modern work is that it is, to some extent at least, Dutch in spirit, and the sort of thing which the Dutch architects might have done had they happened to think of it," stated Embury.[23]

The reproduction of the dutch colonial chair, the York chair, echoed a similar sentiment and offered an equally complicated history. Manufactured by a number of firms as representative of furniture created in rural, Dutch New York, the form, in actuality, owes more to England and New England than Holland in its design. It cannot be termed purely colonial, as it was made long after the conclusion of the revolutionary war, and was largely the product of urban, rather than rural, chairmaking shops. Still, the York chair epitomized New York vernacular furniture and found a warm reception in colonial revival interiors.[24]

Exploration of the role of the Dutch in New York history intensified after the turn of the century. The major public event that ushered in this fascination was the 1909 Hudson-Fulton Celebration, a com-

---

[23] Vincent J. Scully, Jr., *The Shingle Style: Architectural Theory and Design from Richardson to the Origins of Wright* (New Haven: Yale University Press, 1955), pp. 48–49; Embury, *Dutch Colonial*, pp. 20, 7–8, 6, ii, 83, fig. facing p. 82. The Dutch Colonial and other Dutch-inspired revival architectural styles were also used for public buildings. See William B. Rhoads, "Roadside Colonial: Early American Design for the Automobile Age, 1900–1940," *Winterthur Portfolio* 21, nos. 2/3 (Summer/Autumn 1986): 133–52.

[24] Kathleen Eagen Johnson, "The Fiddleback Chair," *Art and Antiques* 4, no. 5 (September–October 1981): 78–83; *Conant-Ball Colonial Furniture Catalogue* (Boston: Conant-Ball Co., [ca. 1930]), p. 53. I thank William B. Rhoads for pointing out that the Sheraton Chair Co. advertised reproduction York chairs in *International Studio*.

memoration of Henry Hudson's 1609 exploration of the river that now bears his name and Robert Fulton's successful launch of his steamship in 1807. The autumn of 1909 was filled with lectures, parades, and exhibitions. The Metropolitan Museum of Art's display of early American fine and decorative arts, in fact, is considered the first by a major museum. The two-week-long celebration ran the length of the Hudson River.[25]

One of the major aims of the Hudson-Fulton Celebration was "the assimilation of the adopted population," and New Yorkers even went so far as to use their Dutch heritage to promote the acculturation of recent immigrants. The commissioners hoped to instill pride and loyalty for American social and political institutions and drove this point home by creating the figure Father Knickerbocker, based on Irving's character Dietrich Knickerbocker, as a focal point of the history of the New York parade. The parade culminated with Father Knickerbocker welcoming all the peoples of the world to New York. As the commissioners remarked, "Historical culture thus materially promotes the welfare of the Commonwealth."[26]

Most of the official commemorative objects and publications for the celebration were designed in a beaux arts, rather than arts and crafts, style, but the two largest artifacts, life-size models of Hudson's and Fulton's vessels, the *Half Moon* and the *North River Steamship* (later referred to as *The Clermont*), reflected an approach in keeping with arts and crafts philosophy. So too did examples of constructive work outlined in a handbook issued by the New York State Education Department, including pictures of children fashioning a birch canoe, wigwam, canal lock, colonial fireplace, and waterwheel and mill in miniature.[27]

In the early twentieth century interest in the colonial Dutch was expressed through a flurry of book illustration. Elbert Hubbard rode the crest of Hudson-Fulton Celebration fever with *Manhattan and Henry Hudson*, a volume that contained an ode by Joseph I.C. Clarke as well as Hubbard's own peculiar reflections on Hudson. Hunter de-

[25] Hall, *Hudson-Fulton*, 2:715–19, 829–43, 844–73, 1:72–73, 198–245, 354–60, 120–25, 345–53, 361–82, 174–97, 180–83; Natalie Curtis, "The Hudson-Fulton Memorial Art Exhibition," *The Craftsman* 17, no. 2 (November 1909): 124–41.

[26] Hall, *Hudson-Fulton*, 1:7, 8, 304.

[27] Hall, *Hudson-Fulton*, 1:75–115; Harland Hoyt Horner, *Hudson-Fulton Celebration* (Albany: New York State Education Department, 1909), p. 11.

signed the volume. In a similar vein, for the poster-style cover of the
1909 *Westchester County Historical Pageant*, Violet Oakley depicted
early New Yorkers in romantic costume inspired by Frans Hals. Rekin-
dled interest in early New York sparked the publication of countless
histories, many in an arts and crafts style.[28]

The antitechnological bent of the arts and crafts philosophy found
ready expression through the widespread proliferation of symbols often
associated with the Dutch, including the windmill and the sailing ship.
Although windmills could be found across Europe and the United
States, the structures were readily identified with the Netherlands.
While the symbol of the sailing ship enjoyed international appeal during
this period, it held special meaning to New Yorkers as Hudson's mode
of transport. His ship, under sail, appeared on the cover of *Manhattan*,
ploughing the waters around the border of a Hudson-Fulton commemorative plate. It was also memorialized in stained glass windows, as seen in
the arts and crafts–style Joseph I. Dowling house, built in Albany in 1909,
and in the Albany Chamber of Commerce's rooms.[29]

The character Rip Van Winkle also symbolized alienation from
a modern world and was appropriated by designers other than book
illustrators. A Rookwood decorator portrayed the actor Jefferson as Rip
Van Winkle on a three-handled cup in 1903. Henry Chapman Mercer,
who had spent part of his youth in the Hudson River valley, designed
and executed fireplace surrounds at the Moravian Tile and Pottery
Works at Doylestown, Pennsylvania, that were based on stories with
deep meaning to Americans. The tale of Rip Van Winkle was a most
appropriate subject.[30]

[28] Elbert Hubbard, *Manhattan and Henry Hudson* (East Aurora, N.Y.: Roycroft
Shop, 1910) contained a poem by Joseph I. C. Clarke, *The Book of the Words, Westchester
County Historical Pageant* (1909). Mrs. John King Van Rensselaer, *The Goed Vrouw of
Mana-ha-ta* (New York: Charles Scribner's Sons, 1898), and Margherita Arlina Hamm,
Famous Families of New York, 2 vols. (New York: G. P. Putnam's Knickerbocker Press,
1902), are two of many such histories.

[29] Hubbard, *Manhattan*; the commemorative plate, the official dinnerware for the
Hudson-Fulton banquet at Hotel Astor, September 29, 1909, is part of the collection at
Historic Hudson Valley; Harvey M. Kaplan, "The Parking Lot at 116 Washington Avenue," *Tiller* 1 (September–October 1982): 18; the Dowling window is now in the collection of the New York State Museum.

[30] Cleota Reed, *Henry Chapman Mercer and the Moravian Pottery and Tile Works*
(Philadelphia: University of Pennsylvania Press, 1987), pp. 147–50; cup illustrated in
Parke-Bernet sale catalogue, "Good Decorative Works of Art, Furniture, and Rugs from

While American arts and crafts proponents sang the praises of the Dutch people, theirs was not necessarily a wholehearted embrace. Many Americans continued to be Anglophiles. The commissioners of the Hudson-Fulton Celebration, for example, chose to focus on two men in the history of New York who were both English by birth.

In the eyes of Americans, the Dutch were ethnic but not too ethnic; picturesque in their provincial dress and dramatic landscape; non-threatening politically and militarily; a stalwart nation of merchants and farmers with a monumental artistic tradition; harnessers of a sometimes cruel Mother Nature; and creators of modest but cozy homes and gardens.

Why, however, did Dutch symbols and styles enjoy national, even international, appeal? The Dutch role in the founding and settlement of New York, the cultural, artistic, and publishing capital of the United States in 1900, was translated into a widespread distribution of this indigenous style. The publicity that accompanied the Hudson-Fulton Celebration further promoted interest in things Dutch. Dutch settlement, of course, was not restricted only to New York but also occurred in New Jersey, Delaware, and some Midwest states, thus prompting a broad range of appeal. Like the Spanish revival in California, the Dutch revival was accompanied by a body of romantic literature, including the legendary stories of Irving and Dodge. Its lure seemed irresistible.

Americans used Dutch objects, symbols, and stereotypes to represent aspects of arts and crafts ideology. The hodgepodge of stereotypes employed—urban and rural, bourgeois and peasant, masculine and feminine, Dutch and Dutch-English-American—reflected what the American proponents and followers considered shared values: the artificiality of drawing distinctions between art and craft; the role of the home as a clean, cozy, family-centered haven; the need to draw inspiration from local, indigenous folklife and adapt aspects to meet the demands of modern living; the advocacy of employing simple, nonthreatening technology; and a yearning for a simpler, golden era. Arts and crafts believers warmly received this idealized Dutch world as expressive of their own social needs and aspirations at the turn of the twentieth century.

1875 and American and European Paintings, Drawings, Watercolors, and Sculpture" (June 11–12, 1980), lot 99.

Aesthetics and Meanings
The Arts and Crafts Movement and the Revival of American Indian Basketry

Melanie Herzog

At the end of the nineteenth century, American Indian arts enjoyed an extraordinary surge in interest. Principal among these arts was basketry. American Indian baskets were acquired by non-Indian collectors in unprecedented numbers. One commonly recognized reason for this interest was the popular concern for the "vanishing Indian," the idea that the Indian way of life was about to be swept away in the onslaught of modernity. This prevalent cultural attitude reflected what was seen as the inevitable outcome of the confinement of Indians to reservations

This study had its genesis in the author's research for "American Indian Art: The Collecting Experience," an exhibition curated by Beverly Gordon at the Elvehjem Museum of Art, University of Wisconsin–Madison. (Beverly Gordon with Melanie Herzog, *American Indian Art: The Collecting Experience* [Madison, Wis.: Elvehjem Museum of Art, 1988]). Many of the ideas contained in this essay are explored more fully in Melanie Herzog, "Gathering Traditions: The Arts and Crafts Movement and the Revival of American Indian Basketry" (Master's thesis, University of Wisconsin–Madison, 1989).

The Elvehjem exhibition and the author's focus on baskets shared the same impetus, a collection of eighty-three American Indian baskets donated to the Elvehjem Museum by the Van Zelst family in 1984. The author thanks Beverly Gordon, associate professor of environment, textiles, and design, and Barbara Buenger, associate professor of art history at the University of Wisconsin–Madison, for their support and encouragement and the Elvehjem Museum of Art for making the Van Zelst collection accessible for her research. She also thanks William C. Bunce, director of the Kohler Art Library at the University of Wisconsin–Madison, for his knowledgeable and generous assistance and for kindly providing access to journals such as *The Craftsman*.

and the intensified efforts to assimilate them into dominant American society.[1] The concept of the vanishing Indian suggested that although individuals of Native American heritage would survive, Indian culture faced a certain death. The increased concern with American Indian arts was thus in part an interest in artifacts of cultures believed to be on the verge of extinction.

Other attitudes also played a crucial role in this proliferation of interest. The height of attention to Indian baskets was reached between 1900 and 1910, concurrent with the broadest influence of the arts and crafts movement in the United States. Arts and crafts proponents admired Indian art and particularly recommended Navajo weavings, Pueblo pottery, and Southwest and California baskets as furnishings for the arts and crafts home. Turn-of-the-century writings on American Indian baskets and basket makers consistently echo arts and crafts sentiments and language and are infused with the nostalgia for a simpler way of life in which arts and crafts ideals were fundamentally grounded.[2]

The often contradictory values that informed arts and crafts thinking led to writings about Indian art and artists that contained complex, multiple meanings for their readers. Spokespersons for the arts and

[1] Brian William Dippie, *The Vanishing American: White Attitudes and U.S. Indian Policy* (1982; reprint, Lawrence: University of Kansas Press, 1991).

[2] For example, see Alice M. Kellogg, *Home Furnishing, Practical and Artistic* (New York: Frederick A. Stokes, 1905), p. 52; "An Arts and Crafts House," *House Beautiful* 25, no. 5 (April 1909): 102–4; Bertha Damaris Knobe, "A House Made with Hands," *House Beautiful* 12, no. 6 (November 1907): 15–16; Charles Keeler, *The Simple Home* (1904; reprint, Santa Barbara and Salt Lake City: Peregrine Smith, 1979), p. 48. On turn-of-the-century interest in Indian art, see J. J. Brody, *Indian Painters and White Patrons* (Albuquerque: University of New Mexico Press, 1971), pp. 60–72; John M. Gogol, "American Indian Art: Values and Aesthetics," *American Indian Basketry and Other Native Arts* 4, no. 4 (December 1984): 4–30; and Edwin L. Wade, "The Ethnic Art Market in the American Southwest, 1880–1980," in *Objects and Others: Essays on Museums and Material Culture*, ed. George W. Stocking, Jr. (Madison: University of Wisconsin Press, 1985), pp. 167–91. On Navajo weaving, see Otto Charles Thieme, "Meaning in Collecting Navajo Weaving," in *Collecting Navajo Weaving*, ed. Otto Thieme, Ruth E. Franzen, and Sally G. Kabat (Minneapolis: Goldstein Gallery, University of Minnesota, 1984), pp. 2–4; on Pueblo potters and their work, see Barbara A. Babcock, "'A New Mexican Rebecca': Imaging Pueblo Women," *Journal of the Southwest* 32, no. 4 (Winter 1990): 400–437; on baskets and their makers, see Marvin Cohodas, "Louisa Keyser and the Cohns: Mythmaking and Basket Making in the American West," in *The Early Years of Native American Art History: The Politics of Scholarship and Collecting*, ed. Janet Catherine Berlo (Seattle: University of Washington Press, 1992), pp. 88–133; John M. Gogol, "1900–1910, The Golden Decade of Collecting Indian Basketry," *American Indian Basketry and Other Native Arts* 5, no. 1 (April 1985): 12–29.

crafts movement were involved in the promotion of American Indian art and publications such as *The Craftsman* and *Handicraft* magazine encouraged the basketry revival. Yet arts and crafts attention to baskets went beyond general interest in Indian arts as "curiosities" or mementos of a disappearing way of life to infuse Indian baskets and their makers with a unique set of meanings. These meanings became prescriptive models for women involved in the arts and crafts and were fundamental in the definition of women's roles within the movement.

During the latter part of the nineteenth century, progressive-minded reformers began to question the assumptions implicit in the United States government's Indian policies and practices—those of European-American social and cultural superiority in relation to indigenous societies and cultures. The reform movement was galvanized by Helen Hunt Jackson's tremendously popular novel *Ramona*, written in 1884, that condemned the treatment of the native peoples of California under United States rule.[3] Jackson's portrayal of her Indian heroine was a romantic glorification of the relationship between Indians and the purifying and strengthening forces of nature. Ramona was also the essence of womanhood, with the domestic inclinations of a properly Christianized late nineteenth-century woman that enhanced her "natural" Indian instincts.

This image of the Indian woman as a paradigm of natural woman-liness, which conflated the image of the "noble savage" and nineteenth-century European-American ideals of femininity, would recur with regularity in the later writings of arts and crafts proponents and other champions of the American Indian. In addition, arts and crafts writers in sympathy with the movement for the reform of Indian policy used the arts of Indian women to argue that Native American cultures should be preserved and that the United States government was wrong to force European-American culture on the Indians.[4]

---

[3] Robert J. Berkhofer, Jr., *The White Man's Indian: Images of the American Indian from Columbus to the Present* (New York: Alfred A. Knopf, 1978); Helen M. Bannan, "The Idea of Civilization and American Indian Policy Reformers in the 1880s," *Journal of American Culture* 1, no. 4 (Winter 1978): 787–99. Helen Hunt Jackson, *Ramona: A Story* (1886; reprint, Boston: Little, Brown, 1928).
[4] See, for example, Frederick Monsen, "The Destruction of Our Indians: What Civilization Is Doing to Extinguish an Ancient and Highly Intelligent Race by Taking Away Its Arts, Industries and Religion," *The Craftsman* 11, no. 6 (March 1907): 683–91.

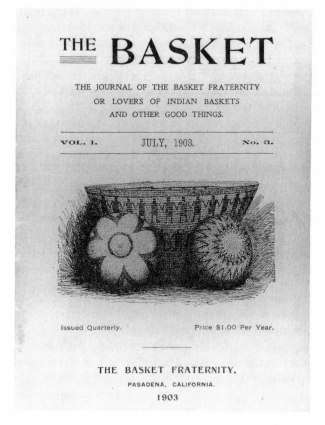

Fig. 1. From *The Basket* 1, no. 3 (July 1903), cover. (Library of the State Historical Society of Wisconsin, Madison.)

It is significant that the creative activities of Jackson's heroine were confined to the beautification of her home according to late nineteenth-century European-American standards. Ramona was not described as a practitioner of traditional Indian arts. If this novel had been written fifteen years later, however, Ramona would most certainly have been a basket maker, and her baskets would have been a manifestation of her virtuous character. In fact, in *Indian Basketry*, first published in

1901, George Wharton James (who was well known for his embellishment and even outright invention) claimed that the heroine of Jackson's novel was still living in the San Jacinto mountains of southern California, that he had known Ramona "for some years," and that he had purchased one of her baskets during the summer of 1900.[5]

In 1903 James began publication of *The Basket: The Journal of the Basket Fraternity; or, Lovers of Indian Baskets and Other Good Things* (fig. 1). James was a fervent promoter and avid collector of American Indian baskets and was also a leading spokesperson for the American arts and crafts movement. As in *Indian Basketry*, he suffused *The Basket* with arts and crafts subjects, imagery, and language. *The Basket* ceased publication in 1904, when James became associate editor of *The Craftsman*.

James wrote a number of articles for *The Craftsman*—on the architecture of the California missions; missions and Indians; Indian houses, entitled "Aboriginal American Homes"; Indian arts, with an emphasis on baskets; and a series of "Simple Life Biographies," including one of William Morris. As a representative of *The Craftsman*, James also lectured on arts and crafts topics such as "William Morris, the Man," and "The Founding and Adorning of an Ideal Home."[6]

In October 1909 James published an issue of *The Arroyo Craftsman*, in many ways a California version of *The Craftsman*. Each issue was to illustrate an Arroyo house, built in the manner of Gustav Stickley's Craftsman homes by the Arroyo Guild, an "Association of Expert Workers in the Applied Arts" of Pasadena, California. Dedicated to Stickley, the contents of *The Arroyo Craftsman* include articles on California arts and crafts houses and domestic landscape gardening, building a "house beautiful," and collecting Indian baskets.[7]

----

[5] George Wharton James, *Indian Basketry* (4th ed.; New York: Henry Malkan, 1909), pp. 220–22; fig. 307, p. 221, is a photograph of "Ramona" holding this basket. On James, see Roger Joseph Bourdon, "George Wharton James: Interpreter of the Southwest" (Ph.D. diss., University of California, Los Angeles, 1966).

[6] "Notes," *The Craftsman* 7, no. 4 (January 1905): 488–90.

[7] See "What is the Arroyo Guild?" *The Arroyo Craftsman* 1, no. 1 (October 1909): 52–54; Robert W. Winter, "The Arroyo Culture," in *California Design 1910*, ed. Timothy Andersen, Eudorah M. Moore, and Robert W. Winter (Santa Barbara and Salt Lake City: Peregrine Smith, 1980), pp. 21–22. George Wharton James, "The Collecting of Indian Baskets," *Arroyo Craftsman* 1, no. 1 (October 1909): 4–11. On James and his role in Pasadena's Arroyo culture, see Bourdon, "George Wharton James"; Kevin Starr,

Much of James's writing is dedicated to the preservation of the cultural heritage of the West, especially its Indian arts and the Spanish missions. His articles appeared in numerous publications, including *The Chautauquan, Out West, Ladies' Home Journal,* and *Sunset Magazine* as well as *The Craftsman.* Between 1881 and his death in 1923, James wrote more than forty books and hundreds of articles and pamphlets about the West, Indian life and arts, and various social and moral issues. These causes are often intertwined in his writing; it is thus impossible to separate James's social activism, arts and crafts advocacy, and championing of the causes of American Indians and their art.

James's final editorship was with the *California Indian Herald,* published beginning in January 1923 by the Indian Board of Cooperation. Among the most progressive of the many social reform organizations dedicated to the Indian cause, this board not only offered assistance but encouraged American Indians to organize for their legal rights. Characteristically, James included in each issue of the publication a retelling of an Indian legend collected during his travels or a chapter from his well-known *Indian Basketry.*

James celebrated Indian baskets as the indigenous American equivalent of the medieval cathedral, extolled by the English arts and crafts movement as the artistic culmination of the Middle Ages and a symbol of an organic unity of artist, society, and spirituality: "Fine baskets, to the older Indian women, were their poems, their painting, their sculpture, their cathedrals. . . . What Victor Hugo strikingly expressed about the cathedrals of Europe when he exclaimed 'The book has killed the building!' could be truthfully applied to the Indian in the expression 'Civilization has killed the basket.'" As did others who mourned the passing of presumably vanishing Indian cultures, James feared the imminent demise of their basketmaking traditions. He saw traditional Indian baskets as symbols of Indian cultures and felt that they served as monuments to the memories of these cultures. "These baskets, thus looked at," James said, "become the embalmed mummies of the mentality and spirituality of ages that are past—of a civilization that would soon otherwise be lost."[8]

Inventing the Dream: California through the Progressive Era (Oxford, Eng.: Oxford University Press, 1985), pp. 107–12; Winter, "Arroyo Culture," pp. 9–28.

[8]James, *Indian Basketry,* p. 16. George Wharton James, "Indian Basketry in House Decoration," *The Chautauquan* 33 (1901): 620.

Fig. 2. Apache basket, Arizona, ca. 1900. Willow and devil's claw; H. 8½″, Diam. 9½″. (Elvehjem Museum of Art, University of Wisconsin–Madison: Photo, Liz Loring.)

With the increasing commercial availability of metal pots and kettles, Indian women were indeed making fewer baskets for domestic use at the turn of the century. By the 1890s most Indian baskets were made for sale to non-Indian collectors. As the demand for such work grew, increasing numbers of Indian women began to make baskets as a means to supplement their household income; these included baskets made in the manner of older cooking, serving, and storage baskets. Those that emulated storage baskets were often smaller in scale but consistent in form, decoration, and technique of manufacture with baskets that had been made for use within their communities of origin (fig. 2). More ornate examples, such as Pomo "gift" baskets, which incorporated traditional materials, forms, and designs, were especially popular (fig. 3). Such baskets were available through mail order catalogues; small baskets, finely made and intricately decorated, often sold for under $10.

Baskets were also made in new shapes—many imitating European-American objects—that innovative basket makers introduced to meet the demands of an expanding market. Using traditional materials and methods of manufacture, they adapted traditional design motifs to forms such as wastebaskets, covered jars, and even tea sets. Some basket

Fig. 3. Pomo "gift" basket, California,
ca. 1900. Willow, sedge and bulrush
roots, clamshell, glass beads, woodpecker
and quail feathers; H. 1¹/₂", Diam. 5¹/₂".
(Elvehjem Museum of Art, University of
Wisconsin–Madison: Photo, Liz Loring.)

makers also incorporated new decorative images, such as letters and
numbers. Basketry teacups did not appeal to arts and crafts proponents,
and some admirers of Indian baskets, including James, saw such objects
as evidence of the debasement of the basketmaking tradition. But baskets made for sale that looked like traditional Indian baskets seem to
have been regarded as manifestations, if not as actual artifacts, of the
basketmakers' art and the integration of art and life that the tradition
represented.

Although in theory James was interested only in baskets made for
domestic use, his own collection must have included some made for
sale. According to Otis Tufton Mason, an expert on Indian baskets and
curator of the Division of Ethnology of the Smithsonian Institution,
James had one of the outstanding collections of Indian baskets in the
United States (fig. 4). It was "especially good in examples from California Missions."[9]

[9] Otis Tufton Mason, *Indian Basketry: Studies in a Textile Art without Machinery*
(New York: Doubleday, Page, 1904), p. 507. This is a reprint of Mason's *Aboriginal
Indian Basketry*, report of the U.S. National Museum, Smithsonian Institution, 1902.
The new title may reflect the arts and crafts concern, shared by Mason, about the issue
of handwork versus machinework.

Fig. 4. George Wharton James basket collection, ca. 1900. From George Wharton James, "Indian Basketry in House Decoration," *The Chautauquan* 33 (1901): 620. (University of Wisconsin Memorial Library, University of Wisconsin–Madison.)

Traditional-style Indian baskets were still being made in other parts of the United States, but the baskets most highly acclaimed were those from the Southwest and California, and to a lesser extent from the Northwest Coast and Alaska. James stated that a satisfactory collection would include baskets made by all the peoples of these regions. Baskets from the Southwest and the Pacific Coast are illustrated in *Indian Basketry, The Basket,* and his other publications. A 1906 article in *The Craftsman* noted the popularity throughout the United States of the baskets made by the "picturesque" Southwest basketmakers. [10]

Much of the fascination with the Southwest and California must be attributed to the West's accessibility by railroad. The arrival in New Mexico and Arizona of the Santa Fe Railway in 1880 was fundamental in the introduction of Indian imagery and art objects into popular culture. To promote local Indian culture as a Southwest attraction, the railway often used design motifs from Indian pottery and baskets as graphic elements in its advertisements. As well, the sense of cultural continuity and stable domesticity evoked by the long-inhabited pueblos of the Southwest drew ethnologists, tourists, and collectors of Indian art to the region to witness and experience "authentic" Indian culture. Few baskets were made by the Pueblo peoples, and the Southwest baskets represented in arts and crafts literature and collections were not from these communities. It does seem, however, that the image of harmonious Pueblo domesticity that appealed to the arts and crafts movement was suggested by other baskets of the region.

Similarly, the romanticized past of the mission era as portrayed by Helen Hunt Jackson in *Ramona* drew many people to California, although in actuality the Spanish missions had thoroughly disrupted the traditional lifeways of many of California's native peoples. ("Mission Indian" is a designation given to a number of southern California Indian peoples whose separate group identities were lost under mission rule.) As a symbol of a lost way of life that was destroyed by the arrival of the Anglo-Americans, the mission ideal, to a large extent, was based in a fantasy that overlooked historical reality. Even so, many non-Indians idealized the mission era as a time of peaceful coexistence between Indians and non-Indians.

[10] George Wharton James, "Indian Basketry," *Outing* 38, no. 2 (May 1901): 179. Charles Frederick Holder, "Some Queer Laborers—Where Peaceful Living is Preferred to Money Making," *The Craftsman* 10, no. 6 (September 1906): 752–61.

For turn-of-the-century "lovers of Indian baskets," those from the Southwest and California were perceived as embodiments of the values represented by these cultures as they were popularly understood. This conviction was reinforced by the material aspects of the baskets themselves, for they represented the "organic" correspondence among design, materials, process of manufacture, and use that the arts and crafts movement espoused.

Gustav Stickley described beauty as "returning to the old frankness of expression, the primitive emphasis upon structure, the natural adaptation of ornament to material."[11] The structure of an Indian basket is emphasized in the method of construction, which establishes rhythms and patterns of form and decoration. Indian baskets are made from indigenous natural materials, with contrasting shades or colors derived from the use of various plant fibers. As Stickley based his designs on the inherent properties of his materials, with emphasis on the straight grain of his preferred native oak, basket forms were based on the techniques and materials used. Although some Craftsman furniture was made using machines, finishing was done by hand, and the marks of handwork were important decorative elements. Joints were not hidden but were used as ornament that was also integral to the structure of the piece. Made by hand, Indian baskets of the Southwest and California were (and are) constructed by either wrapping and stitching fibers to the completed part below, as in coiled baskets, or by twisting fibers around stiff warps or ribs that run vertically from the base to the top of the basket, as in twined baskets. Designs were twined or coiled into the basket as it was being shaped, not applied later to the finished form.

A Chemehuevi basket of around 1900, from the southeastern California desert, can be seen to closely correspond to Stickley's Craftsman aesthetic (fig. 5). Made of willow (the lighter material) and devil's claw (the darker material), every stitch of this coiled basket is visible and is part of the beauty of the finished work. Because of the way that a design is coiled or twined into a basket, geometric and simplified forms predominate. Design motifs are necessarily angular, with curves actually made up of tiny steps. Each step is a stitch or a twist of the material.

The decoration of an Indian basket, frequently consisting of conventionalized natural forms, reflects not only the basket's method of

---

[11] Gustav Stickley, "From Ugliness to Beauty," *The Craftsman* 7, no. 3 (December 1904): 310.

Fig. 5. Chemehuevi basket, California, ca. 1900.
Willow and devil's claw; H. 6¾″, Diam. 6¾″. (El-
vehjem Museum of Art, University of Wisconsin–
Madison: Photo, Liz Loring.)

manufacture but fits the shape of the basket as well. The Chemehuevi
example, ornamented with geometricized, angular corn plants that
swell and contract to harmonize with its subtle curves, is straightforward
in form and design. More ornate baskets, however, also reveal correla-
tions to arts and crafts aesthetics. A Yokuts basket from central California is an example of the fancier "gift baskets" that were often illustrated
and cited in arts and crafts–oriented literature of the time (fig. 6). Its
characteristic rattlesnake design accentuates the basket's more dramatic
contours. Just as arts and crafts furniture makers used inlaid woods and
functional elements such as decorative metal hardware as ornamental
devices, Indian basket makers embellished their products with a variety
of natural materials. The Yokuts basket has quail topknots worked into
the shoulder to enhance its distinct angle.

Although such explicit comparisons do not appear in arts and

Fig. 6. Yokuts basket, California, ca. 1900. Willow, redbud, sedge, quail feathers; H. 6″, Diam. 12½″. (Elvehjem Museum of Art, University of Wisconsin–Madison: Photo, Liz Loring.)

crafts literature, that these aesthetic consistencies were perceived is clear. When Ernest Batchelder offered a series of design lessons in *The Craftsman*, based on his *Principles of Design*, the first example illustrated to represent universal beauty was an Indian basket. The beauty exemplified here, Batchelder wrote, is "invariably sane and orderly in arrangement, clear and coherent in expression, frank and straightforward in an acceptance of all the conditions imposed by questions of use, environment, tools, materials, and processes." Similarly, Mason elaborated on the technical distinction between baskets and Indian pottery. In contrast to the potter's intentional obliteration of the marks of manufacture, Mason wrote, the finished basket displays the results of a process that is deliberately visible, and thus, he implied, more honest in its relationship of construction and finish.[12]

Pueblo pottery and Navajo weaving were similarly assimilated into

[12] Ernest A. Batchelder, "Design in Theory and Practice," *The Craftsman* 13, no. 1 (October 1907): 84. Mason, *Indian Basketry*, p. 131.

the arts and crafts lexicon as symbols of the simple life; in fact, they appear to have been used to a greater degree than baskets in the furnishing of arts and crafts homes. Like baskets, they seemed to offer non-Indian admirers access to the beginnings of humankind and the origins of art.

This sense of timeless continuity and connection with an ancient past was tremendously important to the arts and crafts movement, as emphasized in articles such as "Indian Blankets, Baskets, and Bowls: The Product of the Original Craftworkers of This Continent," published in *The Craftsman* in 1910.[13] Weavings, pottery, and baskets are described as actual manifestations of the craftsman ideal, embodiments of a harmony of intentions that went beyond visual aesthetics to evoke a spiritual and moral harmony within the arts and crafts environment. It was the art of basketmaking in particular, however, that came to be imbued with unique symbolic meaning.

Many arts and crafts adherents were fascinated with the origins of art and felt that "original" art would embody the essential interconnection of life and art that they sought to re-create for their own time. Stickley called for a "vital" art, based in utility, that would transcend historical styles by reaching back to what he referred to as "root principles." The search for the indigenous artistic roots of American art led to recognition of American Indian art as the earliest American art, baskets as the original American art, and basket makers as the original American artists. Mason provided archaeological evidence for the existence of ancient baskets and called basketry "the mother of all loom work and beadwork." James repeatedly argued that basketry was the mother art of both weaving and pottery. Author Neltje Blanchan described basketry as "the oldest and the most universally practised handicraft known" and noted the various uses of baskets in all aspects of Indian life.[14]

[13] "Indian Blankets, Baskets, and Bowls: The Product of the Original Craftworkers of This Continent," *The Craftsman* 17, no. 5 (February 1910): 588–90.

[14] Gustav Stickley, "The Use and Abuse of Machinery, and Its Relation to the Arts and Crafts," *The Craftsman* 11, no. 2 (November 1906): 202. Mason, *Indian Basketry*, p. 3. See George Wharton James, "Indian Pottery," *Outing* 39, no. 2 (November 1901): 154–61; George Wharton James, "Indian Blanketry," *Outing* 39, no. 6 (March 1902): 684–93; and George Wharton James, "Primitive Inventions," *The Craftsman* 5, no. 2 (November 1903): 125–37, reprinted in *The Basket* 2, no. 1 (January 1904): 3–18; George Wharton James, *Indian Blankets and Their Makers* (1914; reprint, New York:

These writers saw baskets as a sort of primeval universal art. At great length, James often described baskets as an integral and essential part of Indian life. Unfortunately his descriptions were not always accurate, for he created an image of general Indianness that disregarded the specific and often disparate cultural activities of different Indian peoples, and he sometimes embellished the truth to impress his readers. Like many contemporary archaeologists, anthropologists, art historians, and aficionados of Indian art, James believed that all art traditions follow a similar evolutionary course. As an original art, Indian baskets were a key to understanding the development of all art. When we study Indian baskets, James wrote, "we are studying humanity under its earliest and simplest phases,—such phases as were probably manifested in our own ancestral history." He regarded basket designs as emblematic of the origins of all artistic conceptions: "From the primitive weaver one may learn how the patterns and designs originated, became conventionalized, and eventually became symbols. . . . Sometimes these basket designs contain as much as the inscription on Assyrian monuments or Egyptian cartouches. They become the historic autographs of the race."[15] The origin and development of forms and designs was a subject of much late nineteenth-century writing on art. Significant in arts and crafts writings on baskets was the way that Indian baskets were held as the artistic equivalent of the forerunners of European art and not simply discussed as ethnographic artifacts or exotic curiosities.

Basketry decoration, according to Irene Sargent, was the source of all design motifs used in the decorative arts, an original art form worthy of serious study as a means to understand the "life-histories" of designs. Sargent saw basket designs as originating in the structure of baskets and the techniques used in their manufacture and subsequently developing as symbols. James believed that basket shapes as well as designs were based in an imitation of natural forms and that designs became increasingly conventionalized as they took on symbolic meaning.[16] He

Tudor Publishing Co., 1937), and James, *Indian Basketry*. Neltje Blanchan, "What the Basket Means to the Indian," *Everybody's Magazine* 5 (July 1901): 561–70, reprinted in Mary White, *How to Make Baskets* (New York: Doubleday, Page, 1902), pp. 181–94.

[15] James, *Indian Basketry*, p. 11. James, "Collecting of Indian Baskets," p. 8.

[16] Irene Sargent, "Indian Basketry: Its Structure and Decoration," *The Craftsman* 7, no. 3 (December 1904): 321–34. "Letter to the Editor on the Subject of American

stressed, however, that basket makers did not merely copy nature. Rather, they adapted natural forms to use. They made baskets to meet essential needs, a paradigm of the synthesis of beauty and utility.

According to James, only "authentic" Indian baskets, made prior to the impact of nonindigenous societies, successfully integrated beauty and utility. To be Indian, James apparently believed, a tradition had to be insulated against outside influence, frozen at an indeterminate point in its evolutionary history. His critique of the effect of non-Indian culture on the basketmaking tradition echoes the arts and crafts analysis of the effect of the industrial revolution on handwork in general. James saw the advent of machine production, the manufacture of objects with no other function than to be visually pleasing, the separation of use from beauty, and the lure of commercialism as contributing to the downfall of the basket tradition. His glorification of traditional basket-making as a pre-industrial legacy often served not only to celebrate the art of basketry but also to provide a forum for sermons preached against the evils of contemporary American culture and its products.

James condemned new forms, materials, and design elements introduced by non-Indian culture. He believed that the use of newly available commercial aniline dyes, rather than the softer natural dyes, resulted in "a piece of Indian work masquerading in gaudy garments that are not really its own."[17] *Indian Basketry* included a chapter entitled "The Decadence of the Art," which discussed the detrimental effect of commercialism on basket makers and their art. In another chapter James urged collectors to discourage the use of aniline dyes and designs taken from non-Indian culture.

The effect of modern society and technology on the basketmaking tradition led another turn-of-the-century writer, Ada Woodruff Anderson, to condemn the role of modern industry in the passing of Indian culture: "We pause on the edge of this labor-saving century to look back with a thrill of sympathy for these patient weavers, the last of a

Indian Basket-Work" was signed "Traveller" and expressed similar beliefs; *International Studio* 20 (August 1903): 144–46. George Wharton James, "Indian Handicrafts," *Handicraft* 1, no. 12 (March 1903): 273; "Primitive Inventions" and "The Indian and Art Work," in George Wharton James, *What the White Race May Learn from the Indian* (Chicago: Forbes, 1908).

[17] James, *Indian Basketry*, p. 90.

people crowded out, all but lost in the rush and whirl of its machinery."[18]

Many people who mourned basketmaking as a dying art saw its
passing as symbolic of the end of an entire way of life that was spiritu-
ally, morally, and aesthetically superior to what James called "machine-
crazed civilization." The lesson of the Indian basket makers went beyond their art, he wrote: "Is it to be wondered at that I regard such
baskets as these as priceless; that money cannot buy them? For they
are not only pretty pieces of basket-work, color, design, weave, shape,
fine specimens of aboriginal digital skill, but there are enshrined in
them the prayers, the longings, the hopes and satisfactions of pure and
simple hearts."[19] The basket maker as well as her art thus became a
true exemplar of the simple life and a symbol of a disappearing aspect
of womanhood, for, while they are aided by men and children in the
gathering and preparation of materials, American Indian basket makers
were (and are) almost exclusively women.

Many at the turn of the century who admired American Indian
baskets felt that their makers also deserved admiration as artists and
inventors. Mason lauded their contributions to the origin and development of native textile arts. "The first and most versatile shuttles were
women's fingers," he wrote. While man was the inventor in "the arts
of hunting and war," James echoed Mason, woman was the inventor
in "the arts of peace."[20]

Such praise of Indian basket makers invariably led to comparisons
of their art with the handwork of modern non-Indian women. James
was explicit in stating his point of view: "I contend that the basket
demonstrates that the Indian woman is not only an artist, but a far
superior artist to most civilized American women." James challenged
these women, "Let the white woman who has scorned the 'rude, dirty,
vulgar, brutal, savage woman' take the finest and highest accomplishments of her race in needlework or any other 'refined' art and place it
side by side with the art manifested in Indian basketry, and she may

[18] Ada Woodruff Anderson, "The Last Industry of a Passing Race," *Harper's Bazar*
32, no. 45 (November 11, 1899): 965.
[19] George Wharton James, *Through Ramona's Country* (Boston: Little, Brown,
1909), p. 268; also James, *What the White Race May Learn*.
[20] Mason, *Indian Basketry*, p. 3. James, "Primitive Inventions," p. 3.

then, perhaps, begin to see how impertinent was her scorn, how igno-
rant her contempt."[21] Arts and crafts ideology held up Indian basket
makers as models of moral and spiritual as well as aesthetic virtue. The
Indian basket maker, James suggested, was more womanly than was
the modern "civilized" European-American woman.

Inherently conservative in its definitions of womanhood and wom-
anliness, the arts and crafts movement promulgated an image of the
Indian basket maker as a paradigm of ideal womanly domesticity for
modern non-Indian women. As the Indian basket maker had twined
or stitched her hopes and dreams into the baskets used by her family,
the modern woman could express her creativity in the objects she made
for her home and at the same time reaffirm her commitment to the
turn-of-the-century domestic ideal.

The arts and crafts celebration of Indian baskets and basket makers
generated a basketmaking craze that swept the United States. Numerous
publications instructed women in the art. Mary White's *How to Make
Baskets* paid homage to American Indian basketry traditions. But White
advised her non-Indian readers to use commercial materials such as
raffia rather than the natural materials used by Indian basket makers.
These, wrote White, "would be useless to us without the Indian
touch." In 1903, *Indian Basket Weaving* appeared under the auspices
of the Navajo School of Indian Basketry. Although unattributed, the
introduction, and probably the entire book, was almost certainly written
by James. "Baskets are the Indian Woman's poems; the shaping of
them her sculpture. They wove into them the story of their life and
love," wrote the author. The introduction echoes themes that appear
elsewhere in James's writings: the "inventive genius of the aboriginal
woman," the use of natural materials to create "useful and beautiful
forms," the many uses of baskets in domestic Indian life, and the
spiritual aspects of these baskets for the Indian basket maker, "making
manifest her ideals and longings for the beautiful."[22]

Indian Basket Weaving was published so that non-Indians could

[21] George Wharton James, "Poetry and Symbolism of Indian Basketry," *The Basket*
2, no. 1 (January 1904): 19. James, "Indian Handicrafts," p. 269; see also Constance
Goddard Du Bois, "The Indian Woman as a Craftsman," *The Craftsman* 6, no. 4 (July
1904): 391.
[22] White, *How to Make Baskets*, p. 169. Navajo School of Indian Basketry, *Indian
Basket Weaving* (Los Angeles: Whedon and Spreng Co., 1903), frontispiece, p. 7.

learn to make "real Indian baskets" using Indian weaves and designs. Yet many of the baskets illustrated and discussed in this work are not related to any American Indian basketry tradition. While James decried the Indian woman's departure from tradition in the use of new forms and decorative motifs, *Indian Basket Weaving* includes instructions for a "small waste-paper basket, eight or nine inches tall," made from date-palm leaves.[23] In essence, what seems to have been important was that European-American women could participate in the artistically valid and morally uplifting process of making an "Indian" basket, but at the same time it was clear that the finished product would not contain the larger meanings signified by true Indian baskets. White women's Indian baskets were not the repositories, after all, of the disappearing cultural values of a vanishing way of life.

While these publications encouraged non-Indian women to draw inspiration from Indian baskets, and even to copy them using patterns and written instructions, Sargent criticized the imitation of the art of another culture without an understanding of its meaning: "It is plain that Indian basketry should be regarded much more seriously and respectfully than it has been our custom to do; that it has a much deeper meaning than has been suspected by the majority of those who have recently counted its stitches and mechanically repeated its symbolic designs, in the effort, made without especial reason, to produce objects of no important value or use."[24] Sargent also saw as meaningless the imitation of objects whose value resided in their fusion of beauty and utility and recognized that non-Indian women's baskets would not be functionally integrated into their lives.

On the other hand, despite some initial misgivings, James felt that non-Indian women making Indian baskets was a positive phenomenon because of what they could learn from the experience. In general, however, he believed that most European-American women were lacking in the time, patience, and knowledge to properly participate in the experience. For James, it was the women of the arts and crafts movement, with an understanding of its underlying principles, who could learn the lessons of Indian design. These women, he maintained, could attempt to make Indian baskets because of the essential kinship between

[23] Navajo School, *Indian Basket Weaving*, p. 95.
[24] Sargent, "Indian Basketry," p. 332.

American Indian aesthetics and principles and those of the arts and crafts movement.

James's writings on basketmaking were really addressed to the women who embraced arts and crafts aesthetics and philosophy. "When the women of THIS civilization began to talk about making Indian baskets I openly and loudly laughed at them," James wrote, but he added: "I have changed my mind materially about the folly of white women attempting the work of the Indian. It is a good thing . . . it will teach us many things besides the twisting of splints and the blistering of our fingers. It will show us the worth of real work, and reveal the value of the efforts of these simple aborigines . . . So, then, to the work of the Indian basket-weaver, to see what she thought and felt, dreamed and longed after, as her busy fingers twisted the splints into the shapes and designs we are learning to think so much of." [25] Responding to such encouragement, non-Indian women made many baskets in the manner of Indian baskets. These appeared in arts and crafts interiors in the same way that Indian baskets were used—as wastebaskets, sewing baskets, or simply as decorative objects. In 1904 *The Basket* ran a basketmaking competition in which readers submitted baskets to be judged by their peers on the basis of suitablity and quality of weave, appropriate and harmonious use of materials, beauty of form, relationship of design to form, color (based on the weaver's description), finish, appropriateness of size to the function of the basket, and general effect. James determined which baskets would be illustrated and voted on by the "basket fraternity." [26] As this fraternity was made up of "lovers of Indian baskets," it was assumed that baskets entered in this competition would look like Indian baskets.

Some non-Indian basket makers were content to use raffia and other commercially available materials, but the use of natural materials was an important aspect of basketmaking for others. A number of arts and crafts societies based in New England and the Midwest made items inspired by American Indian basketry traditions. A report published in *The Basket* on an exhibition by the Primitive Arts Club of Brooklyn, New York, organized in 1903 as part of "the general revival of primitive art that has swept over the entire country," described baskets made by

[25] James, "Indian Handicrafts," p. 270.
[26] "The Basket Prize Competition," *The Basket* 2, no. 3 (July 1904): 119.

members using local natural materials.[27] At times, women in these groups actually employed materials used by local indigenous basket makers. For the most part, however, their visual influences were not the local American Indian basketmaking traditions. Rather, they were inspired by the baskets of the Southwest and California that were better illustrated in arts and crafts publications.

Because vegetable rather than aniline dyes were used by some arts and crafts basket makers, their baskets were perceived, ironically, as superior to some of the baskets made by contemporary Indian basket makers. A 1902 article in *Handicraft* stated that "while primitive peoples are now ruining the quality of their products, once so beautiful, by the use of aniline dyes . . . there is among handicraft workers a wholesome insistence upon native dyes."[28] The arts and crafts handcraft revival had taken hold, and with it came the desire on the part of many women to emulate and revive the accomplishments of American Indian basket makers.

These women responded to the call to devote their creative energy to making aesthetically pleasing objects for use in the home. Inherent in the arts and crafts appeal to women were implicit prescriptive limits; women were to consider the home as their domain and its decoration their highest aesthetic calling. Yet the arts and crafts movement also expanded the culturally acceptable boundaries of creative work for women. Many did not limit themselves to making objects only for their own homes but made and sold work through numerous arts and crafts organizations and devoted themselves to proclaiming the arts and crafts message to others in their communities and beyond.

The model for European-American basketmaking women was a sentimentalized image of the American Indian basket maker. This image was grounded in a synthesis of cultural constructs particular to the

---

[27] Mabel Tuke Priestman, "History of the Arts and Crafts Movement in America," *House Beautiful* 20, no. 5 (October 1906): 15–16; *House Beautiful* 20, no. 6 (November 1906): 14–16; Mary L. Riley, "Arts and Crafts Societies in Massachusetts," *House Beautiful* 18, no. 5 (October 1905): 31–33; Sylvester Baxter, "The Movement for Village Industries," *Handicraft* 1, no. 7 (October 1902): 147–65; and Chester Lane, "Hingham Arts and Crafts: Their Aims and Objects," *The Craftsman* 5, no. 3 (December 1903): 276–81. "Primitive Arts Club, Brooklyn, N.Y.," *The Basket* 2, no. 3 (July 1904): 141. See also Edna Carr, "Pine-Needle Basketry: A New Development in American Handicraft," *The Craftsman* 25, no. 2 (November 1913): 201–4.

[28] Baxter, "Movement for Village Industries," p. 150.

time: an ideologically conservative vision of "natural" womanhood and feminine domesticity combined with the nostalgic mourning of a presumably vanishing "natural" Indian way of life. The turn-of-the-century American Indian basket maker made baskets to meet the needs of her family, but for the most part they were no longer used in the activities of daily life. Instead these baskets were sold to buy food and other necessities. Ironically, the images of woman and of the American Indian that shaped the arts and crafts vision denied turn-of-the-century social and economic realities for both Indian and non-Indian women, even as the popularity of Indian baskets and basketmaking engendered by the arts and crafts movement provided important artistic, social, and economic opportunities for many.

In the way of life represented by Indian baskets, arts and crafts advocates saw the melding of artistry and domesticity and a way of living in harmony with nature that they yearned to re-create in their own lives. For many, American Indian art ultimately came to stand for a whole set of projected sentimental ideals that had more to do with turn-of-the-century European American values and nostalgia than with Indian life itself or the meaning of Indian art for its cultures of origin. Significantly, the words of Indian basket makers do not appear in arts and crafts literature on Indian baskets. Presumably, the baskets speak for their makers, but their meaning is imparted to the reader through the assumptions and values of arts and crafts writers. Thus an image of American Indian baskets and basket makers was created to serve the interests and desires of arts and crafts ideology.

Indian basket makers and their art were not, however, merely nostalgic reminders of simpler, more natural ways of life. Baskets were, indeed, symbols of the simple life, but what made them work as such was the perception of their fundamental accord with arts and crafts aesthetic principles. The aesthetic qualities of baskets were discussed in the same terms used to discuss arts and crafts art objects. That American Indian art is recognized as deserving attention as an essential part of the American artistic heritage is a legacy of the arts and crafts movement.

The arts and crafts fascination with American Indian art was consistent with the cultural climate of the time. Arts and crafts ideals were grounded in nostalgia for a disappearing pre-industrial way of life. The broader concern for the vanishing Indian provided the American arts

and crafts movement with a particularly American focus for this sentiment. A conservative and sentimental late nineteenth-century perspective on the home, the family, and the role of women shaped the arts
and crafts emphasis on the home and its vision of feminine domesticity.
Together, these cultural constructs created a philosophical environment that became the basis for the image of the American Indian basket
maker and her art that the arts and crafts movement created.

Arts and Crafts in the Santa Fe Style

Lonn Taylor

Rural craft revivals were an important part of the arts and crafts movement in both Europe and America. They sprang directly from one of the movement's central themes: that preindustrial rural society was morally superior to industrial urban society. They played a particularly important role in the American arts and crafts movement because their goals coincided with a deep-seated Jeffersonian idealization of rural values and because they were popularized at a time when the Progressive political movement was calling on those values to rejuvenate a corrupt society. Wendy Kaplan points out in *"The Art That Is Life"* that, in this country, "nostalgia for the handicrafts of a pre-industrial period, combined with efforts to give those in poverty a respectable way of earning a living, appealed enormously to upper-middle-class women, who became the chief sponsors of the movement's efforts to save lost souls." Most of the literature on craft revival movements in the United States has concentrated on efforts to revive home textile production in the southern Appalachians and New England, and these movements would appear to fit Kaplan's description. However, two craft revivals in the American Southwest that do not fit that gendered pattern are

The author expresses his gratitude to Ellen Paul Denker, Wilmington, Del.; Lynn Brittner Hutton, School of American Research, Santa Fe; Orlando Romero, Museum of New Mexico, Santa Fe; Rosemary Talley, Santa Fe; and Paul Gonzales, San Ildefonso pueblo, for their assistance with the preparation of this paper. The conclusions, however, are solely the responsibility of the author.

nevertheless intimately connected with the American arts and crafts movement: the revival of pottery making at New Mexico's San Ildefonso pueblo and the revival of Hispanic crafts, particularly cabinet-making, in the neighboring Hispanic villages.[1]

San Ildefonso pueblo is a Tewa-speaking Indian village located on the banks of the Rio Grande twenty-two miles north of Santa Fe. It has been in its present location since about 1300. In 1910 it had a population of approximately 150, most of whom were farmers. Until the 1850s the pueblo raised its own food, but during the late nineteenth and early twentieth centuries, it suffered severe land loss from encroachment, and by 1920 it was estimated that only 6 farmers there raised enough to feed their families. The pueblo did not produce enough agricultural surplus to permit its residents to participate in the cash economy that had developed around it. In addition, the pueblo's people suffered from malnutrition and associated diseases, and they were decimated by the influenza epidemic of 1918. In 1922 the population was at an all-time low of 91.[2]

In the 1880s, however, the women of the pueblo had developed a source of cash income. For generations they had made both ceremonial and utilitarian pottery for their own use and for trade with other pueblos. Complex trade patterns had developed that were still in place when they were recorded by nineteenth-century observers: people at Cochiti pueblo used water jars made at Zia and Acoma pueblos; Taos and Picuris pueblos preferred pottery made at San Juan pueblo; and pottery made at San Juan and Picuris pueblos was carried by Jicarilla Apache traders to the remote Spanish villages in the upper Chama and San Juan river valleys. The arrival of the railroad in New Mexico in 1880 disrupted these established trade patterns by making tinware and cheap stoneware available, but it created new ones by bringing tourists into the region whose desire for Indian souvenirs generated new markets for pueblo potters. Potters began to produce smaller, more brightly colored forms that were easily portable, appealed to tourists' preconcep-

[1] Wendy Kaplan, *"The Art That Is Life": The Arts and Crafts Movement in America, 1875–1920* (Boston: Museum of Fine Arts, 1987), p. 58.
[2] Henrietta K. Burton, *The Re-establishment of the Indians in Their Pueblo Life through the Revival of Their Traditional Crafts* (New York: Columbia University, 1936), p. 51.

tions of "Indian" designs, and, in some cases, were derived from non-Indian sources. In 1881 U.S. Army Capt. John Gregory Bourke described a scene in the Santa Fe Railway's station in El Rito, New Mexico: "The sugar bowls and salt cellars were bric-a-brac that would have set Eastern collectors crazy with envy; they were of ornamental ware made by the pueblos of Laguna, six miles distant. A dozen or more Indians were hanging around the door, waiting to sell their wares to passengers." The Santa Fe Railway, always anxious to promote tourism in the Southwest, gave free passes to Indians who would sell their pottery at railroad stations, and their hotel concessionaire, the Fred Harvey Company, included "Indian Rooms" in several of their hotels where pueblo pottery could be purchased along with Navajo rugs, silver jewelry, and other southwestern and Mexican artifacts.[3]

The women of San Ildefonso begin making pottery for the tourist trade in the 1880s. It was thin-walled polychrome and black-on-red ware, so poorly made that it would not hold water and was often full of cracks and imperfections. It was marketed by being taken into Santa Fe and sold by the wagonload to curio dealers, who would destroy the bad pots and keep the good ones for resale. In 1910 the potters received about $.25 per pot. In order to increase their production, they had abandoned the traditional Tewa slip, which required hours of polishing with a stone, and substituted a slip that could be wiped on with a rag. The years between 1910 and 1915 have been described as "the most degenerative phase in San Ildefonso pottery making" (fig. 1).[4]

In 1907 Edgar Lee Hewett, director of the School of American Research (and, after 1909, the Museum of New Mexico) in Santa Fe, became interested in both pottery making at San Ildefonso and the economic plight of the pueblo. Hewett was an archaeologist, educator, and former teacher's college president who genuinely admired pueblo culture and was equally committed to ensuring its survival and increasing public understanding of it. He felt that the Indian population of the United States was "a valuable cultural asset" whose "normal evolu-

[3]Bourke is quoted in David Snow, "Some Economic Considerations of Historic Pueblo Pottery," *El Corral de Santa Fe Westerners Brand Book 1973* (Santa Fe, N.M.: Santa Fe Westerners, 1973), p. 61; Keith L. Bryant, Jr., *History of the Atchison, Topeka, and Santa Fe Railway* (New York: Macmillan, 1974), pp. 119–21, 327.

[4]Edwin Lewis Wade, "The History of the Southwest Indian Ethnic Art Market" (Ph.D. diss., University of Washington, 1976), pp. 77–78.

Fig. 1. San Ildefonso jar, 1910. Clay with cream slip and black-on-red painted decoration. (School of American Research, Santa Fe, N.M.) The crosses on the upper band are probably adapted from Navajo rugs to make the jar look more "Indian" to tourist purchasers.

tion" had been prevented by the government's assimilationist policies and mercenary attitudes, although he was also opposed to what he called "the emotional efforts of friendly societies" to improve Indian life. He believed that a careful craft revival program could "revive hereditary talents, rendered dormant through several generations of suppression" and enable Indian people to meet the world on their own terms. Unlike most of his scholarly colleagues, who were interested only in "uncorrupted" Indian artifacts, he recognized the constantly changing nature of Indian culture. Finally, he had a prescient understanding of the role that tourism was to play in the economy of the Southwest and of the market value of ethnicity, especially Indian ethnicity. "In pottery," he wrote, "the making of fine ware was encouraged by establishing a market for it and securing fair prices."[5]

Writing in retrospect in 1927, Hewett called the pottery revival program that he initiated at San Ildefonso the "Santa Fe Program" and described it as though he had conceived it as a whole in 1907 and carefully directed its execution over a period of twenty years. In fact, documents in both the Hewett Papers at the Museum of New Mexico and the Kenneth Chapman Papers at the School of American Research as well as interviews with the descendants of some of the San Ildefonso potters make it clear that the program evolved through several stages and was influenced at critical points by a number of people, including the potters Maria and Julian Martinez and several museum employees, chief among them Kenneth Chapman and Countess Verra von Blumenthal, a Russian arts and crafts enthusiast. However, it is equally clear that Hewett provided direction for the program at crucial points and lent to it the prestige and resources of both the School of American Research and the Museum of New Mexico.

The program actually began in 1907, when Hewett was directing a dig at a prehistoric pueblo called Puye, about five miles from San Ildefonso. The diggers were recruited from San Ildefonso, and they included Julian Martinez and several other men who were married to potters. Hewett tried to interest the women in reproducing the designs found on shards of Abiquiu black-on-gray, Bandelier black-on-gray, and Sankawi black-on-cream pottery from the dig, and several potters, including Martinez's wife, Maria, did incorporate the prehistoric designs into their work. They quickly discovered that there was no market for prehistoric pottery reproductions among the Santa Fe traders, and they returned to the more colorful San Ildefonso polychrome and black-on-red ware. However, the Martinezes became fascinated with the process of innovation, and Julian began decorating Maria's pots with designs drawn, but by no means replicated, from prehistoric sources as well as from historic Hopi, Acoma, and Zuni pottery. Ruth Bunzel

---

[5] Archaeological Institute of America, *Official Acts and Administrative Reports of the School of American Research, Santa Fe, New Mexico, U.S.A., 1918 to 1927* (n.p., n.d.), pp. 173–77.

has left us a vivid account of his eclectic methods, recorded during a visit to San Ildefonso in 1925:

At San Ildefonso . . . the men and women were all much interested in the photographs of the old shards which I had with me. Julian's reactions were especially notable. He looked over all the pictures with evident interest and enjoyment. Suddenly he took my pencil out of my hand and tore a page from my notebook to copy a bird that struck his fancy. This bird appeared in a narrow border on a Laguna pot and formed an inconspicuous part of the whole design. Other bits of design he copied for future use were equally fragmentary. . . . He apparently was not interested in new types of decoration or arrangement, but rather in clever little twists that he could embody in his own already highly developed and individual style. There seemed to be no doubt in his mind as to what he could use and could not use.[6]

While the Martinezes were making these design experiments and diffusing the results among other San Ildefonso potters (fig. 2), Hewett's energies were absorbed by other projects, including obtaining a charter from the territorial legislature for the Museum of New Mexico in 1909 and remodeling the seventeenth-century Palace of the Governors in Santa Fe to house it. He did, however, continue his efforts to help the people of San Ildefonso by developing a market for their pottery. Between 1908 and 1912, he invited groups of potters from San Ildefonso to demonstrate their work in the patio of the Palace of the Governors. These demonstrations, which went on for a number of summers, usually lasted two or three days, with the potters and their families sleeping at the museum. In 1912 Hewett was placed in charge of the exhibits at the Panama California Exposition in San Diego, and when the exhibition opened in 1915, the Martinezes were among the Pueblo Indians who demonstrated their craft at the Santa Fe Railroad exhibit, a plywood-and-stone pueblo called "The Painted Desert." This focused national attention on Pueblo pottery in general and on the Martinezes in particular. Finally, in 1917 Hewett devised a scheme to eliminate the Santa Fe curio dealers as middlemen and give San Ildefonso's potters direct access to the public by selling selected pottery at the

---

[6] Ruth Bunzel, *The Pueblo Potter* (New York: Columbia University Press, 1929), pp. 59–60; Richard L. Spivey, *Maria* (Flagstaff, Ariz.: Northland Publishing, 1989), pp. 128–29; for Hewett's attempts to revive prehistoric pottery styles, see Wade, "History," pp. 77–78.

Fig. 2. Maria Martinez, San Ildefonso jar, 1920. Clay with cream slip and black-on-red painted decoration. (School of American Research, Santa Fe, N.M.) Purchased by Kenneth Chapman from the maker in 1920.

museum on commission. When the dealers threatened to complain to the legislature, one of the museum's staff resigned and opened her own gallery to carry San Ildefonso wares.[7]

In the summer of 1917, the pottery revival at San Ildefonso was given a new direction by the arrival there of two Pasadena, California, women, Rose Dougan and von Blumenthal. The two built an adobe home, which included living quarters for potters, on a spur of Tsankawi Mesa just across the Rio Grande from the pueblo. They announced

[7]Burton, *Re-establishment*, pp. 56–58; Archaeological Institute of America, *Organic Acts and Administrative Reports of the School of American Archaeology, Santa Fe, New Mexico, U.S.A., 1907 to 1917* (n.p., n.d.), pp. 163–64.

their intention to improve the production of pottery at the pueblo by selecting two or three potters each summer who would come and live at Tsankawi and receive individual instruction in ceramics. The countess was a native of Russia who had lived in Chicago before moving to Pasadena and was active in the arts and crafts movements in both cities. In 1903 she began purchasing lace and needlework from the peasant art centers being established in Russia by various private and governmental entities to improve those crafts. She attached additional sums to the purchase price for work that she deemed exceptional. This money was used to establish funds at the various centers to benefit the needleworkers. In 1907 she established the Slavic Arts Center in Pasadena, where Russian peasant needlework was sold, and she arranged exhibits of Russian needlework at the national Arts and Crafts Society's 1910 annual exhibit and at the Art Institute of Chicago the following year. Her companion, Dougan, was born in Richmond, Indiana, and was described by the Santa Fe press as a "musician and aviator"; her correspondence in the Hewett Papers shows that she had traveled extensively in Europe and was an advocate of Indian rights as well as a self-described student of pueblo religion. She was a friend of the linguist and folklorist Jeremiah Curtin and assisted his widow in editing his last three books, *The Mongols* (1908), *The Mongols in Russia* (1909), and *A Journey in Southern Siberia* (1909).[8]

It is unclear who von Blumenthal and Dougan originally intended to engage to provide instruction to the San Ildefonso potters, but by September 1918, they had evidently abandoned the idea of bringing potters to their Tsankawi home. Instead, von Blumenthal, after a series of conversations with Hewett, decided to establish a relationship between the Slavic Arts Center in Pasadena and the School of American Research that was similar to the one that the Pasadena center had with

[8]On von Blumenthal's and Dougan's program at Tsankawi, see Kenneth Chapman, "The Von Blumenthal-Dougan Project, 1917–1919," MS, folder 21–1, Kenneth Chapman Papers, School of American Research, Santa Fe (hereafter cited as Chapman Papers); for von Blumenthal's background, see U.S. Consulate, Moscow, *Russia: A Handbook on Commercial and Industrial Relations*, special consular reports no. 61 (Washington, D.C.: Government Printing Office, 1913), p. 60; *El Palacio* 4, no. 3 (July 1917): 93; for information on Dougan, see Rose Dougan to Editor, *El Palacio* 6 (February 5, 1919), and Rose Dougan to Paul A. F. Walter, December 29, 1918, and February 21, 1919, Edgar L. Hewett Papers, History Library, Museum of New Mexico, Santa Fe (hereafter cited as Hewett Papers).

the peasant art centers in Russia. In a letter to Hewett dated September 9, 1918, she announced her decision "to open the Pasadena Center to the productions of pueblo Indians." But, "as the center could only deal with the makers through the assistance of the Archaeological Institute [School of American Research]," she went on, "I propose to appoint a committee of the local artists well acquainted with the best types of the pueblo pottery and other branches of their skill. The appointed artists will have to pass their judgement on the submitted work . . . to increase the existing prices. Such method would speedily establish a tangible link between the makers and their protectors, also would soon eliminate the unworthy overproduction—a very ruinous element in every art bringing it to the level of curios." In other words, she proposed to apply the principle of paying the maker something extra over the asking price for pueblo pottery in return for exceptional quality. At the same time, she promised Hewett that the Pasadena center would pay for the pottery on arrival and would "enlighten the public on the fundamental principles of the Red Man in his art" in order to "bring into the knowledge and imagination of the purchaser the wider conception and wider sympathy for the creative power of the living Indian." The joint venture was to be both economic and educational. Von Blumenthal and Hewett discussed plans to open other centers in Chicago, Detroit, and New York and made arrangements to have an official School of American Research stamp of approval put on the pottery that was transmitted to the centers.[9]

Hewett appointed Chapman, Wesley Bradfield, and Mrs. Harry L. Wilson, all of the School of American Research, to the oversight committee and made Paul A. F. Walter, assistant director of the Museum of New Mexico, treasurer. In November 1918 von Blumenthal sent Walter a check for fifty dollars toward a two hundred dollar contribution for prize money and travel expenses for the committee. The following June a note in the Museum of New Mexico's official magazine recorded that "black luster ware and the highly decorated red and black and cream colored ware" had been brought to the museum from San Ildefonso by the Martinezes and would be "sent to the Art Crafts Center, Pasadena, California of Mrs. Verra von Blumenthal." At this

[9]Verra von Blumenthal to Edgar Hewett, September 9, 1918, Hewett Papers; "Indian Arts Center," *El Palacio* 5, no. 14 (November 16, 1918): 35–36.

point von Blumenthal and the Slavic Arts Center disappear from the record. But the system of rewards that she suggested to Hewett was put into operation by Chapman, and it soon took on a life of its own.[10]

Although the Pasadena retail outlet did not materialize as a permanent fixture of the Santa Fe Program, the committee established by Hewett soon moved the program into a stage characterized by Chapman as "individual help." Between the summer of 1918 and the summer of 1921, Chapman, Bradfield, and a third School of American Research staff member, Odd Halseath, paid frequent visits to San Ildefonso and worked with its potters to solve technical problems inherent in the traditional processes that they used: the selection and mixing of clay; the methods of combining the coils of clay; firing methods and fuels; and ways of avoiding breakage during firing. Chapman, an artist as well as an art teacher, was fascinated by pueblo pottery and had used pottery designs in his art classes at New Mexico State Normal School as early as 1900. He combined his teaching visits to the pueblo with the research on pueblo pottery design that resulted in his monumental *Pottery of San Ildefonso Pueblo* so that the teaching process was reciprocal: he helped the potters with the technical aspects of their work, and they helped him understand the complex design systems. In addition to providing technical assistance, the museum staff offered aesthetic advice and marketing assistance. In the words of Henrietta Burton, who interviewed Hewett about the program in the 1930s for her master's thesis at Columbia University Teacher's College: "In their instructions to the Indian artists, they observed the forms and restricted their products to a few good types, choosing the best of the native shapes . . . [they] continually stressed three necessities: that they discriminate between the good and poor pieces; that they learn to evaluate the white man's idea of aesthetics; and that they set reasonable prices on good vases." These revivalists literally introduced the idea of art as a commodity in the pueblo. Following von Blumenthal's system, Chapman asked the potters to set their own prices on a group of bowls and then offered one or two dollars more for the one that he thought best, explaining why he thought it superior to the others. He also persuaded

---

[10] *El Palacio* 6, no. 13 (June 14, 1919): 215; von Blumenthal to Walter, November 9, 1918, Hewett Papers.

some of the potters to make larger pieces and to price them in relation to the amount of time it took to make them.[11]

Two further developments moved the pottery revival toward the revisionists' goal. In March 1922 Dougan, who was evidently still spending her summers at Tsankawi, notified Hewett that she intended to establish an endowment at the School of American Research that would provide eighty-five dollars annually to be awarded as prizes for Indian arts and crafts. Hewett responded by announcing the first Southwest Indian Fair and Industrial Arts and Crafts Exhibition, to be held in conjunction with the recently instituted Santa Fe Fiesta, September 4–6, 1922. First, second, and third prizes were awarded, and the prize objects were purchased for the Museum of New Mexico's collection. Three years later, in 1925, Tonita Roybal of San Ildefonso sold a pot at the fair for the unheard-of price of $13.20. The Indian fair eventually developed into the Southwestern Association on Indian Affairs' annual Indian Market, now entering it's sixty-ninth year. Finally, in 1922 Chapman, moved by Maria Martinez's comment that Pueblo potters could not remember the old designs because anthropologists had taken all the old pottery away, established the Pueblo Pottery Fund to collect and make available to Indian potters the best examples of old work. In 1925 the name of the fund was changed to the Indian Arts Fund, and the collection purchased with it is now housed at the School of American Research.[12]

The potters of San Ildefonso themselves played an active role in shaping the revival. In 1918, after ten years of experimenting with black pottery finishes, the Martinezes developed a glossy black finish combined with black matte decoration. While pottery with a polished black surface had been made at neighboring Santa Clara pueblo for more than a century, and more recently at San Ildefonso, the Martinezes' innovation was the addition of black matte decoration. This was achieved by painting designs on the slipped-and-burnished pot with a second slip that was made, after a good deal of experimentation, from

[11] Burton, *Re-establishment*, p. 55; Kenneth Chapman, *The Pottery of San Ildefonso Pueblo* (Albuquerque: University of New Mexico Press, 1970), p. 28.
[12] For Indian Fair prizes, see *El Palacio* 12, no. 6 (March 15, 1922): 81; *El Palacio* 15, no. 2 (July 16, 1923): 23; for the establishment of the Pueblo Pottery Fund, see Jonathan Batkin, *Pottery of the Pueblos of New Mexico, 1700–1940* (Colorado Springs: Taylor Museum of the Colorado Springs Fine Arts Center, 1987), pp. 32–33.

Fig. 3. Maria Martinez, San Ildefonso jar, 1925. Clay with polished black finish and black mat design. (School of American Research, Santa Fe, N.M.) An *awanyu*, or horned serpent, is in the center band.

a refractory greenish gray clay. Maria taught this process to her sisters, and black-on-black soon became the characteristic pottery of San Ildefonso pueblo (fig. 3). Years later, when asked to explain the popularity of this pottery with tourists, Martinez replied, "People think that black goes with everything." The potters maximized their profits by selling their wares directly to tourists at the pueblo rather than through dealers in Santa Fe. By 1925 automobile tourism was common in New Mexico, and Martinez opened a sales shop in the front room of her house and encouraged others to do the same or to display their wares in front of their homes. By the mid 1930s the potters of San Ildefonso had become one of New Mexico's best-known tourist attractions. Chapman, considering the reasons for this success, mused in his memoirs on the gendered nature of the tourist pottery trade: "I feel safe in saying that fully 75% of all purchases of Indian crafts were by women . . . so with pottery, most women are considering its use in their homes. Often I have heard a tourist say, particularly of Maria Martinez's polished plain or decorated black ware, 'How lovely! It doesn't look too Indian. It might have been made most anywhere. I like it because it will fit in with my other things, for use, and for its lovely form and finish.' " Chapman went on to say that San Ildefonso pueblo had five advantages over other pottery-making pueblos, "from the woman's point of view." These were: the wide variety of pottery available there (polychrome, black-on-red, and three kinds of black); the ease with which the pueblo could be reached by automobile; the fact that buying a pot there gave the buyer an opportunity to enter a pueblo home and talk to a potter; the presence of a tea room, operated by an Anglo-American woman, just two miles from the pueblo; and the publicity given to the pueblo by the Chamber of Commerce, the hotels, and "particularly the women of Santa Fe, who treat their guests to the trip and recommend it to visitors."[13]

The economic success of the pottery revival brought about significant changes at San Ildefonso. The attention that was focused on Maria Martinez created jealousy among other pueblo residents, for whom individual achievement was never as high a value as group unity. In fact, calling attention to oneself was a most un-puebloan thing to do. Martinez deflected some of this jealousy by opening a small store and arranging credit there for some other San Ildefonso families and by employing relatives at $1.00 per day to assist her by slipping and polishing pots. She also occasionally bought unfinished pottery from other potters, finished it, and sold it under her own name. An equally successful contemporary, Rose Gonzales, shared her new wealth with the pueblo by serving as a godmother to many pueblo children, thus incurring lifelong obligations for their welfare. Still, rivalry among potters

[13] Kenneth Chapman, "Memoirs, Santa Fe II, 1915–1919," MS, Chapman Papers; Carl E. Guthe, *Pueblo Pottery Making: A Study at the Village of San Ildefonso* (New Haven: Yale University Press, 1925), pp. 24–25; Susan Peterson, *The Living Tradition of Maria Martinez* (Tokyo: Kodansha International, 1977), pp. 91–92, 97.

created tensions among pueblo families. An observer in the late 1930s wrote that "feeling has grown to such a pitch that women will not visit other women lest they be suspected of trying to spy on the number of pots their rivals have or be accused of stealing designs. And women say jealously of one another, 'she works night and day on her pottery.' The undercurrent of suspicion has reached a point where the women are not capable of forming a cooperative group to market their wares to advantage."[14]

There is no doubt that this rivalry exacerbated a deep-seated factionalism that was already present in the pueblo between the people of its north plaza and its south plaza, a factionalism that had been apparent to outside observers as early as 1918, when the south plaza was built, and which during the 1930s disrupted both the religious life and civil governance of the pueblo. A 1935 Bureau of Indian Affairs (BIA) report described Martinez and her sisters as "recognized matriarchs" who were leaders of the north plaza faction, while the south plaza leaders were called "agriculturalists, religious men whose wives did not take part in family affairs." South plaza potters Susannah Aguilar and Ramona Gonzales were quoted in the same report as saying that Santa Fe art patrons favored the north plaza potters.[15]

With increased factionalism, however, came prosperity. Figures gathered in 1933 showed that twenty people at San Ildefonso were making pottery; they made 1,800 pots that year and sold them for $9,900. The next largest source of income was farming, at which twenty-two people earned $2,548. Individual income is impossible to estimate, but the BIA report quoted above states that "the second most successful potter [at San Ildefonso] has averaged at least $50 a month from November through May, with the best pottery season still to come." The per-family income at San Ildefonso was $762 in 1933, compared to $290 at neighboring Nambe pueblo, which did not have a pottery industry. One indication of economic change is that in the late 1930s several San Ildefonso women employed Hispanic women to

[14] Quoted in William Whitman, *The Pueblo Indians of San Ildefonso* (New York: Columbia University Press, 1947), pp. 104–6; on Martinez, see Wade, "History," pp. 2–3; information on Rose Gonzalez is from Paul Gonzales, interview with author, Santa Fe, January 24, 1991.

[15] U.S. Office of Indian Affairs, Indian Land Research Unit, "Tewa Basin Study," ed. Eshref Shevky et al., 3 vols. (1935, mimeographed), 1:75.

wash, sweep, and clean for them, which was a complete reversal of earlier roles.[16]

The greatest measurable change, of course, was the increase in the pueblo's income, which permitted its families not only to rise above poverty but to meet the outside world on their own terms. William Whitman, an anthropologist who lived at San Ildefonso in the late 1930s, wrote that "pottery . . . supplies whole families not only with a livelihood but with a surplus over and above the necessities. It buys automobiles, furniture, radios, and sends young men to college." Juan Diego Martinez, Maria and Julian's son, put it somewhat differently. "Before art came into existence," he wrote, "the principal products of the soil were beans, corn, squashes, and pinon nuts." Clearly, the economic goals of the revivalists had been met and surpassed but with unexpected results for the pueblo's social structure.[17]

The Anglo-American attempt to revive Hispanic crafts in New Mexico had its origins not so much in a concern for a people as in a perceived need for a product. While that revival included tinwork, weaving, and woodcarving, it focused heavily on furniture making, a craft that had flourished in New Mexico since its colonization by Spaniards in the seventeenth century. That focus was the result of an Anglo-sponsored architectural revival encouraged, like the pottery revival at San Ildefonso, by Hewett and his colleagues at the Museum of New Mexico. Hewett and his friends admired Santa Fe's old adobe buildings both for their aesthetics and their value as a tourist attraction. During the 1910s they became advocates of the "Santa Fe Style," a mixture of Hispanic and Pueblo architectural elements adopted to Anglo-American needs. The first buildings erected in this style in Santa Fe were public buildings and hotels, but by the early 1920s a few private residences had also appeared. These buildings demanded furniture, but no suitable style existed until 1917, when Chapman and Jesse Nusbaum collaborated to design furniture for the Women's Board Room in the new Museum of Fine Arts. Unlike traditional Hispanic New Mexican furniture, the Women's Board Room furniture had extended mortise-and-tenon joints and painted chip carving, and it included a

Fig. 4. Women's Board Room, Museum of Fine Arts, Santa Fe, N.M., 1917. (Museum of New Mexico: Photo, Wesley Bradfield.) The Spanish colonial revival furniture was designed by Kenneth Chapman and Jesse Nusbaum and built by Sam Huddleson.

totally nontraditional form, a buffet (fig. 4). In creating this furniture, Nusbaum provided Anglo-Americans who were moving to Santa Fe in increasing numbers a style with which to furnish their adobe houses—a style that mixed well with the Hispanic antiques that they were collecting. Nusbaum suddenly became greatly in demand as a cabinetmaker, although his real interests lay in archaeology and historic preservation, to which he made significant contributions. In the early 1920s he and his wife, Ailene, designed furniture for their own use, and in 1923 two wealthy New Yorkers, Amelia Elizabeth White and Martha White, commissioned Nusbaum to make the furniture for the adobe summer home they were building in Santa Fe. Like the Santa Fe style itself, most of this furniture, which Nusbaum described as "in the early Franciscan style," was derived from a combination of Hispanic architectural elements and Pueblo Indian designs. When completed, this furniture was exhibited at the Museum of New Mexico and was the subject of an article in the February 1925 *Good Furniture* magazine.[18]

In the same year that Nusbaum's furniture for the White house was exhibited, Mary Austin, a writer who moved to Santa Fe in 1923, and her neighbor Frank Applegate had a series of discussions about Hispanic crafts—discussions that were held in the context of the successful Indian fairs being produced by Hewett. Austin later recalled that she and Applegate "rapidly got interested in the old and almost dishabilitated arts of New Mexico, touched with a profound regret for their disappearance. In collecting old pieces, Frank had often recourse to native workmen for repair, and by this means came to realize that the capacity for handicraft of a fine and satisfying quality, though overlaid by modern American neglect, had not completely disintegrated. We began to discuss the possibility of reviving it."[19]

Applegate, who was a key figure in the revival movement, was a ceramics artist who had come to Santa Fe in 1921 from Trenton, New Jersey, where he had been head of the Department of Ceramics and Sculpture at Trenton Industrial School. He once had a studio in the arts community of New Hope, Pennsylvania, and had moved to New Mexico to learn about pueblo pottery; however, he immediately became interested in the Hispanic religious art and antique furniture that he saw in the homes of the Santa Fe art colony and set out to collect it. Looking back shortly before his death in 1931, Applegate wrote that "William Morris and the Pre-Raphaelites worked a revolution in the taste of Victorian England . . . in a less ambitious and a more provincial way, the program in the Spanish arts and crafts brought similar gains." Applegate and Austin, with the financial backing of Mrs. Elon Hooker of New York, launched the Society for the Revival of Spanish Colonial Arts in late 1925 or early 1926 (the name was changed to the Spanish Colonial Arts Society in 1929). The society's program was three-pronged: a collection of Hispanic New Mexican furniture, textiles, tinwork, and religious art would be formed to serve as examples for craftsmen; Applegate and Austin would write an illustrated book on

[18] Lonn Taylor and Dessa Bokides, *New Mexican Furniture, 1600–1940* (Santa Fe: Museum of New Mexico Press, 1987), pp. 213–18. "Notable Spanish-Colonial House Furnishings," *Good Furniture* 24, no. 2 (February 1925): 85–87.

[19] Mary Austin, "Frank Applegate," *New Mexico Quarterly* 2 (1932): 214.

Spanish colonial arts and crafts that would stimulate interest in the subject; and an annual craft fair would be held in Santa Fe, at which prizes would be awarded for the best work. There is no evidence that Applegate and Austin's original considerations included improving the economy of the Hispanic villages of northern New Mexico. A fourth, future goal was the establishment of a retail outlet in Santa Fe for the work of Hispanic craftsmen. The society's first exhibit was held in 1926, during the Santa Fe Fiesta, alongside Hewett's Indian fair. There were fifteen entries. First prize of sixty dollars was won by Celso Gallegos, a Santa Fe woodcarver. At the next year's fair the first prize for furniture went to Jose Dolores Lopez of Cordova, whose work was avidly promoted by Applegate and the society.[20]

In 1929 the society begin a permanent collection, and in 1930 they opened a shop, the Spanish Arts Shop, in William Penhallow Henderson's restored Sena Plaza in Santa Fe. Applegate encouraged Lopez, Adolfo Salazar, and Elidio Gonzales to make furniture for the shop, carefully guiding their designs toward adaptations of eighteenth- and early nineteenth-century pieces in local collections. He also established a relationship with the Spanish American Normal School in El Rito, New Mexico, where students began making furniture and weaving blankets for the shop. The society carefully directed the design of these objects by sending the school "albums of photographs and drawings of the old things most suited to reproduction and at the same time most saleable." Applegate suffered a fatal heart attack in February 1931. His and Austin's manuscript on Spanish colonial arts was never published.[21]

The Spanish Arts Shop, under the management of weaver Helen McCrossen, made every effort to be successful. McCrossen tried to publicize the venture through an article in *School Arts Magazine* in which she said, "Much has already been done for the Indian and his arts but so far, this is the first organized effort to help the descendants of the Spanish Colonials." She added, rather apologetically, that "to

---

[20] Applegate is quoted in Ina Sizer Cassidy, "Art and Artists in New Mexico," *New Mexico* 12, no. 6 (1934): 28; Taylor and Bokides, *New Mexican Furniture*, pp. 226–29.

[21] Taylor and Bokides, *New Mexican Furniture*, p. 229; *Spanish Colonial Arts Society Commences Fifth Year of Activity*, broadside, Spanish Arts Shop Papers, Museum of International Folk Art, Santa Fe (hereafter cited as SAS Papers).

some extent the native taste has been corrupted by contact with an alien civilization and cheap, machine-made articles but, in the main, the native worker shows a true feeling for color and design." She tried to persuade craft shops in Scottsdale, Arizona; Berea, Kentucky; Asheville, North Carolina; and Huron, Ohio; as well as in Boston and New York to carry items from the shop's stock, and she attempted to market furniture through Frederick Rummelle, a Carmel, California, interior decorator. Rummelle felt that the pine furniture was unsalable due to the high cost of crating and shipping—which added 67 percent to its cost in Santa Fe—and to its lack of antique finish. "It will be necessary to go over it with tools or sanding and acid to produce the look of crudity, wear, and age that I feel is vitally necessary to make it a saleable item," he wrote.[22]

The society's revival program was not a success. Applegate was able to stimulate production, and some beautiful furniture was made under his guidance, but the local market for Spanish colonial furniture was saturated, and the prices the shop had to charge in order to compensate the cabinetmakers for their labor were simply too high for the tourist market to bear in the depths of the Great Depression. Chests were $40.00 each, tables $15.00, and chairs $5.00 to $20.00. These products were not as portable as Indian pottery, and customers had to make arrangements to ship them home. The shop frequently could not pay its suppliers, and in October 1933 it closed its doors for lack of income. Its place as a retail outlet for Hispanic craft products was taken in June 1934 by a shop called the Native Market, which was owned and subsidized by a wealthy Santa Fe woman, Lenora Curtin.[23]

In 1932 much of the society's craft revival program had been taken over by the New Mexico Bureau of Vocational Education, which had recently come under the direction of a visionary named Brice Seawell. Seawell saw the Hispanic craft revival as a way to rejuvenate the economies of the small Hispanic villages of New Mexico, which had suffered greatly from the depression. His plan was to dramatically expand New

[22] Helen Camp McCrossen, "Native Crafts in New Mexico," *School Arts Magazine* 30, no. 7 (March 1931): 456; Frederick Rummelle to Helen McCrossen, March 16, 1931, SAS Papers.
[23] Taylor and Bokides, *New Mexican Furniture*, p. 231. For the subsequent history of the Native Market, see Sarah Nestor, *The Native Market of the Spanish New Mexican Native Craftsmen* (Santa Fe: Colonial New Mexico Historical Foundation, 1978).

Mexico's vocational education system, using funds from various New Deal agencies to establish vocational schools that would eventually become community handicraft centers in the afflicted villages. The schools were to be open to anyone between sixteen and sixty, and in them, he wrote, "the men can be taught to make useful and saleable handmade products from local resources . . . As soon as these people are thoroughly trained, the teachers are removed and the units cease to operate as a school and become a community workshop." Seawell put together a talented team to advance his objectives, training teachers and persuading communities to donate land and labor to build the schools. By 1938 his office had established schools in more than forty communities. The Taos Vocational School was typical. It was built on donated land with funds from the Federal Emergency Relief Administration; teachers' salaries were paid from a combination of county, state, and federal funds, including money from the Works Progress Administration's Emergency Education Program; students were paid to attend class by the National Youth Administration; and some of the first furniture produced was bought by the Works Progress Administration for the state capitol building in Santa Fe.[24]

Like the Spanish Colonial Arts Society, the Bureau of Vocational Education tried to maintain close control over the design of its craftsmen's products. It achieved this through mimeographed design manuals, including a *Spanish Colonial Furniture Bulletin* issued in 1933 and a manual called *Spanish Colonial Painted Chests* published in 1937. The bulletin was written and illustrated by Santa Fe architect William Lumpkins and included drawings of thirty-seven examples of eighteenth- and nineteenth-century New Mexican furniture from the collections of the Museum of New Mexico and the Spanish Colonial Arts Society. In a short preface, Lumpkins wrote that "this collection of drawings has been compiled that authentic information regarding the old Spanish Colonial furniture may be available to the modern cabinet maker. . . . This type of furniture, with proper adaptations, is particularly well-suited to the Southwestern type of architecture that has been revived and is prevalent in this region."[25]

[24] Brice Seawell, "A New Type of School," *New Mexico School Review* 15, no. 2 (1935): 49; George I. Sanchez, *Forgotten People: A Study of New Mexicans* (Albuquerque: University of New Mexico Press, 1940), pp. 58–62.
[25] Taylor and Bokides, *New Mexican Furniture*, p. 234.

While some excellent furniture was produced in the vocational schools (fig. 5), most of it by students who did not let themselves be bound by Lumpkin's drawings, the schools, with one exception, never became the self-supporting community institutions that Seawell envisioned. Their sales were limited largely to public agencies or to people who wished to decorate their homes in "native style," and there were not enough of either to create a permanent market. The school at Chupadera, about ten miles north of Santa Fe, was the exception. It produced willow and leather patio furniture that became very popular and was probably modeled on some Huichol Indian religious objects in the collection of the Rockefeller-funded, independent Laboratory of Anthropology. For the most part, however, the schools served only as an effective way to bring federal and state funds into depressed communities.

Almost from the beginning of the program, critics questioned the ability of the vocational education handicraft program to meet its goal of creating an economy based on craft sales. In 1935 a federal study of Hispanic villages in the Rio Grande valley reported that in the town of Santa Cruz "thirty-eight [students] are studying woodwork and twenty-three are taking up weaving. One of the teachers estimates that probably ten per cent of these will follow up and attempt to make a living at weaving or woodwork. The reason for this is that the wages per hour on handicraft work remain extremely low, 15 cents at best. . . . for example, an excellent chest with some thirty hours of labor in it will bring $10, and the cost of the wood is $2.50."[26]

In 1937 the Federal government begin requiring state education departments to keep job-placement records for students trained from federal funds. Seawell reported on the first set of records in the *New Mexico School Review*, saying that "placements are showing up well for students trained in the woodworking classes. While few young men have found employment in furniture factories, most of them went into general construction as carpenters' helpers, form builders, etc. This indicates a necessity for students to be trained in general carpentry as well as cabinetmaking."[27]

[26]Marta Weigle, ed., *Hispanic Villages of Northern New Mexico: A Reprint of Volume II of the 1935 Tewa Basin Study with Supplementary Materials* (Santa Fe, N.M.: Lightening Tree Press, 1975), p. 26.
[27]Brice Seawell, "Vocational Education Adjusts Its Program to Meet the Needs of Industry," *New Mexico School Review* 17, no. 6 (1938): 26.

Fig. 5. El Rito Vocational School, chair, El Rito, N.M., ca. 1935. (Mr. and Mrs. John Gaw Meem: Photo, Mary Peck.) The design, especially the carving on the back, is an interpretation of a drawing in the Bureau of Vocational Education's *Spanish Colonial Furniture Bulletin*.

Ironically, at the same time that it became evident to all that a handicraft revival would not revive the economy of northern New Mexico, an industrial upturn on the West Coast begin to absorb the woodworking skills of Seawell's vocational school graduates. Shipyards and airplane factories, gearing up in 1940 for the war effort, needed skilled pattern makers, and New Mexico was ready to supply them. In 1942 an estimated 2,300 former New Mexico vocational students were working in these factories and sending portions of their paychecks home.

What do we find when we compare the pottery revival at San Ildefonso with the Hispanic crafts revival? First, there is a profound difference in their goals. Hewett's pottery revival had clear economic goals, while the Spanish Colonial Arts Society wished to revive crafts purely for the sake of reviving them. Second, after a brief early fling with historic re-creations, Hewett and his colleagues abandoned all interest in the issue of "authentic" versus "inauthentic" objects and concentrated on questions of technical quality and contemporary aesthetic appeal. Proponents of the Hispanic revival, on the other hand, seem to have been obsessed with controlling the design process to ensure conformity to historic examples and guard the craftsmen from the taint of modernity. One could almost say that the pottery revivers trusted their craftsmen's creative impulses but the Hispanic revivers did not. Finally, while Hewett had a clear understanding of the tourist market of his time and its fascination with anything Indian, those involved with the Hispanic revival did not. Their turn was not to come until the 1980s, when eastern designers gave the "Santa Fe Style" national prominence.

Both the pueblo and Hispanic craft revivals sprang from an urge to prolong the conditions of preindustrial society among two ethnic groups in New Mexico. Both were initiated and stimulated by outsiders who were aware of the arts and crafts movement in the East, although in neither case were these outsiders exclusively female. Ironically, neither would have achieved any degree of success without the purchasing power of tourists, itself a product of the industrial society deplored by arts and crafts advocates.

"One Who Has Seen More and Knows More"
The Design Critic and the Arts and Crafts

Beverly K. Brandt

The masterworks of the arts and crafts movement did not spring fully formed from the brains of craftsmen. They were the product of a life-long struggle to put theories of design reform into practice, the result of years of experimentation, of trial and error, of countless returns to the drawing board or bench. Yet, their restrained forms, subdued finishes, and chaste ornamentation belie the long and arduous labor that led to their creation. For that reason, researchers have dwelt upon the finished products as masterpieces—without examining the painstaking process by which they became so.

As they evolved from novices to masters, craftsmen strove to improve their work conceptually, aesthetically, and technically and, in doing so, sought advice from critics whose judgment they deemed superior to their own. By virtue of background, training, and education, or familiarity with emerging theories of design, these critics played an integral role within the design process, serving as both its starting point and its summation. Providing inspiration at the beginning and passing judgment upon finished products at the end, critics functioned as important intermediaries between theory and practice.

The critic's challenge was to promote high conceptual, aesthetic, and technical standards while remaining ever mindful of the crafts-man's limitations to achieving them. Successful design reform depended upon close interaction between critic and craftsman. Thus, the most effective critic was generally a blend of theorist and practitioner. "To be a real critic," wrote Boston connoisseur, author, and educator Denman Waldo Ross (1853–1935), "you must have studied the masterpieces in a way which the man of words cannot understand. You must," he continued, "have analyzed the fine things. You must know exactly what they are made of, and how the materials were put together. To make sure of your knowledge," he argued, "you must have put similar materials together in the same way with approximately the same results. . . . To be a real critic," he concluded, "you must have all the knowledge of the workman." The critic, Ross suggested, could learn as much from the craftsman as could the craftsman from the critic.[1]

Promoting interaction among craftsmen and critics was a goal of arts and crafts organizations both in America and abroad. The Society of Arts and Crafts, Boston (SACB), encouraged such interaction from its inception in 1897, proposing "to open a room in a central position where Artists and Craftsmen [might] meet for consultation and discussion, and where Workmen desirous of advice and instruction [might] at stated times find competent and sympathetic advisers." Many SACB members, such as metalworker Mary C. Knight (b. 1876), took advantage of such services over the years. "A Craftsman might work by himself indefinitely," wrote Knight, "when just a little encouragement and direction from one who has seen more and knows more would help such a lot." Like Knight, many craftsmen welcomed input from those whose historical, cultural, and theoretical awareness was broader than their own.[2]

Among those offering advice in the SACB's early years were accomplished master craftsmen and enthusiastic connoisseurs who supported the organization's interest in design reform. These "masters"

---

[1] Denman Waldo Ross, "The Arts and Crafts: A Diagnosis," *Handicraft* 1, no. 10 (January 1903): 229–43.

[2] Mary C. Knight to Frederick P. Cabot, probably from the spring of 1908, reel 317, frame 381, Society of Arts and Crafts, Boston, Papers, Archives of American Art, Smithsonian Institution, Washington, D.C. (hereafter cited as AAA/SACB Papers). In an untitled prospectus pamphlet, Harold Broadfield Warren discusses the SACB's plan to "open rooms": H. B. Warren, secretary, *[Untitled Prospectus Pamphlet] The Society of Arts and Crafts, Boston, Massachusetts, Incorporated* 1897 (Boston, 1898), reel 300, frame 003, AAA/SACB Papers.

and "patrons" (or "associates" as they were later called) met with novice craftsmen and aspiring amateurs at meetings organized to "quicken the spirit of invention in design and to encourage technical excellence." Some lectured on topics of general interest; others gave demonstrations of a technical nature or offered workshops and classes on design fundamentals. The SACB's varied constituency—billed as "Workmen, Artists and Lovers of Art" in its announcements—ensured that craftsmen and critics had an opportunity to meet regularly.[3]

That design criticism was integral to the mission of such organizations reflects the growth of the field as a specialty during the nineteenth century. The focus in the 1840s of English reformers, design criticism quickly evolved into both profession and pastime in America and abroad. It became particularly lively in the aftermath of the 1851 Great Exhibition in London, an event that provoked critical assessment of the industrialized world's manufactured products and work processes. During the century's latter half, design criticism became inextricably linked with design reform, inspiring new institutions such as museums of industrial arts, schools of practical design or mechanical arts, programs in art education, and numerous publications devoted to design. Improving the character of work processes and products, which was the goal of the design reform movement, demanded evaluation of both from an objective, theoretical perspective. The latter was the role of design criticism.[4]

Ninteenth-century design criticism had strong connections with both history and theory. Many critics were also historians of craft and ornament who used traditional models of craftsmanship as a basis when judging contemporary works. Some were familiar with emerging theories of design secondhand while others were theorists in their own right. All sought to extract from the past timeless principles appropriate to

[3]"For a Permanent Exhibition," *Boston Herald*, April 15, 1897, reel 322, frame 222, AAA/SACB Papers. Another untitled pamphlet offers prospective members information about upcoming meetings; *The Society of Arts and Crafts, Boston, Massachusetts, Incorporated* 1897 (Boston: Thomas Smith Printing Co., 1897), reel 316, frame 586, AAA/SACB Papers.

[4]For further information on design education and design publications in Boston, see Beverly Kay Brandt, " 'Mutually Helpful Relations': Architects, Craftsmen, and the Society of Arts and Crafts, Boston, 1897–1917" (Ph.D. diss., Boston University, 1984), pp. 25–26, 39, 49–53.

creating or evaluating design in an industrial age. In their quest to define good design and to determine how to achieve it, these critics addressed a variety of issues: the character of the product along with that of its maker and its user; what models, if any, could inspire originality in design; the impact of the machine upon form, ornament, construction, and finish; criteria according to which products should be judged; the critics' credentials; and, taste—what it was, who determined it, and what caused it to change. Finally, they debated issues of design education and how it might improve both the public's expectations and craftsmen's capabilities.

Many critics' ultimate goal was to render their own jobs obsolete by educating craftsmen to function as critics in their own right. "The all-round, complete artist, with his knowledge and judgment, his standard and ideals, his knowledge of tools and materials, of ways, means and methods, his power of eye and skill of hand," wrote Ross, "that is the man we want, the man we must have, before we can hope to see the Arts and Crafts alive again, and flourishing." His goal was to encourage craftsmen to approach their work from an intellectual as well as a technical perspective, thereby elevating the overall quality of design to a point where an external critic was no longer necessary to the design process.[5]

Honing craftsmen's intellectual and critical abilities was an ongoing concern of design reformers throughout the lifespan of the arts and crafts movement. Ross's statement reiterates the arguments of John Ruskin (1819–1900), who blamed the separation of thought and action in the creative process upon the division of labor in factories. "We want one man to be always thinking, and another to be always working," he wrote in his seminal essay "The Nature of Gothic" (1853), "and we call one a gentleman, and the other an operative; whereas," he argued, "the workman ought often to be thinking, and the thinker often to be working, and both should be gentlemen, in the best sense." This was easier said than done, however, as Boston design reformer and the SACB's second president, Arthur Astor Carey (1857–1923), pointed out. Most craftsmen, he explained, "have, for the most part, if they want to make a living out of their work, no opportunity of knowing

[5] Ross, "Arts and Crafts," p. 239.

anything about good design, and therefore they cannot learn to appreciate it." Reformers like Ruskin, Ross, and Carey argued that the average worker had little time to intellectualize about design. Thus, honing a craftsman's intellectual and critical abilities was an ideal worth pursuing—but one that was frustratingly difficult to achieve.[6]

Nevertheless, Ross regarded education as essential to refining the design process. He believed that educating workers in the history and theory of their respective crafts would increase their overall capabilities. But, as he wrote in 1903 addressing the existing system of education, "Idealism with its love of righteousness, truth and beauty, and technical ability . . . are widely separated. To achieve the ideal, technically," he admitted, and "to bring it forth as a tangible and visible reality is quite another matter. What we have to do," he offered, "is to give our pupils technical ability of all kinds, and, with it, the finest possible impulses,—the impulses which come from a real thorough knowledge of the best work that has been done in the world and the best thought that has been put into it." Ross viewed museums and libraries as a means of gaining exposure to such achievements since both were accessible to students and practitioners alike; thus, he encouraged craftsmen to take full advantage of them.[7]

Critics may have focused upon the education, training, and work processes of the craftsman, but their vision extended to everyone even remotely associated with making or using everyday objects. Design reform, advised Charles Howard Walker (1857–1936), a Boston architect, educator, and administrator of the SACB, required "education at both ends of the line of training." This meant, he indicated, "cultivating not only the artist, the producer, but also the public, the buyer." He might have mentioned the additional necessity of educating and cultivating participants whose responsibilities fell somewhere *between* those of producer and consumer, such as manufacturers and merchants, collectors and patrons, students and educators.[8]

[6]John Ruskin, "The Nature of Gothic" (1853), in *The Lamp of Beauty: Writings on Art by John Ruskin*, ed. Joan Evans (Ithaca, N.Y.: Cornell University Press, 1980), p. 237. Arthur Astor Carey, "The Past Year and Its Lessons," *Handicraft* 1, no. 1 (April 1902): 3–27.
[7]Ross, "Arts and Crafts," pp. 235, 243.
[8]C. Howard Walker, "The Museum and the School," *Handicraft* 2, no. 2 (May 1903): 29–31.

Herbert Langford Warren (1857–1917), another Boston architect, educator, and administrator of the SACB, described the complex interrelationship of these various participants. "We want to so raise the public taste," he stated in his inaugural address as the society's third president, "that the educated public will demand the qualities which can only be had through hand work. When the public demand that," he predicted, "the great firms that are now our opponents may become our best friends, because they will find it to their advantage to throw much of their machinery out of doors and work by hand." This, Warren explained, would occur "because the public [would] demand artistic works and [because]," he emphasized, "works of artistic handicraft cannot be made by machine." Like many reformers, Warren viewed the educated consumer as a critic whose purchases directly influenced decisions made by designers and craftsmen, along with those of manufacturers and merchants. Like others, he believed that the design process was a finely tuned mechanism in which opinions of all participants were equally important.[9]

One vehicle for raising standards was the public exhibition of arts and crafts—carefully selected, well documented, and tastefully displayed. Following the lead of British organizations, the SACB mounted such exhibitions regularly during its first two decades. Of particular importance were those held in 1897 (figs. 1, 2), 1899, 1904 (at the Louisiana Purchase Exposition in St. Louis), and 1907. The SACB's interest in these events extended beyond self-promotion. Administrators recognized that such "display[s] of ideals" might encourage the public's "appreciation and demand for art in common forms of construction and manufacture" and believed that smaller, ongoing exhibitions might serve as "a constant model for the people, a corrector and a developer of the public taste." Thus, they regarded participation in these events as essential to their organization's welfare and as beneficial to the design reform movement as a whole.[10]

[9] H. Langford Warren, "Our Work and Our Prospects," an inaugural address delivered to the SACB on November 20, 1903, and later reprinted in *Handicraft* 2, no. 9 (November 1903): 179–202.

[10] Henry Lewis Johnson, exhibition director, as quoted on "ideals" in "Arts and Crafts Exhibit: Unique Display to Be Made in Copley Hall in April," *Boston Herald*, January 9, 1897, reel 322, frame 166, AAA/SACB Papers. Otto Fleishner, Boston Public Library staff member, as quoted in "Artists and Artisans: Effort to Encourage Better Work by Mechanics," *Boston Herald*, February 27, 1897, reel 322, frame 178, AAA/SACB Papers. On the SACB display in St. Louis, see Beverly K. Brandt, " 'Worthy and Care-

Fig. 1. Copley Hall, "First Exhibition of the Arts and Crafts, Boston,"
April 5–16, 1897. (SACB Archives, Boston: Photo, N. L. Stebbins.)

Ensuring the quality of such events and interpreting their merits
were among the responsibilities of critics, who served on juries of review
for local, national, and international exhibitions or screened craftsmen's submissions to salesrooms. In addition, critics actively engaged
in related activities to maintain widespread influence: presenting public
lectures and teaching in universities, art programs, or trade schools;
publishing books and articles; and participating as members or officers
in arts and crafts organizations. Some of these arbiters of taste were
social reformers, journalists, educators, and connoisseurs; but, most
were practicing architects, designers, craftsmen, and skilled amateurs.
Despite their different professions or avocations, all hoped to elevate

fully Selected': American Arts and Crafts at the Louisiana Purchase Exposition, 1904,"
Archives of American Art Journal 28, no. 1 (1988): 2–16.

Fig. 2. Alston Hall, "First Exhibition of the Arts and Crafts, Boston," April 5–16, 1897. (SACB Archives, Boston: Photo, N. L. Stebbins.)

tastes among makers and users of everyday items by setting and enforcing the highest standards.[11]

The jury of the SACB—a body of critics to which Ross, Carey, Walker, and Warren all belonged—was established for this purpose concurrent with the society's second major exhibition in 1899 (figs. 3, 4) and following the opening of its salesroom in September 1900. One of the first of its kind in the country, the jury influenced craftsmen and consumers throughout the United States and beyond, in part because of the organization's growing international membership. The group became a model for other juries nationwide, ultimately serving as a prototype for review boards at events such as international expositions. In 1914, after concluding a tour of the western United States, SACB

[11] Influential Boston journalists included Sylvester Baxter of the *Herald*, F. W. Coburn of the *Transcript*, and William H. Downes of the *Transcript*.

Fig. 3. Copley Hall, "Exhibition of the Society of Arts and Crafts, Boston," April 4–15, 1899. (SACB Archives, Boston: Photo, Chickering.)

secretary Percy Macomber (ca. 1881–1960) reported with pride, "The severity of the Boston jury was everywhere quoted, sometimes with complete approval, sometimes with reservations. It was generally admitted," he concluded, "that nowhere else is such strictness maintained as in this city." That strictness extended not only to a product's appearance and style but also to its materials and manner of construction.[12]

The jury's reputation was a credit to its members, many of whom were multitalented master craftsmen (see appendix). Specialists in such areas as embroidery, stained glass, leatherwork, jewelry, metalwork, and carving, they regularly published books and articles on the history and theory of their crafts. As jury members, they struggled to establish,

[12]"Arts and Crafts Work through the West," *Boston Times*, May 19, 1914, reel 322, frame 324, AAA/SACB Papers.

Fig. 4. *Exhibition of the Society of Arts and Crafts, Copley Hall: Boston, Massachusetts, April 4–15, 1899,* cover (designed by Theodore Brown Hapgood). (SACB Archives, Boston.)

maintain, and then elevate standards among the 900 or so SACB members. Although impatient with dilettantes, they cultivated emerging talent in novices, arguing that "ingenuity in expression in bad things is more hopeful under training than the unanimity of the commonplace." If buyers questioned varying standards within the SACB salesroom, the jury rose to the novice craftsman's defense, contending that "the encouragement of recognition to the beginner is as much a part of the duty of the Society as is the presentation of superlative work."

Fig. 5. Salesroom, Society of Arts and Crafts, Boston, 9 Park St., in proximity to the Boston Statehouse. (SACB Archives, Boston.)

The jury adjusted its standards accordingly although it always stopped short of compromising its ideals.[13]

Minutes of meetings and essays published in the society's annual reports attest to the jury's strictness. Both sources document opinions rendered as the jury reviewed submissions by craftsmen wishing to sell work in the society's salesroom (fig. 5) or exhibit under the SACB's auspices. In doing so, the jury considered every aspect of a product's design or execution as well as its price and relative salability, its cultural relevance, and conceptual validity. It insisted that each product reflect a craftsman's highest potential according to that individual's capabilities.

Similarly, the jury insisted that each product reflect the potential of the medium that it represented or the craft tradition from which it had evolved. The group maintained that a hierarchy existed among crafts. "The various classes of objects," it stated in its report for 1914,

[13]C. Howard Walker, "Report of the Critic of the Jury," in *Annual Report of the Society of Arts and Crafts, Boston, Massachusetts, for the Year 1916, 9 Park Street* (Boston, 1917), p. 7.

"are different in intrinsic merit because of the materials and the skill required in the workmanship. It should be obvious," the report continued, "that jewelry and enamels, wood carving and illuminating can be expressed in higher terms than the usual china painting and leather working and coarse basket making." With that attitude in mind, the jury chided craftsmen whose work failed to exhibit the quality expected of a particular craft. "Criticism of Mrs. [Julia de Wolfe] Addison's (1866–1952) embroidery" was noted in the jury's minutes for February 12, 1902. "Embroidery not finely and carefully enough wrought for this class of work." Avoiding such mistakes required thorough knowledge of the medium, its evolution, and its refinement over time. "Learn the nature of your material first—its possibilities and limitations," advised SACB secretary Frederick Allen Whiting (1873–1959), "then learn the traditions of the craft which you will usually find to be closely related to the limitations of the material itself." Craftsmen could gain such knowledge through training and apprenticeships, by carefully observing the masterworks of the past, and by trial and error.[14]

In evaluating an individual's work, the jury consistently upheld the society's mission "to develop and encourage higher artistic standards in the handicrafts." In addition, the jury promoted the "Principles of Handicraft," a brief statement (drafted ca. 1900) that occupied a prominent position in the organization's publications. These principles emerged at the onset of Carey's presidency (1900–1903) because, as he later explained, members had "come to the point when [they] were a little afraid of [the] abstract and somewhat hungry for concrete and tangible facts." Thus they eagerly embraced the society's pledge "to endeavor to stimulate in workmen an appreciation of the dignity and value of good design; to counteract the popular impatience of Law and Form, the desire for over-ornamentation and specious originality, [while] insist[ing] upon the necessity of sobriety and restraint, of ordered arrangement, of due regard for the relation between the form of an object and its use, and of harmony and fitness in the decoration put

[14] Frederick A. Whiting, "Development and Meaning of the Arts and Crafts Movement," lecture manuscript, February 18, 1903, reel 300, frame 038–075, AAA/SACB Papers. C. Howard Walker, "Report of the Jury," in *Annual Report of the Society of Arts and Crafts, Boston, Massachusetts, Incorporated 1897, 9 Park Street* (Boston, 1914), pp. 9–12. "Minutes of the Meeting of the Jury," February 12, 1902, pp. 35–37, reel 316, frame 019, AAA/SACB Papers.

upon it." Such a conservative statement suggests that the jury's chief concern was improving its members' understanding of design fundamentals without promoting any particular style.[15]

The "Principles of Handicraft" are among those with which the jury assessed work of SACB members. But, they by no means constituted its sole criteria. Jurors cognizant of design theory were eager to apply their own principles to the evaluation process. Among these were Ross, author of *A Theory of Pure Design* (1907), and Walker, who lectured on design fundamentals and history at several Boston institutions while maintaining an architectural practice (Walker and Kimball). Walker never wrote a volume articulating his design theory, but essays in the society's annual reports elucidated his views. And he, like Warren and Ross, actively promoted books written by other well-known theorists. With such works at hand, the jury sought to convince their constituents that handicraft was less a craft than an art and less the product of the hand than of the intellect. "Designing is an art to be gained by careful, serious study," warned Walker, "not a fantasy or an amusement, excepting in so far as achievement gives pleasure."[16]

The jury regarded criticism as an equally serious pursuit. At the onset it established strict procedures to follow when reviewing members' works to ensure fairness and impartiality. Members submitting work identified it by number to guarantee anonymity, and, for nearly a decade, the jury met in secrecy behind closed doors. The jury recorded decisions to accept or reject work in a log, commenting on the merits or flaws of particular submissions. Occasionally it conveyed such comments to contributors, sometimes clarifying its points with small sketches.[17]

---

[15] On standards see "Charter and Statements of Criteria," June 28, 1897, reel 300, frame 002, AAA/SACB Papers. The SACB's pledge to uphold good design appears in an untitled document that serves as the prototype for later annual reports; *The Society of Arts and Crafts, Boston, Massachusetts, Incorporated 1897, 14 Somerset Street, 1901* (Boston, 1901). A handwritten note indicates that this was printed by the Merrymount Press on August 7, 1902 (SACB Vertical File, Fine Arts Library, Boston Public Library). Carey, "Past Year and Its Lessons," pp. 3–27.

[16] C. Howard Walker, "Report of the Critic of the Jury," in *Annual Report of the Society of Arts and Crafts, Boston, Massachusetts, for the Year 1917* (Boston: Stetson Press, 1918), p. 8. Denman W. Ross, *A Theory of Pure Design: Harmony, Balance, Rhythm* (1907; reprint, New York: Peter Smith, 1933).

[17] "Minutes of the Meeting of the Jury," January 2, 1901, p. 15, reel 316, frame 009, AAA/SACB Papers.

The breadth of the jury's watchfulness extended especially to matters of technique or construction. Sometimes it found fault with every aspect of a work submitted for consideration, recording such comments as "the design is not good and the whole thing is clumsy." But, on most occasions it questioned just a single characteristic. Among these were the visual or physical connection of parts to the whole: "The pen rack and feet could be made more in harmony with the rest of the piece"; the character, placement, or amount of ornament: "Overcharged and unbalanced in design, no reserve of richness"; the overall form: "Outline unpleasant and pretentious"; proportion or scale: "Rejected: Miss [Jane] Carson's Ring: Lacks delicacy"; or, the draftsmanship and disposition of decorative elements: "The composition has no *organic* value, [and] could not give permanent pleasure." For every specific recommendation offered by the jury, such as the suggestion that one distinct type of molding be substituted for another, or that a cool gray glaze be adjusted to "a *warm* to harmonize," there were others that seemed arbitrary or ambiguous. What did the jury mean when it labeled a color "unfortunate," a glaze "odd," or a shape "lacking in distinction"? What did it hope to convey by suggesting that a piece of jewelry was "lacking in quality" or that a bowl needed "more exquisite treatment owing to the beauty of the subject"? Such statements were well founded but lacked the specificity required to be helpful, especially to the novice.[18]

The jury often overlooked weaknesses in one aspect of a work if it noticed strengths of another sort. "Accepted," it stated regarding article no. 2 of contributor no. 56, "the admirable workmanship rather than the design is commended." "[Approved]," it noted on another occasion, "design of chairs [by Mrs. Dennett and Mrs. Hill] with some criticism of workmanship. [Approved] tables in design; but construction criticized." As this last comment suggests, the jury's tolerance for weakness in design generally surpassed its willingness to overlook flaws in craftsmanship. It paid particular attention to surface and finish, always alert for signs of impatience on the part of the craftsman, or what it

[18]"Minutes of the Meeting of the Jury," August 12, 1902; November 9, 1900; May 28, 1902; April 11, 1901; February 13, 1901; December 19, 1902; March 6, 1901; April 12, 1901; October 22, 1902; November 14, 1900; and September 16, 1901, reel 316, frames 003–051, AAA/SACB Papers.

called "hurried workmanship." It might return a piece of jewelry or metalwork that seemed overly bright, recommending that it "be oxidized" to tone down the coloration, but it would not tolerate pieces that already appeared overworked in any way, having, for example, a "surface too much fussed over." It rejected products having either an "affectation of age" or of "rudeness," expressing particular dislike for "heavy hammer marks" or for any "imperfections that were too obviously intentional." The jury insisted that every surface or finish must be *genuine*, a true reflection of the nature of the material and the technique employed to manipulate it. It disdained artificiality.[19]

Criticism recorded in the jury's minutes set the tone for its essays published in the society's annual reports. Directed at the entire membership, these essays (published yearly after 1906) summarized achievements in general craft categories, often making specific recommendations regarding types of new products needed in the marketplace. Although they varied year to year, these reports often reiterated the same points, as exemplified by that for 1912. "It is absurd," the report began, "to charge a price in excess of that charged for machine work unless some distinctive artistic or skilful character pertains to the article which is not found in machine work. Also, that imitation of the happy accidents of crude craftsmanship," it continued, "is pure affectation, as is likewise the exaggeration of elementary design and workmanship. This applies especially to glazes which do not cover," it indicated, "and to tool marks which should have been worked out. . . . A great deal of the work presented," it concluded, "is of no especial interest, being merely a poor attempt to be original to the point of uncouthness, or else barely meeting the utilitarian requirements." Year after year the jury encouraged its constituents to fabricate works that provided a compelling alternative to machine-made products. It insisted that such works be competitive conceptually, aesthetically, and technically and possess a character reflecting the hand, spirit, and intellect.[20]

These yearly reports encouraged craftsmen to master basic princi-

[19]"Minutes of the Meeting of the Jury," November 9, 1900; December 19, 1900; January 2, 1901; April 11, 1901; March 5, 1902; April 2, 1902; and April 1, 1901, reel 316, frames 003–051, AAA/SACB Papers.

[20]J. T. Coolidge, Jr., "Report of the Jury," in *Annual Report of the Society of Arts and Crafts, Boston, Massachusetts, Incorporated 1897, 1912, 9 Park Street* (Boston, 1913), pp. 16–17.

ples and discouraged them from becoming stylistic innovators. The
jury's critiques consistently questioned products that it deemed "eccentric," "bizarre," "self-consciously aesthetic," or "exclusively novel." It
recognized a "need to improve design, and to develop originality," but
it insisted upon an "originality of idea, not of sensationalism." It advised members against "ambitious flights of fancy" or "launch[ing] into
a sea of new ideas for which they were unprepared." It cautioned them
against *l'art nouveau*, condemning it as "the work of the untrained,
underdeveloped, unstocked brain and the faltering hand." Evidently
the jury's enthusiasm for the latest theories of good design did not
extend to newly emerging styles.[21]

The jury's recommendation for achieving originality was to reject
the new art in favor of studying and adapting the work of the past. It
urged its constituents to examine objects in museums, loan exhibitions,
and private collections, discerning within them principles that were
timeless and universal. "The study of the work of the old masters,"
said the report for 1910, "can be urged as the most important influence
in promoting good handicraft. . . . We have examples of Greek,
Gothic, Renaissance, Chinese, Persian, Japanese, and Moorish craftsmanship all around us," it offered, "in our museums, our collections,
our homes, in books and photographs to inspire and guide the worker."
To learn from such examples, it advised, might require "cop[ying]
directly as a painter copies an old picture, in order to acquire some of
its feeling and skill" or, it continued, studying such examples "to endeavor to reach the point of view of the old craftsman, with his exquisite
sense of appropriateness in form and arrangement, in line and color,
and in surface treatment and the relation of materials." The purpose
of such an approach, it indicated, was to shore up the "insecure foundations upon which the modern movement of the Arts and Crafts rested"
and to replace its "eccentricities and false sentiments" with "a more

[21]"Report of the Jury," in *Annual Report of the Society of Arts and Crafts, Boston,
Massachusetts, 9 Park Street, 1907* (Boston, 1907), pp. 17–18. "Report of the Jury," in
*Annual Report of the Society of Arts and Crafts, Boston, Massachusetts, Incorporated
1897, 1908* (Boston, 1908), p. 19. "Report of the Jury," in *The Society of Arts and Crafts
Annual Report and List of Members, 1906, 9 Park Street* (Boston, 1907), p. 19. On the
jury's conservatism and its impact upon the evolution of a Boston style, see Beverly K.
Brandt, " 'Sobriety and Restraint': The Search for an Arts and Crafts Style in Boston,
1897–1917," *Tiller* 2, no. 5 (Fall 1985): 26–73.

real and sincere knowledge and feeling." To study exemplary work from the past, and more importantly to understand the spirit that led to its creation, was essential, the jury suggested, to producing contemporary products that were both beautiful and useful while remaining technically competent and culturally relevant. To facilitate hands-on exposure to historical artifacts, collectors within the SACB often made available to craftsmen pieces from their personal collections for study or duplication, but only after the jury had approved them. [22]

Three-dimensional objects were the best models for craftsmen desirous of learning from the past. Illustrations in books, however, also served as a valuable resource and an acceptable substitute. To that end, the society's lending library included books on varied subjects to "inspire and guide the worker." Some were devoted to design theory; a few were monographs on individual craftsmen; others were purely technical in nature; and, numerous volumes documented the historical evolution of particular crafts. The society published a bibliography of its holdings in 1907 and 1916 as an example for others wishing to develop their own libraries. [23]

The jury often reminded craftsmen of the benefits of studying "the illustrated literature upon the class of work [they] produced," but it recommended publications selectively. It insisted that some were better than others and grew perplexed when SACB members chose to consult those not on its approved list. "There is one very persistent fact which manifests itself to the Jury," it lamented in 1917, "and that is the inability of the average worker to use a good library, and his ignorance of books of instruction in his own art. Often skill of hand exists, with not even elemental idea of design." The report went on to denounce especially those who "seem[ed] to imbibe ideas [only] from very second-rate sources in weeklies or magazines." In the following year it cautioned its readers: "The Jury wishes therefore especially to advocate the study of Design. Skill is technique and necessary for expression. Design is the best achievement of that expression." And, the best achievements

[22] J. T. Coolidge, Jr., "Report of the Jury," in *The Society of Arts and Crafts Thirteenth Annual Report: List of Members, Boston 1910* (Boston, 1911), pp. 15–16.
[23] "The League Libraries," *Handicraft* 3, no. 4 (July 1910): 136. "List of Books in the Library of the Society," in *Annual Report of the Society of Arts and Crafts, Boston, Massachusetts, for the Year 1915, 9 Park Street, Boston* (Montague, Mass.: Montague Press, 1916), pp. 20–23.

in design, the jury might have added, drew inspiration only from approved models.[24]

The jury's recommendation to study historical models was consistent with theories of design that had evolved internationally since the
1840s. "For your teachers, they must be Nature and History," wrote
William Morris in his essay "The Lesser Arts" (1882), adding that historical understanding was only a means to a greater end. "Let us therefore
study it wisely," he advised, "be taught by it, kindled by it; all the while
determining not to imitate it or repeat it; to have either no art at all, or an
art which we have made our own." Similarly, Walker argued eloquently
that workers must adapt historical lessons to contemporary applications.
Students of history, he wrote in "The Museum and the School" (1903),
"having lived in the art of the past, build up as worthy an art of the present,
founded on the past as all things must be, but on the best of the past, and
permeated by the life of the present, as all active workers must be and
therefore," he concluded, "making the art of the past suffer a change
which makes it the art of the present." This attitude informed Walker's
work as an architect and that of his students at institutions in Boston and
Cambridge. In addition, it influenced his constituents who sought his
advice regarding models that he deemed appropriate in his capacity as the
SACB's official "Critic of the Jury."[25]

Catalogue entries from the society's numerous exhibitions document the historical models to which craftsmen dutifully turned for inspiration. Inspired by a broad range of cultures and time periods, they limited their reach only by the inherent restrictions of the materials in which
they worked or according to the tenets of the craft tradition that they represented. In fabricating work for the society's decennial exhibition (fig. 6),
for example, basketmakers turned to Native American examples produced by the Washo, Pima, and Apache tribes. Glassmakers emulated
Italian and French wares, while jewelers explored a wider range, including Egyptian, "Runic," Gothic, and oriental. Leatherworkers were particularly catholic in their tastes, embracing Celtic, Old English, Elizabe-

---

[24]C. Howard Walker, "Report of the Jury," in *The Annual Report of the Society of
Arts and Crafts, Boston, Massachusetts, Incorporated 1897* (Boston, 1915), p. 10. *Annual
Report for 1916*, p. 7. C. Howard Walker, "Report of the Critic of the Jury" for 1917,
p. 8.
[25]William Morris, "The Lesser Arts," in *William Morris*, ed. G. D. H. Cole (New
York: Random House, 1934), pp. 494–516. C. Howard Walker, "Museum and the
School," p. 41.

Fig. 6. Copley Hall, "Decennial Exhibition of the Society of Arts and Crafts, Boston," February 5–26, 1907. (SACB Archives, Boston.)

than, Flemish, and Venetian models along with those from the Byzantine, Romanesque, Italian Renaissance, and Louis XVI periods. Woodworkers based their pieces on Florentine and Dutch sources or upon the work of Thomas Chippendale II, while metalworkers, weavers, and embroiderers preferred to emulate their colonial predecessors.[26]

Contemporary reactions to such historically based products were generally positive, in keeping with the conservative preferences of northeastern consumers. "Here," wrote journalist Will Hutchins, regarding the decennial exhibition, "the complete absence of either the more brutal styles of 'crafts' furniture, or the more uncontrolled exuberance of the art-nouveau manner is conspicuous. Everything shown," he concluded, "is refined and chaste and . . . carefully executed along the best traditions—for the most part of the eighteenth century." To those who accused the show of being either "too tame," or too "imitative and copied from the past," Walker replied, "Styles of art are so

[26] *Exhibition of the Society of Arts and Crafts: Copley Hall, Boston, February 5–26, 1907, Arts and Crafts Exhibition in Celebration of the Tenth Anniversary of Organization* . . . (Boston: Heintzemann Press, 1907), pp. 1–108.

many that it is difficult to find any work which has not resemblance to antecedents, unless it be monstrous." Softening his tone, he added, "The intention certainly has been to avoid absolute copying, and to be grateful for a sense of appreciation of what is good in the past." What he failed to note was the difficulty most craftsmen experienced in extracting the spirit of the age from a particular model while avoiding line-for-line duplication of its form.[27]

Craftsmen seeking to apply an appreciation of the past to their own work faced numerous obstacles, not the least of which were Walker and his colleagues, who were always quick to point out the failure of contemporary products. Around 1910 the jury chastised the society's jewelers for works that were flawed by what it termed a "perfectly indiscriminate association and treatment of metals and stones" or those inspired by so-called "inappropriate" models. Emulating "picturesque and barbaric peasant work" and that of "village Oriental craftsmen," jewelers had produced pieces that appeared, in the jury's estimation, "thoroughly crude and childish in idea," rendering them ill-suited to the society's discriminating clientele. Presumably, such input caused craftsmen to change their approach, for by 1911 or so the jury had altered its tone, praising their work for demonstrating consistently high standards. And in 1913 a journalist complimented the jewelers and enamelists for abandoning the "heavy and barbaric style of ornament that was more or less prevalent" in the early days of the movement. As these comments suggest, critics' expectations seemed to reflect the traditionally high rank held by jewelry making within the craft hierarchy. Critics attributed its stature as a craft to its association with products fabricated from expensive materials, executed fastidiously, and based upon high-style sources. Accordingly, they were skeptical of any works deviating from a traditional approach.[28]

[27] O.L.E. to Edward H. Clement, ed., "Listener," *Boston Transcript*, ca. February 27, 1907; Will Hutchins, "The Boston Arts and Crafts Exhibition in Copley Hall," *Republican* (Springfield), February 7, 1907; C. Howard Walker to the editor, *Boston Herald*, ca. March 7, 1907 (1907 Scrapbook, SACB Archives, Boston Public Library).

[28] *Annual Report* for 1906, pp. 20–21. *Annual Report* for 1907, p. 19. "Report of the Jury," in *The Society of Arts and Crafts, Fourteenth Annual Report and List of Members, Boston, 1911* (Boston: Merrymount Press, 1912), pp. 14–15. "Jewelry and Enamels," *Boston Transcript*, ca. March 6, 1913, reel 322, frame 316, AAA/SACB Papers.

The jury did not render such opinions without craftsmen's protestations. Many regarded the jury's relentless pursuit of excellence as a threat to their artistic integrity. They spoke out against stylistic censorship, claiming that the appropriateness of vernacular models depended upon a product's end use. "To me the Jury is trying to make all keys fit the same keyhole," complained metalworker Annie C. Putnam (1850–1924). "Therein lies the danger of '*Standards.*' The machine standard which stands for accuracy and perfect finish," she explained, "has to me disastrously affected the handiwork of today. I have seen many beautiful things in Museums," she fussed, "that would never be accepted by the Boston Arts and Crafts Society. Draw some of the beautiful old borders on the metalwork of India and Persia accurately," she offered, "and you destroy the beauty and vitality in them." Reminding the jury that "the use of an article . . . determines its design and execution," Putnam encouraged jurors to allow for greater variety of character among the work that it approved. "A piece of Favrile glass is not in keeping with a bungalo whereas a rather primitive bowl might be. A buckle designed for an outing dress is not suitable with a reception dress," she added. "Nor would we desire the same design and execution for the setting of precious and semi-precious stones." With this challenge, Putnam raised an important issue—that of the jury's limited aesthetic vision. Arts and crafts designers had expressed an abiding interest in vernacular models since the 1860s, but SACB members who chose to do so risked infuriating the jury if their designs appeared crude in technique or rough in aspect. The jury's standards demanded a degree of refinement that discouraged reference to primitive or provincial sources or to anything "commonplace."[29]

For those not wishing to emulate history, nature offered an alternative. Following the recommendations of a host of internationally known theorist-practitioners, craftsmen turned to nature as the ultimate muse that inspired freshness and originality. Although historicism dominated among products displayed or sold under the SACB's auspices, naturalism informed every craft category. With varying degrees of realism, these crafts employed forms, ornament, motifs, and imagery adapted from flora, fauna, and countryside. And, in doing so, they

[29] Annie C. Putnam to the SACB jury, March 14, 1908, reel 300, frame 515, AAA/ SACB Papers.

were among the most innovative and progressive works that SACB members produced.[30]

Success at employing naturalism, however, depended upon the particular craft. According to the jury, leatherwork frequently suffered from ornamentation that was either "of a weak naturalistic type, or of the still worst convolutions of the so-called art nouveau," a fault that it shared with china painting. "In both cases," stated the jury in 1912, "the difficulty apparently is that each [craft] lends itself too readily to any type of design and there is not," it continued, "constructive necessity which tends to create any special type of design. Whenever this is the case," the report concluded, "the designer dives at once into the depth of 'inspiration from nature' failing to realize that naturalistic design is the last word of the skilled designer." Evidently the principles governing a naturalistic approach were more stringent than those controlling one that was historical. But, lacking a foundation in history and theory, few workers knew the underlying principles that dictated success and thus could not make discriminating choices.[31]

The jury elucidated some of those principles to benefit workers having difficulty. To improve leatherwork derived from "poorly drawn, naturalistic sketches," it advised, "The best leather designs of all time have been strongly conventional, with firm, true lines and forms, well suited for naturalistic work." Arguing that wood carving also suffered from "slipshod naturalistic designs," it declared, "Naturalism requires great skill, and with the numberless fine examples of conventional wood carving upon the South Sea Island paddle blades and Dutch and Elizabethan and Jacobean furniture, it would seem wise for the wood carvers to study simpler forms than those they undertake." As both statements suggest, the jury regarded conventionalization as the key to transforming natural elements so that they might enhance an object's form. But even that approach was challenging. "If conventionalized naturalism is to occur, and it must occur in decorative pattern, especially upon small objects," the jury warned, "it would be well to have a knowledge of the natural forms themselves before any conventionalism is attempted." Thus, looking to nature for inspiration, the jury suggested, was as demanding as turning to history. Both approaches

---

[30] For references to naturalism, see the *Exhibition of the Society of Arts and Crafts: Copley Hall, Boston, February 5–26, 1907*, pp. 1–108.
[31] *Annual Report* for 1911, p. 17. *Annual Report* for 1912, p. 17.

required close scrutiny of the subject at hand before transforming and then applying it—both originally and appropriately.[32]

Craftsmen's responses to these and other recommendations varied. Some challenged the jury openly, and a few resigned from the organization altogether, but most took its comments in stride because they believed that their livelihood depended upon conformity to its standards. Many craftsmen entrusted their life's work to the SACB salesroom, so they implemented the jury's recommendations swiftly and without protest. Those who supported the jury process credited it with strengthening their professional development. "I think we can feel that the Society's success is our success, and at the same time . . . that our success is the Society's success," said metalsmith Arthur J. Stone (1847–1938) of the benefits of mutual cooperation among craftsmen, the jury, and the society's administrators.[33]

Stone is one of those whom the jury critiqued regularly throughout his career, despite his designation as a master craftsman and (in 1912–13) as a "medallist"—the society's highest commendation. The jury offered Stone's silver hollowware and flatware as a model to novices and masters alike; yet, it persisted in finding fault with it, often to the point of nit-picking. By stating in its minutes for January 29, 1902, that certain pieces "might be varied a little" or that others might "possibly [be] a *trifle only* too wide and thick," the jury established that even the most accomplished craftsmen must continually upgrade the quality of their work and demonstrated that no one within the organization could escape its discriminating eye. Despite such criticism, Stone enjoyed a sales record exceeding that of any other individual within the organization. He welcomed input from the jury graciously, agreeing with his wife and business partner, Elizabeth, "that no other jury system of equal intelligence exists" anywhere within the United States.[34]

Their vote of confidence did not, however, preclude the Stones from criticizing the jury. They questioned salesroom policies, having a vested interest in its management, and even challenged the jury's effectiveness, claiming that its abstract theories only frustrated and con-

[32] *Annual Report* for 1914, p. 11. *Annual Report* for 1915, p. 9.
[33] Arthur J. Stone and Elizabeth B. Stone to Frederick P. Cabot, July 17, 1912, reel 317, frame 671, AAA/SACB Papers.
[34] "Minutes of the Meeting of the Jury," January 29, 1902, p. 35, reel 316, frame 019, AAA/SACB Papers. Elizabeth B. Stone to H. Langford Warren, February 22, 1908, reel 300, frame 498, AAA/SACB Papers.

fused struggling craftsmen. In that regard their comments paralleled those of Knight, who feared that the jury's criticism was too esoteric. It might be "ever so good," she claimed, "but only one person in two or three at most has the chance to appreciate it." Administrators within the SACB, she continued, might "frankly say that not one of the Crafts-men can draw or design. But the mere saying so does not help this matter, nor publishing it in the A[nnual] R[eport]." Offering criticism that was consistently objective, constructive, and understandable was an art that eluded even the jury.[35]

In offering criticism, the jury had the best intentions, but some SACB members took exception to its tone, claiming that it was unneces-sarily negative. "The Jury has received from various sources a number of suggestions, many of which are excellent," it reported in 1909. "Among them is a recommendation that workers should be encouraged by praise as well as helped by criticism, and that the jury should do this by 'pointing out not only what is bad, but by indicating, as well, that which is good or indifferent.'" The jury obliged by marking exemplary goods in the salesroom "specially commended" and by publishing outstanding crafts-men's names in the annual report. But those who were overlooked labeled the practice unfair, claiming that their work suffered by comparison with pieces bearing special labels and complaining that this jeopardized their livelihood. Such claims trapped the jury between its own goals and its constituents' conflicting needs and abilities. "The Jury would prefer a higher standard than the existing one," it stated in 1913, "but can only work gradually towards it, because it is obvious that a state of excellence beyond the average producing capacity of our members cannot be forced, and so it has been necessary to give some weight to the 'living' side of the question." The need for craftsmen to earn a living caused the jury to set aside its idealistic vision of what *might be* and to promote instead a more realistic standard that a majority of members might achieve.[36]

Ultimately, the relationship between craftsmen and the critics de-pended upon a willingness to compromise. Both groups had to view

[35] Knight to Cabot. Elizabeth B. Stone, "Observations of an Onlooker," *Handicraft* 3, no. 3 (June 1910): 79.
[36] *Annual Report* for 1909, p. 16. J. T. Coolidge, Jr., "Report of the Jury," in *Annual Report of the Society of Arts and Crafts, Boston, Massachusetts, Incorporated 1897, 9 Park Street, Boston* (Boston, 1913), p. 15. "Records of the Meeting of the Council," March 11, 1908, reel 316, frame 441, AAA/SACB Papers.

the creative process from each others' perspectives and to balance individual agendas with the goals of the SACB. Ultimately, craftsmen accepted criticism as a vital part of their work process while critics adjusted their principles to accommodate their constituents' practical needs. As a result, craftsmen expanded their conceptual horizons while critics witnessed their theories implemented with varying degrees of success. In the process, craftsmen came to regard their work more critically, allowing critics to invest their energies in other ventures. "Anyone looking over the reports of the Jury over the past few years would notice a distinct change in their tenor," stated the report for 1911. "Comment and recommendation, in the presence of steady improvement, have taken the place over criticism; and the day seems not far distant when the Jury's report will have to deal more with general conditions of advancement than with particular conditions of criticism. . . . The standards," it indicated, "have been raised and the workers have risen in response." And, in 1913, it reported proudly, "Our productions have a quality not to be found elsewhere in our city, while our few masterpieces would hold their own anywhere." The fact that they have continued to do so decades later in an international marketplace is a testimony to the willingness of craftsmen and critics to work together.[37]

Despite its widespread reputation and influence, the SACB jury was merely one of many similar bodies affecting arts and crafts within and beyond the United States. All deserve the attention of scholars of the arts and crafts movement before the full impact of criticism upon reform will be understood. Criticism informed every stage of the design process, from conception and implementation to completion and distribution, utilization, and ultimately evaluation. The role of critics as arbiters of taste at every stage warrants further exploration to document the transformation of an object from abstract idea to fully realized masterpiece. Comprehending the role of criticism in shaping the arts and crafts movement requires understanding an equally significant subject—the role of design theory as it emerged between 1840 and 1920. Understanding both criticism and theory is vitally important to interpreting the design reform movement today. Their exploration should elucidate further the propaganda of the arts and crafts movement while enhancing an understanding of its work processes and end products.

[37] *Annual Report* for 1911, p. 14. *Annual Report* for 1913, p. 16.

Appendix

Members of the Jury of the Society of Arts and Crafts, Boston[1]

1900–1917

Name	Dates	Occupation	Service as Juror
Carey, Arthur Astor	1857–1923	social reformer	1900–1902
Clark, Henry Hunt	1875–1962	metalworker	1900–1902
Coolidge, J. Templeman, Jr.	1856–1945	designer	1900–1903, 1908–17
Dennett, Mary Ware	1872–1947	leatherworker	1900–1903
Forssen, Carl G.	n.a.	metalworker	1908, 1910
Hale, Frank Gardner	b. 1876	jewelry maker	1910–16
Kendrick, George Prentiss	b. 1850	designer	1903–1908
Kjellstrom, N.	n.a.	wood carver	1900–1903
Longfellow, Alex. Wadsworth, Jr.	1854–1934	architect	1900–1903, 1908–17
Martin, Laurin Hovey	b. 1875	jewelry maker	1900–1903
Morse, Alice J.	n.a.	metalworker	1908–17
Murphy, Herman Dudley	1867–1945	frame maker	1908–9
Peabody, John Endicott	1853–1921	designer	1909–17
Putnam, Annie Cabot	1850–1924	metalworker	1908–12
Ross, Denman Waldo	1853–1935	design, educator	1900–1903
Sacker, Amy M.	n.a.	designer, educator	1903, 1908–13
Sears, Mary Crease	n.a.	designer	1908, 1910–17
Sears, Sarah Choate	1858–1935	embroiderer	1900–1903
Smith, Joseph Linden	1863–1950	designer	1902, 1911–13
Sturgis, R. Clipston	b. 1860	architect	1900
Walker, Charles Howard	1857–1936	architect, educator	1901, 1903, 1908–17
Warren, Herbert Langford	1857–1917	architect, educator	1900–1903, 1908, 1911
Whiting, Frederick Allen	1873–1959	clerk, lecturer	1900–1903, 1908–12
Whitman, Sarah Wyman	1842–1904	stained glass maker	1900–1903

[1]No records of juror's names exist for the years 1904–7, but Coolidge, Kendrick, Longfellow, Ross, Sacker, Walker, Warren, and Whiting probably served during that time.

Sources: For the years 1900, 1901, 1902, and 1903, see reel 316, frame 002, 009, 016, 028, AAA/SACB papers. No records are available for the years 1904, 1905, 1906, and 1907. For the year 1908, see reel 319, frame 464, AAA/SACB Papers. For the years 1909, 1910, 1911, and 1912, see reel 316, frame 036–049, AAA/SACB Papers. For the year 1913, see reel 319, frame 817, AAA/SACB Papers. For the year 1914, see reel 318, frame 864, AAA/SACB Papers. For the years 1915, 1916, and 1917, see *Annual Reports* for 1916, 1917, and 1918.

"The Distinction of Being Different"

Joseph P. McHugh and the American
Arts and Crafts Movement

Anna Tobin D'Ambrosio

"From a purely craftsman's point of view, the Mission Furniture has the excellent quality which is the outcome of good workmanship. The joints and dovetailing are excellently finished, the material is treated as if the worker took a delight in handling it and the articles look as if they begged to be used for the several purposes for which they were intended." "His mission designs were inept and their execution substandard."[1] Neither of these quotes, made nearly a century apart, adequately represents the work of Joseph P. McHugh, the self-proclaimed

The author thanks Catherine Zusy for her initial contribution to my research and her continued guidance. She also gratefully acknowledges Dr. Paul Schweizer, the Munson-Williams-Proctor Institute, and Dr. Jane C. Busch for their support of this project. Her appreciation also goes to Helen Gant for her insightful comments in the preparation of this manuscript. Also see Anna Tobin D'Ambrosio, "The Distinction of Being Different": Joseph P. McHugh and the American Arts and Crafts Movement (Utica, N.Y.: Munson-Williams-Proctor Institute, 1993) for recent discoveries and a complete discussion of Joseph P. McHugh and Co.

[1] The furniture is praised in Temple Scott, "Mission Furniture," *International Studio* (February 1901), which is reprinted in *The "Mission" Furniture of Joseph P. McHugh and Company: Its Origin and Some Opinions by Decorative Authorities* (New York: Joseph P. McHugh, 1901), p. 8. David M. Cathers, *Furniture of the American Arts and Crafts Movement* (New York: New American Library, 1981), p. 15.

originator of American mission-style furniture. Although McHugh's impact on the American arts and crafts movement has gone unexplored, his mass-produced furniture did make a significant contribution to the development of the movement.

The American arts and crafts movement had less of an ideological component than its English counterpart. American manufacturers adapted the style to mass-production and marketing techniques without embracing the corresponding ideals. McHugh typified this approach. His interest in progressive stylistic trends brought him briefly to the forefront of the movement although a comprehensive and interpretive analysis of the man reveals that he was not a proponent of the arts and crafts philosophy. He was, however, a shrewd businessman who capitalized on the movement through stylistic adaptation and used the rhetoric of the period to promote his Popular Shop and his products. McHugh typifies how American manufacturers' industrial compromise contributed to the popularity of the movement in America.[2]

McHugh was a self-taught interior designer and a furniture manufacturer who received his business and interior design training through practical experience. Born in 1854 to Mary Sheehan and Patrick McHugh of New York City, he aquired skills by becoming increasingly involved in his father's dry goods business. After completing four years at the College of the Holy Cross preparatory school in Worcester, Massachusetts,[3] McHugh returned to New York to assist in his father's store, where he worked from 1869 through 1878 without wages. In 1873 Patrick McHugh allowed his son to add window shades and floor coverings to the stock.

By 1875 Patrick had moved the store from Third Avenue to Eighth Avenue at Fifty-second Street and limited the stock to oil cloths, carpets, matting, and shades. Joseph established the Popular Shop in 1878, when, in return for his services in the carpet salesroom, he received a small space in the store where he could produce and sell shades. In 1880 he opened his own business, Joseph McHugh and Company, on Sixth Avenue near Fifty-second Street, expanding his

[2] Leslie Greene Bowman, "The American Arts and Crafts Movement: Industry Applied to Art," *Antiques* 137, no. 3 (September 1990): 506–17.

[3] "Joseph P. McHugh—His Shop," *The Decorative Furnisher* 29 (October 1915): 46–48, 53–54.

inventory to include upholstery and wallpapers and training himself in their installation.

Rooted in the aesthetic movement, McHugh's Popular Shop developed into an arts and crafts retail store that offered a broader range of products than many of its competitors. The shop was an attempt to combine an arts and crafts manufactory with an interior decoration business. Following the course set by his contemporaries, McHugh heeded the prevailing trend in department store development toward greater size and inclusiveness, stressing a holistic approach to interior design. He exhibited this philosophy throughout the development of his product lines along with the decorative arts he imported from Europe. By 1882 McHugh imported Liberty of London furnishings, including William Morris and Walter Crane wallpapers. He also carried Charles Volkmar ceramics from New York, pewter accessories, French Zuber wallpapers, a broad selection of European metalwares and ceramics, and fabrics made to his design and color specifications. Finally, in 1884 McHugh moved the Popular Shop to Forty-second Street and Fifth Avenue, across from the New York Public Library, where it operated until the 1920s.[4]

Numerous contemporary arts and crafts publications have discussed McHugh's proclamation that he was the originator of mission-style furniture. The origin was debated as much in the late nineteenth and early twentieth centuries as it is today. Arguments were put forth by McHugh, Gustav Stickley, and George Clingman.[5] McHugh's claim can, however, be substantiated.

In 1915 a Wanamaker's department store advertisement promoted the Stickley Brothers as "originators of mission furniture in America." McHugh was infuriated and wrote to Wanamaker's requesting a retraction. The printed restatement sparked a flurry of inquiries addressed to the trade publication called *The Decorative Furnisher*. Through a series

[4] "Joseph P. McHugh—His Shop," p. 47. See William R. Leach, "Transformation in a Culture of Consumption: Women and Department Stores, 1890–1925," *Journal of American History* 71 (September 1984): 319–42.

[5] George Clingman to Leopold Stickley, May 26, 1911, Stickley collection, Archives and Library, Henry Ford Museum and Greenfield Village, Dearborn, Mich. In this letter Clingman asserts that he made the first plain piece of American mission furniture in 1885. The Michigan Chair Company was also producing simple, rush-seated chairs in 1898, as illustrated in its catalogue from that year.

of letters among McHugh, his coworkers, and interested parties, the magazine reported what was entitled "Truth about 'Mission' Furniture," supporting McHugh's claim of originating mission-style furniture. McHugh asserted that in 1894 Eudora Martin, a young California decorator, forwarded to him either a sketch of or actual chairs that were to furnish the Swedenborgian Church of the New Jerusalem in San Francisco. The church was designed by the offices of A. Page Brown; Bernard Maybeck served as draftsman. Following either Maybeck's or Brown's design, eighty handmade maple chairs were commissioned to furnish the church. The chairs were constructed without nails, and the seats were woven with tule rushes from the deltas of the Sacramento and San Joaquin rivers. It was from these chairs that McHugh developed his first pieces of mission furniture, sketched by his designer Walter J. H. Dudley and produced by his cabinetmaker Lorenz Licht.[6]

Uncertainty remains concerning the date. McHugh and Licht assign 1894 to the origins of McHughMission. James McCabe, a former salesman at the Popular Shop, attributed an 1896 or 1897 date. Further, a 1921 article asserts that Dudley did not begin to work for McHugh until 1896.[7] It therefore appears that McHugh may have altered the date of origin of the chairs by two years to strengthen his claim. Nevertheless, an 1896 date establishes McHugh as the first manufacturer of American arts and crafts furniture.

Throughout his career, McHugh maintained that Stickley copied his first designs from McHughMission pieces: "In or about 1898, Mr. Stickley, in company with another person, showed me here three small

[6]The advertisement can be found in "Truth About 'Mission' Furniture," *The Decorative Furnisher* 30 (June 1915): 50. "How 'Mission' Furniture Originated," *The Decorative Furnisher* 9 (October 1905): 64b. Othmar Tobisch, *The Garden Church of San Francisco: A Church of the New Jerusalem Swedenborgian and a Description of Its Symbols, Art Treasures, and Excerpts from Historical Documents* (San Francisco: San Francisco Society of New Jerusalem, 1966). According to the church's current pastor, seventy-nine of the original eighty chairs are still in use. An example is illustrated and discussed in Kenneth R. Trapp, *The Arts and Crafts Movement in California: Living the Good Life* (Oakland: Oakland Museum of Art, 1993), fig. 4. McHugh's version of the chair eliminated a small box located on the top back slat. It was intended to hold hymnals or prayer books. "More About 'Mission' Furniture," *The Decorative Furnisher* 30 (July 1915): 50, 53.
[7]On McCabe, see "More About Mission Furniture," p. 50. On Dudley, see Matlack Price, "Practicality, Imagination, and the Designer: A Study of the Work of Walter J. H. Dudley," *Arts and Decoration* 15 (July 1921): 166–68.

pieces of furniture manifestly based upon my sketches and said that they were the first of his line; my recollection is that I bought a sample of each in order to indicate my good will." McHugh also claimed that shortly after the 1901 Pan-American Exposition in Buffalo, Stickley visited the Popular Shop and asked McHugh to sell him unmarked and unfinished pieces, which Stickley could finish and use to fill an order for Wanamaker's. McHugh quoted Stickley as saying, "Of course I could turn out the order from your sketches, but my factory is not equipped for special work and it would cost me more than it would cost you, for you have the drawings and the patterns."[8]

Although there is no documentation to support McHugh's claim, a visual comparison between early Stickley pieces and McHughMission illustrates strong parallels. Both are of similar heavy, angular proportions and feature strong, broad horizontal back slats and stretchers (fig. 1).[9] Stickley further developed and refined his mission designs, whereas McHugh's established mission forms remained static.

The name *mission* came to denote a movement to reform taste. In 1901 the *Upholstery Dealer and Decorative Furnisher* explained, "It is furniture with a mission, and that mission is to teach that the first laws of furniture making should be good material, true proportion, and honest workmanship." The term, however, originated from McHugh's custom of naming all his furniture lines. For instance, within his colonial revival collection, which he produced as early as 1882, each piece received an appropriate description. McHugh promoted John Harvard and Standish chairs, a Priscilla wing chair, and a Nantucket chair. Likewise, he attached imaginative names to pieces with old English flair, such as the King Arthur hall settle and the wave-top vicarage settle. It was only natural, then, for McHugh to name his new line of furniture McHughMission, considering that it originated from a California church and an area noted for its Spanish missions. The strong association lent an aura of romance to the furniture and contributed to its promotion.[10]

At the Pan-American Exposition, McHugh furnished the recep-

<hr>

[8]McHugh is quoted in "Truth About 'Mission' Furniture," p. 50.
[9]See Cathers, *Furniture*, p. 39 for Stickley illustration.
[10]"The Mission Furniture: Its Design and Execution," *Upholstery Dealer and Decorative Furnisher* 1 (October 1901): 53. Cathers, *Furniture*, pp. 14–15.

Fig. 1. Joseph P. McHugh and Company, arm-chair, New York, 1898–1916. Ash with original green finish and rush seat; H. 36″, W. 18½″, D. 18¾″. (Munson-Williams-Proctor Institute, Utica, N.Y.: Photo, Gale Farley.)

tion room of the New York State building. After winning a silver medal, he received considerable commendation in American and European periodicals.[11] It was at the exposition and through extensive advertisement that McHugh popularized the term *mission*. Subsequently, the name became synonymous with American arts and crafts furniture.

Combining his intuitive sense of styles and trends with the influences of English arts and crafts designers, McHugh conformed to the aesthetic of the arts and crafts movement. Yearly buying trips, contemporary periodicals, and imported furniture exposed him to a broad range of English designers. Their influences are apparent in McHughMission. The Popular Shop carried an extensive line of Liberty products that may have included the line of furniture M. H. Baillie Scott designed for Liberty. Scott's and C. F. A. Voysey's attenuated proportions are evident in such pieces as McHugh's Hillair chair and the Mission Prayer and Chamber chairs that are characterized by slender legs and light proportions. Arthur H. Mackmurdo's influence is even more apparent and illustrated in the comparison of a McHugh-designed book table and Mackmurdo's desk (fig. 2).[12] The pieces are of nearly identical proportions, especially in the legs. Although the characteristic McHugh foot, which tapers toward the bottom and flares out to a squashed, square shape, has been referred to as the Mackmurdo foot, McHugh seems to have derived the form from the California chairs.

By 1898 McHugh offered a selection of fully developed mission-style forms. He also modified a number of his earlier pieces, "missionizing" them to conform to the arts and crafts aesthetic. The Princeton study table—a combination table, bookcase, and chair in one piece—is one of the clearest illustrations of such an alteration. An 1897 *New York Tribune* article refers to the table as "for people who want the unusual and useful combined in compact fashion." McHugh labeled the table as odd and described it saying, "A recent manifestation for

---

[11] "More Honors," *Upholstery Dealer and Decorative Furnisher* 2 (June 1902): 59.
[12] For comparative Voysey illustration, see Wendy Kaplan, *"The Art That Is Life"*: *The Arts and Crafts Movement in America, 1875–1920* (Boston: Museum of Fine Arts, 1987), fig. 10, p. 82. For comparative Mackmurdo illustration, see Cathers, *Furniture*, p. 26.

Fig. 2. Bailey-Jones Company, book table (design attributed to Joseph P. McHugh and Company), Jamestown, N.Y., ca. 1908. Ash; H. 26½", W. 28", L. 40". (Private collection.)

the convenience and delight of the student or bookworm is the Princeton table, which admits the occupant of the chair to its midst." He continued, asserting that the piece was "quite practicable and strictly within the bounds of simplicity and good taste." The earliest version of the circular table featured an open shelf along the exterior and a hinged chair on casters that, when pulled in, completed the circle. Its legs were slender and tapered downward. The chair's back slats were in the form of an *x*. The same desk, with some minor alterations, was illustrated in a 1900 *London Furniture Record* article and reprinted

Fig. 3. Joseph P. McHugh and Company, Princeton study table, New York, 1900. From *The "Mission" Furniture of Joseph P. McHugh and Co.* (New York: Joseph P. McHugh, 1901). (Photo, Winterthur Library.)

in McHugh's 1901 catalogue (fig. 3). At this point, the crossbracing encompassed the entire table. The legs remained tapered and slender. A 1902 article from the Austrian periodical *Kunst und Kunsthandwerk* discussed the furniture exhibited at the Pan-American Exposition, including a version of the table with protruding leg posts, broader legs, and the characteristic McHugh foot.[13] By 1904 the table had been completely missionized, as illustrated in the company's catalogue de-

[13] McHugh is quoted in "Some Odd Furniture," *New York Tribune*, May 3, 1897, which is reprinted in *Some Pictures of Quaint Things Which Are Sold at the Sign of the "Popular Shop," and a Few Words about Making the House Beautiful with Homely Material* (New York: Joseph P. McHugh and Co., 1898). Clara Ruge, "Das Kunstgewerbe Amerikas," *Kunst und Kunsthandwerk* (Vienna, 1902): v.

The Princeton Table.

Designed by Jos. P. McHugh & Co.

Fig. 4. From *What a Woman Finds to Write about When She Sees the McHugh (Mission) Furniture* (New York: Joseph P. McHugh, 1904). (Photo, Warshaw Collection of Business Americana, Archives Center, National Museum of American History, Smithsonian Institution.)

rived from *New York Tribune* articles (fig. 4). The crossbracing on the chair was replaced by Wright-like or Stickley-like vertical slats. The seat was changed from wood with a cushion to a more appropriate leather seat, and the file slots were introduced.

In a similar mode, McHugh made minor alterations on other pieces and reintroduced them as part of the mission line. The 1898 dutch drinking chair, a simple form with a triangular seat, three legs, and a T-shape back, was renamed the mission smoke seat by 1904. McHugh added a compartment to the back to hold smoking paraphernalia. The 1898 King Arthur hall settle showed the influence of arts and crafts aesthetics when it was resurrected in 1900 as the mission King

Arthur settle. The table/chair retained its original form, but broader leg posts that protruded through the arms were added, and curvilinear lines were replaced by straight ones. The company no longer carried the 1898 clover muffin rack, but the mission muffin rack was available. By 1901 McHugh had redesigned nearly his entire line of furniture and interior decorating projects. His surviving 1901 and 1904 furniture catalogues concentrate almost solely on mission-style furniture.

McHugh refined other aspects of his stock according to popular taste. Recognizing the potential of his designs, he attempted to capitalize on their popularity through the development of his willow line. In 1893 McHugh was importing willow furniture from the Far East. Not satisfied with the quality, by 1895 he produced his own with reeds from York County, Pennsylvania, where, he said, "the longest and straightest willow sticks" were grown.[14] Soon after McHugh initiated production of this line in a New York City factory, he began to missionize it. He turned the curvilinear forms he had been importing to rectilinear designs with broad, flat surfaces. An assortment of McHughWillow items were produced—ranging from a nursery hedge and a dog hamper to chairs with side pockets and extension footstools. McHugh also meshed mission and willow, resulting in the St. Leonards Group and Craftstyle lines. Both divisions incorporated woven cane panels into wooden frames, creating essentially mission designs. It was the best of both worlds.

Seeing the vigor of his sales after popularizing McHughMission at the Buffalo exposition, McHugh capitalized on his rising national and international acclaim by offering his mission line in a broad variety of forms—everything from a golf-stick holder or a shaving stand to a simple clothes hook and numerous seating forms. As early as 1897 he had patented a mission folding chair. From the nursery to the library to the front porch swing, any room in the house could be completely furnished with McHughMission. Once the name *mission* was set in the minds of customers, McHugh diversified the forms to meet clients' needs, retaining the standardized qualities and applying them to any type of household furnishing. He added crossbracing, keyed tenons, broader proportions, and his characteristic foot and then called the

[14]McHugh is quoted in "Talk on Wicker Furniture," *New York Tribune*, April 5, 1897, which is reprinted in *Some Pictures of Quaint Things*.

piece mission. McHugh saw the potential and believed that the best way to capitalize on it was to create as many forms as possible in the established style.

McHugh conveyed the philosophy of unity in decoration. To this end, his advertisements and catalogues featured entire room settings in the McHughMission style, stating, "Messrs. McHugh Contract for Interior Furnishing in their Own Style, Fitments to Suit Special Requirements." McHugh's intention was to create customized and coherent mission interiors, all of which could be contracted out of the Popular Shop. Carrying a diverse line of goods catering to fashionable tastes, the company was a full-service decorating firm. The goods included iron grillwork, floor coverings, mosaics, and textiles. The shop also exhibited the virtue of decorative harmony by displaying, for instance, McHughMission in a room with an antiqued floor, hewn ceiling beams, and a large brick fireplace.[15]

McHugh did diverge from his established mission style in 1900, when he introduced a stylized branch motif into the same areas that might otherwise be filled with the x motif—on chair backs, under chair arms, or as a decorative feature on cabinet doors (fig. 5). Otherwise the forms remained essentially the same. In an attempt to reach a broader audience, the style linked mission with art nouveau using minor variations of a static product. The variety of pieces produced in the line was not as extensive as the number of mission forms. It was, however, incorporated into interiors designed for McHugh by Dudley, as illustrated in a 1902 mission library where the door paneling pattern echoes the design.

Another manner of the diversification employed by McHugh was to offer the mission line in a broad range of colors and fabrics. His works were available in oak or "strong grained native ash," a wood he claimed was "best fitted to preserve the direct and simple features of the style," its grain providing a pleasing effect to the flat expanses of the furniture. The line also offered "nature's colorings in the fields and forests," including forest green, sealing wax red, "toa brown," dainty

[15] For advertisement, see John Crosby Freeman, ed., *Antique Furniture Handbooks: 5. Mission and Art Nouveau* (Watkins Glen, N.Y.: Century House, 1966). This book contains a reprinted McHugh catalogue along with several of the company's advertisements. *Upholstery Dealer and Decorative Furnisher* 1 (October 1901): 49.

Fig. 5. Joseph P. McHugh and Company, Marquette reading chair, New York, ca. 1904. Oak or ash; H. 44″, W. 31″, D. 33½″. (Mr. and Mrs. Alexander S. Moser: Photo, Gale Farley.)

willow green, a plain varnish, or smoked black with rich brown grain-ing.[16] The selection of seat coverings included rush, haircloth, flax, leather, wooden slats, and merino sheep hide. McHughWillow could be purchased in Spanish yellow, indigo blue, delft blue, or emerald green. Some colors were boiled into the wicker, while others were applied using a varnish. The wide selection of materials and colors allowed McHugh to cater to various tastes while concentrating his pro-duction on one style of furniture.

McHugh's discussion of the materials used in McHughMission attempted to demonstrate the role of the craftsman in the production of his line. He stated that they were "all natural products, prepared and applied by hand." An 1897 article from the *New York Tribune* acknowledges McHugh's awareness of the arts and crafts philosophy. McHugh borrowed the rhetoric that had been used to promote colonial revival furniture styles popular before his mission line, "In furniture the old English and Colonial reproductions bear witness to the industry and good taste of women in collecting the pieces which point to the times when simplicity and directness of construction gave distinction to the art of the cabinet-maker, before the use of machinery made possible the addition of superfluous details, without gain to the comfort or the beauty of the piece."[17] Having found a successful merchandising recipe, McHugh marketed a number of his products using arts and crafts terminology and declared that his "handmade" furniture was appropriate not only for complete mission interiors but also for "old Spanish, Dutch and Early English lines." In promotion, a major com-ponent of the company's success, McHugh effectively used the rhetoric of the movement.

McHugh cleverly put to use a series of comments and reviews taken from 1900 and 1901 to compose his 1901 catalogue. Today they demonstrate that although McHugh never reached the regard accorded Stickley, his furniture was widely praised. Critics such as Temple Scott, writing for *International Studio*, asserted that McHughMission "owes

---

[16]On material and colors, see *The "Mission" Furniture of Joseph P. McHugh*, p. 3; "The Mission Furniture: Its Design and Execution," p. 52.

[17]McHugh is quoted in *The "Mission" Furniture of Joseph P. McHugh*, p. 3; "Woman and the House Beautiful," *New York Tribune*, March 28, 1897, which is reprinted in *Some Pictures of Quaint Things*.

its modern vogue to the movement in house decoration initiated by William Morris." He continued: "but Morris went to European sources direct. Mr. McHugh, however, has gone to those traditions indirectly, and as benefits an American craftsman, has sought inspiration from Spanish missionaries. . . . We welcome Mr. McHugh's efforts, because any attempt to develop a taste for simplicity in life is to be commended." Another author referred to McHugh furniture as a simple, direct, inexpensive, and practical mode of furnishing. Georgia Fraser Arkell was quoted in *Art Education* as stating, "Mr. McHugh's work is quite unique in this country. Its honesty of purpose, its simplicity of effect, its entire usefulness as well as beauty, appeal to those who can appreciate such qualities in the furnishings of a home."[18]

American arts and crafts manufacturers were generally not concerned with compliance to Morris's philosophy and maintained a balance between hand production and machine production. McHugh claimed, however, that his furniture was handcrafted. For all the praise it received concerning superior style and construction, McHugh furniture was mass-produced. It does appear that many pieces were made to order and often customized, as illustrated in several of Dudley's original drawings that retain notations such as "For Mrs. Duncan Eliot, Newport." The survival of numerous small pieces, such as side chairs, indicates that they *were* manufactured in quantity. In addition, McHugh furniture was distributed through wholesale dealers such as Bailey Tables.[19] Like other mass producers, McHugh developed interchangeable parts and industrial production methods, all possible with standardized styles. Handcrafted in all probability referred to the finishing.

McHugh pieces illustrate style over substance—the craftsman was not involved in each step of production. Dudley designed all of the

---

[18]Temple Scott, "Mission Furniture," which is reprinted in *The "Mission" Furniture of Joseph P. McHugh*, p. 6. Georgia Fraser Arkell, "The Mission Furniture—Its Design and Execution," *Art Education* (February 1901), which is reprinted in *The "Mission" Furniture of Joseph P. McHugh*, p. 4.

[19]A McHugh-designed book table (see fig. 2) in a private collection has a "Bailey Tables" paper label. The table appears in several variations in McHugh and Co. advertisements and catalogues. The same desk was featured in the Bailey-Jones Company 1908 catalogue. The connection between McHugh and Bailey-Jones has not been determined, but McHugh may have relied on other manufacturers to provide popular stock designs.

company's output, but that is where his creative involvement ended. Manufactured at an eastern New York City plant, the construction of McHugh furniture is not "substandard," but conscientious changes in manufacturing methods to adapt the furniture to factory production are evident. Mass-produced wooden drawer pulls were used and the *x* or cross elements, which resemble relief carving, were applied with glue and small nails. Freestanding crossbracing was nailed into place. Major expanses of wood were mortised and tenoned together, held by an occasional nail. Keyed tenons were also glued into place and served no true function. The overall look of the pieces was, however, sturdy, angular, simple, and utilitarian—all key words in the promotion of arts and crafts furnishings.

Although McHugh emphasized mission furniture in his catalogues, he never lost sight of his primary business, interior decoration. Throughout the tenure of the Popular Shop, advertisements promoted wall coverings and fabrics that dealers could purchase wholesale. McHugh invited the "trade" to visit his shop and place orders for interior furnishings.

McHugh's product development corresponded to his adoption of reform ideas. By 1897 he had patented Singapore lattice, an openweave fabric suitable as a wall covering or drapery and advertised as ideal for those interested in the reform to simpler interiors. The 1898 catalogue *Some Pictures of Quaint Things Which Are Sold at the Sign of the "Popular Shop," and a Few Words about Making the House Beautiful with Homely Material* was a conglomeration of 1896 to 1898 advertisements and articles from New York City newspapers and magazines such as the *Ladies' Home Journal*. It indicated the influence of reform authors Clarence Cook and Charles Eastlake. The catalogue was divided into thematic sections ranging from color, wall treatment, and decorative accessories to other topics such as "Hints for Summer Homes" and "The Question of Screens." One section, "Woman and the House Beautiful," recalls Cook's 1878 book *The House Beautiful*.[20]

After McHugh's death in 1916, his son and his partner, James Slater, continued to operate the Popular Shop, reducing the furniture

[20] Marsha Crabill McClaugherty, "Household Art: Creating the Artistic Home, 1868–1893," *Winterthur Portfolio* 18, no. 1 (Spring 1983): 1–23. Clarence Cook, *The House Beautiful* (1878; reprint, Croton-on-Hudson, N.Y.: North River Press, 1980).

production and concentrating on interior decoration. Before World War II the business moved and worked on WPA projects and church interiors. Today it operates as a school-furniture distributor, and its current owner knows little of the company's past fame.

We may never know the actual truth about mission furniture. When introduced, McHughMission created a fervor in the decorative arts world. McHugh's designs were, however, unchanged for nearly two decades. By using mass-production techniques to reproduce the English arts and crafts style, Joseph P. McHugh and Company exemplifies the American compromise. It is my contention that McHughMission was the product of a manufacturer who capitalized on the American arts and crafts movement and an entrepreneur interested in the philosophy of the movement as far as it could be used to meet his own ends. He knew the marketing value that attended "the distinction of being different" but also understood and manipulated the distinction between rhetoric and reality.[21] In so doing, he left for posterity a product laden with inherent contradictions, a paradigm for the larger arts and crafts movement.

[21] The McHugh company used the slogan "the distinction of being different" on its letterhead.

Maturity of Design and Commercial Success

A Critical Reassessment of the Work of L. and J. G. Stickley and Peter Hansen

Donald A. Davidoff

The contribution of the firm of L. and J. G. Stickley to the evolution and popularization of the design aesthetic of the American arts and crafts movement has long been underestimated. The oldest Stickley brother, Gustav, was responsible for the dissemination of the philosophy of John Ruskin and William Morris to a wide-ranging national audience. Gustav left us an enormous legacy not only in terms of his furniture but also in terms of his prodigious publications. Nonetheless, it remained for the superior business acumen of his younger brothers, Leopold (fig. 1) and John George, to place physical examples of that philosophy in middle-class American homes and to revitalize the entire "mission aesthetic" for the second decade of the twentieth century.

It is without doubt that Gustav Stickley played a seminal role in shaping the taste of a changing America. Furniture produced by his workshops represents classic American design and in some circles is considered to be the first original expression of American thought in furniture. An examination of Gustav's production over the sixteen years

The author gratefully acknowledges the help of Susan Tarlow, Paul Fiore, Cathie Zusy, Olive (Bets) Hansen, Mike Danial, Bruce Johnson, and Judith Deal.

Fig. 1. Leopold Stickley (1869–1957). (L. and J. G. Stickley Archives, Manlius, N.Y.)

that his company existed independently reveals his debt to the English cottage revival style and the subsequent stylistic modifications he made over that span of years. David Cathers, in his introduction to the reprint of the Stickley Craftsman furniture catalogues and in his pioneering work on the furniture of the American arts and crafts movement, provides a cogent sequential analysis of Gustav's design changes, dividing production into four distinct periods. A similar approach can be employed to examine the work of Leopold and John George.[1]

Such an analysis of the furniture of the L. and J. G. Stickley firm has only recently been attempted. With few exceptions, their work has

[1] Thomas K. Maher, "Gustav Stickley's Early Furniture," *Arts and Crafts Quarterly* 2, no. 2 (Spring 1988): 7. David M. Cathers, "Introduction to Gustav Stickley and L. and J. G. Stickley," in *Stickley Craftsman Furniture Catalogues* (New York: Dover, 1979), pp. iii–viii. David M. Cathers, *Furniture of the Arts and Crafts Movement: Stickley and Roycroft Mission Oak* (New York: New American Library, 1981).

in recent years been much maligned, regarded as derivative and not worthy of serious consideration. These misconceptions emanated from two sources. First was the seeming dismissal of L. and J. G. Stickley's furniture in the Princeton catalogue of 1972.[2] In that influential publication from the exhibition that sparked the current flame of interest in the arts and crafts movement, descriptions of some of L. and J. G. Stickley's furniture alluded to the use of inferior wood, the overuse of veneers, and, especially, the derivative designs themselves. Thus, work by the company has been given relatively short shrift during the current revival. Reinforcing the thrust of these comments has been the relative paucity of documentation of the work by L. and J. G. Stickley.

Gustav took great pleasure in delineating the changes in his furniture. He issued voluminous catalogues detailing both the design adaptations and the philosophical bases for those changes. His monthly magazine, *The Craftsman*, also provided him with an outlet to further chronicle his views and feature his designs. In contrast, Leopold seemed little interested in selling a lifestyle and focused on selling his furniture. Consequently, he issued far fewer catalogues, none of which bore any resemblance to Gustav's treatises on the arts and crafts aesthetic. Most of Leopold's catalogues were undated, with slip-in price lists added so that each catalogue could be used for several years. Knowledge of Leopold's design philosophy derives only from hints provided by his brief introduction in each of the catalogues or from an analysis of the furniture itself. Additionally, while many of Gustav's business records have been preserved, few of Leopold's records dating from 1900 to 1920 have been found. Thus, there has been much confusion over the work of L. and J. G. Stickley.

The supporters of the arts and crafts movement passionately believed that design affects society—that the character of the living and working environment molds the character of the individual. The propo-

[2] Donald A. Davidoff, "The Work of L. and J. G. Stickley: The Mature Period and Design Sophistication," *Arts and Crafts Quarterly* 3, no. 1 (Winter 1989): 6–9; Donald A. Davidoff, "Introduction: A Critical Reexamination of the Work of L. and J. G. Stickley," *Early L. and J. G. Stickley Furniture: From Onondaga Shops to Handcraft,* ed. Donald A. Davidoff and Robert L. Zarrow (New York: Dover, 1992), pp. vii–xix. Robert Judson Clark, "L. and J. G. Stickley Co.," in *The Arts and Crafts Movement in America, 1876–1916,* ed. Robert Judson Clark (Princeton: Princeton University Press, 1972), p. 44.

nents of the movement believed that by restoring honesty and integrity to the objects common to daily living, the quality of life could not help but be improved.[3] The paradox that the movement was unable to resolve, and which is relevant to understanding the contribution of L. and J. G. Stickley, was how to produce goods of integrity at a cost that the common man could afford. The corollary of this issue concerns the commercialization of the movement and the use of machinery in the production of goods.

The English crafts designers, as exemplified by Morris, were often gentlemen and gentlewomen who tended to look down on trade and commercialism. They preferred, instead, to produce exquisite objects in relatively small quantities although that entailed concomitant high prices.[4] The draftsmen and laborers who produced the fine work were unable to afford such items themselves. As a result, the nature of the movement in England had more of a retrospective importance and was significantly limited in its impact at the time.

The two primary reasons why the arts and crafts movement succeeded in America were the democratic nature of our society and the unwillingness of American manufacturers to bind themselves to the philosophical limitations set down by the proponents of the English movement. Realizing the need for mass production to bring the cost of manufacturing down to a marketable level, Gustav and Leopold equipped their factories with planers, drill presses, table saws, joiners, and mortise machines. The use of these was not new; machines were a product of the industrial revolution. In Gustav's opinion, the machine "eliminated the laborious, repetitious tasks associated with woodworking."[5]

As to individual craftsmanship, the ideal often surpassed reality at both the Gustav and L. and J. G. Stickley shops. The layouts of both Stickley factories (Eastwood and Fayetteville, New York, respectively) were planned for a flow of materials that created a natural separation of tasks. It is illogical, for instance, to believe that either Stickley would

---

[3] Beverly Brandt, Introduction, in *The Encyclopedia of Arts and Crafts*, ed. Wendy Kaplan (New York: E. P. Dutton, 1989), pp. 7–18.

[4] John Weidner et al., "Other Paths: A Sampler of European Arts and Crafts," *Arts and Crafts Quarterly* 5, no. 4 (Winter 1993): 30–33.

[5] Gustav Stickley, *What Is Wrought in the Craftsman Workshops* (1904; reprint, New York: Turn of the Century Editions, 1992).

boast of a modern production facility (which they both did) and yet require each cabinetmaker to plane his own lumber.

The arts and crafts movement was in full flower in England when Gustav returned from his trip to Europe in the late 1890s. He observed firsthand the many handicraft guilds that had sprung up in response to the hue and cry raised by Ruskin and Morris. Gustav, with almost fifteen years experience in the manufacturing of furniture, reassessed his ideas on design and created the United Crafts Workshops in 1898 in Eastwood, New York, with his brother Leopold employed as shop foreman. Gustav's first original furniture designs were loosely based on art nouveau models, with some features that presaged his later arts and crafts style. The Gustave Stickley Company (he later dropped the *e*) went into production and exhibited the results at the Grand Rapids Furniture Show in July 1900.[6]

Although Gustav initially attempted to follow in Ruskin's and Morris's footsteps in recreating a medieval crafts guild, he found this structure antithetical to running a successful business in America. He reorganized his company around modern manufacturing processes, woodworking machinery, and the specialization of job duties. He nonetheless felt a debt to Morris and Ruskin and dedicated the first two issues of his soon-to-be influential periodical, *The Craftsman*, to them. Through the incorporation of modern furniture-making technology into his production line, Gustav sought to avoid the pitfall of pricing himself out of the market, as had Morris. In this endeavor, he was initially successful.

Beverly Brandt states that "Gustav Stickley was central in the dissemination of the arts and crafts ideal in America. . . . Of *all* furniture designers he came closest to Morris' life-long goal of producing 'useful' and 'beautiful' home furnishings at modest prices."[7] Yet Gustav ultimately failed commercially, and his venture was absorbed by his brother Leopold's company.

The chronology of the two companies sheds some light on Gustav's bankruptcy and Leopold's commercial successes and ultimate influence on the movement. Gustav and Leopold originally worked together in a variety of furniture concerns for almost ten years before the Gustav Stickley Company was established. The text of an early

[6]Cathers, *Furniture*, p. 34.
[7]Brandt, Introduction, p. 16.

advertisement at the turn of the century indicated that Leopold was not
only the shop foreman but also the principal representative of Gustav's
company to the public. George Clingman, of Chicago's Tobey Furniture Company, admired the first original furniture designs Gustav produced and negotiated an exclusive arrangement wherein Tobey would
market Gustav's "New Furniture" under their name. It is likely, as
Bruce Johnson suggested, that Gustav opted for anonymity in this venture because financial concerns were paramount and shop marks were
a secondary consideration at the time. Yet six months later, in December 1900, Gustav severed his relationship with Tobey in spite of the
favorable notices his furniture had received in the trade journals.[8]

At this point Leopold saw his opportunity and left his position
with Gustav to begin his own company. The Collin, Sisson, and Pratt
Factory on Orchard Street in Fayetteville, New York, was purchased
with the help of a loan from brother Gustav. Leopold's company thus
entered into its early period, which lasted until about 1903 and during
which the company primarily manufactured furniture for a host of
other concerns. Gustav, on his part, was free to develop his own ideas
that he felt were truer in spirit to the philosophies of Ruskin and Morris.

Sharon Darling has speculated that since advertisements for Tobey's New Furniture continued through 1901, it was possible that Gustav's original contract was fulfilled by Leopold's new company.[9] Working drawings for much of the early mission furniture produced by L.
and J. G. Stickley, rediscovered in the attic of the old Orchard Street
factory, lends credence to this theory. Included among these designs
were a number of the New Furniture pieces designed by Gustav, including his "Tree-of-Life" stand and his "Cloud-Lift" taboret. Aside
from these, no other drawings of Gustav's furniture were found in the
attic. Furthermore, these designs were clearly marked "Tobey Furniture Company."

In addition, in 1901 Tobey issued a new catalogue offering a revised
line of "New Furniture in Weathered Oak." This line contained a

[8]As Bruce Johnson states, Gustav Stickley's entire history is one of fierce independence. Only financial considerations could have prompted his anonymous relationship
with Tobey; Bruce Johnson, *The Official Identification and Price Guide to Arts and
Crafts* (New York: House of Collectibles, 1988), pp. 175–76. *American Cabinet Maker
and Upholsterer* (July 1900).
[9]Sharon Darling, *Chicago Furniture: Art, Craft, and Industry, 1833–1983* (New
York: W. W. Norton in association with Chicago Historical Society, 1984).

broader range of designs, from pure mission to colonial to quasi-prairie style. While it has been suggested that all of these pieces were designed by Clingman, manager and chief buyer for Tobey, and produced by Tobey in Chicago, the Fayetteville attic drawings suggest otherwise.

In at least one instance, plans identical to a table labeled by Tobey Furniture Company were found at Orchard Street, and were plainly marked "Tobey Furniture Company."[10] It thus appears that at least one piece of Tobey's New Furniture was manufactured by Leopold's company.

The Russmore line of furniture lends further credence to the existence of a relationship between Leopold and Tobey. By the summer of 1902 Tobey had added a less expensive line of mission-style furniture to their inventory and labeled it Russmore. While it has often been remarked that these pieces bear a striking similarity to early L. and J. G. Stickley pieces, it remained for the old attic to offer up the concrete evidence in the form of furniture plans, clearly labeled Russmore. In addition, a catalogue in the Winterthur library from Tobey—of mission furniture designs done in rough-hewn green cedar—reveals an almost one-to-one correspondence with identical oak and cedar pieces from the L. and J. G. Stickley Company.[11] Taking all this evidence together certainly suggests a close relationship between Tobey and Leopold's new company.

Other plans were found that were labeled by George Flint and Company, John Wanamaker, Jordan Marsh, and Paine Furniture, among others. The pattern emerges that Leopold apparently borrowed Gustav's original business strategy and secured contracts from a variety of furniture companies to manufacture their furniture. Thus, in spite of not producing original designs, Leopold became an important force in the production of mission-style furniture. He could therefore secure a toehold in the furniture industry with little financial risk.

The early period of the company was successful enough to give Leopold the impetus to introduce his own designs. He marketed them under the trademark "Onondaga Shops," named for the New York county in which the factory was located. John George, who had been living in Grand Rapids, Michigan, where he was a partner with his

[10] Darling, *Chicago Furniture*, p. 240.

[11] On Russmore, see Darling, *Chicago Furniture*, p. 240. *Tobey Furniture in Cedar* (Chicago: Tobey Furniture Co., ca. 1903).

brother Albert in Stickley Brothers Company, had in the meantime returned East to be married. John George had already distinguished himself as "the best fancy rocker salesman in America." Leopold quickly took advantage of this fortuitous circumstance and enticed his brother to become his partner. They incorporated as the L. and J. G. Stickley Company in 1904, a date inscribed on the Orchard Street factory office safe. Their Onondaga Shops met with success as reflected by the rapid expansion of both the furniture line and the factory. Their first trade advertisement was placed in *Furniture World* in February 1904; they exhibited at the Grand Rapids trade show for the first time in January 1905; and, three months later, in March, they issued their first catalogue.[12] Onondaga Shops furniture marks the middle period of L. and J. G. Stickley's mission line.

An examination of the production of the Onondaga Shops suggests some reasons for the underappreciation of the work of L. and J. G. Stickley. A comparison with their brother Gustav's work shows that Leopold's output, during this middle period, was often at best derivative and at worst imitative. Sometimes, when he did make design changes, the results were crude or ungainly in comparison with Gustav's fine achievements. When the Onondaga Shops either created pieces not in Gustav's repertoire or departed innovatively from his line, they triumphed. Leopold's drop-front desk #395 suggests an almost architectural approach to expressed form that leaves Gustav's comparable early Chalet desk looking merely cute (fig. 2). Regardless of design, Onondaga Shops furniture was often extremely well made, using the finest-grained quarter-sawn and fumed white oak, and compares quite favorably in this respect with Gustav's early pieces.

One argument often advanced in favor of the pieces produced by Gustav is that they reflect his design imperative as the creator of this new American style. Hence, furniture by the Onondaga Shops cannot possibly be of relevance. This argument is spurious, however, for Gustav modified designs of others as well. He certainly borrowed from the English cottage revivalists, in particular M. H. Baillie Scott, whose designs, too, have clearly traceable roots.

Gustav, in his promotion of a new design aesthetic, certainly helped shape America's taste. He reveled in his role as the apostle of

[12]On John George, see Cathers, *Furniture*, p. 70. Cathers, *Furniture*, pp. 71–72.

Fig. 2. Onondaga Shops, desk #395, Fayetteville, N.Y., ca. 1904. From *Handmade Furniture from the Onondaga Shops* (ca. 1904). (Photo, Donald A. Davidoff.)

the movement, selling not only furniture but a philosophy of living as
well. His interpretation of the arts and crafts credo of surrounding
oneself with "the art that is life" reverberated in everything he published
or produced. Leopold eschewed the role of philosopher for that of the
businessman. Perhaps for that reason there is a less coherent aesthetic
theme demonstrated by the Onondaga Shops furniture. Whereas Gustav strictly adhered to the rectilinear style, examination of the Onondaga Shops catalogue reveals less orthodoxy, as for example, in chair
legs that taper and others that terminate almost explosively in a "Mack-
murdo-style" club foot. Oddly curved slats sometimes seem to subdue,
rather than enhance, the rectilinearity of some pieces. Also of interest
are the crude attempts at plantlike low-relief carving for decoration on
some items, in contrast to the carefully integrated stylized inlays that
Gustav employed. While illustrations in an early catalogue suggest that
a line of carved furniture was planned, almost all of the hand-carved
items discovered to date came from the basement of the factory itself or
from the houses of the various officers of the company. It does appear
that although Leopold occasionally made reference to carved pieces, he
thought better of developing the line beyond some prototypes.[13]

Gustav's designs, at least during his early and middle periods,
were always true to his philosophy about design, ornamentation, and
handwork. Leopold appeared to feel free to adopt or reject bits and
pieces of Gustav's design principles whenever he felt it economically
useful to do so. Thus, when Gustav successfully marketed the virtues
of handwork, Leopold titled his 1905 catalogue *Handmade Furniture*.
His next catalogue downplayed this notion and instead simply focused
on the "frank construction" of the furniture. Leopold experienced no
contradiction in stating in the same paragraph that "some of this furniture has quaint cuttings in place; some has metal work to accent certain
points, and some has an outline so simple and devoid of ornament as
to be almost severe in its plainness."[14] Leopold tried to provide middle-
class America with whatever it wanted. Unlike Gustav, he made no
attempt to create a movement or mold Americans' aesthetic sense.

----

[13] William Price used the motto "the art that is life" as the subtitle of his journal,
The Artsman, published from October 1903 to April 1907. Davidoff and Zarrow, *Early
L. and J. G. Stickley Furniture.*
    [14] Leopold Stickley, "Some Sketches of Furniture Made at the Onondaga Shops,"
in *The Mission Furniture of L. and J. G. Stickley*, ed. Stephen Gray (New York: Turn
of the Century Editions, 1983), p. 44.

In late 1906, Leopold changed the name and shop mark of his furniture from Onondaga Shops to Handcraft. After this change was announced in the October 25 issue of *Furniture World*, no further advertisements appeared for a year. The early L. and J. G. Stickley furniture catalogues graphically illustrate the varied directions Leopold had taken (as with the aforementioned line of carved furniture) as well as the new influences that ultimately shaped his production for the second decade of the twentieth century.[15] The links between his Onondaga Shops line and later work may be seen in the photographs of the prototypes of his new Handcraft furniture found at the end of the Onondaga Shops catalogue and numbered with the Onondaga Shops production numbers. With the publication of his Handcraft catalogue, these prototypical pieces were renumbered according to a new scheme.

The development of these pieces marked a new maturity for the work of L. and J. G. Stickley and a pivotal turn in the commercial arts and crafts aesthetic. The new designs exemplified a fresh approach, whose roots could be traced to three stylistic sources: the prairie style of Frank Lloyd Wright and his contemporaries; the European reform movement espoused by the Viennese architect-designers; and the English arts and crafts masters such as C. F. A. Voysey, A. H. Mackmurdo, and Ernest Gimson. The infusion of these disparate influences, especially that of the prairie school architects, revitalized the simple mission style and pushed the adaptable firm of L. and J. G. Stickley into a new prominence in the marketplace. While the full realization of this new aesthetic would reach fruition over the next several years, the work reproduced in the first Handcraft catalogue does illustrate the roots of these designs.[16]

Quality workmanship was reemphasized. Quarter-sawn white oak was the rule, and older factory workers have handed down stories that Leopold would personally inspect each shipment of lumber when it arrived and reject those boards that he felt did not meet his standards. The factory also developed a laminating technique to showcase the remarkable tiger-striped grain pattern of the quarter-sawn oak on all four sides of furniture legs rather than on just two sides, as with non-laminated legs. All pieces were fumed to further highlight the grain

[15] Davidoff and Zarrow, *Early L. and J. G. Stickley Furniture.*
[16] Davidoff and Zarrow, *Early L. and J. G. Stickley Furniture*, pp. 115–87.

pattern, and even those critical of L. and J. G. Stickley's designs have always acknowledged the superb quality of their furniture's finish.

Even as Leopold's firm was breaking new ground, Gustav's production began to take on an enervated appearance. He designed virtually no new pieces after 1910 and relied on the simplification and distillation of his existing designs. As the economic reality of the furniture business began to encroach on his philosophy, Gustav eliminated costly detailing such as through-tenons and focused instead on designs easily produced by machine. He resorted to cheaper materials, including inferior wood and thinner hardware, and virtually ceased his long-touted but expensive fuming process.

It is likely that much of the innovation in the designs of L. and J. G. Stickley's furniture during their mature period can be traced to Leopold's employment of the twenty-nine-year-old Peter Heinrich Hansen (1880–1947) as chief designer. Hansen was a German-born cabinetmaker who immigrated to the United States at the turn of the century and, in 1904, found employment with Gustav. In 1907 he married Ruth Ann Williams, a Chicago-trained designer who was also working for Stickley. Following a monetary dispute with their employer, the young couple returned to upstate New York, where Ruth Ann had been born. Leopold quickly employed Hansen as both chief designer and shop foreman. Before she died, Leopold's second wife, Louise, recounted how Hansen was instrumental in designing the furniture of L. and J. G. Stickley. Evidence provided by the label of an L. and J. G. Stickley mantel clock (fig. 3) by Hansen as well as three houses designed by him suggest that he was conversant with all of the major design influences apparent in the furniture produced during the mature period.[17]

Among the more important pieces produced by L. and J. G. Stick-

[17] Hansen is discussed in Cathers, *Furniture*, p. 84. On Hansen's designs, see Catherine Zusy, "Shelf Clock," in Wendy Kaplan, *"The Art That Is Life": The Arts and Crafts Movement in America, 1875–1920* (Boston: Museum of Fine Arts, 1987), p. 168; Louise Shrimpton, "Craftsmanship in a Cottage," *Good Housekeeping* (December 1909): 705–11; Louise Shrimpton, "The Handicraft House," *House and Garden* (August 1912): 81–83, 110–11. Of the two documented houses, Hansen designed the interior of the former but the entirety of the latter. A third house also exists that is owned by the daughter of one of the officers of the L. and J. G. Stickley Company. The owner claims to have had the original plans by Hansen. It was in that house that the documented mantel clock was found.

Fig. 3. L. and J. G. Stickley Co., mantle clock #85, Peter Hansen (designer), Fayetteville, N.Y., 1912. Quarter-sawn oak, acid-etched copper over zinc; H. 22″, W. 16″, D. 8″. (Photo, Skinner.)

ley during their mature period are those that reflect a prairie-style aesthetic. A connection between Wright and Leopold has long been suggested. It was rumored that during Leopold's earliest years, his firm
was the manufacturer for the furniture in Wright's Bradley and Hickox
houses. That rumor was put to rest by establishing that the furniture
had actually been made by John Ayres. The confusion probably originated from the fact that some of Wright's clients used Leopold's furniture in secondary rooms of some of his commissions. There was also
a similarity between Wright's veneration of the machine and Leopold's
own philosophy as espoused in his 1914 catalogue. The compatibility
of some of Leopold's furniture with the prairie style was also evidenced
by the use of his furniture in houses designed by the firm of Purcell
and Elmslie and by Walter Burley Griffen.[18]

An examination of the L. and J. G. Stickley prairie-style pieces
reveals that some are direct adaptations of Wright designs, such as a
bed, #104, inspired by one in Wright's 1908 Evans house. Other
items are less derivative and instead are more reflective of the general
principles underlying prairie school design. This style, as Donald Kalec
points out, focuses on a "carefully calculated horizontality" to evoke
the long "horizon line of the prairie [itself as well as] . . . the low long
lines of the earth-hugging Prairie houses." He goes on to say: "The
planes of table, desk and cabinet tops were emphasized by extending
them beyond their upright supports. Their thickness was often exaggerated by using a 3 or 4 inch wide board as the side facing even though
the top was only 3/4 inches thick. . . . [Thus] shelves of table tops with
this . . . strong horizontal could overpower any divergent line or shape
placed upon it. . . . [Those] unifying horizontal lines would 'order' a
room automatically. These thickened edges also reduced the size and
number of supporting uprights which further emphasize the horizontal
line."[19] The interplay of elementary horizontal planes with massive
vertical piers to indicate a rootedness in the earth is emphasized. The

[18]On the Wright connection, see Clark, *Arts and Crafts Movement in America*, p.
44. On John Ayres and Wright, see David A. Hanks, *The Decorative Designs of Frank
Lloyd Wright* (New York: E. P. Dutton, 1979), pp. 41–42. On other prairie school
architects, see H. Allen Brooks, *The Prairie School: Frank Lloyd Wright and His Midwest
Contemporaries* (1972; reprint, New York: W. W. Norton, 1976), p. 252, which illustrates a photograph (1913) of the living room of Walter Burley Griffin's Harry E. Gunn
house showing prominently placed L. and J. G. Stickley furniture.
[19]Donald Kalec, "The Prairie School Furniture," *Prairie School Review* 1, no. 4
(1964): 6.

eye should be allowed long, open vistas, so narrow vertical spindles are used to create screened spaces without impeding the view. Furthermore, dominant horizontal elements with vertical accents are used to break up solid planes into eye-catching patterns. The eye is thus always drawn along the horizontal axes.

L. and J. G. Stickley particularly embraced this aesthetic and produced an entire line of furniture that exemplified these principles. In addition to making a variety of chairs, settles, and tables that used the narrow square spindle, they also, in 1912, manufactured a paneled prairie settle (#220) and chair (#416). The design of these pieces (fig. 4) relates to similar ones Wright designed for the 1909 Robie house and repeated in the Francis W. Little house. The settle's bold horizontal planes established by the overhanging wraparound arms grab the eye and pull it along that axis, and the paneling—due to its recession under the broad overhang of the arms—almost recedes into the background. In comparing the L. and J. G. Stickley settle with Wright's own design, the decorative addition of applied strips and the exaggeration of the horizontal arms on Wright's settle are noted, emphasizing and reemphasizing the basic horizontality.

As with almost all L. and J. G. Stickley pieces, the quality of wood is emphasized. The grain of the quarter-sawn oak in the expansive (but not too expansive) arms makes a statement about the nature and texture of the oak itself. Wright seemed less concerned with selection of wood and finish, preferring to let the design stand on its own.

The prairie settle #220, while clear in its debt to Wright, owes little to brother Gustav's work. Gustav never explored the prairie style to the extent that Leopold did. He did experiment with square spindles, but he used them to emphasize verticality almost to the exclusion of the horizontal. The prairie chair #416 complements the settle and also evokes the geometric simplicity of a cube. As with the settle, the visual emphasis remains horizontal, but the paneling here produces a rhythm that reinforces the almost pure elemental quality of the geometry.

In 1912 Wright designed a spindled settle for the William B. Green house. Square spindles were ubiquitous in prairie-style homes because they served "as a definite link between the furniture and the architecture."[20] Wright notes that the use of spindles created "a sense

[20] Kalec, "Prairie School Furniture," p. 17.

Fig. 4. L. and J. G. Stickley Co., prairie settle #220, prairie chair #416, Fayetteville, N.Y., 1912. Settle: quarter-sawn oak; H. 29″, W. 84½″, D. 26¾″; chair: quarter-sawn oak; H. 27″, W. 39″, D. 35″. (Photo, Christie's.)

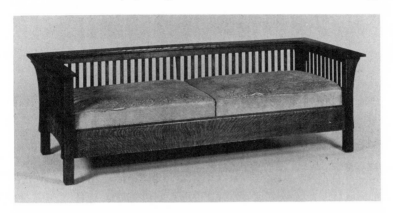

Fig. 5. L. and J. G. Stickley Co., spindled prairie settle #234, Fayette-ville, N.Y., 1913. Quarter-sawn oak; H. 25½", W. 86", D. 34". (Photo, Christie's.)

of visual privacy without bottling up the ever free flowing space." L. and J. G. Stickley, in their 1913 supplement, illustrated their own version (fig. 5) of a spindle settle. As with Wright's piece, the transparency created by the spindles blurs vertical boundaries without impeding the eye. The Stickley settle, however, almost transcends Wright's work as the broad horizontal overhang of the arms borrowed from the paneled settle heightens the visual intensity of that axis. The spindled piece is also 3½ inches lower than the paneled settle; thus, the horizontality of the piece is even further emphasized.

Architects of the prairie school also emphasized pure geometric form and natural materials. Wright and his colleagues designed furniture that focused on the circle, square, hexagon, and octagon. The repertoire of L. and J. G. Stickley also included an abundance of such forms. For example, the interplay of the intersecting horizontal planes of their tall cut-corner stand (#574) best exemplifies the relationship of rotated horizontal axes. And, just as Wright attempted to create a visual privacy screen with his tall-backed dining chairs, so too did L. and J. G. Stickley manufacture a variety of similar chairs.

It is important to note here that there is a major difference between the furniture designed by the prairie school architects and that produced by the L. and J. G. Stickley factory. The design of the former derived exclusively from architecture and only secondarily involved comfort and use as furniture. The L. and J. G. Stickley Company was in business to sell furniture, and comfort was a primary consideration. Leopold, in his introduction to the 1914 catalogue emphasizes this idea, stating, in part, that "chairs are studied from the point of view of many different sitters" and "care is given to your comfort." Wright designed furniture to complement the designs of his houses. While other prairie school architects were, perhaps, less ideological than Wright and did at least attempt to design chairs that served the function of sitting, Wright did remark that "his shins were often rendered black and blue from encounters with chairs of his design."[21] Thus one contribution of the L. and J. G. Stickley Company is the simple synthesis of comfort with design.

It is also perhaps not accidental that Leopold's post-1910 emphasis on machine technique in building furniture echoed Wright's 1901 address to the Chicago Society of Arts and Crafts. In that speech Wright explained how the geometric simplicity of his new American style was ideally suited to mechanized production. Leopold's introduction to the 1914 catalogue noted that "the work of L. and J. G. Stickley built in a scientific manner, does not attempt to follow the traditions of a by-gone day. All the resources of modern invention are used as helps in constructing this thoroughly modern product."[22] It is not known whether Leopold's introduction was a conscious adaptation of Wright's philosophy or whether he simply sensed that America was more accepting of the positive contributions of the machine to society. For whatever the reason, Leopold felt that such statements would help sell furniture.

Had the L. and J. G. Stickley Company only made relatively inexpensive versions of prairie-style furniture, no matter how comfortable, their contribution to the arts and crafts movement might be overlooked. They were, however, also able to expand the vocabulary of the mission style by incorporating a wealth of other influences. They reinterpreted some of Gustav's classic designs. Gustav's earliest version

[21] Leopold Stickley, "Introduction to L. and J. G. Stickley Catalogue," in *Stickley Craftsman Furniture Catalogues* (New York: Dover, 1979), p. 4. Brendan Gill, *Many Masks: A Life of Frank Lloyd Wright* (New York: Putnam, 1987), p. 494.
[22] Stickley, "Introduction," p. 3.

Fig. 6. L. and J. G. Stickley Co., curved-arm Morris chair #406, Fayetteville, N.Y., 1912. Quarter-sawn oak; H. 40″, W. 28″, D. 29¼″. (Susan J. Tarlow: Photo, Donald A. Davidoff.)

of the bow-arm Morris chair, with its reverse tapered legs and massive arms, has been said to capture the essence of early arts and crafts furniture.[23] The L. and J. G. Stickley version (fig. 6) adds a vertical board under the curve of the arm and four slats between that board and the seat rail. In addition, the corbels under the arms are extended down to the seat rail. The effect of these design changes is that the focus shifts to a wall of interspersed solids and spaces. This is combined

[23] Maher, "Gustav Stickley's Early Furniture."

with the horizontal emphasis added by the side facing and the rooted-ness conveyed by the corbels on the vertical piers supporting the arms.

Nowhere is the synthesis of design more successfully accomplished than in Hansen's mantel clock (see fig. 3). The design demonstrates his familiarity with the works of Voysey and F. C. Morawe, the German designer. Voysey used similar trapezoidal forms in his architecture, interior fittings, and furniture but relied on a polychrome finish to enhance his design; Hansen emphasized the form itself for visual impact. The clock also relates to one of Morawe's clocks illustrated in *Dekorative Kunst* (December 1903). Morawe's clocks, however, incorporated decorative carving.[24] Hansen, in contrast, eschewed virtually all decoration save the subtle grain pattern of the quarter-sawn oak itself. By so doing, Hansen clearly follows the spirit of Gustav's philosophy.

The clock also calls to mind Wright's emphasis on natural materials by highlighting the warmth of the fumed oak and dull glow of the etched copper dial. Two simple squares of end-grain oak serve as the only applied decoration. This use reemphasizes the nature of the oak itself, allowing the viewer to appreciate another aspect of the wood. Finally, in the true prairie style, the eye is confronted by the simple unadorned juxtaposition of pure geometric forms: trapezoid, circle, rectangle, and square.

These fresh designs, involving a synthesis of broad influences, together with Leopold's consummate business skill, pushed his firm to ever-increasing financial success. Gustav, in contrast, financially overextended himself, filed for bankruptcy in March 1915, and by May 1916 was essentially out of business. The Stickley family, under Leopold's guidance, formed Stickley Associated Cabinetmakers in 1917 in an apparent attempt to stave off Gustav's financial ruin. The new firm included Leopold as president and Gustav as vice president, with other brothers as officers. Gustav's independent nature, however, allowed him to work for the new concern for only twelve months. At that point he retired to the family house in Syracuse and never returned to the furniture market.

[24]Thanks to Catherine Zusy for this analysis, although Voysey's use of this form predates the Viennese secessionists. Nonetheless, cross-fertilization of design aesthetics ultimately creates unique interpretations of decorative objects; Zusy, "Shelf Clock," pp. 88, 168.

Leopold proved to be the more adaptable brother. Because he only produced and sold furniture, he was able to sense the changes occurring in furniture tastes. As early as 1916 an unpublished catalogue revealed that he had begun the manufacture of oak reproductions of colonial revival furniture. While price lists of 1925 reveal that he was still selling mission furniture, he had begun a phaseout by 1918. His last arts and crafts furniture catalogue was published in 1922. Leopold's first catalogue of Cherry Valley furniture was issued in 1924, showing colonial revival pieces; production of mission pieces had ceased.

The L. and J. G. Stickley Company continues in business today and until 1985 used the same factory that Leopold had bought in Fayetteville. In 1989 the company began to reproduce many adaptations of the mission pieces from both the L. and J. G. Stickley and Gustav Stickley catalogues.

The contribution then of the L. and J. G. Stickley Company to the design aesthetic of the arts and crafts movement in America is a considerable one. In terms of the popularization of the style in the years immediately preceding America's entry into World War I, the commercial appeal of Leopold's products allowed the firm to achieve prominence in the marketplace. Gustav was, in essence, unable to cope with the vicissitudes of the business world. He could not reconcile his role as apostle with the need to retain marketshare, and so the mantle passed to younger brother Leopold.

Leopold's contribution is not only one of commercial success. It is one of innovation and design as well. Even in the context of successful retailing practices, many of the L. and J. G. Stickley pieces well represent the arts and crafts aesthetic. Largely due to the knowledge and skill of Hansen, the company was able to extend the boundaries of the arts and crafts vernacular through the infusion of the aesthetics of the prairie school, the geometry of the Viennese secessionists, and the elegance of English designers.

Gustav will always be recalled for his innovation and his bold statements, both in terms of furniture and philosophy. Yet it was left to the more commercial instincts of Leopold to successfully negotiate the paradox of "the art that is life" and disseminate the products of the arts and crafts movement to the widest audience possible.

The Bradley and Hubbard Manufacturing Company and the Merchandising of the Arts and Crafts Movement in America

Richard Stamm

The arts and crafts style, characterized as resulting from "a quiet revolution [which] protested the mechanized replacement of craft," was ironically adopted by some large manufacturers against whom the movement rebelled.[1] These manufacturers were not then nor are they now considered reformers or even major figures within the movement. They did, however, play an important secondary role: one of dissemination of *style* rather than *philosophy*. The large manufacturers were, perhaps, more successful than the reformers in this endeavor because of the huge market they had cultivated among the great masses of the American middle class. The Bradley and Hubbard Manufacturing Company of Meriden, Connecticut, was one such manufacturer that, because of size, scope, and the inventiveness of its operation, should be considered

---

[1] Leslie Greene Bowman, *Virtue in Design: A Catalogue of the Palevsky/Evans Collection and Related Works at the Los Angeles County Museum of Art* (Boston: Little, Brown, Bulfinch Press, 1990), p. 13.

a leader among large companies in the dissemination of an arts and crafts style.

The name of Bradley and Hubbard is recognized by curators and dealers alike as a major nineteenth-century manufacturer of lighting and household goods, surviving well into the twentieth century. In spite of the relatively little that has been published about this firm to date, much can be discerned about their connection to the arts and crafts movement from the study of trade catalogues and patent documents and the examination of products made by the company in the arts and crafts style. These documents and objects show that while embracing the style, Bradley and Hubbard's methods of production remained consistent with their own philosophy of business.

The introduction of an arts and crafts line by Bradley and Hubbard began at about the turn of the century; however, myriad objects of various styles were produced by the company concurrently with those in the arts and crafts style, as seen in their trade catalogues at the time. Gas and electric lighting fixtures were illustrated representing the neoclassical, Eastlake, rococo revival, Renaissance revival, and arts and crafts style. This great variety reflected the eclectic tastes prevalent at the close of the nineteenth century and emphasized Bradley and Hubbard's ability to capitalize on trends.

As with the development of the arts and crafts movement in general, the adoption of an arts and crafts line by Bradley and Hubbard had its roots in the aesthetic movement of the 1880s.[2] Several objects patented by the firm at that time were clearly aesthetic in design but could easily be attributed to the arts and crafts movement were they not dated. One wonders, in fact, if these designs were later included in a Bradley and Hubbard arts and crafts line.

A cursory look at four Bradley and Hubbard design patents of the 1880s (figs. 1, 2) shows the close relationship between the two design reform movements. An inspection of these documents and their comparison with two items produced by Bradley and Hubbard reveal a few of the company's mass-production techniques used consistently throughout their history. These techniques included the substitution

[2] David Hanks and Jennifer Toher, "Metalwork: An Eclectic Aesthetic," in *In Pursuit of Beauty: Americans and the Aesthetic Movement,* ed. Polly Cone (New York: Metropolitan Museum of Art, 1986), p. 291.

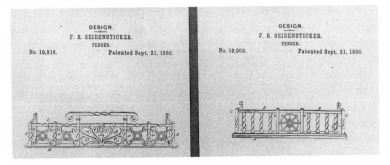

Fig. 1. F. R. Seidensticker, patent papers for fire fenders, assigned to Bradley and Hubbard Manufacturing Co., Meriden, Conn., September 21, 1886.

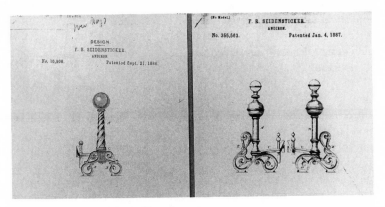

Fig. 2. F. R. Seidensticker, patent papers for andirons, assigned to Bradley and Hubbard Manufacturing Co., Meriden, Conn., September 21, 1886 (*left*), January 4, 1887 (*right*).

of materials that imitated more costly ones, design flexibility, and the interchangeability of parts.

The aesthetic ornamentation of an 1886 fire fender, designed and patented by Frederick Seidensticker and assigned to Bradley and Hubbard (see fig. 1, *left*), is characterized by flat, twisted, and scrolled members, giving the appearance of handwrought iron. The letters of patent describe the craftslike aspect of the twisted design on the uprights and upper frame as well as the representation of open scrollwork between. The top ornament, Seidensticker stated, "may be omitted or changed without departing from the spirit of this design." A comparison of this document to another fireplace fender attributed to Bradley and Hubbard illustrates one of the cost-saving methods used in production. While the second example appears to be handwrought iron, as in the patent drawing, it is actually made of cast iron, representing a cost savings in labor and allowing multiples to be produced in great numbers from one mold.[3] While the second fender is similar to the patent design, significant differences exist in the ornamentation between its twisted uprights. It could be that these inner decorations were intended as expendable design elements, as with the top ornament in the patent drawing, or that this was a completely different design for which a patent was requested but not secured. Yet another possibility is that the fender was the result of "mixing and matching" design elements, either by the customer or the company itself. It is reasonable to assume that such design flexibility created greater product variety and had the effect of increasing Bradley and Hubbard's market appeal.

Bradley and Hubbard also used interchangeable parts in many of their designs, creating even more flexibility. In a second patent for a fire fender also designed in 1886 (see fig. 1, *right*), Seidensticker incorporated some details from the framework of the first but added others, creating an entirely new design that shows a stronger relationship to the arts and crafts movement than that of the first fender. The more severe geometric and linear elements are less fanciful, and the repeated twisted uprights have a structural appearance; both support the arts and crafts principles of "simplicity" and "honesty"—further blurring the differences between the aesthetic and arts and crafts styles.[4]

---

[3] U.S. Patent Office, Washington, D.C., "Design for a Fender," specification of design no. 16,910 by F. Robert Seidensticker, September 21, 1886; term of patent was seven years. The second fireplace fender under discussion, attributed to Bradley and Hubbard Manufacturing Co., ca. 1886, is in a private collection. It is cast iron; H. 11", W. 41¾", D. 12". On the use of cast iron, see "Mining Industry of the United States," in *Eighty Years' Progress of the United States: A Family Record of American Industry, Energy, and Enterprise* (Hartford, Conn.: L. Stebbins, 1867), p. 36.

[4] U.S. Patent Office, Washington, D.C., "Design for a Fender," specification of design no. 16,909 by F. Robert Seidensticker, September 21, 1886.

Two patents for andirons and their comparison to a third andiron attributed to Bradley and Hubbard also illustrate a substitution of materials and design flexibility. The spiral fluting of the tapered column of an 1886 patent design by Seidensticker (see fig. 2, *left*) seems to indicate that the andiron was intended to have the appearance of wrought iron. However, a set of andirons in a private collection, having similar details and attributed to Bradley and Hubbard, are instead made of cast iron.[5] Flexibility is apparent in the design of the set; it is a composite of the twisted shaft from the 1886 patent design and the elaborate scrolled feet from the mechanical patent dated 1887 (see fig. 2, *right*). Most mechanical patent drawings were not representative of the design of an object but rather illustrated a mechanical device or process. In this case, however, the scroll legs drawn are identical in design to the andirons in the private collection. Why this patent was classified as mechanical rather than design is unclear.

Bradley and Hubbard's mass-production techniques did not change with their adoption of the arts and crafts style, a further indication that it was the style rather than the philosophy that the company was embracing. Patent documents and objects they produced reveal the consistent use of production shortcuts and the substitution of less expensive materials, illustrating how this large company merchandised the arts and crafts movement for mass consumption.

What does this tell us about Bradley and Hubbard's relation to the movement? Would a "philosophically pure craftsman" agree with their methods of production? The Bradley and Hubbard Company was, by 1900, well established with a large workforce successfully engaged in mechanized mass production by division of labor. In other words, they made use of techniques rejected by many ardent proponents of the movement.

Gustav Stickley railed against the factory system of production, saying "the production of 'goods' has become evil." Although the processes of production employed by the Bradley and Hubbard factory may not have been, in Stickley's words, "pleasurable" or "instructive," the

---

[5] U.S. Patent Office, Washington, D.C., "Design for Andiron," specification of design no. 16,908 by F. Robert Seidensticker, September 21, 1886. The pair of andirons, attributed to Bradley and Hubbard Manufacturing Co., ca. 1886, are in a private collection. They are cast iron; H. 23″, W. 11¼″, D. 22″.

intent was far from evil. Certainly the conditions that factory workers endured at the turn of the century were brutal compared with today's standards. For example, in 1914, 78 percent of the wage earners in the state of Connecticut worked between 54 and 60 hours per week. There is little compelling evidence to suggest that Bradley and Hubbard was more progressive than other manufacturers at the time, but judging from accounts of the day, both Bradley and Hubbard were held in high regard by the entire community, including their employees. Both men were generous philanthropists, giving time and money to numerous local charities, citizens groups, and institutions.[6]

It is fair to assume that Bradley and Hubbard's sole purpose in producing an arts and crafts line was profit. By designing objects in the style and by producing them more cheaply than their competitors, the firm allowed its customers to become beneficiaries of the cost savings. That the items produced by Bradley and Hubbard possessed a relatively high standard of workmanship causes one to question the movement's philosophical opposition to industrialization. For the studios of the top craftsmen of the movement to make a profit, they had to either charge high prices for hand-crafted items, thereby limiting their market to only the affluent of society, or compromise their ideals by introducing mass-production techniques.

A close look at a few household objects produced by Bradley and Hubbard in the arts and crafts style illustrates how the company combined quality design with cost savings in materials and production techniques. An arts and crafts–style candlestick appears to be constructed of brass and copper but is in fact composed of three metals: cast iron, brass, and white or pot metal (fig. 3, *far left*). The base and bobeche appear to be copper, but traces of brass plating remain on top of the copper. The candle cup appears to be brass, but traces of copper are visible under the brass; close inspection of hidden areas reveals that the candle cup is made of a white metal. The shaft of the candlestick is an extruded hollow brass pipe, hexagonal in section. The candlestick,

---

[6]Stickley is quoted in Barry Sanders, ed., *The Craftsman: An Anthology* (Santa Barbara and Salt Lake City: Peregrine Smith, 1978), 1–4:21. On work hours, see U.S. Department of Commerce, Bureau of the Census, *Census of Manufactures, 1914*, prepared by W. M. Steuart (Washington, D.C.: Government Printing Office, 1918), 1:179. George Curtis and Charles Gillespie, *A Century of Meriden* (Hartford, Conn.: Journal Publishing Co., 1906), pp. 67–74.

Fig. 3. Bradley and Hubbard Manufacturing Co., candlesticks, Meriden, Conn., ca. 1900. Brass, white metal, cast iron, copper, brass plating; (*left to right*) H. 10¾", W. 5⅛", D. 5⅛" (private collection); H. 12½", W. 4⅞", D. 4⅞" (private collection); H. 8½", W. 4⅞", D. 4⅞" (National Museum of American History, Smithsonian Institution); H. 11", W. 4¾", D. 4¾" (private collection).

constructed of three different base metals, was intended to appear as brass overall. Why were the parts plated twice, and why was the candlestick constructed of three different metals instead of solid brass? To acquire a uniform brass appearance, two of the metals required brass plating. However, because cast iron and pot metal are not readily plated with other metals such as gold, silver, or brass, these parts were first covered with copper in a process commonly called flashing.[7] The use of pot metal and hollow brass pipe instead of solid brass represented a cost savings in material, and the use of cast iron for the base provided necessary stability and weight.

[7]Oppi Untracht, *Metal Techniques for Craftsmen* (Garden City, N.Y.: Doubleday, 1968), p. 390.

Two mission-style candlesticks (fig. 3, *center*) were also designed to look like solid brass but were constructed with a copper-plated iron base, brass shaft, and white metal candle cup. These examples demonstrate another factor in cost savings—interchangeable parts. The great difference in appearance of the two candlesticks is the result of the modification of just one part—the brass shaft—and the addition of a collar to the shorter candlestick; the bases and candle cups of both are identical. Therefore, by standardizing component parts of their products, Bradley and Hubbard could easily and cheaply produce several variations of an object, each greatly different in appearance, while still maintaining a relatively high level of quality.

Another example of the use of interchangeable parts to produce a completely different design can be seen in figure 3, on the far right. Although similar to the preceding examples, this candlestick varies slightly in construction and materials. Unlike the others, the base is constructed in two parts: a cast-iron section for weight, topped with a bell-shape hollow brass shell. The candle cup and shaft are the same as the other candlesticks, but the different base alters the appearance greatly. Traces of copper and brass plating are found on the cast-iron base; the candle cup is white metal. The construction of all four candlesticks is similar: the base of the candle cup is threaded to receive a steel rod that runs the length of the shaft through the base, secured with a threaded nut. Uniformity of construction made the use of interchangeable parts possible.

A pair of Bradley and Hubbard brass candlesticks (fig. 4) resembles a design produced by Stickley Brothers Company of Grand Rapids, Michigan, that was featured in their circa 1908 catalogue. Because all the metal objects presented on the pages of the Stickley catalogue were "strictly hand made, no machinery of any kind whatever being used in their manufacture," they bore the marks of the craftsman—hammer marks and irregularity of form.[8] The resemblance of the Bradley and Hubbard candlesticks, with their highly polished finish and perfectly regular shape, to the Stickley example is rendered somewhat superficial by the fact that the component parts were stamped by machine, not handwrought. The candlesticks exhibit none of the characteristics of

[8] Stickley Brothers Co., *Quaint Furniture in Arts and Crafts* (ca. 1908; reprint, New York: Turn of the Century Editions, 1981), no. 147, pp. 66–67, 5.

Fig. 4. Bradley and Hubbard Manufacturing Co., candlesticks, Meriden, Conn., ca. 1900. Brass, H. 4¾″, W. 4⁷/₁₆″, D. 4⁷/₁₆″. (Private collection.)

hand labor; even the brass rivets that secure the handles appear to be machine driven.

Although machine work was disregarded by Stickley and other movement purists, these brass candlesticks ironically seem to fulfill two of the movement's criteria: honesty and simplicity. On these objects, Bradley and Hubbard made no attempt to reproduce hammer marks, which served as proof of handwork and had decorative value on arts and crafts objects. The absence of them, or any other surface decoration, bestows simplicity to their design. Bradley and Hubbard's extensive use of machinery and production cost-cutting techniques also "brought within the means of those with even the most moderate of incomes the possibility of artistic homes."[9]

[9] Stickley Brothers Co., *Quaint Furniture*, p. 4.

The examples discussed so far have emphasized only the production cost-cutting techniques used by the company, not their attention to the customer's needs (utility). A large percentage of the 139 patents for mechanical devices assigned to the company were, however, improvements in products that addressed customer needs and increased efficiency. One such mechanical patent, assigned to Bradley and Hubbard in 1909, was a candlestick with a three-fold purpose, "to produce a convenient article of attractive and novel appearance." The candlestick had a special spring-loaded cartridge that held a candle constantly pressed to the top of the chamber, enabling the candle to be burned completely and allowing for the easy replacement of the burned candle. As for appearance, the candlestick was arguably an attractive arts and crafts design, although not specifically created as such. The inventor stated, "I do not limit myself to candlesticks of rectilinear design as herein shown as the shapes of the parts may be varied without changing the construction."[10] The spring-loaded cartridge was fashioned to look like a candle inserted into the candlestick, answering the criteria of "novelty of appearance."

Bradley and Hubbard's improvements extended to all types of products, including stained glass lamp shades, which became extremely popular early in the arts and crafts movement. By 1905, however, as the patent document for a lamp shade design indicates (figs. 5, 6), there were problems associated with traditional stained glass objects—namely, the great expense of production and the difficulty of repairs to damaged glass by the customer. The patent addressed these concerns by stating that the purpose of the invention was to produce a lamp shade in imitation of traditional leaded stained glass "at greatly reduced costs" and "to enable broken glass to be readily replaced by the owner of the shade." Each triangular section was composed of a frame with "leading" cast as one piece from a soft metal; the sections were then soldered together to form a hexagonal lamp shade. The pieces of colored glass were placed behind the tracery, and metal tabs were bent over the glass to hold them in, thus requiring only three or four pieces of glass to give the illusion of a stained glass panel. Again, in keeping with the desire for flexibility of design and interchangeability of parts,

[10] U.S. Patent Office, Washington, D.C., "Candlestick," specification of patent no. 914,804 by R. F. Crooke, March 9, 1909.

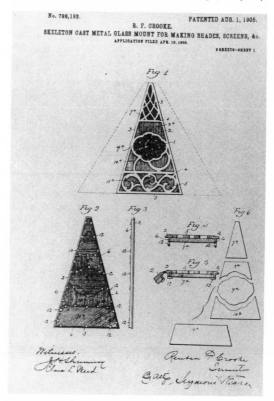

Fig. 5. R. F. Crooke, patent papers for lamp shade, assigned to Bradley and Hubbard Manufacturing Co., Meriden, Conn., August 1, 1905.

the inventor stated that the designs within the frame "may be either geometric, pictorial, floral or arabesque."[11] While the effectiveness of the illusion of stained glass cannot be discerned from the drawing alone, the value of a system for the easy replacement of broken glass can be readily surmised.

The floral design lamp shade of a labeled Bradley and Hubbard

---

[11] U.S. Patent Office, Washington, D.C., "Skeleton Cast Metal Glass Mount for Making Shades, Screens, &c.," specification of patent no. 796,193 by R. F. Crooke, August 1, 1905.

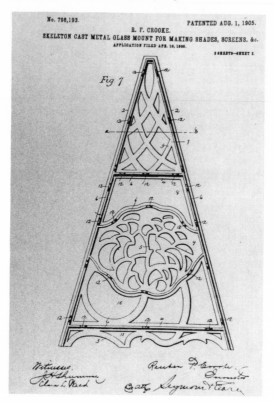

Fig. 6. R. F. Crooke, patent papers for lamp
shade, assigned to Bradley and Hubbard Manufacturing Co., Meriden, Conn., August 1, 1905.

lamp (fig. 7) readily illustrates the effectiveness of these patent claims.
From a distance the use of multicolored slag glass contributes to the
illusion of leaded glass. The illusion, however, is not totally successful
when viewed at a close distance. The overall design of the lamp is arts
and crafts and employs a base and column similar to those of the
hexagonal candlestick (see fig. 3) but is larger in scale. As with that
candlestick, the base on this lamp is brass-plated cast iron, and the
hollow column is brass. Although similar to the patent drawing of
1905, this lamp was patented on October 8, 1908, and represents a

Fig. 7. Bradley and Hubbard Manufacturing Co.,
lamp, Meriden, Conn., ca. 1905. Brass, cast iron,
brass plating, multicolored slag glass and leading;
H. 23″, Diam. 20½″. (Private collection.)

slight improvement over the earlier design. This later patent was by
the same inventor who stated that its pictorial design "is an effect far
beyond the reach of [traditional] leading."[12] It allows the design to be
more complex.

Bradley and Hubbard not only produced household goods cheaper
by mass-production techniques but also addressed the needs of their
customers with innovative and well-designed products. Whether these

[12] U.S. Patent Office, Washington, D.C., "Glass Mount for Shades and Kindred
Articles," specification of patent no. 901,690 by R. F. Crooke, October 20, 1908.

innovations were completely successful in their stated intent is not of primary importance here. That these patents were designed for objects in the arts and crafts style and that they served to disseminate that style to people who could not otherwise afford similar objects produced by hand is of greater importance.

Bradley and Hubbard's choice of the arts and crafts style raises several theoretical questions. No evidence exists to suggest that they were active participants in either the social or design reform movements of the time, but they nevertheless used design reform elements in their products. What characteristics of Bradley and Hubbard's arts and crafts–style objects were at odds with the tenets of the movement? Specifically, the use of cast iron in imitation of wrought iron, the employment of plated metal finishes as substitutes for solid metals, and the use of applied ornamentation are all in direct conflict with the ideas of honesty of materials and simplicity of design held so strongly by Stickley and the other members of the movement. In an article entitled "Utility—Simplicity—Beauty," Stickley stated, "And so we might pass on through the list of household furnishings; condemning with justice those that copy and imitate; those that are wanting in honesty and originality; or again when decoration simulates constructive principle."[13]

Indeed, the very capitalist factory system that Bradley and Hubbard built was in conflict with Stickley's philosophy. It was not the use of machinery for production that Stickley found objectionable in the factory system, for he stated that "as a matter of fact, given the real need for production and the fundamental desire for honest self-expression, the machine can be put to all its legitimate uses as an aid, and a preparation for, the work of the hand." It was the fact that, as he put it in *The Craftsman*, "Capitalism presents a hostile attitude toward all efforts to restore the conditions of healthful, pleasurable, beautiful workmanship."[14] Bradley and Hubbard were, after all, capitalists in every respect.

A fundamental flaw in Stickley's argument against capitalism may be found in his statement that "wage slavery deprives the producer of all desire to improve his product." Had this been the case, there would

[13] Sanders, *Craftsman*, 1–4:16.
[14] Stickley is quoted in Sanders, *Craftsman*, 11–15:187–88; 1–4: 23.

have been no need for Bradley and Hubbard to exert time and effort patenting new designs and improving mechanical devices for their products. Their success was proven. Furthermore, the patentees of those innovations, in most cases, were employees whose position with the company was not that of "designer" but rather "department foreman." Bradley and Hubbard, it seems, did promote a desire among their employees to improve the products they produced, fulfilling Stickley's desire for the "union in one person of the designer and the workman."[15]

Stickley also stated that the people to whom he made his plea for a "democratic art" were the members of the "great middle classes, possessed of moderate culture and moderate material resources."[16] Who, then, better served the masses: an idealistic producer of higher cost, hand-crafted items of great integrity, or the manufacturer who, through mass production, made utilitarian objects, perhaps derivative in design but available to virtually everyone in society, including the so-called wage slave? The philosophical conflict of a large capitalistic company embracing a fundamentally socialistic movement might then appear to be reconcilable.

[15] Stickley is quoted in Sanders, *Craftsman*, 1–4:23. On the union of designer and workman, see Stephen Gray and Robert Edwards, eds., *Collected Works of Gustav Stickley* (1981; rev. ed., New York: Turn of the Century Editions, 1989), p. 47.

[16] Sanders, *Craftsman*, 6–10:121.

Louise Brigham
Developer of Box Furniture

Neville Thompson

Louise Brigham, the author of the 1909 book *Box Furniture: How to Make a Hundred Useful Objects for the Home,* was one of those fascinating figures without whom movements and styles would simply be isolated episodes. Her book sold widely, remained in print for at least ten years, and was even translated into Danish. Brigham vigorously publicized her design and construction theories through demonstrations, lectures, and the examples of furnishings in her own apartments and in the settlement houses and children's camps she outfitted. The Winterthur library is fortunate to have acquired Brigham's own copy of the 1919 printing of *Box Furniture,* with additional ephemeral material and her extensive annotations for a projected future edition. Since Brigham is little known today, the copy of her book has provided valuable clues for the reconstruction of her life and career.

Brigham was born in Boston in 1875 (fig. 1). She studied at Pratt Institute; her experience there seems to have been formative, although she is not recorded as a graduate. By her own account, she was enrolled as a scholarship student in the Kindergarten Department (where great emphasis was placed on teaching with the Froebel toys so well known

For advice, assistance, and encouragement the author thanks Cheryl Robertson and Bert Denker, co-chairmen of the conference at which this paper was presented; Birgit Kagstrom Janson, curator, Carl Larsson Garden, Sundborn, Sweden; Birgitta Hagstrom, librarian, Uppsala Universitetsbibliotek, Uppsala, Sweden; Margot Karp, reference librarian, Pratt Institute, Brooklyn, N.Y.; Bente Jacobsen, Winterthur; Katharine Martinez; and my colleagues in the Winterthur library.

© Moffett, Chicago.

The Woman Who Makes Furniture From Boxes

Fig. 1. Portrait of Louise Brigham. From *Illustrated Lectures by Louise Brigham, Author of "Box Furniture"* (n.p., n.d.), p. 1. (Winterthur Library.)

today through their association with Frank Lloyd Wright's kindergarten years) and in the Domestic Science and Domestic Art departments. Pratt in those early years stressed manual training, crafts, and practical experience with the residents of the Astral, the settlement house operated by the school. The Astral was provided with specially designed foldaway kitchen furniture—a theme that would appear in Brigham's own design work.[1]

While in charge of a settlement house in Cleveland called Sun-

[1] The author is indebted to Margot Karp, reference librarian, Pratt Institute, for information on Pratt's early years and for pointing out that Brigham's name does *not* appear on the institute's list of graduates.

shine Cottage, Brigham improvised her first piece of box furniture, a high chair hastily fashioned from a wooden packing box. According to *The Craftsman,* Brigham became interested in learning more about the immigrants she worked with through their native handicrafts. She put this notion into practice with a daunting series of academic and practical experiences in many European countries, including study with Charles Rennie Mackintosh in Glasgow and courses in the national handcrafts schools of Denmark, Holland, Norway, and Austria. Her work with the designer Josef Hoffmann in Vienna seems to have meant the most to her; in her book she states that she used "the Hoffmann method" in conceiving her own interior and furniture designs.[2] In some obvious ways, Hoffmann's own furniture, beautifully finished and destined for an upper middle-class clientele, was very different from Brigham's, but his use of the square as the basis for his design was obviously well suited to the requirements imposed on Brigham's work by her use of boxes as raw material, which by their very nature come as rectangles or squares.

Brigham traveled widely during those European years, visiting (among others) the Swedish painter Carl Larsson and his wife, Karin, to whom Brigham later sent an inscribed copy of her book. (This book still exists in the library at Sundborn, Larsson's home, now a museum.)

Brigham's correspondence with the Larssons survives in the Larsson archive in the University of Uppsala, Sweden. Her letters project a vivid sense of a person who was busy, warmhearted, full of projects, and always on the move. She proclaims her devotion to the Larssons, to whom she sent a gift of pottery from the hands of Anton Lang, the Oberammergau potter famous also as the Christ of the Passion Play in that city. Brigham even suggests the publication of a book to be written by her and illustrated by Larsson—which unfortunately was never realized—and discusses attempts to interest American publishers in issuing translations of Larsson's popular illustrated books. It is tempting to think that Karin Larsson, who herself designed some of her own furniture, might have found a compatible acquaintance in Louise Brigham. It is true that the well-known flower stand at Sundborn, designed by

[2]"Making Box Furniture: Its Practical and Ethical Value," *The Craftsman* 21, no. 2 (November 1911): 218–21. Louise Brigham, *Box Furniture: How to Make a Hundred Useful Things for the Home* (1909; reprint, New York: Century Co., 1910), p. 6.

Karin and executed by a village carpenter, does indeed resemble a window seat in *Box Furniture*.

Brigham says she perfected box furniture on an unlikely site, the treeless island of Spitzbergen in the Arctic Ocean, while she was the guest (possibly in 1907) of the manager of coal mines on the island. Alternately, one of her obituaries states that she found herself in this remote location as a guest on the icebound yacht of the owner of the mines, a Bostonian described in *Who Was Who in America* simply as "capitalist." Although this connection cannot be proved, it is not surprising that Brigham might have chosen to downplay the circumstance, given her profession of social worker. At any rate, she apparently asked to make use of the ubiquitous packing crates in which everything needed for daily life had to be shipped onto the island and, perhaps remembering the Cleveland high chair, created a variety of furniture forms for the manager's newly arrived prefabricated house. Box furniture had been born. Before Brigham left the island, her work had been seen and admired by a number of visitors, from the Prince of Monaco to the members of an American polar exploration team, who acclaimed her as having created the "northernmost civilized home in the world."[3]

Returning to New York City, Brigham settled in a series of apartments, each named "Box Corner." Her first was at East End Avenue and Eighty-ninth Street, then far beyond the pale of polite society. She furnished the apartment entirely with box furniture she made herself and then proceeded to write a book and a series of magazine articles about her creations. The first edition of *Box Furniture* appeared in 1909, to a receptive audience and excellent reviews (fig. 2). That of *The Independent* was typical: "The book has a seriously helpful purpose . . . it is also a surprise book of delights for boys and girls, a useful course in manual training, and a refuge for those who seek in simple physical occupation relaxation of mental strain." Many of the reviewers commented on the practicality of Brigham's designs, their good looks, and the unpretentious charm of her writing. The *New York Times* added that it was "one of the few indications of the birth in this country of a tendency toward less wastefulness of raw material," an idea that

---

[3] *Who Was Who in America: Vol I: 1847–1942*, s.v. "Longyear, John Munro." On Brigham's life, see "Louise Chisholm, Crafts Expert, 81," *New York Times*, March 31, 1956. Brigham, *Box Furniture*, p. xviii.

Box Furniture Making School at Panama Pacific International Exposition, San Francisco.

Fig. 2. From Louise Brigham, *Box Furniture: How to Make a Hundred Useful Articles for the Home* (1909; reprint, New York: Century Co., 1919), cover. (Winterthur Library.)

was fundamental to Brigham's work. On the other hand, the preface to the Danish edition emphasized above all the recreational value of her projects, adding, "there's no word more true than selfmade is well done."[4]

Box furniture is based on the simple concept of disassembling wooden packing boxes of many sizes into their component parts and reassembling these parts into furniture through simple carpentry. Around 1910 just about everything came in wooden boxes of standard measurements; Brigham could therefore call for "silk boxes" or "butter boxes" in her directions, confident that this terminology would be generally understood. Most packing boxes then were simply nailed together and could easily be taken apart; Brigham cautioned against use of the

[4]"Literary Notes," *The Independent*, July 29, 1909. "A Book of Boxes," *New York Times*, June 5, 1909. Louise Brigham, *Kasse-mobler: Hvorledes man selv af brugte Pakasser kan lav en maengde nyttigt Bohave til sit Hjem* (Copenhagen: N.C. Roms Forlagsforretning, [1909]), p. 7. I thank Bente Jacobsen of Winterthur for her translation of the publisher's preface to the Danish edition of Brigham's book.

new dovetail-jointed boxes as unsuitable raw material. Her book's first projects used boxes in their original form, and the text then proceeded through increasingly complex combinations and permutations of the basic box shape. Only a few simple construction methods were called for. Throughout, Brigham stated that her principal aim was to develop furniture that could be made easily by amateurs, even children. Elaborate finishes and decorative details were not required, only the use of overlaid wood strips along joints and edges, the filling in of nail holes and sanding of the surfaces, and the application of paint (often white) as a finish, a popular method of treating furniture that was appropriate for these pieces, since they were made of inferior wood. Brigham herself said that she did not grow up with a command of woodworking tools, a fact that probably was helpful in keeping her methods so easy. Having published *Box Furniture*, she enthusiastically promoted her creations at the 1912 and 1913 Woman's Industrial Exhibit in New York, Chicago, and Buffalo; at Rochester in 1911 through 1913; and at the Panama-Pacific Exposition in 1915, where she was awarded a medal of honor. In a pamphlet of 1914 or 1915 she advertised illustrated lectures on the subject, which must have been a success, for she is said to have spoken on box furniture in such exotic locales as Japan, China, and Egypt.[5] Brigham produced pragmatic proof of the ease of construction of box furniture through her creation of the Home Thrift Association, which she founded for the children of the immigrant families of her neighborhood. She led this group in the unlikely quarters of Gracie Mansion (not yet the mayor's residence). Here she taught boys to make box furniture and toys and instructed girls in sewing and braiding raffia, an irony apparently lost on the association's female founder. Also for association members, she designed "Tak-Apart" portable furniture for summer camps, to be transported in boxes that were then used as seating furniture.

In 1916 Brigham married steel company executive Henry Arnott Chisholm and moved to Cleveland, where she is said to have introduced Christmas Eve "at homes." During World War I she returned to New York to engage in occupational therapy with wounded veterans, for which she was officially commended. In 1920 Chisholm died in

[5] *Illustrated Lectures by Louise Brigham, Author of "Box Furniture"* (n.p., n.d.), pp. 1–16.

Yokohama, Japan; after his death, Brigham returned to New York to live. This time she settled in a studio apartment in MacDougall Alley that was fitted out with box furniture and with the spoils of her many trips abroad. MacDougall Alley, nicknamed the "Art Alley de Luxe" in 1917, then provided home or studio space to Daniel Chester French, Gertrude Vanderbilt Whitney, James Earle Fraser, and many other creative New Yorkers. Here Brigham lived in high-class pre-war "village" style, while also maintaining residences in Bermuda and Venice, holding locally famous Sunday afternoon receptions, and reputedly spending her Christmas eves in Bethlehem. It was even claimed that she was "the first woman to have entered the tomb of King Tutankhamen after its discovery." In a 1929 interview she said that "making every inch count has become her ruling passion." "Efficiency is the most important thing in life," she stated, "whether in business or in homemaking," and her interviewer was eloquent about her clever transformation of closets into bathroom and kitchen. "Housewives would admire . . . [her] concept of a dining room table, in the shape of a Greek cross . . . whose four sides let down. In each of the four corners is a tall pillar, surmounted by an electric candle, and each pillar contains a plug for table appliances such as toasters, grills, and so on." The interviewer was referring to the Greek cross tea-table from *Box Furniture*, apparently her favorite design, for she devoted an entire article in the *Ladies' Home Journal* to describing the twelve configurations that could be achieved through manipulation of the fold-down leaves and separate tall candlesticks (figs. 3, 4). "I want to spend the rest of my life in New York," Brigham said, "It's the most exhilarating city in the world." The impressed reporter felt sure that there she would continue to preach her doctrine of "making simple, efficient furniture, and showing others how to assemble simple things into a harmonic unity."[6]

The proposed new edition of *Box Furniture* seems never to have appeared; perhaps the flush times of the postwar era were not right for

[6]On the King Tut claim, see Eleanor Clarage, "Main Street Meditations," *Plain Dealer* (Cleveland), February 4, 1929. Document furnished by the Cleveland Public Library from its clipping files. On the 1929 interview, see Clarage, "Main Street Meditations." Louise Brigham, "What Can Be Done with One Table," *Ladies' Home Journal* 27, no. 2 (March 1910): 39.

Fig. 3. *The Greek Cross or Four-Leaf Table.* From *Illustrated Lectures by Louise Brigham, Author of "Box Furniture"* (n.p., n.d.), p. 8. (Winterthur Library.)

such intentional simplicity. Brigham seems so much a person of another age that it is almost a shock to learn that she did not die until 1956, at the age of eighty-one. At her death she was reported to have been a member of many writers' organizations, but her innovative furniture was the highlight of her obituary accounts. She was survived by a sister and by her book.

Brigham did not originate the idea of furniture made from boxes; her improvisation from found materials is an honorable tradition that constantly reappears in American culture, even during periods of ex-

BOX FURNITURE

GREEK-CROSS TEA-TABLE

Fig. 4. From Louise Brigham, *Box Furniture: How to Make a Hundred Useful Things for the Home* (1909; reprint, New York: Century Co., 1910), p. 202. (Winterthur Library.)

cess, the *New York Times* review notwithstanding. Long before Brigham's day, housewives were turning barrels into chairs and boxes into cribs. If this were all her book embodied, it would simply stand as another popular craft instruction manual for amateurs. Because of Brigham's sensibility, however—and that of one other person—it is an uncommonly elegant production. When composing her furniture, Brigham was obviously aware of arts and crafts design dicta and dutifully stated in her preface that even in Spitzbergen she felt anew the truth "that work to be of real value must be honest, useful, and beautiful, and Ruskin and Morris spoke as clearly in the arctic regions as in the settlements and studios of New York."[7] Indeed, the squares and

[7] Brigham, *Box Furniture*, p. xviii.

rectangles into which her raw material was disassembled, when reassembled into furniture bore a striking resemblance to that of, for instance, Frank Lloyd Wright at the same period as well as to pieces mass-produced in Grand Rapids in the mission style. But it is not only the extent to which Brigham's designs echo some of the most innovative furniture of the day that catches our eye; it is their presentation as well.

Brigham's most original contribution lay in her actualization of the concept of box furniture and her popularization of it to audiences that wanted and needed inexpensive but tasteful furnishings. She came from a background of settlement work, and it is from this perspective that her participation in the arts and crafts movement derived. It is telling that she dedicated her book to the social reformer Jacob Riis and acknowledged as well the encouragement of Hoffmann. The book, however, owes much of its visual distinction to its illustrator, who, I think, must have contributed significantly to its most interesting feature: the completely furnished room settings shown at the beginning of each chapter. These interiors are elegantly drawn, and the entire decorative scheme is meticulously described down to the color of the flowers each room contains (figs. 5, 6). These illustrations were the work of Edward H. Ascherman, "from designs by the author." It is unclear why Brigham did not furnish her own illustrations, but these suggest strongly that Ascherman had a considerable part to play in the visualization of her ideas. Ascherman, born in Saint Paul, Minnesota, in 1878, also studied in Vienna with Hoffmann (Brigham may have known him there), at the Academie Julian, and with Robert Henri and Frank Alvah Parsons.

At the time *Box Furniture* appeared, Ascherman was already practicing as an interior designer in New York, as his advertisement in *The Craftsman* in 1908 testifies. His own work as a decorator is strong evidence for his possible contribution to the context of the room settings in *Box Furniture*. One example, the living room of a house in Forest Hills, New York, appears in an interesting article by Ascherman in *International Studio* called " 'Modern' Interior Decoration in American Homes." Ascherman, in characterizing this style, says "The 'Modern' treatment is hampered by no set of rules; it aims above all . . . to make each expression individual and personal, and to have the settings appropriate, simple, and cheerful. The lines are mostly straight, and the treatment of the walls and furniture fearless and telling." This could

Fig. 5. Dining room. From Louise Brigham, *Box Furniture: How to Make a Hundred Useful Things for the Home* (New York: Century Co., 1909), p. 248. (Winterthur Library.)

be the description of any of the interiors in *Box Furniture*. The house decorated by Ascherman is strikingly unlike either the Craftsman or colonial revival interiors then appearing in current American periodicals. The color scheme of the living room is gray, white, black, and orange; that of a bedroom in the same house is black and white. Ascherman even imported Viennese furniture for these particular interiors, not content with emulating the Continental style with American artifacts. Brigham's own decorative taste is best set forth in a series of four articles called "How I Furnished My Entire Flat from Boxes," which appeared in the *Ladies' Home Journal* in 1910. While her sense of color seems to have been interesting, her interiors appear more quirky and personal and less Viennese than Ascherman's; she covered her living room walls in brown wrapping paper and based her kitchen color scheme on the gray and white of her graniteware and the red of her soup can labels. Her kitchen walls bore painted slogans reminiscent of those still seen today in the Larsson house, which very probably served

The Dining=Room

FLAG WALL RACK	CHINA CLOSET

ALLENDALE SIDEBOARD
GREEK-CROSS TABLE   MINIATURE PLANT-BOXES
VINE VASES
ROLLING SOILED-DISH STAND   BABY'S HIGH CHAIR
PICTURE FRAME NO. 2

Color Scheme:
  Flemish oak.
  Soft green.

Woodwork:
  Flemish oak.

Furniture:
  Flemish oak.

Walls:
  Soft green.

Drop Ceiling:
  Light green, with motif stenciled in moss green.

Hangings and Table-covers:
  Russian crash, with motif appliquéd or stenciled in
  same color as walls.

Curtains:
  White.

China:
  White.

Pottery:
  Green.

Floor:
  Stained same color as furniture.

Plants:
  Growing ivy and plants with crimson blossoms the
  same color as the flags; yellow or old-rose flowers if
  flags are not used.

Fig. 6. From Louise Brigham, *Box Furniture: How to Make a Hundred Useful Things for the Home* (New York: Century Co., 1909), p. 249. (Winterthur Library.)

as her inspiration. She also, however, created at least one black-and-white room in one of her "box corners," a room that was thought to be very Viennese and one that could have been designed by her mentor, Hoffmann.[8] In any case, Brigham's and Ascherman's common experience of Austrian design training may have reinforced each other's decisions when putting together the book's illustrations, resulting in a publication of notable style.

So we have not one, but two, figures from these years who deserve to be better known: Brigham for her creative response to the arts and crafts ideal of making handsome household articles available to those with little space or money and Ascherman for the Continental elegance of his graphic work and interior schemes. Brigham's dedication of her book "to all who care for simplicity and thrift, utility and beauty" sums up her dual inspirations.[9] She used her extensive design training as a means to an honorable end, one that surely fulfills the goals of the arts and crafts movement in its most appealing sense. There are, however, contradictions in Brigham's life. Since most of what we can learn of her today comes from her own writings, we are seldom reminded that the creator of box furniture also had a vacation home in Bermuda, a privileged education, and wealthy friends. We must remember that the picture we see in contemporary accounts is to a great extent a self-portrait. Nevertheless, there seems to be no doubt about the sincerity in her devotion to her profession and to her immigrant neighbors. Her career reminds us that contributions to the movement came from many sources, and disparate motivations lay behind them. Those of Louise Brigham can still command our interest and deserve our respect.

[8]*The Craftsman* 14, no. 3 (June 1908): ix. E. H. and G. G. Aschermann, " 'Modern' Interior Decoration in American Homes," *International Studio* 53, no. 212 (October 1914): 81. Louise Brigham, "How I Furnished My Entire Flat from Boxes," *Ladies' Home Journal* 27, nos. 10, 12, 14, 16 (October–December 1910). This series of four articles describes her apartment in detail. On the black and white room, see *Illustrated Lectures*, p. 9.
[9]Brigham, *Box Furniture*, p. xxi.

The Handicraft Guild
of Minneapolis
A Model of the Arts and Crafts Movement

Marcia Gail Anderson

The Handicraft Guild of Minneapolis (HG) was not founded until 1904, but its origins are rooted much earlier in the cultural life of the twin cities of Minneapolis and Saint Paul, Minnesota. Between 1870 and 1890, the once prairie towns of Minneapolis and Saint Paul had swelled in population from 33,000 to nearly 300,000. By the 1880s, less than a generation after Minnesota had become a state, the two fledgling metropolises were ready to take on the visage of cities that had truly arrived.[1]

Prior to this time the arts activity in Minneapolis was sporadic and tentative, limited to music, lecture series offered at private clubs, gallery showings by collectors or small groups of artists, and occasional visits from artists and performers in dance and theater. Fine arts were displayed at the state fair as early as the 1850s. While many celebrated artists showed their work over the years, it was not until 1887 that a fire-safe, brick gallery was built on the fairgrounds to attract the loan and exhibition of high-quality works.

When the 1878 art exhibition at the fair was judged an embar-

---

[1] Articles of Incorporation of Handicraft Guild, April 25, 1905, Incorporation Records Secretary of State, Saint Paul, Minn. William A. Lass, *Minnesota: A Bicentennial History* (New York: W. W. Norton, 1976), p. 120.

rassment, local collectors and aficionados pooled their resources to present an improved exhibition in 1879, which was followed by others. An art loan exhibition series, formally initiated in 1883, marked the beginning of a concerted movement to bring a broad spectrum of the arts to Minnesotans.[2]

Supporters of the arts in Minnesota in the late nineteenth century believed that it was more important to establish art schools initially than to develop art museums and great collections. Schools, it was thought, would demonstrate the community's commitment to art and bring a growing, ever-changing pool of artists and ideas to the state. The HG emerged as the opportunity to put these goals in practice in the Twin Cities.

Close study of the patrons, officers, founders, instructors, and alumni of the HG and Minnesota's other early arts organizations and schools reveals a large number of committed working women who remained involved in the arts for many years, whose names appear again and again in one organization after another, and who dedicated their lives to creating the broadest possible base of artistic enterprise and appreciation.[3]

The Minneapolis Society for Fine Arts was founded in 1883 and gave birth to the Minneapolis School of Fine Arts (MSFA) in 1886. William M. R. French, of the Art Institute of Chicago, played an instrumental role in the planning of the new school and in the selection of a director and faculty. Douglas Volk, the school's first director, came highly recommended, with a reputation as a fine painter and distinguished instructor at Cooper Union in New York. Although the school struggled in its early years to build a strong curriculum and staff on a limited budget, the efforts were rewarded. In its first six years the school's enrollment increased from 20 to 134 students, and by the 1890s it was operating at a profit, with a growing constituency. The school's early program included foundation work in the traditional "academic method" that emphasized the study of and proficiency in draw-

---

[2] Karal Ann Marling, *Blue Ribbon: A Social and Pictorial History of the Minnesota State Fair* (Saint Paul: Minnesota Historical Society Press, 1990), pp. 228, 230; Jeffrey A. Hess, *Their Splendid Legacy: The First One Hundred Years of the Minneapolis Society of Fine Arts* (Minneapolis: Minneapolis Society of Fine Arts, 1985), p. 4.

[3] *Minneapolis Journal*, January 12, 1903.

Fig. 1. From Emma E. Beard, "The Recent Exhibition of the Minnesota State Art Society," *International Studio* 28 (1906): cxvii. Mrs.
Ambrose E. Helnick, Minneapolis, chest designer and maker.

ing the human body. By 1899, however, under its new director, Robert
Koehler, even the MSFA was adding classes in industrial art.[4] Other
early arts organizations and schools had less-auspicious origins.

The personal papers of founder Nellie Trufant, which contain
newspaper articles, correspondence, and ephemera, are the only known
documentation of one of America's earliest arts and crafts societies—the
Chalk and Chisel Club of Minneapolis. The club was founded in
January 1895 by a group of women with an interest in wood carving.
As interest in handicrafts grew, the club expanded its focus to include
members from various crafts disciplines (fig. 1).[5]

On November 16, 1898, the club held Minnesota's first major

[4]Hess, *Their Splendid Legacy*, pp. 11, 14. Horace B. Hudson, ed., *Half Century
of Minneapolis, with Numerous Views and Portraits* (Minneapolis: Hudson Publishing
Co., 1908), pp. 124–25. Isaac Atwater, ed., *History of the City of Minneapolis, Minnesota*, pt. 1 (New York: Munsell, 1893), p. 164.

[5]*The Constitution of the Society of Arts and Crafts, Minneapolis, Minnesota*, 1900,
Nellie Trufant Papers, Minneapolis History Collection, Minneapolis Public Library;
Minneapolis Journal, January 26, 1901.

arts and crafts exhibition at the Beard Art Gallery in Minneapolis. "The Chalk and Chisel Club, as we called it," recalled Mrs. A. E. Helmick, "wrote very timorously to all the big craftsworkers in the East, and we were overwhelmed by the enthusiasm of the acceptances and the flood of exhibits sent in." Artists and firms from nine other states and England were represented, including Rookwood Pottery, Grueby Pottery, Dedham Pottery, Bulger, and the Deerfield Society of Blue and White Needlework. Along with similar events in Boston and Chicago, the exhibition was one of the earliest of its kind in this country.[6]

Following the 1899 exhibit the club reorganized, adopted new bylaws, and changed its name to the Arts and Crafts Society of Minneapolis (ACSM) to reflect the growing interest of its members and the community in the applied arts. "The object of the Society," read its bylaws, "shall be to encourage the production of artistic handicraft, to establish mutual and helpful relations between designer and craftsman, and to stimulate the appreciation of harmony and fitness in design."[7] Trufant became secretary of the ACSM, and Mary Moulton Cheney served as treasurer. Meetings were held in an old frame building on Sixth Street in downtown Minneapolis. The building was jointly owned by several club members and doubled as a workshop for the patrons and artists.

A few years later, in 1903, the Minnesota State Art Society (MSAS), or Commission, was established, making Minnesota one of the first states with such a program. Members of the original governing board included the familiar names of Cheney, Robert Koehler, and furniture maker William Youngbauer. The objectives of the MSAS were "to advance the interests of the Fine Arts, to develop the influence of art in education and to foster art in manufactures."[8] The society intended to accomplish these by producing an annual exhibition to be held in several venues throughout the state and by building an art collection that would be housed in the Capitol Museum in Saint Paul.

[6] *Minneapolis Journal*, March 29, 1925. *An Exhibition of the Arts and Crafts under the Auspices of the Chalk and Chisel Club* (Minneapolis: Chalk and Chisel Club, 1898), pp. 1–30.
[7] *Constitution*, Trufant Papers.
[8] "The Beginning of the Minnesota State Art Commission," *Minnesotan* 1, no. 1 (July 1915): 24, 26. *The Constitution and By-Laws of the Minnesota State Art Society* (Minneapolis, 1903).

The collection would travel to augment the annual exhibition or be lent on request.

In 1912 the ACSM became an extension committee of the MSAS. Its new responsibilities were to take over the traveling exhibition circulated throughout the state and to carry on the handicraft movement that it had so capably fostered in the past. In 1914 the MSAS gave its annual exhibition in conjunction with the state fair. This popular exhibit, which enabled its supporters to accomplish their goal of reaching a broad audience, continues to the present day as the fair's Fine Arts Department. For a brief time (1915–17), the MSAS also published a monthly magazine called the *Minnesotan,* which was an important, if temporary, vehicle for the arts and crafts movement in the state.[9]

Little is known about similar crafts schools in Saint Paul. It is clear from their representation in exhibition catalogues, however, that such schools were active and were doing fine work as well. The Saint Paul School of Fine Arts was begun by a group of women in 1890 and was later absorbed by the Saint Paul Institute (also known as the Saint Paul Institute of Arts and Science or the Saint Paul Institute of Art). After its completion in 1907, the elegant Saint Paul auditorium served as home for classes and exhibitions for this organization as well as for shops and studios for several artists and craftspeople. While its emphasis was primarily on the fine arts, the school did offer a normal art course and training in pottery, jewelry, metal, basketry, and leather. Another organization, the Art Workers' Guild of Saint Paul established itself in 1902 with the goals "To encourage the worker in art. To forward the interest of art. To develop in the community a love of beauty in every form." Although photographs of the Art Workers' Guild activities have survived, little written information exists.[10]

The HG traces it immediate origins to the development of design at the MSFA. While the design department of MSFA grew steadily, its cramped quarters made it impossible to take the program to its next logical phase—instruction in the actual techniques and processes of the various handicrafts. The demand for this instruction, made espe-

---

[9] Ray P. Speer and Harry J. Frost, *Minnesota State Fair: The History and Heritage of One Hundred Years* (Minneapolis: Argus Publishing Co., 1964), p. 63.

[10] *Art Workers' Guild of St. Paul* (1906), pp. 1–8. This booklet contains the 1906 annual and treasurer's reports, plans for 1906–7, membership list, and bylaws.

cially by teachers in the public schools, was a factor in the founding of the HG. Grace Margaret Kiess was listed in late 1904 as the HG's president. In 1905 Cheney, then president of the ACSM, Mary Linton Bookwalter, Mary Emma Roberts, and Florence Wales formed the corporation and served as president, treasurer, secretary, and vice president, respectively. In its first published advertisement, the HG offered instruction in clay modeling, leatherwork, and Irish embroidery and sold handwrought objects in leather and metal as well as pottery, embroidery, and textiles from artists throughout the country.[11]

The HG was officially incorporated on April 25, 1905, with the stated purpose of furthering the "intimate relation between the theory and practice of art." Bookwalter, a frequent contributor to *The Craftsman*, became the HG's first director. Its first real home, the guildhouse, was located in the former residence of Thomas S. King in downtown Minneapolis. The guildhouse provided the space for studios and shops for artists and craftsworkers and made tangible the hope that the HG would become the center of the art industries in Minneapolis and the region as well as the finest school for teachers of art, designers, and craftsmen. The drawing room of the home and a large room behind it were modified into a permanent exhibition room and lecture hall. The interior was finished in an arts and crafts palette—soft shades of greens and natural browns—and was simply furnished with handsome rugs and artwares. The front room served as a sales shop where the guild featured Newcomb pottery and Berea Fireside Industries embroidered linens. The rear portion of the building was used by potters and metalworkers. The pantry served as a drying room; the refrigerator was used for storing clay; and the woodshed held the built-in and portable kilns. Studios for the artists and craftswomen were located on the second and third floors.[12]

The first summer school design course, from June 19 to July 19, 1905, was announced in *The Craftsman* in May 1905. The staff in-

---

[11] *Minneapolis Journal*, December 3, 1904. *Fourth Exhibition Catalogue for the Society of Arts and Crafts, Minneapolis, Minnesota* (November 1904).

[12] A designer, consultant, and decorator-architect, Bookwalter, later Mrs. Frederick Lee Ackerman, was stockholder and principal designer in development of the cooperative flat Harperly Hall at Central Park West and 64th St. in New York, 1909; Mary Linton Bookwalter Papers, private collection, Pasadena, Calif. On the guild house, see *Minneapolis Journal*, July 1, 1905; March 1, 1905; September 2, 1905; March 27, 1905.

Pottery designed by Miss Florence D. Willets, of the Handicraft Guild of Minneapolis.

Fig. 2. Handicraft Guild of Minneapolis, pottery, Florence D. Willets (designer), Minneapolis, ca. 1906. From *The Bellman* (November 24, 1906): 471. (Minnesota Historical Society, Saint Paul.)

cluded course director Ernest A. Batchelder of Throop Polytechnical School, Pasadena, California, who taught core courses in design. Batchelder states that his goals for the new program were: "1. To stimulate the imagination. 2. To impart sufficient technical skill to develop the limitations and possibilities of leather, metal, and clay as means of expression. 3. To induce pupils to think in terms of lines, areas, and tones. 4. To lead the individual expression of an idea in accordance with sound principles." Other faculty included James H. Winn of Chicago, who taught jewelry making; Florence Willets, assistant to James T. Webb at the Art Institute of Chicago, who taught pottery (fig. 2); and Nelbert Murphy, a native of Minneapolis then with the manual training department of the East Orange, New Jersey, public schools, who offered instruction in craftwork adapted for public school curricula. These respected instructors and artisans were assisted by local guild members, including Cheney in design, Edith Griffith and Winifred Cole in bookbinding, Kiess in pottery, Bertha Lum in woodblock printing, and Corice Woodruff in sculpture and painting.[13]

In the HG's first summer school, hundreds of pieces of pottery were produced from the native clay of Red Wing, Minnesota, and enough were of worthy quality to make the program a success. The

[13] "Summer School Handicraft Guild," *The Craftsman* 8, no. 2 (May 1905): 266–67; *Minneapolis Journal*, March 27, 1905.

opportunity to accomplish such work in the new facility was largely due to the efforts of Webb, who spent a week in April 1905 setting up the seven wheels (using sewing machine frames and treadles) and directing the placement of the kilns. Guild ceramic pieces were marked with its monogram, and a Minneapolis newspaper article described the output as popular pottery forms including lamp bowls (low and rounded with three short hands) and jars.[14]

While pottery was the primary product of the first summer session, metalwork and leatherwork were also shown. Each student in metalworking completed a small bowl, a tray, a plate with an etched border, and a sconce with a hammered pattern. Leatherwork included card cases, belts, bags, billcases, and covers. Significantly, nearly all of the established local craftsworkers attended the summer school, and many of the other local students were principals or teachers in the public schools. At the close of the first summer term, guild officer Roberts announced that the school would be held again in the summer of 1906 and that Batchelder would return to provide the foundation course in design. Batchelder, meanwhile, left immediately for a study tour of Europe's trade, technical, and industrial art schools.[15]

The success of this first structured program at the HG reinforced the community's belief in the need for an industrial art school in the area.[16] And while the program was still experimental in form, there was great encouragement and support for their plans to expand both the program and facilities. Already unable to accommodate the requests for quarters in the guildhouse from architects, other art professionals, and students, the HG initiated plans to construct a new building and establish the school on a permanent basis with a year-round course of study.

The new building, at 89–93 South Tenth Street, was built at a cost in excess of $30,000 and opened in November 1907. With this facility, the HG strengthened its position as an essential element in the

[14]On pottery at the school, see Martha Scott Anderson, "A New Art Industry May Grow from the Pottery Work of the Handicraft Guild," *Minneapolis Journal*, September 5, 1905; April 19, 1905; September 2, 1905.
[15]On students, see *Minneapolis Journal*, July 19, 1905. On Batchelder, see *Minneapolis Journal*, July 20, 1905; February 22, 1907.
[16]*Minneapolis Journal*, July 1, 1905.

Fig. 3. Handicraft Guild building, 89–93 S. Tenth St., Minneapolis, ca. 1909. (Minnesota Historical Society Collections, Saint Paul: Photo, Elgin R. Shepard.)

development of artistic taste in Minneapolis (fig. 3). The structure provided the most modern and tasteful spaces in the city for study, studios, permanent exhibitions, sales, artists' get-togethers, and lectures. It was conveniently located near the public library at the edge of the downtown retail district. The front of the building held a luncheon room and tearoom and a long salesroom, painted a neutral brown. It had a beamed ceiling and a wide fireplace made of tiles produced by guild pottery workers. A passage that led to the back of the building was flanked by workshops and classrooms, with those for the noisier crafts of jewelry and metal at the very back. The second and third floors contained studios occupied by craftsworkers, designers, a rare books dealer, and a painter. The assembly hall accommodated up to 400 people, and the artistic quality of its dark rafters and beams poised against the rich yellow ceiling made it a much-sought-after meeting place for local organizations. The HG was now firmly established as the center of artistic activity in Minneapolis, a city that strongly believed that art was not a luxury but a necessity.[17]

The HG summer program of 1908 was attended by 140 students who came from all over the United States and Canada. The full school term extended from September to May, with the summer session set at five weeks. Batchelder continued to direct the summer program through 1908 and taught at least through the spring of 1909.[18] In October of that year *The Craftsman* began to run advertisements for Batchelder's Craft Shop and School of Design and Handicraft in California. According to Robert Winter, an authority on California arts and crafts, it was the love of the woman who became his wife that pulled Batchelder away from Minneapolis in 1909. His unique style remained at the HG as his legacy and manifested itself in ceramics and metalwork marked by pierced work and the presence of negative and positive design spaces (fig. 4). The typical HG copper bowl with pierced panels and grape and leaf design, the Dutch motif ships with full masts, and the peacocks and other birds, executed alone or in the mirror images so popular with HG students and faculty, will always attest to Batchelder's influence.

In 1911 Maurice Irwin Flagg of Massachusetts was made permanent director of the school. Trained at the Museum of Fine Arts, Boston and the Institute of Technology, Worcester, Flagg had been a director of the Swain School of Design, New Bedford, before directing the HG summer school in 1910. By the fall of 1911, the HG curriculum was enlarged by the addition of a Normal Arts Department to serve students from the MSFA who sought practical instruction and the use of the guild shops.[19] By 1913 the normal art program was dropped entirely from the school of fine arts curriculum, and all stu-

[17] On the new building and its facilities, see *Minneapolis Journal*, July 28, 1907; Florence N. Levy, ed., *American Art Annual* (Washington, D.C.: American Federation of Arts, 1917), 14: 154; John Alden Bradford, "Books: The Shop and The Man," *The Bellman* (March 14, 1908): 288–90; "Society Biographies: The Handicraft Guild, Minneapolis," *Handicraft* 3 (December 1910): 341–42; Elisabeth A. Chant, "The Handicraft Guild," *The Bellman* (March 21, 1908): 317–19.

[18] Elisabeth A. Chant, "The Summer Session of the Handicraft Guild," *Palette and Bench* 1 (October 1908): 23–25. *Minneapolis Journal*, December 9, 1908.

[19] *Minneapolis Journal*, June 13, 1912; *Minneapolis Society of Fine Arts and School of Art Circular of Information Regarding Instruction, 1911–1912* (Minneapolis, n.d.), p. 8.

Fig. 4. Handicraft Guild of Minneapolis, bowl.
H. 2³/₁₀″, Diam. 7¹/₁₀″. Stamped: HANDICRAFT GUILD/
MINNEAPOLIS. (Private collection.) Bowls of this type fre-
quently have glass liners and were part of nut bowl sets.

dents interested in this field were encouraged to attend the HG for
certification. The HG course prepared students to become instructors
in drawing and handicrafts or supervisors of art education in public
and normal schools. The HG was the only such school in the upper
Midwest at this time to make a serious effort at meeting the increasing
demand for teachers trained with a specialty in art. As early as 1912
there was a long list of HG-trained teachers, designers, and craftsworkers who were spreading the school's principles throughout the country.

The 1914–15 catalogue for the school included courses in normal
art (a two-year program); design (composition, color theory, and practice); watercolor; jewelry; stenciling; leatherwork; clay modeling; metalwork; pottery; woodblock printing; weaving; and public-school music.
Tuition ranged from $5 for a ten-week Saturday class in elementary
design to $210 (plus supply and book costs) for a diploma course from
the normal art program. Fifteen students, several from other states,
graduated in the spring of 1914 with certificates in normal art.[20]

[20] *School of Design Handicraft and Normal Art: Tenth Annual Session, September
21, 1914–May 28, 1915* (Minneapolis: Handicraft Guild of Minneapolis, n.d.), pp.
1–15.

Flagg continued as HG director until 1914, when he took on the directorship of the MSAS, and in 1915 Ruth Raymond replaced Flagg in that position. With her experience as a graduate and former instructor at the Art Institute of Chicago, and as an instructor at the Chautauqua Summer School in New York and the Classical School in Evanston, Illinois, Raymond represented the integrity and high qualifications of the HG faculty.[21] She served as principal until 1918, when the HG was dissolved and absorbed by a new art education department at the University of Minnesota. She was head of that department until her retirement thirty years later.

Peak years for the arts and crafts movement in Minnesota were 1914 and 1915. City directories and publications were full of advertisements for stores carrying, or specializing in, custom handicrafts from around the country. Other notices appeared for businesses that sold supplies or services for china painting, leatherwork, and firing of pottery; schools that offered focused curricula or classes; and individual artisans who gave classes or sold their designs for use by others.

In their roles as contributors to this trend in Minneapolis, pottery and metalwork became the HG's most recognized commercial products. Perhaps the greatest reason for the success and development of the HG's broad foundation was its active exchange with other groups from coast to coast, which succeeded in spreading its reputation. Guild work received generous praise in publications, including *Arts and Decoration, International Studio, The Craftsman,* and *Keramic Studio,* and was sold or shown in shops, galleries, and exhibitions nationwide. In spite of this recognition, descriptions of a definitive style or technique in the HG's work remain elusive.[22] The pottery was recognized for its graceful lines, beauty of form, and quiet, rich color and was judged to be artistic as well as functional. While decorative features included incised lines and impressed, stylized images, much of the work relied

[21] Levy, *American Art Annual,* 14:154, 300. Officers are listed as M. Emma Roberts, President; Florence D. Willetts, Vice President; Florence Wales, secretary/treasurer.

[22] "Art stores in Philadelphia and New York turn over bits of pottery, brass, and copper bowls, richly colored tiles, for the purchaser to see the hall-mark of this Minneapolis workshop on the bottom. What Rookwood has done for Cincinnati and Dedham ware has done for a little town in Massachusetts, this guild is doing in half a dozen commodities for Minneapolis" ("Minneapolis: The Art Center of the Northwest," *Arts and Decoration* 6, no. 2 [May 1912]: 240).

on unique and layered glazes and simple vessel forms rather than applied or added decoration. Faience tiles produced by the HG were used by architects for fireplace mantels; and jars, inkwells, bookends, lamp bases, jugs, sconces, flower frogs, candlesticks, and vases were produced employing hand building, molding, or throwing methods (fig. 5).

Metalwork was produced primarily in copper and brass with jewelry executed in silver and gold with precious and semiprecious stones and enameling. Exceptionally fine examples featuring pierced work, repoussé and mirror imagery of birds—particularly identifiable HG traits—were regularly illustrated in journals of the period (fig. 6). Custom lighting work was commissioned for residences and other new construction. Pierced, hammered, etched, and repoussé techniques were employed in the creation of nut bowl sets, pierced bowls, smoking sets, desk sets, coffee sets, spoons, lamps, bookends, sconces, plates, porringers, candlesticks, trays, vases, and jewelry.

Interviews with Gladys Pattee, a former student of the HG, suggest a possible answer for the scarcity of identified examples of guild work. Because technique and honest craftsmanship were the goals, students were actively discouraged from marking or signing their work. While some particularly fine examples of marked work have been located, it may be that many others were unmarked and have not yet been located or identified as HG products. The HG was also inconsistent about styles or techniques used for marking. The cipher of an *H* over a contained *G*, metal and ceramic stamps that read "Handicraft Guild/ Minneapolis," a small brass plaque that repeats the phrase, a crude engraving of the HG cipher, and a paper label that combines the cipher and the phrase have all been found as marks on HG pieces. In 1916 a newspaper article referred to the HG as a little Greenwich Village. Even after its dissolution on September 20, 1918, the building continued as a center for artists, musicians, dancers, and craftspeople. It remained actively occupied in this manner well into the 1950s.[23]

In addition to its successes as a school for training teachers in the arts and crafts, the HG left a legacy in the form of groups and individuals who laid the foundation for the rich arts and cultural life in Minne-

[23]Gladys Pattee, interviews with author, 1984–90. *Minneapolis Journal*, December 3, 1916.

Fig. 5. Handicraft Guild of Minneapolis, student ceramic work. From *School of Design Handicraft and Normal Art: Twelfth Annual Session*, 1916–17 (Minneapolis: Handicraft Guild of Minneapolis, n.d.), p. 6.

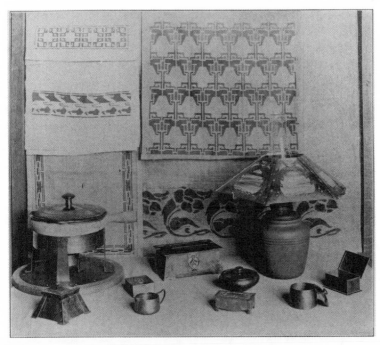

Fig. 6. Handicraft Guild of Minneapolis, metalwork, stenciling, and designs, Minneapolis, 1908. From Elisabeth A. Chant, "The Summer Session of the Handicraft Guild," *Palette and Bench* 1 (October 1908): 24.

sota today, especially in the Twin Cities. HG alumni went on to found programs, schools, and other guilds as well as to direct arts education programs that trained thousands of aspiring artists. Margaret Cable, for example, established a celebrated ceramics program at the University of North Dakota School of Mines at Grand Forks. Cheney opened and managed the Artcraft Shop and taught at and directed the MSFA. Flagg founded the MSAS. Other important teachers and alumni included Raymond; Roberts, instructor and supervisor of art appreciation in the Minneapolis schools for twenty-four years; Henrietta Barclay Paist, teacher, painter, contributor to and assistant editor of *Keramic Studio* for four years, and author of *Design and the Decoration of Porcelain;*

and Pattee, public school teacher, World War I Army occupational therapist, and founding member of the Rochester Art Center.[24]

The success of the Handicraft Guild and other related early arts organizations established a strongly democratic or populist tradition in the arts in Minnesota. Opposed to the arcane, rarified, occasionally elitist atmosphere of many fine art museums, the HG sought to broaden Minnesotans' conceptions of what art was, bringing it out of the gallery and into the community for all to experience and enjoy.

[24] Margaret Kelly Cable was employed in pottery work at the Handicraft Guild between 1907 and 1910; Margaret Libby Barr, Donald Miller, and Robert Barr, *University of North Dakota Pottery: The Cable Years* (Fargo, N.D.: Knight Printing Co., 1977); Mary Moulton Cheney received her training at the Museum of Fine Arts, Boston, and emerged as a key figure in Minnesota arts organizations during the late nineteenth century and first quarter of the twentieth century; Mary Moulton Cheney Family Papers, 1841–1929, Minnesota Historical Society, Saint Paul; Henrietta Barclay Paist, *Design and the Decoration of Porcelain* (Syracuse, N.Y.: Keramic Studio Publishing Co., 1916); Pattee interviews.

Charles Rohlfs and "The Dignity of Labor"

Michael L. James

It was, without question, the Princeton University Art Museum exhibition of 1972 that initiated the rise of the arts and crafts movement to its current position by reintroducing its philosophy and proponents. The exhibition included a broad sampling of the movement's products and generated excitement and curiosity about that period. Regional exhibitions followed, examining many of the artists and craftsmen more closely and introducing others to an expanding audience.

This necessary and valuable study has continued, but it has been overshadowed by an increasing tendency to focus on a few craftsmen who have been singled out as representatives of the movement. This practice, particularly in the area of furniture design, has extended to the ranking of manufacturers and their work according to their "purity" of form and perceived adherence to movement principles. Furnishings of lower rank are viewed as less desirable for either aesthetic appreciation or scholarly study. Ironically, this preoccupation with objects has relegated the movement's philosophical tenets—that inspiration and process are even more important than product—to a position of secondary interest and importance.

I believe that it has been this tendency, coupled with the perception that his work is physically incompatible with other arts and crafts furnishings, that has relegated Charles Rohlfs (1853–1936) to the fringes of the movement's mainstream. Known for his work rather than his philosophy, Rohlfs has been increasingly viewed by many as an interesting eccentric who was, at best, loosely tied to the movement. This belief is understandable, considering that his work ranges across a spectrum of styles.

Rohlfs, however, deserves the position of respected spokesman of the arts and crafts movement that was accorded to him during his lifetime. That he played such a role can certainly be argued on the basis of contemporary press coverage and his international recognition alone. The principles that guided his work are fully aligned with the movement's mainstream ideals. His stylistic individuality supports rather than contradicts Rohlfs's role as designer and manufacturer.

Unlike some of his contemporaries, notably Elbert Hubbard and Gustav Stickley, Rohlfs did little proselytizing and did not leave to future generations a large body of published work. He did, however, grant a number of interviews and often spoke to small gatherings in the Buffalo, New York, area. It is from those magazine and newspaper accounts that we can understand the essence of his philosophy.

Briefly stated, the foundation of Rohlfs's life and work was his strong belief in what he termed "the dignity of labor." This concept, delineated in several prepared talks, has two aspects. First, he viewed labor itself as having great inherent value and satisfaction, more as a process than as simply a means to an end. This held true for all types of labor, from industrial to artistic. "Work is the great thing," he maintained, and he took pride in the fact that he worked in his shop more than ten hours a day until he was well into his seventies (fig. 1). More important is the aspect of work that gives dignity to the labor performed. According to Rohlfs, there is always one thing that an individual can do better than anything else. Determining that appropriate field is the first, crucial step that each person must undertake. When it is discovered, it should be performed with inspired, purposeful effort. This inspiration was to be gained by seeking what Rohlfs termed "the absolute truth," recognizing it in your soul and putting it into your work. Only then could an individual realize the dignity, as well as the joy, of labor. Rohlfs maintained that this joy "is of Divine origin and can not die. It must not and it can not rest."[1]

---

[1] Rohlfs's thoughts on work are quoted in *Chautauqua Assembly Herald*, July 15, 1902. On the joy of labor, see Deshler Welsh, "Charles Rohlfs, Laborer," *Honey Jar* (August 1910): 68–69.

Fig. 1. Charles Rohlfs in his workshop, 198–200 Terrace, Buffalo, N.Y. From *Twentieth Century Buffalo: An Illustrated Com-
pendium of Her Municipal, Financial, Industrial, and General
Public Interests* (Buffalo: J. N. Mathews Co., 1902), p. 170.

Before examining in greater depth this idea that motivated Rohlfs, it will be helpful to survey its beginnings and its development through his early life and the first two of his three careers. Rohlfs dreamed of a life on the stage from a very early age. That dream, although partially realized, was interrupted often by various demands of practicality. His father, a cabinetmaker, cautioned him against such a life and strongly urged that Rohlfs learn an industrial trade. His father's death when Rohlfs was twelve left him no choice but to help support his family at various jobs, including messenger boy and machine shop laborer. He continued to advance his formal education, however, by enrolling in night classes at New York's Cooper Union in 1867.

While it was necessity that motivated Rohlfs to enter industry rather than the arts, it was his experience at Cooper Union that taught him that a satisfaction beyond monetary rewards could be achieved in such work. Peter Cooper had established his school, functioning mainly at night, to provide working men and youth, such as Rohlfs, with the opportunity to remain in school, improving their skills and self-esteem. Rohlfs combined courses in chemistry and physics with others such as ornamental design, which would profoundly affect him. His proficiency in the latter was such that he became known as the best draftsman in the school.

It was Rohlfs's early experience as a wage earner and a student at Cooper Union that developed his belief in the value of work as a process rather than merely a means to an end. The school in particular remained a source of guidance throughout his subsequent careers in industry and the arts and inspired the way in which he merged them. Rohlfs later affirmed that to Cooper: "I owe everything, my training, my art,—for without the early training, the art would have been still undeveloped, and my determination to succeed in every smallest thing undertaken."[2]

Rohlfs applied his Cooper Union education to the cast-iron stove industry, entering that field as a designer. New York and Boston-area firms employed his services directly or purchased the rights to his patented improvements. He honed his design ideas and skills on stoves over a twelve-year period. This early training provided Rohlfs with his

[2] *Buffalo Times*, January 8, 1909.

skills and determination, but it was his stage career that intensified his belief in total commitment to work. He had continued to nurture his theatrical dream and embarked on that second career in 1877, working at it both alternately and concurrently with his stove designing. Performing in support of such leading figures as Lawrence Barrett, Mary Anderson, and Edwin Booth, Rohlfs immersed himself in the study and performance of Shakespearean drama. Although the theater and the stove industry seem poles apart, Rohlfs believed that they shared a common principle. When asked years later to compare his career as a craftsman with that of an actor, he stated that "it is important in both professions that the worker puts himself in such an attitude that the result of his toil creates a responsive throb which testifies to a singleness of purpose, a warm sincerity of feeling. . . . to do work that is the outcome of a cultivated sense emboldened by his efforts to secure extension in his labor."[3]

The extent to which he would pursue this singleness of purpose can be seen in his statement to another interviewer that he immersed himself into the manufacture of furniture as fully as he had once immersed himself into a Shakespearean part: "If I make a chair, I am a chair" (figs. 2, 3). The effect was not merely intensified effort; by merging himself so fully with his work, he believed that it became a Rohlfs chair, bed, or door. It was as much the effort of his labor as it was the design that made the piece identifiable as Rohlfs's furniture. Emotion, feeling, and the power to wholeheartedly give expression to the mind were essential to making the craftsman an artist.[4]

Rohlfs's dramatic experience and love of literature continued throughout his years as a designer of cast-iron stoves and, finally, furniture. He advocated mental and spiritual cultivation through the study of great literature, noting that the work of Ralph Waldo Emerson, Robert Browning, Percy Bysshe Shelley, and, above all, Shakespeare had forged his own creative spirit. This potent combination of study and performance, coupled with the inspiration he found in nature, influenced the later furniture designs that critics described as dramatic.

[3] Welsh, "Charles Rohlfs," p. 69.
[4] Rohlfs is quoted in Clara Ruge, "Kunst und Kunstgewerbe auf der Weltausstellung zu St. Louis," *Kunst und Kunsthandwerk* (December 1904). "Personality Tells," *Buffalo Express*, March 12, 1902.

Fig. 2. Charles Rohlfs in a theater publicity photo, 1895. (Rosamond Rohlfs Zetterholm.)

Fig. 3. Charles Rohlfs, chair, ca. 1898. Oak; H. 54″,
W. 16″, D. 15″. (Rosamond Rohlfs Zetterholm.)

The full development of Rohlfs's ideas can be seen in his furniture design. The stated reason for this third career was the family's need for affordable furnishings, following his 1884 marriage to novelist Anna Katharine Green and the birth of their first child. It is possible, however, that a greater motivation was Rohlfs's dissatisfaction with the creative limitations of factory-produced cast-iron stoves. Although he made some strides in that field—breaking it loose from the aesthetic it shared with Victorian furniture—it is likely that his continued involvement in the medium would have frustrated his need to fully merge art and industry. The innovative designs that he introduced gained some exposure but remained a small part of the steadfastly traditional production of the nineteenth-century's waning years. It was evident that it would be some time before his ideas would be widely accepted in that field.

It appears that Rohlfs did find satisfaction in the small-scale production of custom furniture. His minimal production was due not to limited demand but rather to his adherence to two principles of artistic design and production: inspired expression develops at its own, natural pace, not upon demand; furniture must reflect the lifestyle and needs of the client as well as the vision of the artist. Rohlfs's initial inspiration for a design was often spontaneous, coming to him from "a chance word here, a thought there, a necessity perhaps."[5] The idea then progressed through a painstaking process. A workman made a small model from his original design. Rohlfs then studied it, made functional and artistic improvements, and had another model built. This process was repeated until he was satisfied. His belief in the primacy of individual, inspired expression motivated the proud insistence on made-to-order production that resulted in such an amazingly broad and varied spectrum of design (see fig. 4).

Rohlfs was reluctant, in both words and craftsmanship, to dictate to others what they should have in their homes. As he once told an audience, "I can do very little or nothing for you on the subject of furniture: I can do very much for myself. This is and must be an individual matter, after all."[6] Whenever possible, he visited a client's

---

[5]Lola J. Diffin, "Artistic Designing of House Furniture," *Buffalo Courier*, April 22, 1900.
[6]*Chautauqua Assembly Herald*, July 15, 1902.

office or residence to determine the best means of combining his design with its intended function and surroundings.

Individuality being as essential to the client as it was to the craftsman in developing the artistic home, Rohlfs believed that it was important to aid both in seeking and recognizing the "true" in life and all its choices. He tried to guide those seeking such truth by offering a caveat that they should heed in making their choices:

We make the mistake to think that what has given us pain and care must be proportionately good. The inferior poet labors twice as hard as the able one. The one works out the happiness in his soul, the other his misery, and mistakes effort for effect. We seem to value the thing that has caused us pain more than the thing that has come because we could not prevent its coming. Yet the things produced in the glow of enthusiasm are the things that have stood the test of time, because they have been natural to the producer.[7]

Following the sciences, books, and rules was prerequisite to a degree, but ultimately the soul was supreme. An individual had to break beyond the rules to express himself in ways uniquely his own. "Soul must be put into any work to make it what it should be." It was crucial that the public recognize this distinction and join with artists and craftsmen in identifying and seeking out what is truly important in their work. This would facilitate the process of separating the true from the false and allowing it to flourish. In Rohlfs's words, "Our prayer should be that the scales be removed from our eyes so that we would be able to see the soul of the craftsman in his work; see the good and help him to eradicate the false by first knowing ourselves what is and what is not true and so rise out of the slavery of our own ignorance into the freedom with which the Creator has endowed us all."[8]

Rohlfs believed that the arts and crafts movement was fostering an environment beneficial to that process and furnishing the artist and craftsman with the opportunity to achieve dignity and honest pleasure in his or her labor. He praised the movement for educating the public to respect the artist and craftsman and to encourage their merger of art and industry. He described the movement as "the stone thrown in the

---

[7] *Buffalo Morning Express*, April 20, 1900.
[8] Rohlfs's thoughts on separating true from false are quoted in *Buffalo Enquirer*, March 12, 1902. *Chautauqua Assembly Herald*, July 15, 1902.

mill pond, small in itself yet causing waves that spread to the uttermost parts of the pond. The movement instills into the workingman a desire for artistic labor, that expresses his own individuality, and it prompts the public to look to the artistic in making their purchases. It is the leaven which keeps alive the artistic sense."[9]

The movement's success would have a three-fold effect. It would free the laborer from the mind-numbing repetition of contemporary industrial production, encourage him to express his soul in his work, and benefit the public by enhancing their lives with the resulting artistic creations.

Did Rohlfs accurately perceive the role and intent of the arts and crafts movement? Are his views in alignment with the philosophy of its mainstream? Let us compare his belief in the dignity of labor to the words of John Ruskin:

Every action, down even to the drawing of a line or utterance of a syllable, is capable of a peculiar dignity in the manner of it, which we sometimes express by saying it is truly done. . . , so also it is capable of dignity still higher in the motive of it. For there is no action so slight, nor so mean, but it may be done to a great purpose, and ennobled therefore; nor is any purpose so great but that slight actions may help it, and may be so done as to help it much, most especially that chief of all purposes, the pleasing of God.

Rohlfs personally believed in, and thought that the movement promoted, the idea that an individual's soul must be put into the chosen craft if the finished product is to be true. He often spoke on the "true and false" in furniture, emphasizing that the true, in the sense of a work's artistic honesty and integrity, was not to be sought in its degree of ornamentation or the richness of its finish. It could be of plain design and simple construction. The truest and most artistic furniture had to be "individual, expressive of workmanship that was a pleasure rather than toil that was irksome." Rohlfs's words again parallel those of Ruskin. In a similar vein, Ruskin wrote that

if the man's mind as well as his heart went with his work, all . . . will be in the right places, and each part will set off the others; and the effect of the whole, as compared with the same design cut by a machine or lifeless hand will be like that of poetry well read and deeply felt to that of the same verses

[9]*Chautauqua Assembly Herald*, July 15, 1902.

jangled by rote . . . For we are not sent into this world to do anything into which we can not put our hearts. We have certain work to do for our bread, and that is to be done strenuously; other work to do for our delight, and that is to be done heartily: neither is to be done by halves and shifts, but with a will; and what is not worth this effort is not to be done at all . . . [H]e who would form the creations of his own mind by any other instrument than his own hand, would also, if he might, give grinding organs to Heaven's angels, to make their work easier.[10]

If these sentiments represent the essence of the arts and crafts movement, and I believe that they do, then even a craftsman as individualistic as Rohlfs can be regarded as not only an adherent but one of its pioneers and spokesmen. Rohlfs went beyond words, however, producing a body of work that exemplified his philosophy that art should be "expressive of workmanship that was a pleasure rather than toil that was irksome." That pleasure had to extend beyond the designer to the laborers who actually produced the piece. Rohlfs believed that harmony within the workshop was necessary to turn out truly artistic furniture. The co-workers had to be in sympathy with the designer and "work with the feeling that they are part of a plan."[11] The workers, then, would also achieve dignity in their labor, and the result of their cooperative efforts would be true (fig. 5). Rohlfs was convinced that the "responsive chord" that his furniture struck with his patrons attested to the truth of his expression. Certainly there was no doubt then, nor is there now, regarding its uniqueness among the furniture of the period. It therefore meets Rohlfs's dual criteria of being inspired by the individual and produced with dignity.

It is particularly ironic that a man who represented the arts and crafts movement so closely in word and deed is today considered to be less a part of it than others who abandoned it. While Rohlfs adhered to the principles of originality, honest materials, and handiwork, the profit motive drove many of his contemporaries to embrace mass production and marketing. He lamented that the concepts of craft and craftsmanship had been irreparably cheapened, rendering the arts and

[10]John Ruskin, *The Seven Lamps of Architecture* (London: Ward, Lock, 1911), pp. 27–28. Charles Rohlfs, "Address to Arts and Crafts Conference," *Chautauqua Assembly Herald*, July 15, 1902. Ruskin, *Seven Lamps*, p. 198.
[11]On Rohlfs's philosophy, see *Chautauqua Assembly Herald*, July 15, 1902. On co-workers, *Buffalo Enquirer*, March 12, 1902.

Fig. 4. Charles Rohlfs, Imperial Chinese *(left)* and Martha Washington candlesticks. Imperial Chinese: mahogany and brass; H. 39″; Martha Washington: mahogany, brass, Kapa shell; H. 25″. (Photo, Rosamond Rohlfs Zetterholm.)

Fig. 5. Charles Rohlfs (*third from left*) and craftsmen in workshop, 198–200 Terrace, Buffalo, N.Y., ca. 1903. (Rosamond Rohlfs Zetterholm.)

crafts movement meaningless. Rohlfs never expanded his work force beyond a handful of "fellow laborers," as he called them. He resisted the adaptation to newer production methods or more popular styles that had seduced some of his counterparts. Although he shared their descent into oblivion, he was satisfied that he had held to those principles that he shared with the arts and crafts movement.

Rohlfs, his products, and the labor he expended to create them all exemplify the dignity that one man believed to be essential in his search for the truth. Inspired and highly original, his "artistic furniture," as he called it, articulated in wood what Rohlfs the craftsman saw in his soul.

Henry Chapman Mercer
Technology, Aesthetics, and Arts and Crafts Ideals

David B. Driscoll

Recent scholarship on the arts and crafts movement has portrayed a diverse and multifaceted group of idealists, reformers, craftsmen, and entrepreneurs that defies easy categorization. Some participants in the movement have been described as overt reactionaries, others as harbingers of modernism. While some were primarily concerned with correcting societal ills, others were more interested in making a fast buck from a stylistic trend. In various degrees and combinations, participants in the movement addressed themselves to the alienation of industrial workers, to the perceived degradation of contemporary design, and to the economic and social inequities of the age. As a group, these men and women redefined the American stylistic vocabulary and established new social and economic roles for designers and craftspeople. One of these pioneers was Henry Chapman Mercer.

Mercer (1856–1930) was the founder and guiding force behind the Moravian Pottery and Tile Works in Doylestown, Pennsylvania, one of the longest-lived and most influential arts and crafts tile factories in America (fig. 1). Founded in 1898, the business flourished until Mercer's death and managed to survive in somewhat reduced circumstances until the mid 1950s. Production was revived in the mid 1970s, and the Moravian Pottery and Tile Works continues to produce Mercer's designs today.

Educated at Harvard under Charles Eliot Norton, cofounder of

Fig. 1. Moravian Pottery and Tile Works, Doylestown, Pa., ca. 1918. (Photo, Bucks County Historical Society.)

the Society of Arts and Crafts, Boston, and a friend of John Ruskin, Mercer received a solid grounding in archaeology, history, and art. This served him well throughout a diverse yet remarkably focused career. At various times during his life, Mercer was an archaeologist, historian, writer, collector, scholar, museum founder, folklorist, architect, businessman, and artist. He came late to ceramics, beginning the manufacture of tile when he was forty-two years old. Mercer's interest in ceramics grew out of his ethnographic study of local preindustrial crafts, including that of the Pennsylvania German potter. "Archaeology . . . turned me into a potter," he explained to one reporter.[1] Despite his circuitous arrival at tile making, Mercer's designs and methods of manufacture were a natural culmination of his aesthetic and historical vision.

Mercer is a compelling object of study because his life is so well documented. He was thoroughly versed in the English origins of the arts and crafts movement and wrote extensively, although not systematically, on topics of concern to it. In addition to his published writings

[1] Mercer is quoted in Rose C. Feld, "Unique Museum Links Antiquity to Our Day," *New York Times*, February 19, 1928. Linda Dyke, "Putting Mercer in Context: An Examination of the Contemporary Architectural and Intellectual Movements Which Shaped His Work and Thought" (Fonthill Museum, Doylestown, Pa., manuscript); the definitive biographical and artistic study of Mercer is Cleota Reed, *Henry Chapman Mercer and the Moravian Pottery and Tile Works* (Philadelphia: University of Pennsylvania Press, 1987). Henry C. Mercer, "Notes on the Moravian Pottery of Doylestown," *Bucks County Historical Society Papers* 4 (1917): 482.

and his personal correspondence, the business records, notebooks, design sketches, and equipment of the pottery survive largely intact. Thus, perhaps more so than for any contemporary potter, it is possible to gauge Mercer's rhetoric against his actual practice. An exploration of the interconnections between Mercer's aesthetic vision and the technology he developed to execute it will hopefully elucidate his practical resolution of the tensions—present to some degree in *all* craft work—between design and execution, machine and hand labor, and aesthetics and cost.

Mercer's career and character echo those of the arts and crafts movement's spiritual founder, William Morris. Both widely talented, complex, and sometimes contradictory men, they shared a deep faith in the importance of a beautiful environment and an aesthetic vision that integrated architecture, furniture, and decorative objects. Mercer's aesthetic critique of contemporary culture, however, never took on Morris's explicitly political focus; moreover, Mercer's preference for working alone, without collaborators or students, has limited his popular legacy. Nevertheless, like Morris, Mercer was able to balance his idealism with economic practicality and establish a successful and enduring craft enterprise.[2]

Toward the end of his career, Mercer summarized his goals in undertaking tile manufacture. "The Moravian Pottery was established in 1898 for the making by hand of tiles used in the decoration of pavements and walls. From then until now [1929] it has successfully maintained against all modern conditions of mass production and financial gain its principle that such tile have been and should be works of art and that a work of art never can be made by machinery."[3]

The key word in this statement of purpose is *art*. Although Mercer addressed a variety of concerns related to mechanization, work, and the role of the craftsman in his writings, he generally resolved any

[2] Peter Stansky, *Redesigning the World: William Morris, the 1880s, and the Arts and Crafts* (Princeton: Princeton University Press, 1985). On Morris's business organization, see Charles Harvey and John Press, "William Morris and the Making of Art," *Business History* 28, no. 4 (October 1986): 36–54.
[3] Henry Chapman Mercer (hereafter cited as HCM) for the Washington, D.C., Chapter of the Daughters of the American Revolution, 1929 Mercer Papers, Spruance Library of the Bucks County Historical Society, Doylestown, Pa. (hereafter cited as MPSL).

Fig. 2. American Clay Machinery Co. brick auger (*right*) and combination cutting table (*left*), 1903. (Photo, Jet Lowe for the Historic American Engineering Record, 1987.)

conflicts according to his aesthetic convictions. These convictions had a great deal to do with machines. In one interview he claimed that his tiles were "made in the same way that a less hurried civilization made them. You will hear no noise or see any machinery in the pottery works. You will find fifteen individuals working quietly as individuals."[4]

Actual practice did not bear this out. Despite the assertion, Mercer did not entirely exclude machines from his pottery. A steam engine powered the factory's clay mixers and pigment grinders, and steam from the boiler heated a tile-drying room. A variety of different presses and jigs were used in manufacture, and quarry tile cutters and plaster tile molds removed the responsibility for shaping the final product from individual workers. Clay mixing, the most arduous process at the pottery, was mechanized almost immediately (fig. 2). It was managed

[4]Feld, "Unique Museum."

Fig. 3. *Pressing Steel Plate,* tile mosaic from the floor of the Pennsylvania state capitol, Harrisburg, Pa., 1906. (Photo, Bucks County Historical Society.)

using horse power for the pottery's first five years and mechanically after the acquisition of a steam engine in 1903.[5]

His reservations about machinery and art aside, Mercer admired human ingenuity and its ability to devise new ways of doing things. His tile floor at the Pennsylvania capitol, which depicts the flora, fauna, and historical development of the state, includes mosaic images of blast furnaces, steel mills (fig. 3), locomotives, automobiles, linotype machines, and telephones. In some instances, Mercer even thought machine-made goods improved upon similar goods made by hand. He

[5]On the use of a steam engine, see David B. Driscoll, "The Moravian Pottery and Tile Works" (Report for the Historic American Engineering Record, Project HAER PA–107, March 1990); Frank K. Swain, manuscript notes for Henry C. Mercer's "Notes on the Moravian Pottery," 1917, Fonthill Manuscripts (hereafter cited as FM), ser. 19:4, MPSL.

wrote in 1920, "For a long time I have thought that the machine has more or less justly superseded all domestic arts and crafts which do not depend upon art for their reasonable existence and that for instance there is not enough art in a piece of homespun to enable handspinning and weaving to survive in an open market."[6]

Mercer's aversion to machines was clearly not absolute. Machines that eliminated drudgery and produced goods of no artistic ambition were perfectly acceptable to him. Nor did he object in principle to a system of manufacture based upon the productive capabilities of machines. Lewis Mumford, among others, has argued that the machine is not simply hardware or apparatus but is fundamentally a social system of organizing humans for work.[7] Having chosen his technology, Mercer carefully organized his own pottery for efficient production. In this sense, Mercer fully embraced "machinery." Rather than detesting machines, then, he delighted in handwork for other reasons.

As for Mercer's claim of "individuals working quietly as individuals" at the pottery, actual practice refutes this. In theory, Mercer endorsed the classic arts and crafts assertion that the designer and the producer of objects ought to be the same person. In 1918 he wrote, "I feel that in my work the design and the craft should go together and that the former should be produced in the first place with reference to the latter which does not happen where two persons are at work from different points of view . . . the final result could stand for neither the designer nor the potter."[8]

Mercer himself came close to living out the idealized vision of the independent designer/craftsman who personally controlled his work from idea to completion. In 1897 Mercer apprenticed himself briefly to a neighboring redware potter and hired another local potter to teach him use of materials and processes. He subsequently spent fourteen months on his own, experimenting with glaze recipes, firing techniques, and tile designs. Mercer sought advice when he needed it, most notably in obtaining one of his standard glaze recipes from another

[6]HCM to Jane Teller, ser. 29–30, April (?) 29–30, 1920, MPSL.
[7]Lewis Mumford, *The Myth of the Machine, Vol. I: Technics and Human Development* (New York: Harcourt, Brace, Jovanovich, 1967), p. 191; Langdon Winner, *Autonomous Technology* (Cambridge: MIT Press, 1977).
[8]HCM to Mr. Renwick, November 27, 1918, MPSL.

leading arts and crafts tile maker, William De Morgan, and in hiring
John Briddes, an English potter, to supervise construction and firing
of his first commercial kiln. In 1906 he explained, "By repeated trials
I discovered old colors and old glazes and invented new ones. All these
delicate shades and these rich colors that you see seated around are the
fruits of many attempts, but at last I have brought the art to the point
where I know exactly what I am doing and can do exactly that which
I want."[9]

Thus, like many other arts and crafts practitioners, Mercer first
taught himself the technical skills needed to execute the tiles he envisioned. Although he eventually relinquished most of the day-to-day
responsibility for production to his manager, Frank Swain, Mercer
reserved all of the pottery's design work for himself. His personal experiences as an archaeologist, scholar, and collector provided the design
inspiration for virtually all of the factory's output.[10]

Mercer understood, as Morris did, that allowing his workers complete control over their labor was an impractical business strategy. Mercer used unskilled or semiskilled laborers drawn from the farms surrounding Doylestown. The factory employed eighteen men at its peak,
averaging about a dozen through its first thirty-two years. Some employees, like Swain, worked at the pottery for many years and developed a
great deal of skill and experience; others worked seasonally or for brief
periods.

Like its larger and better-known contemporary, Rookwood Pottery
of Cincinnati, Ohio, the Moravian Pottery and Tile Works relied upon
a hierarchy of duties and a division of labor. Business records list at
least twelve different job titles at the pottery, ranging from "foreman,"
"modeler," and "burner" to the unspecific "maker." The pottery had
a sliding wage scale based on responsibilities and experience. These
job titles dispel the notion that each worker controlled his work from
beginning to end. The institution in 1911 of a quota system, establishing a standard day's output for quarry tile, further emphasized that the

[9]On Mercer's experiments and glazes, see Indian House Record of Experiments,
Moravian Pottery and Tile Works Records (hereafter cited as MPTW), ser. 10, vol. 2,
MPSL; Mercer, "Notes on the Moravian Pottery," p. 485; *Philadelphia North American*
6 (July 1906).
[10]For a detailed analysis of the sources for Mercer's designs, see Reed, *Henry Chapman Mercer*, pp. 89–166, 191–229.

pottery was a factory, not a guild of craftsmen. Despite a philosophical belief in the unity of designer and craftsman, Mercer employed wage labor at his pottery for the execution of his own artistic designs.[11]

Despite Mercer's assertion that "art" had nothing to do with financial gain, running the business on a sound and profitable economic basis was a fundamental concern of his from the outset. "My first effort therefore was to invent new methods of producing hand made tiles cheap enough to sell and artistic enough to rival the old ones. None of my friends and no architects have taken the slightest interest in the technical or practical value of any of these processes, upon which the success of my effort has depended from the start."[12]

The cost of labor was a critical issue for Mercer, one at odds with his explicit endorsement of hand methods. In fact, he sought ways to minimize the amount of hand labor that went into each tile. Using molds to create relief tiles rather than hand painting designs on flat tiles was one method. Another was the "staining" or smoking process he devised (fig. 4). Mercer also patented a technique for making tile mosaics, which resemble stained glass windows, by cutting shapes from large slabs of clay (see fig. 3).[13] A key component of this patent was the plaster mold, which allowed numerous copies of the same design to be pressed quickly and easily. In this method, large fields of color eliminated the need for hand painting, and the thick grout lines eliminated precise fitting.

Mercer's efforts at cost saving were successful. The pottery's account books show that the business lost money in only one month between its founding and Mercer's death. William H. Graves, a former partner in Grueby Faience Company, recognized the success of Mercer's business approach. "You have enjoyed a greater success than the others because you recognized the economic fact—which we didn't—

---

[11] On the division of labor, see Eileen Boris, *Art and Labor: Ruskin, Morris, and the Craftsman Ideal in America* (Philadelphia: Temple University Press, 1985), pp. 140–43. On job titles, see Sharon McGrath-Bernhard, "Henry Chapman Mercer, the Moravian Pottery and Tile Works, and the Work Ethic of the Arts and Crafts Movement" MPTW, May 26, 1989, typescript), p. 10. On the quota systems, see Frank K. Swain, annual report, 1911, FM, unbound ser. 19:7, MPSL.

[12] HCM to William Hagerman Graves, November 14, 1925, MPSL.

[13] Mercer received two patents for his tile mosaic technique: U.S. Patents 733,668 (July 14, 1903) and 763,064 (June 21, 1904).

Fig. 4. Moravian Pottery and Tile Works, *Tiles of the New World* panel, Doylestown, Pa., ca. 1912. H. 5′, W. 9′1″. (Photo, Jet Lowe for the Historic American Engineering Record, 1987.) Pressed from plaster molds, these tiles were fired using Mercer's smoking technique.

that the [labor intensive] methods were precluded in the United States on account of the high cost of labor."[14]

A commonly voiced strain in the arts and crafts movement's rejection of machine work was the belief that machine production degraded the worker. It is likely that Mercer shared this point of view. Throughout his career, he took a deep interest in traditional craft skills. Before taking up tile making, Mercer had assembled an ethnographic collection of preindustrial American hand tools that he exhibited under the title of "The Tools of the Nation Maker." The title's implication that the United States had been built by its laborers is clear. This conviction was reiterated in Mercer's guidebook to the Moravian tile floor of the capitol in Harrisburg. Describing the numerous mosaics of agricultural

[14]William Hagerman Graves to HCM, December 6, 1925, MPSL.

and craft workers, Mercer wrote, "It is the life of the people that is sought to be expressed; the building of a commonwealth economically great, by the individual work of thousands of hands, rather than by wars and legislatures." Yet Mercer was too much of an individualist to follow his incipient populism very far. Throughout his life, he insisted upon complete control of his work and felt that labor unions only served to challenge rightful authority and raise prices.[15]

Mercer's understanding of the degradation of labor under the factory system was founded in aesthetics rather than politics. In describing the factories he illustrated in the floor of the Pennsylvania capitol, he made more note of their offensive appearance than their often oppressive working environments: "Factories do not represent architecture of beauty for man or state. They offer a stern confusion of irregular roofs, windy galleries, soot-dimmed windows and smoky towers, black, gigantic, and significant, which rise against the sky above the modern city. They mark the dominance of machinery over human hand labor since 1820."[16] Thus, for Mercer, the triumph of machine labor was primarily an issue of art and design. To the extent that he did reject machines and embrace handwork, he did so for aesthetic reasons.

On numerous occasions, Mercer vehemently expressed his distaste for the aesthetic qualities of machine-made tiles. Describing the founding of the pottery, he explained that the dreadful state of contemporary tile design provided him a market niche: "The time was very opportune. One the one hand, owing to the reintroduction of fireplaces by modern architects into all the fine dwelling houses, a large demand for ornamental tiles had suddenly sprung up. On the other, the repulsive colors, decadent designs, mechanical surface and texture, and chilling white background of most of the tiles then on the market, had so thoroughly disgusted modern architects of taste, that many of them refused to ornament fireplaces with tiles, and built and faced the latter with plain

---

[15] Mercer is quoted in Henry C. Mercer, *Guidebook to the Tiled Pavement in the Capitol of Pennsylvania* (Harrisburg, 1908). "The Tools of the Nation Maker" exhibition became the core of the extensive collection of American craft technology now housed at the Bucks County Historical Society's Mercer Museum in Doylestown, Pa. On labor unions, see Reed, *Henry Chapman Mercer*, pp. 72–74; McGrath-Bernhard, "Henry Chapman Mercer," pp. 10–15.

[16] Mercer, *Guidebook* (rev. ed.; State College, Pa.: Pennsylvania Guild of Craftsmen, 1975), p. 42.

bricks." In his idiosyncratic 1916 history of American tile making, Mercer was more specific about the causes of such debased work:

Their defects arose, not because the designs were bad, or the color receipts radically different from those of the ancient potter, but because the tiles were the products of machines and not men . . . Bad public taste soon permitted mechanics equipped with air brushes and dust mills, patent bodies, frits, printing presses, stencils, englobes, etc., who appear never to have tried to copy the work of Delft or Spain or De Morgan, to flood the country with imitations of the most mechanical of the English . . . tiles.[17]

Of particular distaste to Mercer was Richard Prosser's dry-dust pressing process, invented in 1840 and standard in "art" tile manufactories at the end of the century. Mercer acknowledged that the technique was "destructive of shrinkage" but argued that it was "fatal to the beauty of tiles." Perhaps Mercer's definitive commentary on machines and art was given in a 1928 interview: "Machinery can't make art. It can make automobiles and radios and telephones, but it can't create art. Art needs the touch of a human hand, its failings as well as its skill. A tile should show the individuality of the potter. A machine has no individuality. It has efficiency. It can repeat itself numberless times. It will earn money for its owner. But art has nothing to do with money making schemes."[18]

Like many other arts and crafts practitioners, Mercer fell into the trap of using a terminology referring to motive power to analyze what was essentially an aesthetic issue. Of course, manufacturing technique and product appearance are closely related as Mercer himself recognized. "The art and technique of this craft are so closely interwoven, that to describe one without the other never gets us to the bottom of the subject."[19] What Mercer's writings fail to address, however, is the specific nature of the connection between technology and aesthetics. What was it, then, about the appearance of hand processes that Mercer particularly treasured, and how did he organize his production to achieve this visual quality?

[17] Mercer, "Notes on the Moravian Pottery," p. 483. Henry Chapman Mercer, "Notes on Decorated Mural and Pavement Tiles in the United States," *Faenza, Bollettino El Museo Internazionale Delle Ceramiche in Faenza* 4 (October–December 1916): 112–14.

[18] On dry-dust pressing, see HCM to Graves. Feld, "Unique Museum."

[19] HCM to Graves.

In his groundbreaking book *The Nature and Art of Workmanship*, David Pye developed a detailed terminology essential to discussions of the visual quality of craft objects. He begins by pointing out that a hand versus machine dichotomy is not only difficult to define clearly but is essentially irrelevant. At issue is not motive power but the intent of the design and the worker's degree of control. The regular, identical ceramics to which Mercer objected were produced by what Pye calls the "workmanship of certainty"—strictly controlled motions whose outcome, whether powered by a worker's hand or by a machine, is certain. In contrast, the varied and diverse wares Mercer prized were generally produced by the "workmanship of risk"—any manufacturing technique in which the worker can determine the outcome.[20] Where it would have little impact on the final appearance of the tile, Mercer was happy to employ the workmanship of certainty. His use of machines to mix clay is an example. In most other processes, however, especially those affecting the final appearance of his tiles, Mercer employed the workmanship of risk.

Virtually all Moravian tiles were shaped by the workmanship of certainty. Quarry tiles were cut from a slab of clay whose thickness had been established by a form, using sheet-metal cutters of a fixed pattern. The worker had no control over the size or shape of these tiles, nor could he control the shapes of the pottery's relief or "brocade" tiles, all of which were pressed from plaster molds (see fig. 4). Pressing tiles from stamp molds did require that a worker judge the tile's thickness, but again the mold, not the worker, determined the tile's design. It is instructive to compare Mercer's work to that of De Morgan. De Morgan's London business suffered when he moved to Italy for health reasons, so he developed an imaginative process: designs were hand painted onto bits of paper in Florence and then were shipped to England, where they were laid onto tiles and fired. These designs, although applied as decals, still allowed the painter a certain leeway in determining the tile's final appearance.[21] They also emphasized the need for skilled, and therefore more costly, laborers.

---

[20] David Pye, *The Nature and Art of Workmanship* (Cambridge, Eng.: Cambridge University Press, 1978), p. 24.

[21] For the technical distinction between "press" and "stamp" molds at the Moravian pottery, see Reed, *Henry Chapman Mercer*, pp. 57–63. On Mercer's relationship to De Morgan, see Reed, *Henry Chapman Mercer*, pp. 33, 42–43, 235–36. On De Morgan's work, see John Catleugh, *William De Morgan Tiles* (London: Trefoil, 1983).

At Mercer's pottery, once the tiles had been pressed, the workman-ship of risk became more common. Drying them could be hazardous; the placement of wareboards near stoves or the sun and the frequency of turning the tiles influenced their likelihood to warp, crack, and develop salt scumming. Glazes and slips were applied by dipping or pouring and were sometimes partially wiped away; the results varied with the individual worker and with the mix of each batch of materials. Perhaps the most difficult area to control was the firing. Atmospheric conditions, the moisture and setting of the ware, and the quality of the fuel all affected the course of the firing. In his kiln manual, Mercer discussed many of the potential problems and ways to prevent them. [22] Among the possible flaws mentioned were frosting, overfluxing, crack-ing, scumming, burning, and blotching.

Although the terms *workmanship of certainty* and *workmanship of risk* are useful for defining what Mercer meant by "hand made," they refer to technique only. As we have seen, Mercer was more interested in appearance than in process. Two other terms used by Pye help us understand the appearances Mercer sought in his tiles: "free workman-ship" and "regulated workmanship." According to Pye, in regulated workmanship "the achievement appears to correspond exactly to the idea," while in free workmanship there is some visual approximation between idea and execution. [23] Since in the right hands even the work-manship of risk can yield very regular and consistent results, it is clear that Mercer valued not the workmanship of risk per se but free work-manship. The approximate nature of free workmanship can produce objects with a pleasing diversity of shape, surface texture, or color, without destroying the overall intent of the design. Throughout his career, Mercer prized free over regulated work, precisely because it yielded a much broader range of effects and fostered an engaging rich-ness in tile installations.

In free workmanship, the relationship between design and execu-tion is central. A lack of precision is a serious flaw in a design that demands precision; it is no flaw where the design does not require it. The appropriateness and aesthetic success of Mercer's manufacturing techniques have much to do with the historical origins of his designs. Many were copied from coarsely cast and often weathered cast-iron

---

[22] Kiln manual, MPTW, ser. 9, vol. 12, MPSL.
[23] Pye, *Nature and Art*, p. 24.

stove plates (fig. 5), from centuries-old medieval tiles, and from a variety of objects Mercer collected in his travels.[24] Because his models were so often worn, damaged, or never intended as tile decoration, Mercer's designs were rarely very precise and hence lent themselves well to free workmanship. The Harrisburg mosaics, many of which were drawn from photographs, are less effective. In these there can be a dissonance between the scale and detail of the image and the necessarily approximate nature of the rendering.

In general, Mercer's own tile designs were simple, graphic, and stylized. They retained their overall effectiveness despite substantial variations among individual tiles. The Moravian tile floors of the Isabella Stewart Gardner Museum in Boston demonstrate Mercer's taste for diversity, tolerance for the sometimes unruly behavior of the clay, and aesthetic standards that embraced what others might see as flaws. Although undeniably attractive, the tiles are so warped and uneven that they would probably violate modern building safety codes.

It is worth noting that although a worker's judgement and dexterity had a major impact on the final appearance of a tile, there was very little actual risk involved. Mercer made allowances for the vagaries of the production process, and if a tile warped a bit in drying, if its edge was ragged from the tile cutter, or if its underglaze was blotchy, the tile was not necessarily discarded. Aside from breaking a tile during manufacture or ruining it in the kiln, workers had a relatively wide latitude in the precision of their work.

Mercer consciously developed production methods that would maximize the amount of free workmanship that could be used. Nevertheless, production at the pottery was by no means chaotic or laissez-faire. Despite the fact that many of the techniques were obsolete or intentionally "primitive" when he adopted them, Mercer melded these into a tightly controlled and integrated production system that maximized the aesthetic qualities he sought while efficiently controlling costs for labor and materials.

Three production areas in particular demonstrate how efficiency in production method could yield Mercer's characteristically variegated tiles. The first of these was smoking. Smoking, which Mercer called

[24] Reed, *Henry Chapman Mercer*, pp. 89–166, 191–229.

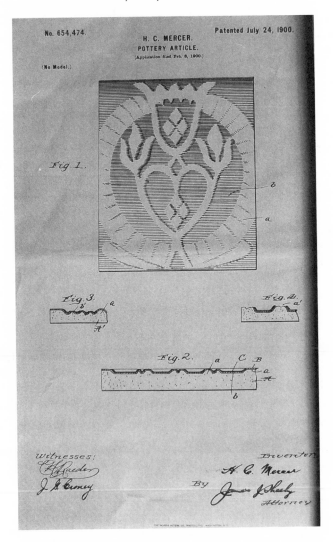

Fig. 5. Henry Chapman Mercer's U.S. Patent for underglaze, granted 1900. (Photo, Bucks County Historical Society.)

staining, was a technique in which green tiles were fired in a sagger with ground coal and sawdust. The tiles emerged in soft, mottled grays and blacks (see fig. 5). Using this technique, a wide range of finished tiles were produced in a single firing without using applied colorants. Smoking saved the cost of pigments, the labor in applying them, and the loading and unloading for multiple firings.

Mercer appears to have derived the smoking technique directly from his archaeological experience with unglazed, pit-fired Native American and African earthenware.[25] In such ware, flash and burn marks appear irregularly over the surface, producing a mottled effect. Mercer's achievement was in developing a technique that produced a similar primitive appearance within his regular production system. He did this by, in effect, reversing the traditional European use of saggers. Instead of using saggers exclusively to keep fly ash and other impurities away from the ware, Mercer used them to concentrate these impurities upon certain wares for decorative effect. With only slight modifications in loading the kilns, smoked tiles could be fired in the regular glaze kilns. Although the inspiration for this process was historical and aesthetic, Mercer developed it into a practical, inexpensive technique that yielded a product unlike anything his competitors were producing.

The diversity of Mercer's tile finishes and the economy of his production methods are also evident in the pottery's most characteristic finishes, the underglazes. Underglazes are an elaboration of a Pennsylvania German slipware technique in which red earthenware is decorated with white and colored slips and then covered with a clear glaze. In 1900 Mercer patented his own technique for applying slips, underglazes, and clear overglazes to relief tiles (see fig. 5). In the underglaze method, a red clay tile was dipped into a buff slip and allowed to dry. If desired, varying amounts of the slip could be scraped away. Next, the tile was dipped into a colored, matte underglaze, which was wiped off the raised portions of the tile, leaving the raised design a buff color and leaving colored underglaze in the recessed portions of the tile. When dried, the tiles were biscuit fired. Finally, a clear glaze was applied over the entire tile, and it was fired a second time. Because of the many layers of colorings, underglazed ware is unusually varied,

---

[25] A description of Mercer's experiments with the smoking technique appears in David Randall MacIver and C. Leonard Woolley, *Areika* (Philadelphia: University Museum, 1911), pp. 16–17.

often showing traces of the red clay body, the buff slip, the colored underglaze, and the clear overglaze. No two tiles prepared this way leave the kiln alike. None of Mercer's contemporaries used layers of colors in this way on their ware, and in a 1925 note in the margin of a book, Mercer himself wrote that this technique "made my fortune at the Pottery."[26]

The underglaze technique was not just an aesthetic success, however. By varying the combination of clay body color, slip thickness, underglaze color, and overglaze, Mercer was able to offer a great range of colors and finishes with a limited number of ingredients. He used, for example, two clear glazes, one essentially colorless and another, furnished by De Morgan, that contained a large quantity of red lead.[27] The yellowish De Morgan glaze dramatically altered the colors below it, changing blue to green, buff to orange, and so on. Thus, by adding a single glaze to his repertoire, Mercer effectively doubled the number of underglaze finishes he could offer. As in many other instances, Mercer managed to rationalize an aesthetically striking technique into a simple, inexpensive, and efficient system of production.

The most elaborate and important technical devices at the pottery were the five coal-fired kilns. The first was built in early 1899 by Briddes, who was hired for the job. Subsequent kilns were built by a local Doylestown mason following the original pattern. All the kilns at the pottery are bottle-shape, combination updraft/downdraft kilns. They are no doubt derived from English sources, possibly from the "Minton's oven" patented in 1873, but are small for industrial kilns and were probably obsolete by the turn of the century. The scarce industrial literature of the time tends to focus on much larger, more sophisticated designs, including continuous and tunnel kilns, while the arts and crafts literature deals with tiny, usually muffle, kilns more suitable for china painting.[28]

[26] In December 1925, Mercer wrote this comment about layers of color in his copy of R. L. Hobson, *Collection of English Pottery in the Department of British Medieval Antiquities and Ethnology of the British Museum* (London, 1903), which is quoted in Reed, *Henry Chapman Mercer*, p. 68. Mercer's technique for slips and glazes is documented in U.S. Patent 644,530 (February 27, 1900).

[27] Mercer, "Notes on the Moravian Pottery," p. 484.

[28] The discussion here of the loading and firing of the kilns is based upon Adam Zayas, "The Processes and Formulae of the Moravian Pottery and Tile Works as They Relate to Henry Chapman Mercer's Original Catalog Offerings," (MPTW, 1989, typescript). On Briddes, see Mercer, "Notes on the Moravian Pottery," p. 485. On sources,

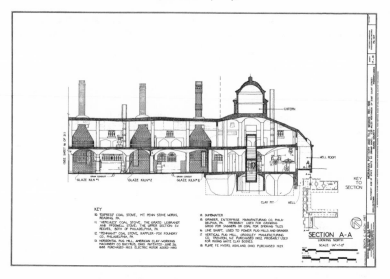

Fig. 6. Cross-section of the Moravian Pottery and Tile Works, Doylestown, Pa., showing the three glaze kilns and the clay mixing area (*first floor, right*). (Drawing, Benita C. Welch for the Historic American Engineering Record, 1987.)

Although the kilns Mercer chose would have been inadequate for producing large quantities of a single type of tile, they were well suited to his range of ware. The two larger kilns fired only unglazed work, while glazed, underglazed, smoked, and biscuit tiles were all fired together in the three smaller kilns (fig. 6). In these, each type of finish had its own set of optimal firing conditions, and each affected the firing conditions of the ware around it. Moreover, firing temperatures varied from place to place inside each kiln. The variables to be controlled in any given firing were considerable.

All ware was fired in saggers, which in the glaze kilns were set in six columns, or "bungs," stacked seven saggers high. Placement of

see Daniel Rhodes, *Kilns: Design, Construction, and Operation* (Radnor, Pa.: Chilton Book Co., 1968), pp. 51–52. Alfred Broadhead Searle, *The Ceramic Industries Pocket Book* (London, 1920) is an example of the technical literature, and Adelaide Alsop Robineau's periodical *Keramic Studio* is representative of the turn-of-the-century "artist's" literature.

individual saggers inside the kiln was critical. The colored glazes did best at high heat and so went in the top of the kiln. Of these, blues and yellows needed the most heat and were placed highest. Whites and browns went slightly lower, while greens could be placed as low as the fourth sagger. In contrast, the De Morgan clear glaze required low heat and was fired in the bottom three layers of saggers. The underglazed ware had a similar stratigraphy of optimal placement. The lowest three layers were also used for biscuit and smoked ware; the lower in the kiln smoked ware was fired, the blacker the result.

The overall proportion of ware inside the kiln was important as well. A kiln containing more than one-third smoked tiles tended to overflux clear glazes and burn the color out of underglazes. Another danger was "frosting," or the undesired appearance of a dry, matte finish on glazed tile. This happened if the overall proportion of biscuit ware in the kiln was too high or if a sagger of smoked tiles was placed immediately above or below a sagger of glazed tiles. Frosting could be prevented, however, by placing a sagger of plain biscuit ware between the glazed and smoked tiles or by moving the glazed ware to the adjacent bung.

Managing the kilns well was essential to the success of the business. Obtaining consistently good results from the pottery's kilns demanded considerable skill and experience as well as the ability to think in three dimensions. To maintain control over firing, specific employees had the responsibility for loading and firing. As important as skilled workers were to the successful operation of these kilns, the factory's product mix was also critical. Even if Mercer had desired it, his kilns would not have been capable of producing exclusively glazed, underglazed, or any other single type of tile. The smoked and underglazed tiles, in addition to their notable aesthetic merits, maximized the saleable yield from each firing by using the lower, cooler levels of the kilns. Similarly, because biscuit ware was useful in mitigating frosting and other firing problems, Mercer was wise to develop a line of tile— the underglazes—that made use of a biscuit firing. Mercer's thorough understanding of his kilns and materials and his ability to tailor his output to their idiosyncracies allowed him to both maximize the factory's output and execute the diverse and varied ware he prized.

Thus, rather than simply rejecting machines in favor of the handmade, the Moravian Pottery and Tile Works possessed a carefully chosen and developed technological system. Its primary features were low capital investment, relatively cheap operation, and the ability to produce a diverse range of wares, most of which were unique to the pottery.

The system of organization and manufacturing used at the pottery helps us in defining Mercer's personal arts and crafts vision. Despite both a romantic and a scholarly attachment to the past and a sympathy to arts and crafts reformist ideals, Mercer did not look to a medieval model of the social relations of production. His fundamental interest was in the visual and sensory variety of the built environment. He believed that hand production or, more precisely, free workmanship within the workmanship of risk was the best way to achieve this variety but did not object to labor-saving machinery in areas of production that did not affect the final appearance of the tile. Indeed, Mercer consciously sought to rationalize and economize his manufacturing system in ways that did not impinge on the aesthetic integrity of his product. Mercer's tight control over process and attention to the economic impact of his technical decisions were instrumental in both the artistic and long financial success of the Moravian Pottery and Tile Works.

Cornelius Kelley of Deerfield, Massachusetts

The Impact of Change on a Rural Blacksmith

Ellen M. Snyder-Grenier

Late nineteenth-century technological innovation brought about massive changes in America. Among them was the transformation of traditional trades. In Deerfield, Massachusetts, Cornelius Mahoney Kelley's work as a blacksmith offers an example of how this modernization affected one particular tradesman. Trained to shoe horses and fix farm equipment, Kelley was faced with overwhelming circumstances when the decline of farming and the rise of the automobile in the early

The author began work on this paper, which was supported by a grant from the Elizabeth Fuller Fellowship Fund, as a fellow in the Historic Deerfield Summer Fellowship Program in American History in 1980. She gratefully acknowledges the assistance of Donald Friary; J. Ritchie Garrison; Thomas Michie; Norma Woods; David Proper; Timothy C. Neumann; Suzanne Flynt; Louise Perrin; Catherine Zusy, whose research on Deerfield's arts and crafts community was extremely helpful; Kenneth L. Ames; and Alan Crawford. This study would not have been possible without the help of those who knew Kelley. In particular, the author thanks Richard W. Hatch, Mr. and Mrs. Alec Ciesluk, Frank Ciesluk, Mr. and Mrs. John Comins, Mrs. Scott Keith, Mrs. Thomas Herlihy, James Cleary, Harriet Harris, Mrs. Richard Arms, Sr., Mrs. Herbert Marsh, Raymond Keyes, Betty Boyden, Mrs. S. W. Childs, Mrs. Mark Crean, Mrs. Ritchie Whitney, Mrs. Philip Ball, Mr. and Mrs. Donald Sullivan, Nathan Tufts, Mrs. J. Douglass Abercrombie, Mrs. Franklin Thorne, Mrs. Sheldon Howe, Mr. and Mrs. Richard Wilby, and Mr. and Mrs. Emmet Cooke.

twentieth century forced him to make a choice: adapt his traditional livelihood or perish as a blacksmith.

With the flourishing arts and crafts activity in turn-of-the-century Deerfield as his backdrop, Kelley chose to redirect his talents. "By the twenties there wasn't a horse in the place," noted Kelley's friend and former Deerfield resident Richard Hatch. "It's my opinion that he was one of those smart blacksmiths who saw the handwriting on the wall. He beat the game . . . before all the horses were gone he was building up his business in wrought iron."[1] From a sporadic participation in Deerfield's arts and crafts scene, Kelley became a full-time craftsman producing colonial revival ornamental ironwork.

For Kelley, the arts and crafts movement presented, more than anything else, a job opportunity in the face of economic change. While his situation—and reaction—were hardly unique, they underscore the fact that participants in America's arts and crafts movement were motivated by a variety of reasons.[2] Kelley's transition, the style his work took, and his place in community memory add a note of complexity to the type of story sometimes simplified in arts and crafts scholarship.

Born in 1874 in Glanworth, County Cork, Ireland, "Con" Kelley was described by a friend as "a child of rural Irish poverty." Fifteen when he arrived in America, he was part of a great, second wave of Irish immigrants that entered the United States between 1860 and 1900. By 1890 he was living in Greenfield, a small business and manufacturing town in western Massachusetts particularly known for its manufacture of cutlery and home to a sizeable Irish population.[3]

[1] Richard Hatch, interview with author, Orleans, Mass., July 1980.

[2] For a concise overview of the arts and crafts movement, see Cheryl A. Robertson, "The Arts and Crafts Movement in America," in *Decorative Arts and Household Furnishings in America, 1650–1920: An Annotated Bibliography*, ed. Kenneth L. Ames and Gerald W. R. Ward (Winterthur, Del.: Henry Francis du Pont Winterthur Museum, 1989), pp. 343–47. For information on the arts and crafts in Deerfield, see Margery Burnham Howe, *Deerfield Embroidery: Traditional Patterns from Colonial Massachusetts* (New York: Charles Scribner's Sons, 1976); Catherine Zusy, " 'Against Overwork and Sweating, Against the Apotheosis of Cheap and Shoddy': Als ik Kan, The Arts and Crafts Movement in Deerfield, 1896–1941" (Pocumtuck Valley Memorial Association Library, Deerfield, Mass. [hereafter cited as PVMA Library], 1981, typescript).

[3] Richard Warren Hatch to Mollie Wells, May 21, 1960, Pocumtuck Valley Memorial Association Museum, Deerfield, Mass. (hereafter cited as PVMA Museum); *Greenfield Marriage Ledger, 1892–1913*, #102, Court Clerk's Office, Greenfield, Mass.; United States Bureau of the Census, 12th census of the United States, Franklin County, Mass., 1900. Paul Jenkins, *The Conservative Rebel: A Social History of Greenfield, Massachusetts* (Greenfield: By the town, 1982).

Kelley initially trained with others, first apprenticing for a carriage, wagon, and sleigh maker, and then working for a blacksmith. By 1897 he was operating on his own. In 1899 his mother, Margaret, came to live with him, and in June 1899, he married Ellen (Nellie) Josephine Connole, a twenty-three-year-old table- and housemaid from County Clare, Ireland. The following year the Kelleys moved several miles south to the village of Deerfield, which was smaller and more rural than Greenfield.[4] A photograph taken about this time depicts Kelley as a serious young man (fig. 1).

While Kelley is listed in the 1900 census as being unemployed, it was not long before he found work as a general blacksmith. Written in a small, neat hand, the entries in his earliest extant account book, from 1902, show such tasks as "debit Charles Ashley for shoeing two horses, $2.50"; "for setting wagon tire $.75"; "debit Theodore Childs $.25 to hammer strap on cart"; "mend chains, $.20."[5]

By the time Kelley was establishing his blacksmithing trade, two newcomers, Margaret Whiting and Ellen Miller, had begun to lay the groundwork for Deerfield's participation in the arts and crafts movement. Well-to-do and well educated, these two New Englanders had moved into stately old homes along the main thoroughfare, the village "Street," near Deerfield's center, in 1893. They were part of the changing face of the town's population. A decline in commercial agriculture after the Civil War coupled with the financial panic of 1873 had hurt Deerfield farmers. Many were forced to sell their farmhouses along the Street. In their place came summer residents, drawn by Deerfield's rural beauty but little interested in actual farming.[6]

Intrigued by examples of American colonial crewel embroidery

---

[4]*Greenfield Directory* (Worcester, Mass.: Fitzgerald Publishers, 1891); *Greenfield Directory, Volume III* (Boston: W. E. Shaw, 1899); *Greenfield Directory, Volume I* (Boston: W. E. Shaw, 1895–96); *Greenfield Directory, Volume II* (Boston: W. E. Shaw, 1897); *Greenfield Marriage Ledger, 1892–1913*. Deerfield's population in 1900 was 1,969, versus Greenfield's 7,927 (*Vital Records of Deerfield and Greenfield* [Boston, 1920]).

[5]12th census of the United States, Franklin County, Mass., 1900. Cornelius Mahoney Kelley account book, 1902–16, PVMA Library. There are five account books in the collection, ranging in date from 1902 to 1945. There is a gap from August 1916 to September 1922, which can be explained in part by Kelley's tenure in Pittsburgh from 1916 to 1917.

[6]Howe, *Deerfield Embroidery*, pp. 15, 18–20; J. Ritchie Garrison, "Farming in Deerfield," *Antiques* 127, no. 3 (March 1985): 691–92.

they had found in the local historical society, Memorial Hall Museum, Whiting and Miller decided to replicate the old pieces. They soon found there was interest in purchasing their reproductions. The two decided to adapt to Deerfield arts and crafts spokesman John Ruskin's vision of workers producing honest articles within a utopian society without machines and smoking factory chimneys. Whiting later wrote that "the notion came that a society for the reproduction of these designs should be founded, a society whose work should be honest in every detail, produced for the love of good work, and carried on for the mutual advantage of all its members."[7] In 1898 they created the Deerfield Society of Blue and White Needlework.

Within a year of the founding of the society, neighbors, almost all women, began to produce other crafts such as baskets, woven rugs, and silver and copper work. These craftspeople eventually formed a separate group, the Society of Deerfield Industries. Their constitution, compiled in 1915, regulated that they maintain "a standard of excellence of design and integrity of workmanship" and prohibited copying commercial designs.[8] Crafts were sold out of members' homes and at a yearly sale held in the summer.

According to author Margery Burnham Howe, who conducted numerous interviews with Whiting, it was Whiting who first approached Kelley about joining the Society of Deerfield Industries. Howe recalls Whiting saying, "I bullied him into making andirons and they brought him so many orders that as blacksmithing stopped he became a prosperous wrought iron worker."[9]

At the annual summer exhibition in 1901, Kelley displayed a lantern (fig. 2) and the hardware on a reproduction Hadley-type chest (fig. 3) in the Village Room of the Martha Gould Pratt Memorial Building, a newly built community structure located along the Street. "In previous exhibitions [Cornelius Kelley] has had some excellent examples of wrought iron-work," noted a 1902 issue of *Handicraft*, a journal published by the Society of Arts and Crafts, Boston, "but his

[7]On interest in the replication, see Howe, *Deerfield Embroidery*, pp. 15, 18–20. Whitney is quoted in Howe, *Deerfield Embroidery*, p. 20; Margery Burnham Howe, "Deerfield Industries" (PVMA Library, 1977, typescript), p. 5.

[8]Constitution of the Society of Deerfield Industries, 1915, PVMA Library.

[9]Howe, *Deerfield Embroidery*, p. 28.

Fig. 1. Cornelius Mahoney Kelley, ca. 1900.
Photograph with charcoal and chalk accents.
(Pocumtuck Valley Memorial Association, Me-
morial Hall Museum, Deerfield, Mass.)

occupation with more routine activities had this year obliged him to
suspend for the time-being his efforts in that direction," thereby con-
fining his work to the "well-shaped hinges" made for the chest, and
the wrought-iron lantern.[10]

The oak and pine chest referenced by *Handicraft* was made by a
local Deerfield doctor, Edwin C. Thorn, and a farmer, Caleb Allen. It
was patterned after a seventeenth-century chest exhibited in Deerfield's
Memorial Hall Museum. "The bride's chest of oak and soft wood . . .
with old iron hinges matched by the village blacksmith [Kelley] with
iron draw-handles and key-plate, occupies the place of honor in front

[10] *Handicraft* 1, no. 7 (October 1902): 153.

Fig. 2. Cornelius Mahoney Kelley, lantern, 1901. (Pocumtuck Valley Memorial Association Library, Deerfield,
Mass.: Photo, Frances Allen and Mary Allen.)

of the chimney" (fig. 4), noted the *Springfield Daily Republican* in its
review of the exhibition. "It is a beautiful specimen of true craft, made
in the same spirit of honest thoroughness that belonged to the makers
of the [original seventeenth-century] chest." The *Daily Republican* also
described the lantern, calling it "boldly simple in form, without ornament, but so well proportioned and excellently true in workmanship
that it is truly satisfactory to the eye."[11]

[11]"In and about Springfield," *Springfield Daily Republican*, 1901, PVMA Library.

Fig. 3. Edwin C. Thorn, Caleb Allen, and Cornelius Mahoney Kelley, chest, 1901. Oak, pine, wrought iron; H. 36″, W. 47″, D. 20″. (Historic Deerfield: Photo, Amanda Merullo.)

The exhibition was extremely successful. The 1902 issue of *Handicraft* noted that as a result of the display, Deerfield's fame had "spread all over the land," and that "orders for work of all the various kinds have come in great number from many parts of the country." It observed that "several orders for copies of the bridal chest have been given, one coming from England."[12]

Given that Deerfield was already a mecca for summer residents, tourists, and history lovers drawn to its peaceful surroundings and its authentic colonial relics (as well as a destination for parents visiting sons attending the local, private boys school, Deerfield Academy), it is hardly surprising that the craft group quickly gained a national reputation, with invitations to exhibit wares or send goods on consignment

[12] *Handicraft* 1, no. 7 (October 1902): 153–54.

Fig. 4. Arts and crafts exhibition, Village Room, Martha Gould Pratt Building, Deerfield, Mass., 1901. (Pocumtuck Valley Memorial Association Library, Deerfield, Mass.: Photo, Frances Allen and Mary Allen.)

coming from arts and crafts organizations in Philadelphia, Providence, Salt Lake City, and elsewhere.[13] Tourism to the area itself was also given a boost when the Greenfield-Northampton trolley line was laid through Deerfield in 1903.

In 1904 the Kelleys moved from their rented quarters into a small cottage they had bought on Academy Lane (now known as Memorial Street) from Maria J. and Marion F. Kennedy, themselves Irish immigrants. The distance from the Street was short but symbolic and emphasizes the reality that while Kelley participated in the arts and crafts societies founded by residents of that prestigious avenue, his private life revolved around a different community. Across Academy Lane from him was a Polish farmer and his wife, who became his friends. On

[13] Correspondence, Society of Deerfield Industries, 1903–16, PVMA Library.

Sundays he went to Mass at Saint James Church in South Deerfield—home to a sizeable Irish and Polish immigrant population—and not to the Protestant services in Deerfield's White Church.[14]

In 1905 the *Springfield Daily Republican* reported that "Cornelius Kelley exhibits some superior forge work, finely finished . . . a pair of andirons among them as good art as one could wish to see." But Kelley continued to participate only sporadically through the 1910s as he continued to devote most of his time to shoeing horses and general jobbing. All this abruptly changed in 1916. Kelley and his wife (his mother had died in 1914) left Deerfield when he accepted a teaching position in the School of Applied Industries at Carnegie Institute of Technology in Pittsburgh, Pennsylvania. According to one Deerfield resident, he was invited by school founder Andrew Carnegie himself, who had visited Deerfield one summer and was impressed by Kelley's work. Kelley assumed the title of "Assistant Instructor in Forge Shop," where he taught students such skills as making fires and tools; simple welding; how to determine wrought iron, low carbon and high carbon steel; forging; and a wide variety of other tasks.[15]

In what may remain a mystery, Kelley stayed at the school only two years before returning to Deerfield. Why the sudden departure? Locals had varying opinions: Ellen Kelley was shy and homesick; the couple missed the country; they wanted to be near the gravesite of an infant son, buried in Greenfield. Local farmer and neighbor Alec Ciesluk quoted Kelley as saying that he would "rather be out in the shop, pounding away," than closed in, teaching.[16]

---

[14]Most Irish in Deerfield in 1900 lived outside the village in South Deerfield; see Barbara A. Curran, "A Community Within: Irish and Irish Americans in Deerfield, ca. 1900" (PVMA Library, 1988, manuscript), p. 13.

[15]*Springfield Daily Republican*, 1905, PVMA Library. *Annual Report of the·Town Officers of Deerfield for the Year Ending January 1st, 1915* (Deerfield, Mass.: E. A. Hall, 1915), p. 58; "The Society of Deerfield Industries, Deerfield, Massachusetts, 1915," circular, PVMA Library; Mrs. Thomas Herlihy, interview with author, Deerfield, July 1980. *Carnegie Institute of Technology Directory for 1916–1917*, p. 8, University Archives, Hunt Library, Carnegie-Mellon University, Pittsburgh, Pa. *Carnegie Institute of Technology School of Applied Industries General Catalog for 1917–1918 with Announcements for 1918–1919*, p. 48, University Archives, Hunt Library, Carnegie-Mellon University, Pittsburgh, Pa.

[16]Margery Burnham Howe, telephone interview with author, July 1980; Hatch to Wells; Herlihy interview; Alec Ciesluk, interview with author, Deerfield, Mass., July 1980.

Within five years after his return, Kelley made an almost complete transition to ornamental ironwork. While it is possible that the change was at least in part inspired by the Pittsburgh years, more centrally at play were the decline of the horse and the rise of the automobile. Additionally, according to Ciesluk, Kelley had been kicked by a horse, making it difficult for him to handle the large animals. The change is reflected in Kelley's business papers: instead of the invoices of his earliest days—plain or simply ornamented with a workhorse—invoices and business cards of the 1920s and 1930s represent him as an "ornamental" ironworker. The words *hand* and *handmade*, no doubt references to the arts and crafts movement's emphasis on the superiority of handcrafts, figure prominently. His record books from the early 1920s are almost completely filled with orders for ornamental work alone: items such as candlesticks, fireplace tools such as pokers and tongs; bridge lamps; sconces; coat racks; candle rush holders; jointed sconces; andirons; and kettle stands. Traditional colonial forms, rush holders and kettle stands, are listed alongside more contemporary forms such as magazine racks and fern stands. Prices penciled into Kelley's account book give a sense of his fees: March 1924, one pair braided bridge lamps, $36.00; jointed sconces, four for $10.00; September 1922, tongs and poker, $6.00; July 1924, lantern, $3.00; December 1927, smoking stand, $10.00.[17]

Kelley was now a full-time ornamental ironworker. His shift points up the difference in the motivations and experiences of Deerfield arts and crafts movement participants. At one end of the spectrum were people like Whiting and Miller. For them the movement was in many ways what historian T.J. Jackson Lears characterizes as a "revivifying hobby for the affluent" instead of "an alternative to alienated labor."[18] Whiting's motives were probably much less inspired by ideas about workers than by a desire to capitalize on an enjoyable pastime. Kelley was at the other end of the spectrum. For him, the arts and crafts movement developed a market that enabled him to continue to earn a living as a blacksmith, to retain his basic identity even as his product

[17] Ciesluk interview; Kelley account book, 1925–27, PVMA Library; the prices are from his "Record" book, pp. 6, 29, 35, 115.
[18] T. J. Jackson Lears, *No Place of Grace: Antimodernism and the Transformation of American Culture, 1880–1920* (New York: Pantheon Books, 1981), p. 93.

changed. There were other differences as well. In addition to the fact that this was a job and not a hobby for Kelley, he was Catholic and Irish in a largely Protestant New England town and male in a female-dominated craft industry.

Clearly, the way Kelley tied into the arts and crafts movement was through the objects he made, items that were predominantly colonial revival in style. Deerfield's arts and crafts leaders had consciously used the colonial past for design sources. Behind their principle of handicraft was a longing for old standards of craftsmanship and integrity then thought to be embodied in things colonial. "Although Mr. Kelly has frequently wrought according to his own design," noted the *Deerfield Scroll* (a student newspaper at Deerfield Academy) in November 1928, "he is primarily concerned with copying to quite some extent the productions of early colonial America. These designs he has not only found in books and museum specimens, but many of his customers have themselves brought him old pieces of iron work, candle molds, candlesticks, and andirons, from which he has constructed many beautiful copies." Kelley's friend Richard Hatch believed that Albert H. Sonn's 1928 exhaustive compilation of drawings of seventeenth-, eighteenth-, and nineteenth-century ironwork from the eastern United States, *Early American Wrought Iron*, had particularly influenced Kelley.[19]

Kelley was good at duplicating old pieces. He was, however, also adept at uniting the colonial with the contemporary to satisfy the needs of a modern audience. In one instance he combined a colonial candlestand with a 1920s bridge lamp (fig. 5). Kelley forged together three legs to create a support for a single, upright, vertical rod, a major element of a colonial American floor candlestand.[20] He used colonial-inspired hearts as decoration (the configuration bears close resemblance to a 1714 weathervane from Mulberry Castle, Oakley, South Carolina, illustrated by Sonn). But instead of a horizontal yoke to hold two cups for candles, he created the neck of a modern electrified lamp.

A combination candlestand/smoking stand (fig. 6) is another example of Kelley's innovation. There are allusions to an American colonial candlestand: the base, the upright vertical, an iron cup similar in

[19] *Deerfield Scroll*, November 3, 1928. Hatch to Wells.
[20] Henry J. Kaufman, *Early American Ironware Cast and Wrought* (Rutland, Vt.: Charles E. Tuttle Co., 1966), p. 65.

Fig. 5. Cornelius Mahoney Kelley, electric bridge lamp, ca. 1930. Wrought iron with electrical fittings; H. 60⅞". (Historic Deerfield: Photo, Robert J. Bitondi.) Each foot is marked "K," the only record of Kelley's use of a mark.

form to those seen on horizontal yokes with two cups (although the cup is iron, not brass, and its drip dish is smaller than colonial prototypes). But the holder for matches and an ash tray are twentieth-century elements, reflecting the vogue that came in at the turn of the century. Somehow, it still manages to look old.

A conversation with one-time Deerfield postmaster John Comins led me to believe that Kelley saw the irony in fabricating eighteenth-

Fig. 6. Cornelius Mahoney Kelley, candlestick/smoking stand, ca. 1930. Wrought iron; H. 39⅝″. (Historic Deerfield: Photo, Robert J. Bitondi.)

century types in the twentieth century. Comins related how Kelley once told him that a woman walked into his shop, commenting that she couldn't understand how Kelley could have so many old things. "Con laughed," said Comins, and told her that he never made anything "less than 150 years old."[21]

One of the real ironies of Kelley's participation as a revivalist is

[21] John Comins, interview with author, Deerfield, Mass., July 1980.

that the colonial revival was in many ways a reaction against mass European immigration at the end of the nineteenth century (of which Kelley was a part), a reaction grounded in anxiety and fear of foreigners. The press coverage of Deerfield's arts and crafts that extolled the old and the American aspects actually ignored participants like Kelley, a relative newcomer, choosing instead to honor a mythic return to pioneer roots. "These people are not following blindly some new or foreign craft," noted an article in *New Ideas Woman's Magazine*. "They are taking up again the handiwork of their Colonial ancestors, following closely the spirit, methods and beautiful craftsmanship of the days before the war." As Florence Griswold summed it up in the 1912 *Independent*, "These people have simply *returned* to their original crafts."[22]

Kelley's work with the Society of Deerfield Industries continued into the late 1920s and 1930s. His forge continued to draw customers, some of whom made small drawings on index and business cards of items they wanted to order. The writing in Kelley's account books in different hands suggests that patrons often placed orders directly into the books. Such an entry is one for September 1928, where a visitor records an order for "one blacked copper lantern fitted for an electric light (like the one on display) and a black bracket to hold it for Dr. Robert J. Joplin/Mass. General Hospital/Boston, Mass." Customers came from near and far: "The ash tray was swell," wrote Irvin D. Foos of Washington, D.C. "The visit to your shop was a bright stop on our trip." In another letter, tucked inside one of Kelley's account books, a customer from Detroit writes in 1933 that "you may recall that Mrs. Meginnity and I called on you on Sunday morning, November 5th and ordered some andirons to be made up by you and also an ash tray with a twisted pedestal and a hearth set also with the twisted effect." Kelley became so well known for his skill that the *Deerfield Scroll* wrote that he "has to turn away many more orders than he now fills. . . . Samples of his work are all over this country as well as in India, Japan, and Egypt."[23]

[22] Mary Emily Curtis, "The Crafts of Deerfield," *New Ideas Woman's Magazine* [ca. 1910]: 19; Florence K. Griswold, "Home Industries in Old Deerfield," *Independent*, November 7, 1912.
[23] Irvin D. Foos to Cornelius Kelley, November 15, 1941, PVMA Library; Robert Meginnity to Cornelius Kelley, November 24, 1933, PVMA Library; Kelley account book, 1928–37, PVMA Library. *Deerfield Scroll*, November 3, 1928, p. 4.

While the end date for the arts and crafts movement in America has been put at World War I, Deerfield's groups were active well beyond that time. The Society of Blue and White Needlework did not disband until 1926. The Society of Deerfield Industries continued to operate into the early 1940s, with some lapses. In June 1939 the group met and noted that "after a lapse of five years interest has been revived in the Society of Deerfield Industries."[24] There are scattered references to their existence as late as 1944, but their activities had drastically dwindled. Kelley's accounts show that he continued to make ornamental ironwork into the late 1930s, but entries were becoming sparse. By the early 1940s, in place of orders for ornamental pieces, there are occasional orders for small repairs, such as fixing a mower.

Kelley's career had come full circle. But this time, there was no outlet. By the 1940s he was in his late sixties. According to Hatch, he suffered from an illness that robbed him of the necessary motor control for his work. Ciesluk recalls that with the onset of World War II Kelley could no longer obtain the high-grade quality of iron he needed.[25] And the crowds of tourists were gone. The last entry in Kelley's account book is for August 1942.

In Kelley's later years, Ciesluk remembers seeing the former blacksmith sitting on his porch each evening in "his easy chair, reading his paper. The farmers would be coming home, but there Mr. Kelley would always be." Times were hard. In 1952 Kelley and his wife had to grant their property to the town in return for old-age assistance.[26] In 1954 Kelley died, followed six years later by his wife.

Kelley's work survives today. His memory also lives on, often intertwined with the objects he created. As I visited with people who had known him, many showed me ironwork they had bought or received from the blacksmith. A fire fork evoked the story of how Kelley gave it as a wedding gift. A lamp with a twisted base appeared, and I would hear about the Kelley weave, a technique that involved forging together four pencil-thin pieces of iron. "He could braid iron," recalled Kelley's godson, James Cleary, of Greenfield, a proud owner of a Kelley lamp;

---

[24] Society of Deerfield Industries records, 1915–34, PVMA Library.
[25] Ciesluk interview.
[26] Ciesluk interview. On old-age assistance, see Historic Deerfield, Deerfield Home Lot file (compiled by Amelia F. Miller), Historic Deerfield Library.

"He could braid it like braiding hair." This four-ply braid (see fig. 5) was the blacksmith's signature design. The 1928 *Deerfield Scroll* referred to it as "the famous Kelley weave, a very intricate but beautiful four ply braiding." Hatch took great pride in the fact that, as he told me, he was the only person with whom Kelley had shared the technique. At the same time, Hatch realized that the method could be learned by another blacksmith. "Nothing is a secret that can be taken apart," he reflected.[27]

Above all, for most of those who remembered Kelley, he seems to have symbolized a simpler time. At the turn of the century he had made a living creating objects in the colonial revival style—old ironwork thought to represent a simpler, better time. Eighty years later, Kelley himself became a symbol of an earlier age and the appealing simplicity of old-time craftsmanship. Issues of gender, religion, and economics (the differences between Kelley and Deerfield's arts and crafts founders) almost never came up. Kelley became the simple, talented, honest craftsman so venerated by the arts and crafts movement. In a sense, people's reaction to Kelley in the 1980s was a reaction to modernism, in the same way the arts and crafts movement was in 1900. As Cleary put it, these recollections of Kelley were "nice memories . . . of course this was before computerization and mass production."[28] Their memories honored Kelley but overlooked the complex nature of his life and his work.

Kelley's story was complex. He was an active part of Deerfield's arts and crafts societies, which benefited from his participation. But for him, the movement was more of a job opportunity than an ideology or a principle. His particular artistry was born out of the dynamic relationship among changing times, economics, personal choice, and talent. And while the arts and crafts movement had endeavored to reinterpret traditional definitions to give crafts the same dignity as fine arts, Kelley, to the minds of his customers and probably himself, walked the line between artist and craftsman. Perhaps the person who most eloquently addressed the dichotomy was Kelley's friend Hatch. I asked him about Kelley as an artist, and he laughed. "I think he would have

[27] James Cleary, telephone interview with author, July 1980. *Deerfield Scroll*, November 3, 1928, p. 4. Hatch interview.
[28] Cleary interview.

chuckled if you had called him an artist," he explained. "I don't think that's the kind of word he would have wanted. He couldn't pose. Artists always get a touch of the 'poseur' sooner or later. Instead, call him a master craftsman, an extraordinarily talented individual with a reputation for excellence."[29]

[29] Hatch interview.

The Grammar of Nature
Arts and Crafts China Painting

Ellen Paul Denker

Most students of late nineteenth-century American decorative arts know the charming story of how the ladies of Cincinnati were inspired to pursue ceramic art by a set of china paints brought to art class by teacher Benn Pitman and by the foreign ceramic exhibits they saw at the Philadelphia Centennial International Exhibition of 1876. Eventually, this new interest in ceramics led one of Cincinnati's ladies to create Rookwood Pottery, which became an internationally recognized art industry that preceded the establishment of arts and crafts potteries in many of America's major cities. The art of china painting, however, was not left behind during the years that these potteries flourished. Indeed, far more women were involved in the practice of this venerable skill as artists, teachers, and amateurs than were ever employed by the art potteries. Did they see themselves as artists, decorators, amateurs, or professionals? What criteria did they use to define their art? How were they trained? Which models did they hold in esteem? And finally, what happened to the movement after 1910? The answers to some of these questions can be found in the numerous instruction manuals and periodicals for china painters that defined the art, explained the craft, provided design sources, reported on exhibitions, and editorialized on

The author is grateful to the staff of the Winterthur library for all the cheerful assistance they have rendered and to Kenneth R. Trapp, Regina Blaszczyk, Nina Walls, and Paul Staiti for reading early drafts. Some of the research for this paper was supported by a Forman Fellowship from Winterthur.

the state of the art between 1870 and 1920. Further insight may also
be gained from exploring the biographies of many china painters. What
emerges is a complex picture of women who drew on the standard
nomenclature and techniques of the fine arts but developed a wholly
separate category of creative expression that involved knowledge of design history, the natural world, psychology, and geometry.[1]

Before examining these instructional manuals and periodicals,
some definitions and explanations are in order. The amateur interest in china painting, described popularly as "the ceramic mania,"
derived from two issues that concerned women of the middle and upper
classes: first, the use of watercolor and oil painting by these women
as an artistic pastime or as a source of income, and, second, the
necessity for fashionable women to know ceramic history in order
to choose proper tablewares and decorate their homes during a period
that valued the revival of past styles.[2] For the most part, women who
took up china painting were not expecting to work as decorators in
china factories where mundane tasks such as applying transfer prints
or filling in colors on the prints were generally performed by working-class women.

Many china painters, noted one periodical, were "attracted to
the art because of the wondrous store of historical information with
which the slightest investigation of ceramics must be associated"
(fig. 1). China painting became fashionable during the third quarter of the nineteenth century, first in Europe and England and later
in America among genteel women who were seeking an artistic
outlet that was perceived as more stylish than needlework. In addition, women of the same class, but facing limited income, were also

[1] For more information on the women's art movement in Cincinnati, see *The Ladies, God Bless 'Em: The Women's Art Movement in Cincinnati in the Nineteenth Century* (Cincinnati: Cincinnati Art Museum, 1976); and Kenneth R. Trapp, "Toward a Correct Taste: Women and the Rise of the Design Reform Movement in Cincinnati, 1874–1880," in *Celebrate Cincinnati Art: In Honor of the One Hundredth Anniversary of the Cincinnati Art Museum, 1881–1981*, ed. Kenneth R. Trapp (Cincinnati: Cincinnati Art Museum, 1982), pp. 48–70. Estimates of the total number of china painters in the United States alone during the 1890s range between 4,500 ("White China for Amateurs," *Crockery and Glass Journal* [May 17, 1895]) and 25,000 (Jeanne M. Weimann, *The Fair Women* [Chicago: Academy Press, 1981], p. 416). The higher number is probably the more accurate.
[2] "Porcelain-Painting," *Harper's New Monthly Magazine* 61 (November 1880): 903.

Fig. 1. From Sidney T. Whiteford, *A Guide to Porcelain Painting* (London: George Rowney, 1877), frontispiece. (Winterthur Library.)

attracted to china painting as a skill from which they could earn a suitable living, since it could be done privately in the home.[3]

On the other hand, professional studio china painters (also known as practical decorators), who were largely foreign-born men, painted china on order for customers of the potteries or specialized china and glass dealers. Some also served this large amateur following by firing china, giving lessons, and writing manuals and magazine articles. Venetian artist Dominick M. Campana, for example, joined the large china decorating workshop of the Pickard China Studio in Chicago in 1900 but established his own studio two years later. From there Campana decorated china to order, taught amateur china painters, developed and sold a line of china painting supplies, and published numerous books for teachers of various arts.[4]

A number of American women were also successful as professional china painters and teachers whose work was painted largely on order or for exhibition purposes only and who made their livings from teaching, writing, and sometimes developing and selling a personal line of china paints. Dorothea Warren O'Hara (1875–1963), for example, learned her art in Kansas City, Chicago, Munich, and London before settling in New York City shortly after 1900. In New York she taught china painting classes, contributed essays and designs to *Keramic Studio* for sixteen years and *Ladies' Home Journal* for seven years, and developed a method of decorating American belleek china by applying opaque enamels in conventionalized patterns individually adapted from the motifs of European and primitive cultures. Capitalizing on the reputa-

[3] On the historical connection, see "China Painting in Chicago," *Crockery and Glass Journal* (June 11, 1896): 17, 19. See Anthea Callen, *Women Artists of the Arts and Crafts Movement, 1870–1914* (New York: Pantheon Books, 1979), p. 8, for a discussion of the necessity for English gentlewomen to learn a skill among women of their own social class and to practice that skill in the home as a way of earning a living. Gentlewomen were not expected to mix with working-class women to earn a living. Some of the same attitudes could be found in the United States.

[4] Sharon Darling, *Chicago Ceramics and Glass* (Chicago: Chicago Historical Society, 1979), pp. 37, 39. For information on male china painters working in the ceramic industry in the United States, see Alice Cooney Frelinghuysen, *American Porcelain, 1770–1920* (New York: Metropolitan Museum of Art, 1989); and Ellen Paul Denker, *Lenox China: Celebrating a Century of Quality, 1889–1989* (Trenton: New Jersey State Museum, 1989).

tion generated through china painting periodicals, O'Hara successfully sold a line of china painting enamels and published a manual of designs and instruction in the art in 1912. The National Society of Craftsmen, noting that "her talent is quite remarkable," awarded O'Hara the Life Membership Prize in 1916.[5]

At a time when women were beginning to take art seriously as a legitimate career, china painting served their purposes as well as those of the male-dominated art establishment. Women educated in art academies could practice their art as painters on objects that were patently identified with the home rather than the salons where canvas painting and sculpture were exhibited. The early career of Cecilia Beaux (1855– 1942), noted society portrait painter of Philadelphia, provides a good example of this phenomenon. Born into an American family of declining fortune, Beaux was given some formal art instruction and allowed to follow an aunt and cousin into the arts as a way of providing for herself. Her early professional career included the teaching of drawing to girls, lithographic illustration for scientific texts, painting of china plaques, and portrait sketches from photographs. After "a month's lessons in china painting" under Frenchman Camille Piton in Philadelphia in 1879, Beaux developed a method of so beautifully painting children's portraits, almost life size on large ceramic plaques, that "parents nearly wept."[6] Rosina Emmet, another American painter known for portraits, beginning in the 1890s, worked first in china paints on ceramic plaques during the late 1870s and 1880s (fig. 2).

Despite its importance for the development of her career toward oil portraiture, Beaux later described her china painting as "the lowest

[5] Dorothea Warren O'Hara, *The Art of Enameling on Porcelain* (New York: Madison Square Press, 1912); for more on O'Hara, see Wendy Kaplan, *"The Art That Is Life": The Arts and Crafts Movement in America, 1875–1920* (Boston: Museum of Fine Arts, 1987), pp. 254–55; for the award, see Haswell C. Jeffery, "The National Society of Craftsmen Random Notes," *International Studio* 58 (March 1916): xxix–xxx.

[6] For background on women's position in the fine arts, see Ann S. Harris and Linda Nochlin, *Women Artists: 1550–1950* (New York: Alfred A. Knopf, 1977). Cecilia Beaux, *Background with Figures* (New York: Houghton Mifflin Co., 1930), pp. 84–85. For more on the role of design instruction in Beaux's art, see Tara Tappert, *Choices—The Life and Career of Cecilia Beaux* (Ph.D. diss., George Washington University, 1990). For an illustration of a plaque decorated with a child's portrait by Beaux, see *Philadelphia: Three Centuries of American Art* (Philadelphia: Philadelphia Museum of Art, 1976), p. 427.

Fig. 2. Rosina Emmet, portrait plaque of M. B. Brown on blank by Josiah Wedgwood and Sons, England, ca. 1881. Earthenware; Diam. 15⅛″. (Metropolitan Museum of Art, Sansbury-Mills Fund, 1991.)

depth [she] ever reached in commercial art."[7] At the time she resented that her success came through a medium that she associated largely with amateurs—women who did not need to develop their skills to earn a living but only to amuse themselves or expand talents that made them marriageable. Furthermore, male academic artists did not hold china painting in high esteem. On the other hand, an examination of

[7] Beaux, *Background with Figures*, pp. 84–85.

the history of china painting during this period shows that the women who practiced it as a decorative art, whether amateur or professional, were actually on the leading edge of art theory, where decorative art was being elevated to the same plane as fine art by proponents of the arts and crafts movement.

Instruction manuals for professional china and glass decorators appeared early in the nineteenth century, and those written especially for amateurs were more numerous after 1870. Published in both England and the United States, these manuals for amateurs were offered through dealers in artists' supplies, where the enthusiast could also purchase china blanks, china colors, and a variety of paraphernalia.[8] Frequently these dealers also arranged for firing for those painters who did not have a kiln at home. A large mail-order business, directed at women living distances from the specialty dealers in large cities and including all the same materials, also developed during the late nineteenth century.

Both professionals and amateurs read the specialized periodicals written and produced in the United States, beginning with *The China Decorator*, first published in June 1887 (fig. 3). Issued from New York City and edited by china painter and teacher Mrs. O.L. Braumuller (lately arrived from Atlanta), this magazine set the format for subsequent periodicals that featured editorials, news stories, descriptions of historical and contemporary potteries both here and abroad, exhibition reviews, and instructions for copying designs published in black and white and color. *The China Decorator* was issued monthly until 1901, when its popularity was eclipsed by a rival periodical. *Keramic Studio*—issued from Syracuse, New York, and edited by china painter, teacher, and later renowned ceramist Adelaide Alsop Robineau and china painter and teacher Anna B. Leonard—was established in 1899 and continued with the same format until 1924, when its name became *Design*, reflecting a change in focus. *Ceramic Monthly*, issued first from Chicago and later from New York between 1895 and 1900, also served the large audience interested in both china painting and art

---

[8] For more details on the mechanics of china painting, see two similar articles by Cynthia Brandimarte, "Somebody's Aunt and Nobody's Mother: The American China Painter and Her Work, 1870–1920," *Winterthur Portfolio* 23, no. 4 (Winter 1988): 203–24; and Cynthia Brandimarte, "Darling Dabblers: American China Painters and Their Work, 1870–1920," *American Ceramic Circle Journal* 6 (1988): 7–27.

Fig. 3. From *China Decorator* (January 1889), cover. (Winterthur Library.)

pottery. These magazines helped china painters communicate with one another, promoted the careers of talented and aggressive professional artists, and served to define china painting as a separate and serious art with its own language, methods, and leaders.

China painting, however, was not entirely segregated from the broader developing interest in art during the period. Magazines like *Art Amateur, International Studio, Brush and Pencil, Arts and Decoration*, and others frequently carried news and sometimes critical reviews of exhibitions held by local organizations of china painters or arts and crafts exhibitions that included china painting in Chicago, New York, Detroit, and elsewhere. They also featured articles on china painting techniques and designs.

Throughout china painting manuals and periodicals, the relationship between canvas and watercolor painting and china painting was mentioned continually. Amateur china painter M. Louise McLaughlin (1847–1939) described Haviland's Limoges underglaze painted wares on view at the Philadelphia Centennial International Exhibition as having the "appearance of a painting in oil, to which a brilliant glaze has been added." Writers disagreed on whether both media were similar or dissimilar to china painting. Some, like English designer and educator Lewis F. Day, stressed the similarity to watercolors by noting that the "liquid and transparent quality in water-color, which every water-color painter wishes he could retain beyond the wet stage of his picture" could be obtained in china painting.[9] Indeed, china painting is most similar visually to watercolor because both depend on the support for their luminous effects; however, the fact that decorating enamels change in color when fired separates china painting from oil and watercolor painting in terms of technique. Despite these differences, all authors did stress that drawing was the basis for all three art forms.

Because of the close association between china painting and oil and watercolor painting, the vocabulary used to instruct the techniques

[9]M. Louise McLaughlin, *Pottery Decoration under the Glaze* (Cincinnati: Robert Clarke Company, 1880), p. 41. Lewis F. Day, *The Application of Ornament* (London: B. T. Batsford, 1888) as cited in O'Hara, *Art of Enameling*, p. 11. O'Hara was a pupil of Day's during her studies in London; see Lida Rose McCabe, "Rise of American China Painting," *Art World* 2 (April 1917): 93.

of china painting was taken entirely from the fine arts. Color theory was usually reviewed in china painting manuals, and students were instructed in the grinding and mixing of colors, the setting of the artist's palette, and the use of easels, maulsticks, and other rests. Brushes were interchangeable among all three media. Furthermore, students were encouraged to establish a portfolio of sketches from nature to use in composing decorations. Decorative motifs were drawn separately and transferred to the china form by using tracing papers or pouncing through cartoons, in much the same way that canvas painters worked.

The correspondence between these art forms was basic to the attraction of the students who became artists. China painting was frequently offered alongside painting and drawing in the art and design academies that were being created around the country in addition to the hundreds, or perhaps thousands, of classes taught by china painters in their homes and studios.

A large number of women china painters were also involved in the fine arts before, during, and after their work in china painting. St. Louis china painter and teacher Kathryn Cherry (1871–1931) attended classes at Washington University School of Fine Arts in St. Louis, New York School of Arts, and the Pennsylvania Academy of the Fine Arts, Philadelphia, before studying china painting with Robineau and Marshall Fry in New York City at the turn of this century. Her career as a china painter and teacher was distinguished, including several terms as instructor in china painting at the American Women's University in University City, Missouri, and as the teacher of china painting at Robineau's Four Winds Summer School in Syracuse. By the late 1910s, however, she returned to easel painting and became prominent during the 1920s in the central Midwest, winning many prizes for her landscapes in local and regional competitions. Maria Longworth Nichols Storer, who founded Rookwood Pottery in 1880, also worked in oils, watercolor, tapestry, and metals.[10] Cherry and Storer are just two among many others who could be cited here.

China painting did offer one great advantage over painting on

---

[10] For more on Cherry, see Kaplan, "*Art That Is Life,*" pp. 329–30. Cherry is recorded in *Who Was Who in America: Vol. 1* (Chicago: Marquis Who's Who, 1960), p. 215. Kenneth R. Trapp, "The Bronze Work of Maria Longworth Storer," *Spinning Wheel* 28, no. 7 (September 1972): 14–15.

paper or canvas. Because the china colors were fixed to the porcelain surface by the heat of the kiln fire, the colors were permanently retained and could not be darkened by aging varnishes or faded by sunlight. Thus, the original artistic concept was lost only if the piece was broken or the glazes abraded through carelessness. "Painting on china, may not offer the same facilities for the truthful rendering of nature as oil or water-color painting," wrote McLaughlin, "but it has other compensating advantages in the beauty of the enamel, and the enduring qualities of the pigments, when fixed by the fire. . . . In other times the greatest artists exercised their art upon this material, which, seemingly so frail, has preserved their work unharmed for ages."[11]

In addition to these obvious connections to the painterly arts, china painting had a close relationship with an illustrious and artistic ceramic past. "There is nothing more fascinating and romantic to read than the history of ceramics. There is no guild on earth as old as the potters' guild," wrote china painter, teacher, and entrepreneur Susan Frackelton (1848–1932) of Milwaukee in her manual *Tried by Fire* (1886).[12] Apart from the ancient practice of pottery in general to which Frackelton referred, the special nature of porcelain—its translucency— placed it at the pinnacle of the ceramics hierarchy. The painting of porcelain was the highest form of the potter's art. Furthermore, the production of porcelain in China was centuries old, while its manufacture in Europe was relatively recent in 1870. By that time, European manufacturers had been working in porcelain for little more than 150 years, and their operations had been underwritten for most of the period by kings and princes. Psychologically, all of these associations placed china painters of the late nineteenth century clearly at the forefront of the ceramic art in the West.

China painting also appealed to educated women of this period for overtly sentimental reasons. Granted, the embellishment of decorative and useful forms for home furnishing in any medium was considered an appropriate and thoughtful activity for women. However, the

[11]M. Louise McLaughlin, *China Painting: A Practical Manual for the Use of Amateurs in the Decoration of Hard Porcelains* (Cincinnati: Robert Clarke Company, 1877), pp. vi, vii.
[12]Susan S. Frackelton, *Tried by Fire: A Work on China-Painting* (New York: D. Appleton, 1886), p. 12. Frackelton used either S (for Stuart, her middle name) or G (for Goodrich, her maiden name) for her middle initial.

Fig. 4. Bertha (Mrs. Elbert) Hubbard (*right*) painting china with her daughter-in-law, Alta Fattey (Mrs. Elbert) Hubbard II, in 1899 in East Aurora, N.Y. (Robert and Kitty Turgeon Rust, Roycroft Shops.)

comments of F. B. Dickerson regarding such matters in *Treasures of Use and Beauty* (1883) give some notion of the high esteem especially associated with products of amateur china painters, since the forms they chose so often went to the heart of the home (fig. 4):

When you have bought an ornamental [dinner] service in a shop, you have already borne testimony to the superiority of your taste. But your money alone has procured you a satisfaction which is common enough after all—that is, eating out of another's dishes—only those who have painted and decorated their own services can truly be said to eat out of their own dishes. How much more valuable then, will these objects become whereon you have put your own work, and which you keep round you or give as friendly presents to those you love or by whom you are beloved—objects that no one else could procure at any price.[13]

---

[13] F. B. Dickerson, *Treasures of Use and Beauty: The Choicest Gems of Wisdom, History, Reference, and Recreation* (Detroit: By the author, 1883), p. 282.

Under the circumstances, the sources used by china painters at this time were numerous. Certainly, illustrated books on ceramic history provided obvious models, and a number of these on the great pottery centers of Asia and Europe were published for collectors during the second half of the nineteenth century. Twenty-two books on various aspects of ceramic history are included in the list of thirty-eight reference works (nearly 60 percent) recommended to readers by the editors of *Keramic Studio* about 1900.[14] Writers of instruction manuals and periodical articles also encouraged china painters to collect reproductions of works of art that were available in books as well as chromolithographic prints that could be purchased at artists' supply stores. And, as mentioned earlier, china painters were encouraged to develop their own portfolios of sketches.

The appropriate style and arrangement of these accumulated elements on china, however, was subject to artistic opinion. Some artists favored the naturalistic rendering of subjects to create an illusion of reality much like painting at the time (fig. 5). Other china painters believed strongly that natural motifs should be conventionalized; that is, the essential characteristics of a flower, for example, should be summarized, flattened, and repeated as ornament (fig. 6). A comparison of these two approaches should illuminate the basis of many aesthetic decisions made in the late 1800s. Two manuals are especially instructive because they are relatively early books by American china painters who represent two ends of the china painter's spectrum: McLaughlin's *China Painting* and Frackelton's *Tried by Fire*.

Although McLaughlin and Frackelton were born at the same time into wealthy, or at least comfortable, midwestern families, their backgrounds and interests in china painting derived from very different sources, and their attitudes toward subject and style also diverged. McLaughlin was the definitive amateur, while Frackelton was the consummate professional. During her career, McLaughlin, who was a member of that fateful Pitman class in Cincinnati, also decorated furni-

---

[14]Titles of books on ceramic history and historic ornament as well as exhortations to read and collect them began with the first number of *Keramic Studio* in May 1899; a formal list first appeared with the masthead of volume three (February 1902). Many of the books endorsed by the editors could be purchased through the Keramic Studio Publishing Company.

Fig. 5. Charles Volkmar, *Teal Ducks with Blue Flags and Cow Lillies*, ca. 1890. For Mrs. L. Vance-Phillips, *The Book of the China Painter: A Complete Guide for the Keramic Decorator* (New York: Montague Marks, 1896). (Winterthur Library.)

ture and pottery, made porcelain in a backyard kiln, and wrote several books on European history. Frackelton, on the other hand, was drawn to ceramic decoration through her husband's wholesale china and glass importing business and her father's brick yard. By 1877 she had established Frackelton's China Decorating Works, as an adjunct to her husband's business, with a staff who decorated and fired more than 1,500 pieces a week in 1883. Potter, china painter, and teacher, Frackelton was also an inventor of gas-fired home kilns (1888) and a proselytizer

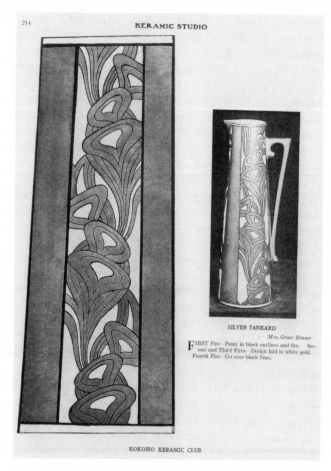

KERAMIC STUDIO

SILVER TANKARD

Mrs. Grace Bruner

FIRST Fire—Paint in black outlines and fire.   Second and Third Fires—Design laid in white gold.
Fourth Fire—Go over black lines.

KOKOMO KERAMIC CLUB

Fig. 6. Mrs. Grace Bruner, painted tankard and its original design, Kokomo, Ind., Keramic Club. From *Keramic Studio* 11 (February 1912): 214. (Winterthur Library.)

for the National League of Mineral Painters, which she helped to create in 1892. Thus, Frackelton's book of 1888, written "for the amateur," represents the views of a seasoned commercial artist.[15]

Both McLaughlin and Frackelton cited nature as their primary inspiration and source for decorative designs. In the nineteenth century, nature in the form of flowers, birds, and landscapes was deemed appropriate for interpretation by women. The female temperament had long been identified with nature (as opposed to culture), and women were expected to be more sympathetic to the subject in art. Moreover, human figures in painting and sculpture were more difficult for women to render since women had little, if any, training in anatomy, either through dissection or nude life-classes in traditional art academies. Such instruction for women was considered socially and morally inappropriate.[16]

In spite of their agreement on nature as the preferred subject, Frackelton and McLaughlin each interpreted it differently. Frackelton thought that nature should be rendered naturalistically on china while McLaughlin espoused conventionalization. Frackelton shuddered at the thought of bowing "entirely at the altar of 'purely conventional,' and there also have I lost the desire to apply geometry to all the works of the Most High. Even the correct designs on English wall-paper, though they please, and there is great good in them, fail to conquer the hot Philistinism which burns in my blood."[17]

Her attitude may have been a reflection more of her readership than her own opinion, however, as her stoneware art pottery is mostly conventional in decoration. For example, Mrs. L. Vance-Phillips, another practical decorator, noted in her 1896 manual, *Book of the China Painter*, that "the strong love of the American for the beauties of the floral world . . . usually asserts itself . . . in china painting . . . in the selection of semi-natural plant and flower forms as motives for decoration. For what may strictly be called conventional ornament," she

---

[15] For more on McLaughlin, see Kaplan, "*Art That Is Life*," pp. 249–50; and "Mary Louise McLaughlin," *American Ceramic Society Bulletin* 17 (May 1938): 219–20. For more on Frackelton, see Kaplan, "*Art That Is Life*," p. 323; and George A. Weedon, Jr., "Susan S. Frackelton and the American Arts and Crafts Movement" (Master's thesis, University of Wisconsin, 1975).

[16] See Harris and Nochlin, *Women Artists*, for an extended discussion of these ideas.

[17] Frackelton, *Tried by Fire*, p. 14.

continued, "there is little inclination among our amateurs."[18] Frackelton, the businesswoman, no doubt was influenced to some degree by prevailing taste in her decisions about how to approach the subject of style outlined in her book.

On the other hand, McLaughlin believed that conventionalized ornament had important uses in ceramic decoration. "As a general rule," she wrote, "it may be said that for all ceramic objects conventional designs are in the best taste, but practically, the question resolves itself into that of the destination of the decorated object. If a plaque or panel is to be hung upon a wall, there seems to be no valid objection to the painting of a naturalistic design upon its surface." She recommends later that "the human figure is the noblest subject" for these forms. The plaque or panel "occupies the same position as a picture, and there can be no reason why it should not be treated as a piece of paper or canvas." She continued, however, that "articles for use should be decorated with simple natural, or what is still better, with conventional forms." Furthermore, she noted that "for articles of ordinary utility designs should be drawn from lower forms of life. For this purpose flowers and plants offer the most available as well as beautiful subjects." Frackelton's conservative opinion is similar to and may draw upon the theories of John Ruskin in which he expounded that the fine and the decorative arts should be treated in the same way in terms of appropriate subject matter and style in order to unite the two. McLaughlin's view, however, reflects a sophisticated understanding for the period that appropriate decoration was based upon historic ornament derived from natural forms and rendered geometrically. First propounded by A.W.N. Pugin in the early 1840s, this idea was later illustrated lavishly in books, such as Owen Jones's *Grammar of Ornament* of 1856 and Heinrich Dolmetsch's *Ornamental Treasures* of 1887, both reprinted many times, which provided solid evidence that the great cultures of the past relied on nature for the shapes used to create repeatable conventionalized motifs for decoration.[19] Jones's the-

[18] Mrs. L. Vance-Phillips, *The Book of the China Painter: A Complete Guide for the Keramic Decorator* (New York: Montague Marks, 1896), p. 2. For illustrations of Frackelton's art stoneware, see Kaplan, "*Art That Is Life*," p. 323; and Paul Evans, *Art Pottery of the United States* (rev. ed.; New York: Feingold and Lewis, 1987), pp. 105–8.
[19] McLaughlin, *China Painting*, pp. 92–95. Owen Jones, *The Grammar of Ornament* (London: Day and Son, 1856); Heinrich Dolmetsch, *Ornamental Treasure* (New

ory synthesized science, geometry, and botany in a way that appealed visually and intellectually to his followers. Further study of historic ceramics specifically confirmed this concept for china painters.

Both Jones's and Dolmetsch's books appear in *Keramic Studio*'s recommended reading list, which also included Albert Racinet's *Polychromatic Ornament* (1870) and Jones's *Examples of Chinese Ornament* (1867).[20] Even at the relatively late date of 1900, these books formed an important segment of the china painter's reference library.

For sophisticated china painters, historical geometric ornament and the stylized asymmetry of the Japanese approach to design were powerful influences. At first these china painters were content to copy Turkish rug designs, picturesque prunus branches, and swirling fish from the pictorial sources that were coming into the United States from Europe and Asia. But by 1900 the urge to create new designs by fully conventionalizing natural forms was rapidly gaining ascendancy. Designers in the United States and England had long been applying the lessons of historic ornament and Japanese design. Christopher Dresser's important and influential plate 98 in Jones's *Grammar of Ornament* had inspired a number of studies during the 1870s and 1880s. In this plate, Dresser presented a variety of familiar flowers and their leaves— iris, rose, daffodil, honeysuckle, lily, periwinkle, and others—above and from the side, reduced to the elements essential for their recognition and flattened to two dimensions.

More important, perhaps, than the visual pleasure of abstraction alone was the intellectual process that Dresser described in *The Art of Decorative Design* (1862). Conventionalization of plants to create "purely ideal ornament," he wrote, is "wholly a creation of the soul; . . . utterly an embodiment of mind in form." For Dresser, decorative art required the same intellectual commitment as fine art and, thus, was in no way a minor art on some lower level in an artistic hierarchy. Furthermore, the influence of Japan on the American artistic intellect

York: Hessling and Spielmeyer, 1890), originally published as *Der Ornamentenschatz* (Stuttgart: J. Hoffmann, 1887). These books are discussed in John K. Jerpersen, "Owen Jones's *The Grammar of Ornament* of 1856: Field Theory in Victorian Design at the Mid-Century" (Ph.D. diss., Brown University, 1984).

[20] Albert Racinet, *Polychromatic Ornament* (London: H. Sotheran, 1870), first published as *L'Ornament Polychrom* (Paris: Firmin Didot Freres, Fils et Cie, 1869–73); Owen Jones, *Examples of Chinese Ornament* (London: S. and T. Gilbert, 1867).

specifically had been strong throughout the 1890s, when Arthur Wesley
Dow was developing the theory of design he based on the teachings of
Far-Eastern scholar Ernest Fenollosa and published in 1899 as *Compo-
sition.*[21]

In addition to the historic design and ceramic pictorial sources on
Keramic Studio's recommended reading list, Walter Crane's *Basis of
Design* (1898), Dow's *Composition*, Day's series on design, ornament,
and their application to decorative objects, and Lilley and Midgley's
Book of Studies in Plant Form (1895) were included.[22]

For china painters who read art magazines, attended summer
schools such as Dow's, which began in 1900, and followed the design
books published in England, the modern approach to design was intox-
icating. China painting was initially a way for women to paint in a
medium that was acceptable in the domestic sphere. Dresden and
Sevres flowers, Boucher putti, landscapes, and portraits, although copied, referred to the fine arts in their subject matter at least, and women
were content to paint anything that could be exhibited. Even if their
work did not appear alongside that of men in the salons, it was shown
with pride in their homes and entered in the competitions sponsored
by local ceramic and arts and crafts organizations. Eventually, however,
the intellectualization of decoration through conventionalization of
natural forms was liberating in itself. By following the ideas of Jones
and Dresser, women china painters could participate intellectually in
the male worlds of science, geometry, and psychology even if painting
and sculpture were still largely closed to them.

Thus, the relationship of china painting to the fine and decorative

[21] Christopher Dresser, *The Art of Decorative Design* (London: Day and Son, 1862),
pp. 39–40. Arthur Wesley Dow, *Composition: A Series of Exercises Selected from a New
System of Art Education* (New York: Doubleday, Page, 1899). See also Frederick C.
Moffatt, *Arthur Wesley Dow (1857–1922)* (Washington, D.C.: National Collection of
Fine Arts, Smithsonian Institution, 1977). For more on the influence of Japanese design,
see Clay Lancaster, *Japanese Influence in America* (New York: Abbeville Press, 1983).
[22] Walter Crane, *The Bases of Design* (London: G. Bell and Sons, 1898); Lewis F.
Day, *The Anatomy of Pattern* (London: B. T. Batsford, 1887); Day, *Application of
Ornament*; Lewis F. Day, *Every-day Art* (London: B. T. Batsford, 1882); Lewis F. Day,
Nature and Ornament (London: B. T. Batsford, 1892); Lewis F. Day, *The Planning of
Ornament* (London: B. T. Batsford, 1887); A. E. V. Lilley and W. Midgley, *A Book of
Studies in Plant Form with Some Suggestions for Their Application to Design* (London:
Chapman and Hall, 1895).

arts was not simple. While china painting was part of the arts and crafts movement by virtue of its embrace of conventionalized decoration and its moralistic emphasis on creating artistic objects for display and use in the home, the form and style a china artist chose classified her (or his) work as either fine art in its conservative Ruskinian definition or decorative art in its modern idiom. The china painter who looked at her work as an extension of oil or watercolor painting in their academic sense developed skills of representational illusion applied to plaques and tiles that were displayed on the wall-like paintings. Conversely, the artist who accepted china decoration as a decorative art characterized by conventionalization was clearly a member of the new legion that placed decorative art on the same high plane as fine art.

After 1910, artists who would have classified themselves as china decorators in the latter sense were drawn increasingly into the university art programs that fostered studio ceramics and trained industrial designers. Those who remained or became china painters in the traditional sense—those who espoused naturalism—continued to organize themselves into groups separate from the art or university establishments. Increasingly, the use of naturalistic decoration by these china painters has been seen by outsiders as "a sign of either immaturity or decadence."[23] Thus, the work of thousands of contemporary American china painters is dismissed by the university art community as an amateur craft, and the important role that china painting played at the turn of the century in both bridging and defining the distinctions between the fine and decorative arts, especially for women, has been largely forgotten. Continued critical examination of the china painting phenomenon, however, should yield more insights into the way the definition of fine art has grown in the last century to embrace decorative art, design, and women.

[23] "Arts and Crafts at the Louisiana Purchase Exposition," *International Studio* 23 (1904): cccxc.

American Tonalism and Rookwood Pottery

Anita J. Ellis

The fine and decorative arts have traditionally been viewed as separate aesthetic expressions; however, this view is not necessarily correct. In the case of American tonalism, the aesthetic expression remained the same in painting and Rookwood ceramics; American tonalism as expressed in painting was equaled in the vellum glaze line of Rookwood Pottery. Moreover, Rookwood added a dimension to the aesthetic. These assertions will become apparent through a discussion of American tonalism, a technical examination of Rookwood's vellum glaze, the investigation of Rookwood as tonalism, and, finally, an analysis of the aesthetics of tonalism in Rookwood, demonstrating its contribution to the movement.

Tonalism flourished in the United States from about 1880 to 1910 or slightly later. Clark Ruge, writing for *International Studio*, called it the "national school of landscape painting." The style was in marked contrast to the earlier midcentury Hudson River school that depicted landscapes as colorful panoramic vistas, dramatic and grandiose. For example, in *The Falls of the Tequendama near Bogota, New Granada* (1854) by Frederic Church, the view is commanding as it centers on the forceful power of the falls. There is a scientific realism as flowers,

---

Kenneth R. Trapp should be given credit for being the first to recognize the tonalist philosophy in Rookwood's vellum glaze line. The first to publish the connection between tonalism and Rookwood was Todd M. Volpe in "Rookwood Landscape Vases and Plaques," *Antiques* 117, no. 4 (April 1980): 838–46.

Fig. 1. John H. Twachtman, *Springtime*, Paris, 1883–85. Oil on canvas; H. 36⅞", W. 50". (Cincinnati Art Museum, gift of Frank Duveneck.)

rocks, and the crash and flow of the water are picked out clearly and factually. Tonalist painters reacted to such an approach. Their landscapes were not commanding or awesome but rather quiet and personal. *Springtime* (fig. 1), painted between 1883 and 1885 by John Henry Twachtman, is intimate and peaceful. Unlike *The Falls of the Tequendama*, the scene is not geographically specific. The location is of minor importance. It could be anywhere where there is a stream and trees. What is more important is the mood that is rendered. The hazy suggestion of land and water has been substituted for the earlier hard-edge realism to express a mood of reverie. Church's landscape creates a public relationship with nature; Twachtman's incites an extremely personal one. The former is scientifically factual; the latter is poetically truthful. The midcentury painters were celebrating the grandeur of the land. Theirs was an age of national optimism and development as the doctrine of manifest destiny postulated the continued territorial expansion of the United States. The age of the tonalists was different. It was a time of industrialization and pollution. While the tonalists never lost sight of the romantic in nature, theirs was not a public celebration of the land. It was a personal escape to peace and quietude. Depicted themes were intimate—as pools in the woods or a clearing highlighted by a soft snow or a quiet rain. The mood of reverie was essential. The arrangement of paints on the canvas was within a narrow color range with one predominating hue, often gray or blue. The predominating hue gave the composition not only its color tone but its psychological tone as well. It reflected the painter's feelings of melancholy derived from an unfulfilled longing to be at one with nature in its preindustrialized state. The all-important mood was enhanced by the color tone and the atmospheric quality of the image. Dawn and dusk were the two most-depicted times of day. Evocative half-lights suggestive of mist, fog, or moonlight were also used to obscure detail and incite a subjective response. Landscapes were hushed and motionless. They offered a quiet atmosphere of subtle luminosity. The tonalist reproduced not only what he saw but his emotional response to it as well. George Inness, an early and influential tonalist, believed that the real greatness of a work of art consisted in the quality and force of this emotional response.[1] Subtle lighting diffused through atmosphere created a personal, peaceful, meditative moment. Nature was its underlying structure. By using the blurred, quiet suggestion of appearance, tonalists combined subjective sentiment with objective fact to create a powerfully felt mood of reverie and longing.

To appreciate Rookwood's tonalist expressions, it is important to understand the vellum glaze that enabled Rookwood's decorators to work in a tonalist mode. Vellum is a translucent matte glaze that was developed by the pottery at the time of the arts and crafts movement, when matte glazes were at the height of ceramic fashion. Rookwood's chemist Stanley Gano Burt began experiments for the glaze in 1900, and the line was officially introduced in 1904 at the Louisiana Purchase

---

[1] Clark Ruge, "The Tonal School of America," *International Studio* 27, no. 107 (January 1905): 58. Inness discusses his views in Ruge, "Tonal School," p. 60. For a detailed discussion of American tonalism, see Wanda M. Corn, *The Color of Mood: American Tonalism, 1880–1910* (San Francisco: M. H. De Young Memorial Museum, 1972).

International Exposition in St. Louis. The glaze was called vellum
since "it partakes both to the touch and to the eye of the qualities of
old parchment." It was remarkable because unlike other mattes, vellum
was translucent; an underglaze slip decoration could be seen through
it. Research to date suggests that Rookwood was the first pottery to
develop such a glaze. By their nature matte glazes are opaque. For
Rookwood to make one that was translucent was like inventing cold
fire or dry water. One reviewer at the St. Louis exposition recognized
the enormity of this feat by stating the "mat glaze on pottery could
develop no further." Indeed, with this glaze line Rookwood received
two grand prizes at the exposition.[2] What is important to the discussion
of tonalism is that the glaze was devoid of lustre and exhibited a slight
haze. For example, in a vellum plaque decorated by Edward Hurley
(fig. 2), there is a slight fogginess to the composition. Along the bottom
edge of the plaque a milky horizontal line is visible. This is where the
glaze pooled and is thicker. The thicker the glaze is applied, the milkier
it becomes, providing a gauzelike veil over the composition. It is this
hazy quality that contributes so well to the tonalist aesthetic. A glaze
is not necessary for an atmospheric effect in a slip-painted composition,
where the effect can be rendered with the proper painting technique
alone. The glaze, however, will enhance or diminish the result. Vellum enhanced the result in two ways: it intensified the hazy appearance
because of its milky quality, and it promoted reverie with its soft matte
sheen. At the time, no other glaze could produce such an effect. All
other translucent glazes were of the high-gloss variety. A glossy finish
could not enhance the atmospheric look of a landscape—since it was
reflective—nor intensify the misty appearance of the composition un-
derneath. The evocative, quiet tonalist mood would be lost with the
ineluctable flash of light created by a glossy surface. The absolutely
necessary meditative mood could not be sustained, if achieved at all.

When introduced, the vellum glaze line displayed no landscape

[2] For a detailed discussion of the vellum glaze line, see Anita J. Ellis, *Rookwood
Pottery: The Glorious Gamble* (New York: Rizzoli, 1992), pp. 56–57. The naming of
the glaze is discussed in a mail order sales catalogue, *The Rookwood Book* (Cincinnati:
Rookwood Pottery Co., 1904). On the inclusion of the vellum glaze at the exposition,
see "Louisiana Purchase Exposition Ceramics," *Keramic Studio* 6, no. 9 (January 1905):
193; Corporate Minutes of the Rookwood Pottery Co., November 18, 1904, p. 88,
collection of Art and Rita Townley, Michigan Center, Mich.

Fig. 2. Rookwood Pottery Co., plaque, Edward Timothy Hurley (decorator), Cincinnati, 1948. Ceramic; H. 12½", W. 14½". (Cincinnati Art Museum, gift of the Fleischmann Foundation in memory of Julius Fleischmann: Photo, Ron Forth.)

decoration. In early test trials the glaze was applied to objects originally intended for Rookwood's standard and iris glazes, that is, predominantly floral compositions, but also some marine depictions probably influenced by Rookwood's sea green glaze line. It did not take long, however, for the pottery's decorators to recognize vellum's tonalist potential. In 1905 Albert Valentien painted the first landscape under the vellum glaze.[3] Prior to this, landscapes had been painted for the iris glaze, but they were generally experimental and extremely rare.

[3] S. G. Burt, *Rookwood Pottery in the Cincinnati Art Museum in 1916* (Cincinnati: Cincinnati Historical Society, 1978), p. 158, no. 8.

Great skill was required to produce a tonalist scene under the vellum glaze. The design was first sketched on the greenware with india ink, which subsequently fired out. An atomizing cup was constantly used to keep the object and its composition at the right point of moisture at all times. Slips used for the decorations were very different in color before firing. To use them effectively required much practice and many trials, especially for subjects as complicated as landscapes. In the Cincinnati Historical Society library there is a small notebook of vellum results by decorator Edward Diers.[4] The pages contain sketches of vases with discussions of various trials of applied slip decorations under the vellum glaze. Vellum landscape decorations were so complex in their application that decorators, like Diers, often noted the results of a wide range of slip trials until the technique was mastered. Compositions could take a few hours or many days to complete. Once decorated, a piece was allowed to dry and was then biscuit fired. Afterward it was dipped in the vellum glaze and fired a final time.

From 1905, when Valentien painted the first scenic vellum—as they came to be known—floral vellums began to disappear. Products of the vellum glaze line were soon decorated almost exclusively in tonalist landscapes. The fact that Rookwood decorators were able to apply a fine arts expression to a decorative arts product reflects their backgrounds. Virtually all of the Rookwood decorators who worked in the tonalist expression attended the Art Academy of Cincinnati, with its fine arts curriculum. Also, most began employment with the pottery as young artists in the 1890s and early 1900s when tonalism was a mainstream aesthetic in the United States. Decorators were aware of the tonalist movement through their connections with the art academy as well as through colleagues. For example, Rookwood decorator Hurley knew tonalist and fellow Cincinnatian Twachtman and often visited Twachtman at his Greenwich, Connecticut, studio.[5] Another means

[4]For a detailed discussion of the glaze process, see William Watts Taylor, "The Rookwood Pottery," *Forensic Quarterly* 1, no. 4 (September 1910): 209–11. Edward George Diers's memoranda of vellum results, ca. 1905–31, Rookwood Pottery Collection, Cincinnati Historical Society library (hereafter cited as RPC/CHSL).

[5]The Harley/Twachtman connection was elucidated by Mrs. Joan Hurley O'Brien (daughter of Edward T. Hurley), interview with the author, Cincinnati, June 4, 1990. Catalogues for these annual exhibitions of American art and annual exhibitions of the Society of Western Artists can be found in the Mary R. Schiff Library, Cincinnati Art Museum.

of exposure to tonalism was through exhibitions. There were no fewer than ten exhibitions at the Cincinnati Art Museum between 1895 and 1922 in which tonalist works by John White Alexander, Ralph Blakelock, William Merritt Chase, Willard Metcalf, Birge Harrison, Childe Hassam, Inness, Twachtman, James Abbott McNeill Whistler, and others could be seen. Exhibitions also included tonalist photography by artists such as Edward Steichen, Alfred Stieglitz, and Clarence H. White. Many of these same exhibitions displayed Rookwood pottery as well as paintings and sculpture by Rookwood decorators. In the spring of every year from 1894 until 1941, the Cincinnati Art Museum held the Annual Exhibition of American Art comprised of works from across the nation. Included in the earlier years were paintings and sculpture by Rookwood artists Matt Daly, Anna Bookprinter Valentien, Albert Valentien, Hurley, Irene Bishop, and John Dee Wareham. In these same exhibitions for 1896, 1898, 1899, 1900, and 1903, Rookwood pottery was displayed along with the fine art that included many tonalist examples. Moreover, from 1897 until 1913, eighteen annual exhibitions of the Society of Western Artists were staged at the Cincinnati Art Museum. The society was a federation of midwestern artists who were called western because at the time the Midwest was referred to as the West. Little research has been completed on this group, but they too exhibited examples of the tonalist aesthetic. Rookwood artists exhibiting painting and sculpture in this group were Bruce Horsfall, both Valentiens, Artus Van Briggle, Hurley, Bishop, Harriet E. Wilcox, and Wareham. The exhibitions for February 1897, October–November 1897, December–January 1898–99, December–January 1902–3, November–December 1904, and December 1911 included Rookwood pottery. In the 1911 exhibition, sixteen Rookwood objects were vellum examples.

In Cincinnati in the 1890s and early 1900s, it would have been virtually impossible for a young, active artist, having studied at the Art Academy of Cincinnati, not to be aware of, indeed, not to be a part of the American tonalist aesthetic. The point that must be emphasized here is that Rookwood decorators came out of a fine arts tradition and often exhibited as easel painters. Their backgrounds did not consist of apprenticeships in china painting. It was their art backgrounds and their undeniable familiarity with tonalism that enabled them to transfer that aesthetic to ceramics. Once the vellum glaze was developed, it took barely a year for the artists to realize its tonalist potential. No other pottery in the world had the same combination of artist-decorators, and a translucent matte glaze.

A vase decorated by Hurley in 1908 displays a quiet, intimate, peaceful scene (fig. 3). The prevailing color is gray. As in all tonalist compositions, the scene invites a personal relationship. Psychologically the viewer wanders alone into the woods. The attraction holds also in a plaque decorated by Sarah E. Coyne (fig. 4). Here the predominant color is gray-blue. The hushed atmosphere obscured in the diffused moonlight gently urges the viewer to a state of reverie. There are no people in the scene. People are rarely depicted in tonalist landscape paintings, and it is highly unusual to see them in the vellum glaze line. Somehow the presence of human figures negates the intimacy for the viewer. More likely to be seen are placid animals such as the black swans on a vase by Carl Schmidt (fig. 5). They add to the poetry of the silent, secluded, foggy setting. Evocative half-lights incite a subjective response. The aesthetic expressed in Rookwood pottery is exactly the same as that expressed in the art of the tonalist painters; the personal quality, diffused light, quiet setting, and limited color range are used in both.

Did Rookwood decorators see themselves as part of the tonalist movement? To answer this it must be realized that the tonalist painters themselves were not an organized group. They had no manifesto, written or announced. They were not unified nor did they consciously promote a group movement. Consequently, Rookwood decorators could not see themselves as a part of a specific, narrowly defined group. Bear in mind also that at Rookwood Pottery, the decorators were a small component of the production process. In their own commercial setting they were not regarded as a major ideational force. Nevertheless, they did not work in ignorance of current aesthetics. In his memoranda of vellum results, Diers describes a vase as a "fine tone piece." Because of their training and interests, Rookwood decorators saw themselves as part of tonalism in general. It must be noted that vellum-glazed wares were profitable for Rookwood and continued to be made until 1948. Needless to say, there came a time when the expression was outdated in terms of the mainstream. Yet for reasons of profit, and perhaps old loyalties to the aesthetic, tonalist vellums continued to be produced at Rookwood as long as decorators who came of age as artists during the

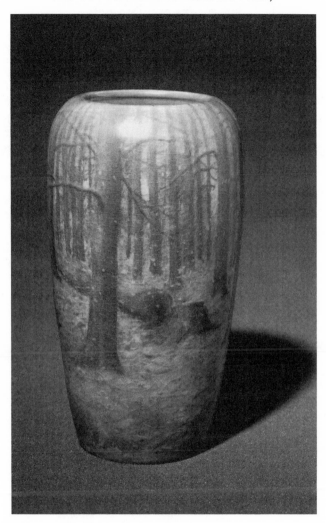

Fig. 3. Rookwood Pottery Co., vase, Edward Timothy
Hurley (decorator), Cincinnati, 1908. Ceramic; H. 9″,
Diam. 5¼″. (Dr. and Mrs. William E. Heil collection:
Photo, Jeff Bates.)

Fig. 4. Rookwood Pottery Co., *A Pale Evening Moon*, plaque, Sarah E. Coyne (decorator), Cincinnati, 1915. Ceramic; H. 6¼″, W. 8¼″. (Cincinnati Art Museum, gift of Mr. and Mrs. Gerald Gordon in memory of Joseph E. Bell: Photo, Ron Forth.)

tonalist era remained at the pottery. In all, the line was produced for forty-three years, with interruptions during the Great Depression, the company's ensuing bankruptcy, and World War II. The last example was created by Hurley in 1948, the year he retired from Rookwood.[6]

Given the long association between the two, what were tonalism's contributions, if any, to Rookwood, and, conversely, Rookwood's contribution to tonalism? In general, tonalism remains the same in the two-dimensional forms of paintings on canvas and ceramic plaques. In

[6]On the tonalists, see Corn, *Color of Mood*, p. 4. Diers memoranda, RPC/CHSL. I have seen more than 10,000 pieces of Rookwood. Of the vellum examples, none have dated later than 1948, and all the 1948 examples have been by Hurley. The fact that he retired in 1948 can be found in Herbert Peck, *The Book of Rookwood Pottery* (New York: Crown Publishers, 1968), p. 145.

Fig. 5. Rookwood Pottery Co., vase, Carl Schmidt (decorator), Cincinnati, 1915. Ceramic; H. 11¼″, W. 5¼″. (Cincinnati Art Museum, gift of Cincinnati Art Galleries: Photo, Ron Forth.)

Fig. 6. Rookwood Pottery Co., *Edge of the Forest*, plaque, Lorinda Epply (decorator), Cincinnati, 1913. Ceramic; H. 4½″, W. 8¼″. (Cincinnati Art Museum, Jane Herschede Memorial Fund: Photo, Ron Forth.)

two-dimensional forms of paintings on canvas and ceramic plaques. In fact, at Rookwood plaques were signed on the front by the artist (see figs. 2, 4). They were fitted by the pottery in typical arts and crafts oak frames (fig. 6) and meant to be hung on a wall. Moreover, each plaque was given a title, which was typed on paper and glued to the back of the frame. Even when the glaze crazed, as it did in *Edge of the Forest*, it was seen as no different from the crazing of paint on canvas. There were no attitudinal differences brought to bear in the creation and display of Rookwood's vellum plaques and tonalist paintings. There was, however, one major visual difference. Paintings were measured in feet whereas plaques were measured in inches. The smaller size of the plaques was the result of technological limitations in ceramics that prohibited the successful firing of large pieces. The distinction in size slightly alters the viewer's relationship. It is important to remember that in the tonalist aesthetic the mood is the subject. When the work is large the extension of mood is empowered by the subject. That is to say, one stands in front of a large painting at a distance far enough away to view the entire composition. The bigger the painting, the farther away one stands. Physically there may be many viewers, but psychologically each is alone in the quiet reverie of the composition.

When the object is small, the extension of mood is empowered by the viewer. One stands in front of the pottery plaque at a distance close enough to view the composition. Physically the viewer is alone because the object is too small to accommodate any real communal viewing. The viewer is also psychologically alone in the reverie of the composition. It is a personal experience in which the viewer physically dominates the object. The ultimate difference between the two is the variation of empowerment in the relationship. Whether activated by the object or the viewer, however, the mood still extends from the work of art to the beholder. The tonalist aesthetic of the powerfully quiet, meditative evocation remains the same.

Once the relationship is activated, physical distance gives place to psychic proximity. In the art of painting, psychic proximity is common, if not in fact expected. One does not look *at* a painting but rather *into* a painting. This tradition can be traced as far back as the fifteenth century, when Leon Battista Alberti insisted that a painting should be like a window onto the world.[7] Psychologically the viewer enters the illusional three-dimensional space of the landscape. The psyche approximates the space and time of the painted impression.

In the decorative art of ceramic plaques, psychic proximity is not a traditional expectation. Historically, plaques were meant to be looked *at*, not *into*. There are exceptions with nineteenth-century plaques with overglaze enamels such as those produced by the Konigliche Porzellan Manufacture, but with plaques painted in underglaze slips the illusion is never as complete as in paintings. With paintings on canvas the illusion completely transcends the materiality of the structure. For example, when viewing Twachtman's *Springtime* one does not see paint on canvas but rather a landscape. However, when viewing traditional ceramic plaques, the ceramic structure is never totally lost to the viewer. If nothing else, the barrier of the reflection caused by the shiny gloss of the glaze obscures the illusion with its demanding presence. In painting, one traditionally sees the concept first and the

[7] For a detailed discussion, see Leon Battista Alberti, *On Painting* (New Haven: Yale University Press, 1956).

materials second, if at all. In most ceramics, one sees the medium
first and the concept second, if at all. Tonalism in combination with
Rookwood's vellum glaze, however, allowed the composition to transcend the materiality of the plaque to a degree never achieved before
in underglaze slip decoration. When looking into a tonalist plaque one
does not see ceramic, slips, and glaze but rather a quiet landscape.
The viewer, drawn by the tonalist landscape, looks into the plaque and
remains looking because the vellum glaze offers no distracting reflection
of light that forces a recognition of the material. One observes the
concept first and the medium second. This is what American tonalism
did for Rookwood ceramics in particular and American ceramics in
general. It allowed for a concept-first approach to art. The overall
concept rather than the material alone became the inspiration for the
aesthetic. In the history of American ceramics the whole was becoming
greater than its parts.

   What, if anything, did Rookwood offer tonalism? To answer this,
one must look to three-dimensional vase forms. Unlike plaques, which
were seen as small paintings, vases were approached differently in their
creation and display. Decorators' signatures were rarely, if ever, applied to the compositions. They were hidden on the bottom of the
vases. Landscapes on the vessels were very rarely given titles. And, of
course, vases were never intended to be displayed in the same manner
as plaques. The source of these distinctions lies with the three-
dimensional quality of the form.

   Transferring the aesthetic from a planar to a volumetric form
posed a problem. The composition had to extend around the vase
without disruption. Consider a tonalist painting on canvas wrapped
around a cylindrical vase whose circumference equals the width of the
canvas. Where the edges of the canvas meet, the compositional lines
will not match. To resolve this problem Rookwood decorators created
landscapes in which the compositional lines were aligned where they
met to encircle the vase. Consequently, one sees no beginning or end
to the depiction. It is a continuous, infinite layout that offers a multi-
plicity of readings.

   Returning to the distinctions between plaques and vases, it becomes clear why vases were signed on the bottom instead of on the
main body. Signatures on plaques were always at the lower left (see
fig. 2) or lower right (see fig. 4) so as not to interfere with the main

thrust of the composition. Tonalist vases, with their continuous composition, could not be discreetly signed.

In addition to signatures, plaques were given titles. This was not the case with vases simply because they offered no practical location on which to glue a label. With plaques, labels were always glued to the frames, never on the ceramic.[8] Vases could only offer a ceramic surface, and the only locations free of the composition were the interior, which was not readily visible, and the bottom, which was generally not spacious enough for a title.

A further difference between plaques and vases is the means of display. Like paintings, plaques were meant to be hung on walls. Vases, however, were to be held or placed on flat surfaces where they could be viewed in-the-round. This is not merely an important distinction between vellum plaques and vases but is the most important distinction between tonalist paintings on canvas and Rookwood ceramics. The physical extension of the object creates a field of real space that includes the viewer. Relating to the form one still experiences the concept first and the material second, but, not being able to see the whole composition at once, the viewer is forced to encircle the form or to turn it in his or her hands. There is no visual beginning or end to the composition. Where to start or stop around the vase is arbitrary. After one revolution the urge is to continue, drawn by what is not seen as much as by what is. The vase form adds a dimension both literally and metaphorically to American tonalism. The participant becomes lost in a powerfully felt poetic mood that visually and psychologically never ends. This is Rookwood's contribution to American tonalism. It broadened the aesthetic to include an infinite loop of mood extension.

Rookwood's vellum landscapes were not merely a by-product of American tonalism. They were very much a part of it. They were not a secondary manifestation of the aesthetic, but integral to it. Rookwood's tonalism was produced by artists working in the same culture and incited by the same philosophy that produced the paintings on canvas. It was a vital part of American tonalism that unified the fine and decorative arts.

[8]When a frame was removed or replaced, the plaque lost its title. This is why many plaques are noted as untitled.

Frederick S. Lamb's Opalescent Vision of "A Broader Art"
The Reunion of Art and Craft in Public Murals

David Adams

I suppose that few, if any, art historians would readily recognize the stained glass window *Religion Enthroned* by Frederick Stymetz Lamb (1863–1928) as a product of the American arts and crafts movement (fig. 1). Using the example of Lamb, an artist and art activist working in New York City from about 1885 to 1922 in the border region between art and craft, I want to question and perhaps to expand the boundaries of existing definitions of the American arts and crafts movement. Withholding premature generalizations—while examining the ideas and activities of a specific designer associated with the movement—will help to ground these considerations in historical reality and avoid constructing a past that never existed.

We are gradually recognizing that the turn of the century was a complex period in the history of American art and design. Most of the neat stylistic classifications we have recently come to recognize for this era—arts and crafts, Gothic revival, American Renaissance, the City Beautiful movement, colonial revival, American impressionism, the aesthetic movement—were not necessarily distinguished as separate movements by the artists, designers, and art lovers of the period. In fact, these stylistic classifications are to some extent merely an added convenience of art historians.

Fig. 1. Frederick Lamb, *Religion Enthroned*, J. and R. Lamb Studios, New York, 1899. Leaded glass; H. 18′, W. 12′. (Brooklyn Museum: Photo, J. and R. Lamb Studios.)

A quick overview of Lamb's career will make apparent the variegated, but not necessarily unusual, nature of his artistic entanglements.
When Lamb was born in New York in 1863, his English-born father,
Joseph, had only six years before founded the J. and R. Lamb Studios
in New York City, in collaboration with his brother Richard. J. and
R. Lamb was reportedly the first American firm to specialize (although
not exclusively) in ecclesiastical decoration and artwork.[1] Their artistic
direction in the beginning followed the lead of the Gothic revival movement inspired by A. W. N. Pugin in England, also the womb of the
British arts and crafts movement. In its earlier years Lamb Studios
worked in wood, stone, and embroidered cloth. After Frederick's older
brother, Charles Rollinson Lamb (1860–1942), began designing for
the studios at age sixteen, the firm expanded into stained glass, glass
mosaic, and stone monuments as well as extensive secular commissions
and began designing in a more eclectic mix of styles.

When Frederick completed his artistic training at the Académie
Julian in Paris in 1885, he had been thoroughly imbued with the
virtues of loosely brushed Barbizon landscape painting, figure drawing,
and French academic mural painting, especially religious mural painting, the most highly valued genre of the French academies. Upon his
return to the city of his birth, Lamb rented an atelier in the Holbein
Studios, where he shared quarters with painters such as George Inness,
Kenyon Cox, and Elliott Daingerfield and soon was on friendly terms
with most of the other New York–based artists of the "American Renaissance" movement. Struggling to make a living as a young painter in
America, he also executed church mural work for the family business.[2]

Lamb soon learned of the experiments in a new type of stained
glass medium being conducted at the Decorative Stained Glass Company

[1] *Catalogue on Figure Glass Work* (New York: J. and R. Lamb, 1893), p. 4, quotes
Moses King, *King's Handbook of the United States* as follows: "The rapid development of
ecclesiastical art in the United States is largely due to the efforts of two brothers, young
Englishmen, who, in 1857, founded their business under the name of J. and R. Lamb.
They were the first to formulate in the United States the idea of religious art as a specialty."
[2] Information on Lamb's biography has been gathered from, among other sources,
art reference works, period J. and R. catalogue booklets, and [Charles Rollinson
Lamb ?], "Frederick Stymetz Lamb: In Memoriam," *Bulletin of the Stained Glass Association of America* 23, no. 9 (October 1928): 8–9. I also gratefully acknowledge the kind
assistance and sharing of information about Frederick Lamb and Lamb Studios on the
part of Barea Lamb Seeley, Condie Lamb, the late Adrian Lamb (son of Frederick
Lamb), Mabel Lamb, and Donald Samick (the current president of Lamb Studios).

on Washington Square (not far from the studios of J. and R. Lamb, off south Sixth Avenue) under the direction of his father's friend, the painter John La Farge. Lamb became one of the most enthusiastic of the young painters who observed the daily development of La Farge's efforts to adapt semi-opaque opalescent flat glass to leaded window design.[3] Soon Lamb was creating opalescent glass windows as well as glass mosaics as head of the Stained Glass Department at J. and R. Lamb.

Lamb also participated actively in the growing American arts and crafts movement. He helped host British visitors C. R. Ashbee and Walter Crane at Lamb Studios, executing with Crane between 1889 and 1891, for Saint Paul's Methodist-Episcopal Church in Newark, New Jersey, what was reported at that time to be the largest stained glass window in America. Lamb showed stained glass designs at the first exhibition of the Society of Arts and Crafts, Boston, in 1897. He also served as a juror and exhibitor at the arts and crafts exhibition organized by Gustav Stickley's United Crafts enterprise in 1903, held at the Craftsman Building in Syracuse, New York. He included a small window depicting parrots in the reorganized version of this same exhibition shown just afterward at the Mechanics Institute in Rochester, under the direction of Harvey Ellis (fig. 2). A founding member of the National Arts Club, Lamb also helped organize the National Society of Craftsmen, which assumed the arts and crafts activities of the National Arts Club in April 1906. Lamb reviewed at length their third annual exhibition in New York, in December 1910, and also belonged to the New York Society of Craftsmen. He apparently was on friendly terms with Stickley and authored eight substantial articles for Stickley's journal, *The Craftsman*, between 1902 and 1906.[4]

For sixteen difficult years Lamb served as president of the Decorative Glass Manufacturer's Association (later called the Stained and

[3] Lamb later wrote a monograph on La Farge in two versions: "John La Farge: With Examples of His Latest Work in the State Capitol, Minn., and the John Harvard Memorial, London," *The Craftsman* 8, no. 3 (June 1905): 312–23; and "John La Farge," *Stained Glass: A Series of Illuminated Monographs* 1 (March 1913): ii–viii.

[4] *St. Paul at Athens Preaching on Mars Hill* was a 35-by-25-foot opalescent glass window designed by Crane: Lamb executed the cartoon and window construction. See "The Murphy Window," *Newark Sunday Call*, cited in *Catalogue on Figure Glass Work* (New York: J. and R. Lamb, 1893), pp. 22–23; Walter Crane, *An Artist's Reminiscences* (London: Metheuen, 1907), pp. 388–89, 391. Crane visited the Lambs in 1892. The Newark window was destroyed in 1936, as reported in Isobel Spencer, *Walter Crane* (New

Leaded Glass Association of New York), the largest local chapter of the Stained Glass Association of America. With his brother Charles he also helped organize the National Society of Mural Painters in 1895. In addition to these activities, Lamb was a busy lecturer and activist in the City Beautiful movement for better civic design. Among other positions, he served as president of the Architectural League of America and vice president of the Architectural League of New York and belonged to the New York chapter of the American Society of Architects. He was secretary and a leading figure in the Municipal Art Society in New York, and he organized and chaired its Committee on Permanent Work in 1908.[5]

It is, in fact, with the issue of municipal or public art that we can find a helpful link or bridge between the various facets in the artistic

---

York: Macmillan, 1975), pp. 119, 174, 176. C. R. Ashbee, in "The Ashbee Journals" (King's College Library, Cambridge, Eng.), April 30, 1896, f. 121, mentions his visit to Lamb Studios of 1896. He also mentions conversations with Charles and Frederick Lamb during his tour of 1900 in C. R. Ashbee, *A Report by Mr. C. R. Ashbee to the Council of the States on the Council's Behalf* (London: Essex House, 1901), p. 13. I am indebted to James E. Benjamin for these Ashbee references. Karem Evans Ulehla, comp. and ed., *The Society of Arts and Crafts, Boston: Exhibition Records, 1897–1920s* (Boston: Boston Public Library, 1981). On the 1903 exhibitions, see Coy L. Ludwig, *The Arts and Crafts Movement in New York State, 1890s–1920s* (Hamilton, N.Y.: Gallery Association of New York State, 1983), p. 57. Lamb's *Parrots* is depicted in an exhibition photograph from the Mechanics Institute show in the archives of the Wallace Memorial Library, Rochester Institute of Technology, Rochester, N.Y., and is listed in the exhibition catalogue as *Casement Window in Opalescent Glass*. I am grateful to Rebecca Lawton for making me aware of this photograph and catalogue entry in a letter of June 30, 1983. The window may also have been included in the earlier Syracuse show. After Lamb's death the parrots window was exhibited with other bird-theme windows by Lamb at the Grand Central Art Galleries in New York City. See "Lamb's Art," *Art Digest* 5 (May 1, 1931): 13; "Lamb Memorial at Grand Central," *Art News* 29 (April 18, 1931): 14; and "Exhibition of a Group of Bird Panels, Grand Central Galleries," *International Studio* 99 (June 1931): 67. "Arts and Crafts Exhibition," *Magazine of Art* 1 (1910): 95–97. Articles by Lamb are: "The Beautifying of Our Cities," *The Craftsman* 2, no. 4 (July 1902): 172–88; "Lessons from the Expositions," *The Craftsman* 3, no. 1 (October 1902): 49–58; "The Painted Window," *The Craftsman* 3, no. 6 (March 1903): 341–49; "The Flower Memorial Library," *The Craftsman* 7, no. 4 (January 1905): 378–99; "Modern Use of the Gothic: The Possibilities of New Architectural Style," *The Craftsman* 8, no. 2 (May 1905): 150–70; "The Architectural Discussion: Reply," *The Craftsman* 8, no. 6 (September 1905): 804–8; "John La Farge"; and "The Making of a Modern Stained Glass Window—Its History and Process; And a Word about Mosaics," *The Craftsman* 10, no. 1 (April 1905): 18–31.

[5] [Lamb], "Frederick Stymetz Lamb," p. 9; Otto W. Heinigke, acknowledgment letter for Frederick Stymetz Lamb adopted by the Stained and Leaded Glass Association of New York, August 2, 1928 (Barea Lamb Seeley, Tenafly, N.J.). Lamb was also active in organizing the New York City Improvement Commission and was a trustee for the American Society for the Preservation of Scenic and Historical Places.

Fig. 2. Frederick Lamb, *Parrots*, J. and R. Lamb
Studios, New York City, ca. 1902. Leaded glass;
H. 44″, W. 36″. (Morse Gallery of Art, Winter Park,
Fla.; Photo, J. and R. Lamb Studios.)

career of Lamb and, perhaps, of others like him from this period. To
accomplish this, we must consider Lamb's ideas regarding art and craft
and, especially, public art, which will suggest a certain continuum
of thinking among the arts and crafts movement, the City Beautiful
movement, and the academically influenced mural decoration of the
American Renaissance artists. This, in turn, will provide a framework
for a brief consideration of the range of Lamb's own artwork.

In his 1902 *Craftsman* article, "The Beautifying of Our Cities,"
Lamb complained that what was then recognized as "art" proper was
largely isolated from everyday life and placed in the unnatural light of

museums and galleries, where it was seldom seen. "Art is what can be exhibited in the Salon; all else is commerce," he commented. He noted that in the Middle Ages and in early Renaissance Italy there were no differentiations between "high art, municipal art, or applied art." Art was simply recognized as a force contributing to the welfare of the community, and every craftsperson under the guild system was also an artist. By the nineteenth century the academies of art had established the dictum that, while crafts such as mosaics, fresco, and stained glass could be designed by a "master" of art, their execution was a craft to be left to others. Indeed, this was one of La Farge's sharpest criticisms of the British arts and crafts movement's practice in creating stained glass windows, as observed in the methods of Edward Burne-Jones. In response, La Farge personally supervised every step of the design and manufacture of his stained glass windows, especially the artistically important steps such as glass selection. Lamb followed suit.[6]

Lamb noted with approval that La Farge had trained his artisans in stained glass "to the point of capacity and interest in artistic work that makes them artists without their losing the character of the workman." He also registered his approval at the decision (on which he had, in fact, exerted some influence) of the upcoming 1904 Louisiana Purchase International Exposition in St. Louis to include galleries for a wide range of crafts mediums in its Department of Art and to make no distinction "between 'what has commonly been considered as Fine Art and that which has been termed Industrial Art.'" "Here is a broader definition of art than has been believed possible," exulted Lamb. "Four hundred years have rolled around and the craftsman is again to take his place among the artists." He noted that the expositions of the period, as a whole, had shown "a tendency to again unite the aesthetic and the practical—to redeem art by making it real and vital."[7]

[6]Lamb, "Beautifying of Our Cities," p. 175. John La Farge, "Reply to Bing," La Farge Family Papers, Yale University Library, New Haven, Conn., as quoted in H. Barbara Weinberg, *The Decorative Work of John La Farge* (New York: Garland, 1977), p. 341. Lamb described his own level of involvement—typical for most American opalescent glass designers—in his articles "Making of a Modern Stained Glass Window"; "Painted Window," pp. 347–48; and "Stained Glass in Its Relation to Church Ornamentation," *Catholic World* 74 (February 1902): 670–74. See also Charles Rollinson Lamb, "How an American Stained Glass Window Is Made," *Chautauquan* 29, no. 6 (September 1899): 515–20.

[7]On training, see Lamb, "John La Farge," p. 320. Lamb, "Lessons from the Expositions," pp. 57, 50.

Yet a reunion of divided art and craft was only one result of the healing Lamb hoped would occur in the larger rift between art and everyday life. Lamb pointed to the historical roots of the present division between art and life, focusing on the period from the seventeenth to the nineteenth centuries: "Commercialism in art commenced when art lost touch with commerce; when art ceased to answer the legitimate demands of the age in which it existed, decadence set in. Art degenerated into an aristocratic adjunct and was viewed with distrust by the people." In Lamb's analysis the artist had gradually drifted from direct dealings with the patron or consumer ("the working, living world") and had to trust commercial middlemen. Then the creative focus shifted from the ability of the artist to the skill of the middleman at commercial exploitation and art market competition. Lamb concluded, "Art, instead of answering the healthy demands of the masses, pandered to the wants of the luxurious few. 'Art for art's sake,' became the cry." The artist alone defined what art should be, cut off from everyday life, so that art exhibitions became, in Lamb's judgement, "mere mannerisms," "tiresome, . . . the endless change of fashion." These sentiments clearly show the marks of an acquaintance with the ideas of William Morris and the British arts and crafts movement, and yet Lamb had made the thoughts his own.[8]

"How can art be revitalized?" Lamb asks in a 1902 article and answers his own question several pages later, as follows: "Let him [the artist], instead of answering unasked questions, meet the conditions of the times. Art is tempered and purified by use; by use it becomes real and vital." In the Middle Ages, emphasized Lamb, "art sprang from the merchant, the magistrate, the artisan; then art was 'of the people, for the people, by the people.'" He argued that authentic art must be related "to the problems of the day in which it exists" and must be "an answer to some legitimate demand." Lamb even went so far as to claim,

[8]Lamb, "Lessons from the Expositions," pp. 49, 50. One example of a similar analysis can be found in William Morris's lecture "Art and Labour"; see Eugene D. Lemire, ed., *The Unpublished Lectures of William Morris* (Detroit: Wayne State University Press, 1969), esp. pp. 105, 111. Lamb may also have been echoing the opinions of one of his teachers at the Académie Julian, Gustave Boulanger, who opposed the abuse of "originality at all costs" in a speech in the early 1880s, when Lamb was his student; see Albert Boime, *The Academy and French Painting in the Nineteenth Century* (New York: Phaidon, 1971), p. 184.

"All great art is public art." Yet, in turn-of-the-century America, he lamented, "how art has drifted from the realization that it is in any way an integral part of our city! How little thought of the effect of color, form, light and shade on the mind of the citizen!"[9] Lamb here announced two further themes to be considered, themes that represented the answers to the dilemma of art's irrelevance and would be pursued in much of his own design work, theoretical writing, and lecturing: civic art and the educational or moral effect of such public art.

Lamb and many other American artists and designers evinced few of the misgivings of Morris about commercializing their handiwork and attempted through example, education, and persuasion to influence existing public and private sponsors of building projects and city planning to improve their aesthetic standards. However, both British and American approaches exemplified Gillian Naylor's assessment that the most significant influence of the arts and crafts movement on twentieth-century design was "to see the problems of design within a social context."[10]

What did Lamb expect from a reformed municipal art? His ideas, in part at least, attempted to apply arts and crafts movement principles to the larger scale of urban planning and design. The magazine that first spread the word of the movement in America was *House Beautiful*, started in 1896. Lamb wanted to extend the arts and crafts philosophy in domestic aesthetics, in the "house beautiful" to the "city beautiful." He wrote in 1902: "We appeal for the monumentalizing of the great utilities of a city. What finer memorial could there be in a city than one of its great bridges properly designed? What finer monument than one of our great buildings properly created?" Three years later he appealed for an architecture that no longer tried to hide its actual iron or cement block construction behind a simulated traditional stone or brick

[9]Lamb, "Lessons from the Expositions," p. 57. Lamb, "Beautifying of Our Cities," p. 180; in addition to his reference to Lincoln's *Gettysburg Address*, Lamb here was perhaps also recalling a repeated sentiment of William Morris, who, for example, called for an "art made by the people and for the people"; G. D. H. Cole, ed., *William Morris Centenary Edition* (London: Nonesuch Press, 1948), p. 545. Lamb, "Lessons from the Expositions," p. 58. Lamb, "Beautifying of Our Cities," p. 185.
[10]Gillian Naylor, *The Arts and Crafts Movement: A Study of Its Sources, Ideals, and Influence on Design Theory* (Cambridge: MIT Press, 1971), p. 7. On Morris's misgivings, see Lionel Lambourne, *Utopian Craftsmen: The Arts and Crafts Movement from the Cotswolds to Chicago* (New York: Van Nostrand Reinhold, 1982), p. 25.

facade.[11] One can readily recognize an expression here of the basic arts and crafts values—extending from Ruskin to Morris to Stickley—of honest use of materials and exploitation of inherent structure and material quality rather than applied ornament.

At the same time, many of the specific suggestions Lamb made for city planning reflected an ideal that Coy Ludwig has called one of the two main concerns of the arts and crafts movement in America: "How to preserve human values in a rapidly expanding society." Among other measures, Lamb recommended diagonal or radiating city streets for the opportunities they provided for extended vistas; pedestrian "isles of safety" and public monuments; piercing solid city blocks with street arcades and galleries to provide more light, air, garden space, pedestrian circulation, and service access; legislation limiting building height, interrelating cornice heights between buildings, and requiring setbacks of buildings from the street line; tablets or monuments commemorating significant events in each locality of a city; greater recreational area in parks; and a general concern for the artistic design of all city amenities from subways to lampposts to park seats.[12]

It is no accident that many of Lamb's City Beautiful recommendations also accord with the beaux arts influenced urban aesthetics of the American Renaissance movement, such as grand vistas with impressive terminal points and isolated monuments. Both municipal art and architectural ornamentation provided a common ground between these two related "movements." With his family background in Gothic revival design and his interest in arts and crafts simplification, however, Lamb was no special advocate of the revived classical and neoclassical styles

[11] Lamb, "Beautifying of Our Cities," pp. 188, 172. Lamb, "Architectural Discussion," p. 805.
[12] Ludwig, *Arts and Crafts Movement*, p. 107. Lamb, "Beautifying of Our Cities," pp. 179–85. Lamb further argued in lectures and writings that municipal art was "a paying investment": good design cost no more than bad, and it augmented a city's public image, welfare, and commercial success. Most of these suggestions had been advanced somewhat earlier, and thereafter more prominently, by his brother. See, for example: Charles Rollinson Lamb, "Civic Architecture from Its Constructive Side," *Municipal Affairs* 2 (1898): 46–72; "New York—The City Beautiful," *Metropolitan Magazine* 12, no. 5 (November 1900): 593–600; "City Plan," *The Craftsman* 6, no. 1 (April 1904): 3–13; and "Saving the Sunshine in the City's Valley of Shadow," *New York Herald*, August 9, 1908, magazine section. Further discussion of Lamb's involvement in New York City improvement efforts, through such organizations as the Municipal Art Society and the Citizens Union Committee, may be found in Gregory Gilmartin, *Shaping the City: New York and the Municipal Art Society* (New York: Clarkson Potter, 1994).

of architecture associated with American Renaissance urban design. He recognized that times were changing and that artistic design must begin to change correspondingly. His 1905 article in *The Craftsman,* "Modern Use of the Gothic: The Possibilities of New Architectural Style," occasioned an extended debate among several authors, most notably Louis Sullivan, regarding the potential for a new, modern style of architecture. The debate focused on whether certain principles inherent in Gothic construction (Lamb suggested tallness, elaborate fenestration, and location of weight on isolated points) could provide a more useful starting point for a new American architectural style than the "rude and rudimentary forms of construction" of the post-and-lintel system underlying "cold, unresponsive" revivals of classical architecture. None of the old architectural styles were an "adequate expression of present conditions," said Lamb, and a new style of design was called for to respond to new, contemporary functional demands of, for example, tall office buildings, railway terminals, and post offices.[13]

Even in the crafts Lamb felt it important to meet the challenge posed to technique and design by the development of new technology. "To make beautiful the product of the machine has been the problem given to us, and unless solved, the machine will dominate the age to the detriment of the individual," wrote Lamb in 1902. But Lamb's own design endeavors rarely called for use of any mechanical technology.[14]

In his architectural discussions Lamb touched on another theme dear to both American arts and crafts designers and American Renaissance artists: the need to create an authentic national artistic expression—in Lamb's words, an architecture that expressed "the energy and enterprise of the American people." Lamb declared, "No true American but would welcome with gladness an architecture that was truly American, but can anyone claim, in all seriousness, that the architec-

---

[13] Lamb, "Modern Use of the Gothic," p. 150.

[14] Lamb, "Lessons from the Expositions," p. 57. Despite a popular but oversimplified impression to the contrary, William Morris shared similar views, writing, for example, that "men should be masters of their machines, and not the slaves as they are now"; see the discussion in Lambourne, *Utopian Craftsmen,* pp. 22, 29. J. and R. Lamb catalogues from the late 1880s announced the addition of a new gas-fired kiln with a glass cart that moved in and out of the kiln on a short rail track. The earliest catalogue with this announcement is entitled *Church and Household Stained Glass* (undated).

ture of to-day 'is what the American people think?' No, a thousand
times no. Architecture, to-day, is more scholastic, more pedantic, more
precedent ridden than at any time in the history of the world."[15]

National "schools" of art were viewed as representing the artistic
and moral level of a people, so there was no small measure of nationalistic pride in the widespread discussions during this period regarding
the development of a truly American art, informed by but not imitative
of European precedents. In the decorative arts and architecture this
sentiment often took the form of an appeal to produce a genuinely
"democratic" art, something called for and essayed by, for example,
both Stickley and Sullivan.[16]

Within the pages of *The Craftsman* a discussion took place in
several articles between 1904 and 1906 emphasizing that mural decoration was a democratic and public form of art and was, in fact, the
medium where we could most expect to develop an American art. To
the extent that the American arts and crafts movement harbored ambitions of also transforming fine art along the lines of arts and crafts
principles, these ambitions were primarily focused on mural decoration. *The Craftsman* discussion was launched in the October 1904
issue with an article authored by Charles M. Shean, a designer who
worked for J. and R. Lamb. While calling for a greatly expanded development of mural decoration in the United States, Shean also con-
tended the following: "Monumental art in this democracy can never
be a toy for the rich, nor will it ever be a field for the exploitation of
studio reminiscences and echoes of the old classical and academic art
of Europe. . . . It must have for its base the broad support of popular
pride and appreciation. This, the condition of its existence and full

---

[15] Lamb, "Architectural Discussion," p. 807.

[16] See, for example, Gustav Stickley, "The Craftsman Movement: Its Origin and
Growth," *The Craftsman* 25, no. 1 (October 1913): 18; or Gustav Stickley, "Thoughts
Occasioned by an Anniversary: A Plea for a Democratic Art," *The Craftsman* 7, no. 1
(October 1904): 42–43, 48, 53. Among many pieces written by Louis Sullivan, see his
first formal essay, "Characteristics and Tendencies of American Architecture," of 1885;
"The Young Men in Architecture" of 1900; "The Possibility of a New Architectural
Style" of June 1905; "What Is Architecture: A Study in the American People of Today"
of 1906; and "Is Our Art a Betrayal Rather than an Expression of American Life?" of
January 1909. The 1905 and 1909 pieces were published in *The Craftsman*; all may be
found in Robert Twombly, ed., *Louis Sullivan: The Public Papers* (Chicago: University
of Chicago Press, 1988).

development will, in the end, control its tendencies and govern its choice of subjects."[17]

Shean asserted that mural work paid for by public funds must have a higher purpose than mere embellishment to justify the expense and command public approval. "Except as they personify the ideas of the people," he opposed the "foreign accent" of "tiresome collections of classical paraphernalia: Fame with her trumpet. The winged victory. The laurel crown and the palm of victory," which were popular in academic and American Renaissance mural design of the time. Instead of these "well worn and over-used allegories and personifications, characterless figures of no particular age or clime," Shean urged that authentically American murals portray scenes and figures from American history and life, "the golden records of the nation's story." Those American Renaissance admirers of the genteel tradition of ideal art would have replied that, for presentation of uplifting and noble images of universal ideals, the artist must draw upon the universal language and history of humanity rather than the specific realism of one moment or geographical locality.[18]

Stickley's collaborator Irene Sargent, in another *Craftsman* article in this series, repeated Shean's call for a democratic mural art, which, unlike "aristocratic," inaccessible easel paintings, would keep before the minds of American citizens "the effort, self-sacrifice and unity necessary to the maintenance of a commonwealth or community." Lamb, who portrayed both American historical and ideal allegorical figures in his murals, also argued for the Ruskinian morally and historically educational values of public art, which was another concept shared by the American Renaissance, City Beautiful, and arts and crafts movements. Many of his own artworks as well as thousands of others in different mediums by J. and R. Lamb memorialized American his-

[17]Charles M. Shean, "Mural Painting from the American Point of View," *The Craftsman* 7, no. 1 (October 1904): 21. Shean (d. 1925), who may have ceased working for J. and R. Lamb sometime during the 1890s, was a New York mural painter who also designed some stained glass windows and other decorative art.
[18]Shean, "Mural Painting," pp. 25–27. On the American Renaissance viewpoint, see the discussion in Richard Guy Wilson, Dianne H. Pilgrim, and Richard N. Murray, *The American Renaissance, 1876–1917* (New York: Pantheon Books, 1979), pp. 29–30, 41–46; Kenyon Cox, *The Classic Point of View* (1911; reprint, New York: W. W. Norton, 1980); and Edwin Howland Blashfield, *Mural Painting in America* (New York: Charles Scribner's Sons, 1913), p. 18.

torical events and personages. Lamb's father had been a pioneer in the cause of historical preservation and commemoration. Lamb lectured on "The Educational Influence of Mural Painting" and on more than one occasion defended the importance in public art of literary subjects and even of "lessons to be taught," as opposed to a pure "language of form and color." "While there is a distinct language of form and color," he wrote in 1902, "the possibility of using it is dependent upon the subject and its arrangement."[19]

Lamb's content-oriented viewpoint stemmed also from his personal assessment of the artistic task in America. He argued that the Puritans' dislike of visual art had resulted in an exclusively literary mode of education, with the result that American children "lost all power of observation." Moreover, he understood the Anglo-Saxon peoples as a whole—among which he apparently included the American people at a time when it was more common to overlook the other races living in the United States—as an essentially literary culture with regard to art. He continued, "We Anglo-Saxons always demand an intellectual element in our art. In order, therefore, to arouse the people from their general apathy toward art it is necessary to give it an intellectual character, to connect it with our national life and large ideas. The mere form counts for little in comparison." Elsewhere he added that public art in churches could help new immigrants not yet fully conversant in English to keep before their minds important scriptural lessons. Mural work could perform a useful public function by supplaning the spoken and written word with "sermons on wall and in window."[20]

[19] Irene Sargent, "Comments upon Mr. Sergeant's 'Mural Painting from the American Point of View,'" *The Craftsman* 7, no. 1 (October 1904): 32. In a similar vein Stickley stated that "badly-constructed, over-ornate, meaningless furniture" in the home led a person "away from the sound qualities which make an honest man and a good citizen" (Gustav Stickley, "Catalogue of Craftsman Furniture" [1910]) in *Stickley Craftsman Furniture Catalogues* (New York: Dover, 1979), p. 3; see also Stickley, "Thoughts Occasioned," p. 53. On historical preservation, see the memorial booklet probably written by Charles Rollinson Lamb, *In Memoriam—Joseph Lamb* (New York: J. and R. Lamb, [1898]). Lamb lectured on May 11, 1899, at the Bridgeport, Conn., public library, as reported in the *Bridgeport Evening Post* of the same date. I thank David W. Palmquist, head of historical collections at the Bridgeport Public Library, for bringing this to my attention in 1985. Lamb, "Painted Window," p. 348. Lamb, "Stained Glass," p. 75.
[20] "Art in a Cafe," *New York Community Advertiser*, November 25, 1899. On murals, see Lamb, "Stained Glass," p. 677. Some of these sentiments were also voiced by Edwin Blashfield in "A Definition of Decorative Art," in *Brochure of the Mural Painters—A National Society* (New York: National Society of Mural Painters, 1916), p. 10.

These latter comments remind us that the greater part of Lamb's own artwork was executed for ecclesiastical edifices. In addition to creating mural paintings and glass mosaics, between 1883 and 1921 he designed or supervised for J. and R. Lamb more than two thousand stained glass windows for buildings in almost every state of the union. Nearly all of these were fabricated with the new opalescent glass adapted to flat-glass manufacture and design by La Farge, beginning in 1877 and popularized soon after through the aggressive promotion of Louis Comfort Tiffany.

In contrast to traditional, transparent "pot metal" or "antique" colored glass used in leaded windows since the medieval period, opalescent glass is cloudy and translucent. It contains opaque particles that float in colloidal suspension. These modulate the opacity of the glass and scatter light, sometimes giving an iridescent effect. The layered structure allows two or more different colors to be blended irregularly within one sheet of glass, giving rise to a tremendous variety of pictorial effects.

While most studies of the American arts and crafts movement have recognized opalescent glass windows as a unique national element, to fully appreciate their role I believe we must come to see the opalescent glass movement belonging as much to the history of mural art as to the history of stained glass craft. The extent to which opalescent glass windows and other large-scale, two-dimensional public artworks (such as mosaics and tapestries) were at the time considered to be only alternative varieties of mural painting has scarcely been mentioned in arts and crafts literature.

Yet, not only Lamb but all of the major opalescent glass window designers—collectively referred to as the "American School"—were Paris-trained and practicing easel and/or mural painters (such as La Farge, Tiffany, D. Maitland Armstrong, Mary Tillinghast, and Joseph Lauber). Lauber commented in 1912, "Nearly all the artists who have essayed mural painting have worked in this medium [opalescent stained glass] some time or other; more as a labor of love, I should say, because compared with painting, it is a decidedly underpaid art."[21] Even many well-known easel painters of the period occasionally designed windows (including Elihu Vedder, Kenyon Cox, Will H. Low, and Robert Blum).

[21] Joseph Lauber, "European Versus American Color Windows," *Architectural Record* 31 (February 1912): 145.

Similar aesthetic ideas were advanced for both mural painting and stained glass. Writers about stained glass as well as the authors of the two major mural painting texts of the period—Pauline King's *Mural Painters in America* of 1902 and Lamb's friend Edwin Blashfield's *Mural Painting in America* of 1913—affirmed the same artistic ideals of large scale, undisguised flatness, allover surface unity, and harmonious relation to surrounding architecture in terms of color, depth, and lighting. With no further comment or distinction, both Blashfield's *Mural Painting in America* and the 1916 brochure of the National Society of Mural Painters illustrated opalescent glass windows side by side with painted murals.[22]

Most of the reasons why La Farge conceived and developed flat, opalescent window glass related to the quest for more sophisticated pictorial means in stained glass, largely to meet the demands of patrons and clients for detailed, naturalistic forms and figural designs. To overcome expressive limitations apparent in the heavily painted antique glass windows of British artists, La Farge attempted to avoid violating the intrinsic nature of the glass with obscuring paint, while still achieving mural-like representational results. The new opalescent medium was used by American artists as much to attain a luminosity and intensity of color not achievable in pigment painting as it was used for genuinely craft, decorative, or architectural window effects. Lamb wrote, "Instead of the jeweled effect of primary colors [medieval windows] or the inadequate painted figure [more recent European windows], we have a gorgeous bloom of color in large 'washes,' so to speak, in which figures and landscape bathe in an atmosphere that the painted canvas can never realize, for the low amber glow behind purple mountains, represented with pigment, cannot possibly have the luminosity of real light shining through."[23] Indeed, the scale of brightness possible through the transmitted light of stained glass is thousands of times wider than that possible from the reflected light of pigment painting.

Lamb referred to the stained glass artist as "a painter without a

---

[22] Pauline King, *Mural Painters in America* (Boston: Noyes, Platt, 1902), pp. 5–10; and Blashfield, *Mural Painting in America*, pp. 86–87, 186. For stained glass writers, see my forthcoming *Voices from the Opalescent Era: An Anthology of Period Articles on the American Opalescent Glass Window Movement*. Blashfield, "Definition of Decorative Art."

[23] Lamb, "Making of a Modern Stained Glass," p. 19.

brush" who "uses light itself for his combining medium" and has his
or her pigment suspended in glass rather than in oil or another medium.[24] In opalescent glass windows the milky texture, streaky soft
blends of color, and subtle transitions in value caused by varying glass
opacity and surface thickness can remind us of tonal effects of oil
painting, while the combination of colors from overplating two or more
differently colored sheets of glass is reminiscent of multiple watercolor
washes. Moreover, an array of new techniques and applications had
further expanded the paintlike repertoire of the American glass artist:
cast or molded glass forms, chipped and faceted glass nuggets and jew-
els, "confetti" glass, mottled glass, folded "drapery glass," patterned or
"corrugated" glass, avoidance of heavy dividing lines through use of
copper foil or tiny heat-fused glass pieces set in fine metal wires, and
graphic use of lead cames for linear and chiaroscuro effects, including
backplating of lead lines behind another piece of glass to suggest softened linear shadows.

Lamb reflected the nationalistic pride of the American School
when he extravagantly claimed that these "crystal canvases" were "the
finest expression of the painter's art that the world has yet seen" and
that "the glassworker's art stands side by side with the painting of the
greatest masters and [is] of equal importance." Opalescent glass windows were, in fact and not in rhetoric only, both pictorial and decorative, both art and craft, a unique and challenging American fusion of
what are still today largely considered separate practices.[25]

Many aspects of opalescent glass window art evinced principles of
the arts and crafts movement. The handcrafted windows were often
placed in Craftsman houses and were attractive to architects and designers, in some cases, for their nostalgic associations with medieval craft

[24]Lamb, "Making of a Modern Stained Glass," p. 19; Lamb, "Painted Window,"
p. 347.
[25]Lamb, "Stained Glass," p. 667. Some critics, especially European authors of the
period, argued that too often the "art" side of the art-craft equation was qualitatively
weak. See Cecilia Warren, "The Industrial Arts of America: The Tiffany Glass and
Decorating Company," *International Studio* 2 (1897): 156–65; 5 (1898): 16–21; Ed[ou-
ard] Didron, "Les Vitraux a L'Exposition de 1900," *Revue des Arts Decoratifs* 20 (1900):
276. For critic Julius Meier-Graefe's opinions, see Robert Koch, *Louis C. Tiffany: Rebel
in Glass* (New York: Crown, 1982), p. 58.

traditions.[26] Opalescent windows avoided applied decoration (painted) and relied on the inherent qualities and colors of the glass and lead themselves. Good designs emphasized the material's intrinsic flatness, usually with some concessions to three-dimensional pictorial effects, and related to their surrounding architecture, space, and lighting as an orchestrated decorative unity. The opalescent windows were a unique American art form, and La Farge had even chosen the dense layered glass material in part to temper the particularly brilliant American light better than European applied paint was able to do. As public, civic art—placed in churches, libraries, restaurants, and government buildings as well as houses—opalescent windows were fully capable of imparting uplifting moral lessons and historical or literary information. The move to opalescent glass window design was, moreover, a perfect response to the exhortation of many American artists to use a cosmopolitan awareness of past artistic traditions to selectively forge a new genuinely American art form.

Lamb's own mural work in oils, stained glass, and glass mosaic illustrated nearly all of these arts and crafts features. He also favored the arts and crafts value of simplification. Like most of the other American muralists, Lamb was strongly influenced by the restrained and dignified decorative approach, simplified figures, and chalky coloration of French mural painter Puvis de Chavannes. In Lamb's case this was tempered somewhat by his admiration for the realistic detail and stronger colors of La Farge and by the large patterns of light and shade found in the compositions of English painter Frank Brangwyn. Within buildings he decorated, Lamb generally opposed an excess of architectural detail and "in the fenestration an over-mullioned effect."[27]

Through his knowledge of the family decorative arts business, his exposure to mural art in Europe, and the early opalescent glass experiments of La Farge in New York, Lamb was unusually well pre-

[26] Gustav Stickley's artistic collaborator Dard Hunter even apprenticed at J. and R. Lamb in October 1903 to learn the craft; see Dard Hunter, *My Life with Paper* (New York: Alfred A. Knopf, 1958), pp. 32–33. I am grateful to Bruce Bland for pointing out to me Hunter's stint at Lamb Studios and his later stained glass work.

[27] Stickley pleaded "for simplicity in all that pertains to the environment of material life under a democracy," in "Thoughts Occasioned," p. 42. Sargent applied the concept to mural painting, recommending "the austere lines and color schemes" of Puvis de Chavannes (Sargent, "Comments upon Mr. Shean's 'Mural Painting,'" p. 31). La Farge and Brangwyn were discussed by Adrian Lamb, interview with author, New York City, May 14, 1980. Lamb, "Stained Glass," p. 670.

pared for creating mural decorations. He is credited with designing more complete glazing programs for buildings than any other American stained glass artist of the period.[28]

Lamb also worked in another uniquely American mural art medium of the period, glass mosaic. Although usually designed by American artists, mosaics were typically executed by Italian artisans. In 1906 Lamb gave a brief account of American innovations in the mosaic art, mentioning the following: use of pieces of opalescent glass instead of, or in addition to, stone or tile tesserae in order to give more subtlety and variety of color and size (such as Tiffany's use of iridescent Favrile glass in mosaics), use of large or irregular sheets of marble, and design conceptions that conveyed effects of lighting and atmosphere quite different from Byzantine and Roman mosaics.[29]

Lamb often called for collaborative and unified decorative efforts among architect, decorative artists, and client. However, work for churches was complicated by the involvement of the priest and the donor. It was one thing for an artist to have clearly conceived ideals and intentions. The possibility of realizing them in large-scale works of public art, however, depended primarily upon the commissioned work that came to the artist. Here Lamb registered a number of complaints regarding the whims and interference of window donors. "But how seldom do the ideal conditions exist which make it possible for the artist to demonstrate his ability!" he lamented. "More often the subject is dictated, the color insisted upon, and the treatment held subordinate to the wishes of the donor." In addition, the tremendous pressure exerted by the seemingly insatiable demand for stained glass windows during this period must have forced Lamb, as it did others, to sometimes reuse earlier cartoons and designs or take other artistic shortcuts. In 1891 alone, for example, he received orders for 174 windows at J. and R. Lamb.[30]

Given these restrictions and caveats, a brief look at a few examples illustrating the range of Lamb's mural decoration work, which was sometimes executed in collaboration with his brother Charles, a "deco-

[28]Charles Rollinson Lamb, "The Romance of American Glass," *Brooklyn Museum Quarterly* 16, no. 4 (October 1929): 30–31.
[29]Lamb, "Making of a Modern Stained Glass Window," pp. 30–31.
[30]Lamb, "Stained Glass," pp. 672, 674. J. and R. Lamb, *Glass Order Book* (Philmont, N.Y.: J. and R. Lamb Studios, 1891–94). A microfilm copy is available in the library of the Corning Museum of Glass, Corning, N.Y.

rative architect," will demonstrate how Lamb struggled to realize his ideals within the often difficult contexts of patron demands, specific building functions, or predetermined mural art subjects or purposes. A round window titled *The Arts* is typical of one type of Lamb subject, featuring allegorical personages in classical garb (fig. 3): Literature with quill pen and paper, flanked by upright Art holding a brush and palette, and Craft working on her embroidery with an actual wire "thread." The window was also known as *Women's Work in the Arts* and *Apotheosis of Woman*, and was created in 1896–97 for the main staircase landing of the Woman's Building at the 1897 Tennessee Centennial and International Exposition in Nashville. It later won a medal at the 1902 Esposizione Internazionale in Turin, Italy (where the German periodical *Deutsche Kunst und Dekoration* mistakenly attributed it to Tiffany).[31]

A compositionally related but more complex window of this same type was *Religion Enthroned* of 1899 (see fig. 1).[32] This rectangular exhibition window won two gold medals at the Exposition Universelle in Paris in 1900. The three iconic, classically clothed figures (the central seated Religion with the armored Church Militant to the left and the robed Church Triumphant to the right) are naturalistically treated but are embedded in a more visionary, spaceless world that draws them into an overall surface pattern that is more energized and mobile. In 1901 *Religion Enthroned* formed the centerpiece of J. and R. Lamb's gold-medal-winning chapel in the Mission Building at the Pan-American Exposition in Buffalo. The window was flanked there by Lamb's painted murals of *The Church* and *The State*, which further extended the theme of the Church Triumphant and the Church Militant.

An earlier three-light version of *Religion Enthroned*, first shown at the 1893 World's Columbian Exposition in Chicago, was included in the foyer area of the extensive decorative scheme designed by the Lamb brothers between 1908 and 1911 for the First Presbyterian Church in Or-

[31] The window in situ is illustrated in Herman Justi, ed., *Official History of the Tennessee Centennial Exposition* (Nashville, 1898), p. 147, and in the souvenir booklet on the Woman's Building, Public Library of Nashville and Davidson County, Tenn. The erroneous German attribution is in Georg Fuchs, "Eindrücke aus der americkanischen Abteilung," *Deutsche Kunst und Dekoration* 11 (1903): 190. In addition, see the in-progress illustrations in Lamb, "How an American Stained Glass Window Is Made."
[32] See my forthcoming booklet on this window, *Religion Enthroned: A Rediscovered 1899 Stained Glass Window by Frederick Stymetz Lamb*, to be published in 1995 or 1996 by the Brooklyn Museum, in whose collection *Religion Enthroned* now resides.

ange, Texas, where it was flanked by two fifteen-by-fifteen-foot, oil-on-canvas murals by Lamb entitled *Faith* and *Charity*. *Faith* and *Charity* seem to have been combined with the church and state themes from Lamb's Buffalo murals to emphasize the appropriate religious virtues. Lamb also created thirty-three additional windows for this church and its Sunday school, illustrating the life of Christ as rendered in popular nineteenth-century European religious paintings. The glazing program was capped by Lamb's approximately thirty-three-foot-diameter opalescent glass dome depicting angels hovering above the sanctuary.

Lamb had earlier used some of the same window subjects in one of the largest stained glass commissions of the period: nineteen large and thirty-six smaller figure windows for the Stanford Memorial Church at Stanford University, created between 1899 and 1903.[33] The larger windows, which illustrate scenes from the life of Christ, were designed in connection with surrounding wall mosaics that portray Old Testament scenes. The smaller windows lining the clerestory represent, on opposite sides of the church, Old and New Testament figures.

When allowed by patrons, Lamb seemed to prefer more nontraditional decoration schemes and window subjects. One effective example was his design for the complete glazing program of the Washington Street United Methodist Church in Columbia, South Carolina, of 1912–13. There Lamb filled the approximately twelve-foot-tall windows with landscapes corresponding to settings of New Testament events. Lamb noted the landscape window as a subject that was entirely modern and a unique contribution of the American school. "The effect of landscape produced in the modern glass," he wrote, "is a kind of vivid, intensified realism that is yet dream-like."[34]

Another purpose called for a completely different type of window mural. For a window placed in a fraternity house as a memorial to Cornell University alumni who had died, Lamb drew on the appropriately scholarly subject from Homer's *Iliad* of the Greek hero Achilles

---

[33] See Gail Stockholm, *Stanford Memorial Church: An Appreciative Guide for the Not-So-Casual Visitor* (Stanford, Calif.: Stanford University, Memorial Church and Office of Public Affairs, 1980). On the mosaics, designed by Antonio Paoletti of Salviati and Company, Venice, see Carol M. Osborne, *Museum Builders in the West: The Stanfords as Collectors and Patrons of Art, 1870–1906* (Stanford, Calif.: Stanford University, 1986).

[34] Lamb, "Stained Glass," p. 30.

Fig. 3. Frederick Lamb, *The Arts*, J. and R. Lamb Studios, New York, 1896–97. Leaded glass; Diam. 104″. (La Belle Verrière Restaurant, Winter Park, Fla.: Photo, J. and R. Lamb Studios.)

mourning his slain friend Patroclus (including a quotation from the original Greek in the window design). A different literary architectural setting and function logically demanded a different type of mural decoration. The decoration of the Flower Memorial Library in Watertown, New York, between 1901 and 1904 under the direction of Charles Lamb, was cited by several *Craftsman* authors (Shean and Sargent among them) as a notable example of the promise of an American mural art. This attention was due partly to the various murals and friezes on local history painted in the upstairs rooms by several different hands, but Frederick Lamb's painting of the main rotunda dome was singled out for especially detailed discussion in the January 1905 issue of *The Craftsman.*[35] This editorial appreciation was appended to an article by Lamb on the decoration project as a whole. Although no author was given, it is apparent that the writer—whether Sargent or Stickley, or someone else—had been somewhat prompted by Lamb himself.

The anonymous writer noted that Lamb had studied the greatest dome decorators from Michelangelo to Paul Baudry and thus was well prepared to handle the optical and compositional challenges of large curved surfaces seen from below. Lamb had handled "his composition *architecturally . . . constructing in color*" and had created in both design and color a simplified, ordered, and balanced arrangement following the architectural framework, thus rendering "the decorative subservient to the structural scheme, as should always be the case." Four figures in "almost medieval costume . . . executed in a deep and rich tonality" were placed on the dome at the main axis of the building, personifying history, romance, religion, and science. These were separated by intermediate figures "more classic in detail" in "a lighter and intermediate color" representing lyric and epic poetry, fable, and drama. With a modern "feeling for Nature, such as could not have been conceived by the old decorators," Lamb used trees to structure the dome into eight arched panels and balanced the upright tree trunks with the horizontal foliage of orange trees fronted by names of representative authors of each type of literature.[36]

Comparisons are extravagant. The anonymous author compares Lamb's composition to that of the Sistine Chapel ceiling, his colors to Titian's, and claims that his figure of Religion "is worthy of the times of the great mosaicists, whose manner it recalls without losing that freshness of conception which marks it as an original work. It is beautiful and majestic." It is also quite similar to his later figure of Charity in the foyer mural in Orange, Texas. *The Craftsman* author also cor-

[35] The 61-by-30-inch window is in the central stairway landing of the Delta Chi chapter of Delta Kappa Epsilon house in Ithaca, N.Y. I acknowledge the help of H. William Fogle, alumni secretary and historian of Delta Chi chapter, in locating this window in 1988. Shean, "Mural Painting," p. 24; Sargent, "Comments upon Mr. Shean's 'Mural Painting,'" p. 33. The other artists who contributed were H. Peabody Flagg, George W. Breck, and brothers Leon and Scott Dabo; special attention was also given in *The Craftsman* article to the mural painting *The Open Book* by Ella Condie Lamb, Charles Lamb's wife.

[36] Lamb, "Flower Memorial Library," pp. 397, 390, 394.

rectly notes in the subtle color handling "the long experience gained by Mr. Lamb in his treatment of painted windows."[37]

In 1907 with another, less well-funded library decoration commission—the Jones Memorial Library in Lynchburg, Virginia—Lamb again created a series of personifications of the different branches of library literature, but this time in opalescent glass windows. Lamb also tackled the American historical subject matter called for by Shean, Blashfield, and others. He painted a three-panel, ten-by-thirty-foot mural about 1915 for public school number 5 in Brooklyn, and entitled it *The Conference of Washington and His Officers at the Battle of Long Island*. His largest commission on an American historical theme was the series of twenty-seven windows designed for the Plymouth Congregational Church in Brooklyn between 1906 and 1914. This glazing program illustrated the history of the Congregational church in America, including the church's famous founding pastor, Henry Ward Beecher, and the Pilgrims. In each window in the auditorium, the colored image panel was approximately six-by-three feet, but a large, light-colored border was added to let light into the colonially styled interior.[38]

These examples represent only a small sampling of thousands of mural decorations designed by Lamb. Most of his artistically productive life was devoted to bringing this sort of mural art into public buildings and to promoting artistic decoration in everyday life within the mediums of his artistic training. Are we willing to include such public mural art within the arts and crafts "canon" or should the arts and crafts movement be seen as only one distinctive stylistic pattern integrated among others within the complex art historical fabric of the turn-of-the-century period in America? However this may eventually be decided, we may continue to reflect on how Lamb, like other American arts and crafts practitioners, envisioned "an art broader than the art we have today—an art that touches the lives of the people; an art that will be in their streets, in their parks, in their homes."[39]

[37]Lamb, "Flower Memorial Library," p. 397.
[38]Before being installed in the public school in Brooklyn (now known as George Westinghouse Vocational and Technical High School), the oil-on-canvas mural was exhibited in the Department of Fine Arts at the Panama-Pacific International Exposition in San Francisco in 1915. It was apparently removed from the school and probably destroyed during remodeling in 1963; Lewis A. Rappaport, principal of George Westinghouse Vocational and Technical High School, interview with author, New York, January 2, 1991. The Brooklyn church is now known as Plymouth Church of the Pilgrims.
[39]Lamb, "Beautifying of Our Cities," p. 172.

"Color in the House"
Painted Furniture of the American Arts and Crafts Movement

Catherine L. Futter

Although the contemporary theorists of the American arts and crafts movement rejected the use of the type of excessive applied ornament and decoration in interior design that had predominated during the mid nineteenth-century revival styles, a small group of artists and craftsmen did produce furniture and decorative accessories with painted designs in the arts and crafts style. Beginning in England with the writings and designs of William Morris and continuing in America with Gustav Stickley, Elbert Hubbard, and many others, writers advocated honesty of construction; restraint in applied ornament; emphasis on the beauty of natural materials; and unity of color, texture, and materials in architecture and the decorative arts. The majority of American furniture in the arts and crafts style is solid, simply constructed, and has a minimum of applied ornament although some pieces, such as those by Arthur and Lucia Mathews in California, Sidney Burleigh in Rhode Island, and the Byrdcliffe Colony in New York, incorporated painted scenes or designs. Upon a thorough examination of the painted accessories and furniture of the period, two distinct categories of decoration are revealed. The first derives from English models of the 1850s, in which simple forms produced by anonymous craftsmen served as canvases for paintings by celebrated artists. In the second group, painted ornament was more successfully integrated into the form; the artist and craftsman were often one and the same. In the former, the exuberant and colorful paintings were usually landscapes or portraits; restrained and conventionalized floral motifs were incorporated into the latter.

American arts and crafts designers and cabinetmakers, including Stickley, advocated the use of subdued colors as the harmonizing element in interior design. In one of Stickley's early writings, he expressed his reservations about employing color in the interior—rejecting its use on wood—as he felt that it concealed and obliterated "the exquisite work of Nature; actually violating the substances created by the Divine Intelligence and perfected by cycles of years." In the same article, of October 1904, however, he wrote that the eye could be soothed or excited to pleasure by the correct use of color and favored educating the public. Stickley acknowledged Morris's successful introduction of textiles and wallpapers in a wide variety of colors in his revolution of English interior design. Stickley himself employed the natural tones of the wood, leather upholstery, and textiles to obtain color effects in his interiors.[1]

Stickley's theories of interior design are revealed in a discussion of a Craftsman house that was published in his book *Craftsman Homes*, in 1909. In the volume he describes a large living room with a great fireplace, open staircase, casement windows, built-in seats, cupboards, bookcases, and a sideboard unified by "soft rich restful color, based upon the mellow radiance of the wood tones and sparkling into the jeweled highlights of copper, brass, or embroideries." The overall tonality of the room was intimate, muted, and warm because of the dark paneling and the subdued lighting of the fixtures. In an article of 1906, in his magazine *The Craftsman*, Stickley had suggested a moss green stain for the woodwork to contrast with the darker green floors, walls of yellow verging on brown, and a stenciled frieze of green and peach. The earth tones, or soft, muted colors derived from nature, which decorate so much of the American painted furniture in this style, were thought to be appropriate for the American consumer. In an article entitled "Color of Furniture," published in May 1888 in *American Architect and Building News*, an unidentified author wrote that subdued tones were suitable for American furniture as they "furnish enough light to enliven" the American people, yet "are of especial

[1]Gustav Stickley, "Thoughts Occasioned by an Anniversary: A Plea for Democratic Art," *The Craftsman* 7, no. 1 (October 1904): 47, 46, 55.

benefaction to the nervous American race by reason of their quieting influence."[2] The bright, coal-tar dyed colors, so popular in the mid nineteenth century, were rejected in favor of much more natural hues.

In the September 1902 issue of *The Craftsman*, two articles addressed the theme of color in interiors and decorative arts. In the first, "Color in the House" by Walter A. Dyer, the author discussed three principles of decoration central to the arts and crafts movement. The first and most important was harmony; the second, simplicity, resulted from the harmony of colors. Dyer wrote that "over-ornamentation, like over-dress, is a sign of poor taste. A bright color does not necessarily offend against simplicity, but an obtrusive color, or a too glaring contrast does." Dyer's third principle for successful decoration was "consistency of color with the style or type of ornamentation." He summarized his aesthetic theory: "A decorative style which is in keeping with the character of the room, carried out with simplicity and harmony, will invariably be beautiful."[3]

In the same issue of *The Craftsman*, Irene Sargent, an editor and frequent contributor to the magazine, examined color in the artworks of Italy and the Pre-Raphaelite painters as well as Morris and his circle. In her article, "Color: An Expression of Modern Life," she concluded that color sense was deeply influenced by climactic conditions. This influence and that of geography played an important role in the work of the American arts and crafts movement and was especially obvious in the paintings and objects of the Mathews. Sargent singled out the English Pre-Raphaelite painter Dante Gabriel Rossetti as the first artist to take steps toward the improvement in aesthetics. In his paintings Rossetti employed colors taken from nature, including browns, yellows, and greens. Through his association with Morris, these hues were employed in both artists' art industries and handicrafts. According to Sargent, through the efforts of Morris the homes of the English middle class had been transformed into "places of delight, rich in suggestive

[2] Gustav Stickley, *Craftsman Homes* (New York: Craftsman Publishing Co., 1909), pp. 196–97. Gustav Stickley, "Craftsman House Number Two," *The Craftsman* 9, no. 5 (February 1906): 717–18, which is cited in Mary Ann Smith, "The Craftsman Interior," *Tiller* 1, no. 1 (September–October 1982): 36–37. "Color of Furniture," *American Architect and Building News* 23, no. 648 (May 26, 1888): 245.

[3] Walter A. Dyer, "Color in the House," *The Craftsman* 2, no. 6 (September 1902): 304, 305.

Substance of Style

color." She continued that "the presence of good color is, in itself, an incentive to 'The Simple Life'; for from it results that sense of quiet, rest and satisfaction which calms the unwholesome longing after many things."[4] The introduction of harmonious color, especially in subdued earth tones, was integral to the concept of a unified interior in arts and crafts design.

Morris and Rossetti were two members of a group of English architects, painters, and designers who joined together during the 1850s to combat contemporary commercialism and bad taste. The group included the painters Edward Burne-Jones and Ford Madox Brown and the architects Philip Webb and William Burges, who collaborated on the design and execution of decorative objects for private residences as well as churches and other public spaces. Morris and the others produced furniture that unified the fine art of painting with the decorative arts. The earliest furniture by these architects and painters was massive and inspired by medieval forms, but later works moved away from a total commitment to medievalism and exhibited an eclectic mix of culturally and historically diverse motifs. These included elements from Greek and Japanese art as well as the English decorative tradition from the Middle Ages up to the early nineteenth century. Also incorporated were influences from the Italian Renaissance and contemporary aestheticism. Many works the group produced during this period combined both the subjects and the styles of pagan and classical themes with those of medieval imagery. In the complete interiors and pieces of furniture, a unity of spirit, intent, color, and form prevented the individual elements from clashing; each room and object was given a specific color scheme selected from a wide variety of tertiary colors. These tones, which were subtly blended to form a unified whole, included mistletoe green, sea green, rose-amber, pomegranate flower, and various shades of yellow and brown.

For the American artists and craftsmen of the arts and crafts movement, the Gothic or medieval sources that their British counterparts looked to for inspiration may have been honestly constructed, simple, and useful, but they were not part of an American tradition. Therefore, what most Americans took from these British examples, and further

[4]Irene Sargent, "Color: An Expression of Modern Life," *The Craftsman* 2, no. 6 (September 1902): 261–70.

Fig. 1. Sidney Burleigh, *Shakespeare Chest*, Providence, ca. 1890. Enameled oak, painted panels; H. 21¾", W. 40", D. 21⅝". (Museum of Art, Rhode Island School of Design, gift of Ellen D. Sharpe.)

developed, were the fundamental principles of functionalism, simplicity, and craftsmanship as well as the color palettes used by Morris, Burne-Jones, and Rossetti.

At least two American artists, however, derived their style and subject matter directly from the medieval tradition drawn upon by members of the English arts and crafts movement. The work of Burleigh, of Providence, and that of Will H. Low of New York, displayed an American adaptation of the Gothic influence that had been so popular in Britain. A chest designed by Burleigh, circa 1890, shows not only medieval subject matter but also a medieval form (fig. 1). Burleigh, best known as a painter, designed a simple ebonized oak chest with painted panels depicting characters from Shakespeare's plays *The Merry Wives*

of Windsor and *The Merchant of Venice*. On the front of the chest are
three brightly colored portraits of Slender, Sir John Falstaff, and Mrs.
Anne Page from *The Merry Wives of Windsor*, all painted on wooden
panels set within a simply carved and ebonized framework. All of the
figures are depicted humorously with exaggerated characteristics and
settings indicating specific scenes within the plays. Burleigh employed
predominantly red and brown tones with green and blue accents also
seen in the work of Morris and his followers during the 1860s. Of the
American painted furniture of the arts and crafts movement, this chest
is probably the closest to the medieval tradition both in its massive,
simple form as well as subject matter and displays a strong affinity with
early English arts and crafts furniture.

    Also in the style of the English arts and crafts movement, espe-
cially the work of Morris and Webb, is a cabinet by Low (fig. 2). Low,
a popular New York painter who is best known for his collaboration
with John La Farge on the interiors for the New York City residence
of Cornelius Vanderbilt II, produced this piece in 1882. The bold
architectural form of ebonized cherry contrasts strongly with the painted
panels of idealized maidens in a classically inspired pastoral scene set
beneath additional painted panels of floral decoration. The form of the
cabinet is much less medieval in inspiration than its earlier English
counterparts or the Burleigh chest and is simpler, more architectural,
and more elegant. The floral decoration of large yellow, red, and pink
roses against a dark background helps to make the transition from the
ebonized framework and the brightly colored women in scarlet, emerald, gold, and black classical robes set in a light-filled landscape of
cypress trees. The painted figures, although clearly reminiscent of Morris, Burne-Jones, and Rossetti, are classically inspired and not medieval
in either theme or style, although the color tones are very similar to
those found on English examples.

    The short-lived artistic colony of Byrdcliffe, in Woodstock, pro-
duced a small amount of furniture from 1904 to 1905. The colony was
the combined effort of Ralph Radcliffe Whitehead, who was the heir
of a wealthy British industrialist; Hervey White, a writer and socialist;
and Bolton Coit Brown, a painter and professor of art at Stanford
University. The three men hoped to create a place where craftspeople
could escape from the "artificial life of commercialism" and create an
environment that would encourage cooperation among the partici-

Fig. 2. William H. Low, cabinet, Providence, 1882. Ebonized cherry, painted panels; H. 52″, W. 42″, D. 17½″. (Virginia Carroll Crawford Collection, High Museum of Art.)

pants. The community, founded in 1902, was to be made up of independent craftsmen in the natural, peaceful, and inspirational setting of the fields and hills of upstate New York, where these men and women would be able to combine manual and intellectual labor. Whitehead had studied with the theorist and critic John Ruskin at Oxford and traveled with him to Italy. The influence of Ruskin's study of nature can be seen in many of the pieces produced at Byrdcliffe, especially in the use of motifs taken from local New York plant life. About fifty pieces of furniture were manufactured at Byrdcliffe. The simple, rectilinear forms were usually constructed of poplar or quartered oak and designed by Whitehead or a Canadian designer, Dawson Watson.[5] Most of the furniture was decorated with stylized plant forms carved into the wooden panels and stained with transparent colors similar to those found in nature. On a linen press designed by two graduates of the Pratt Institute of Art, Zulma Steele and Edna Walker, the overall framework of the piece is stained a celery green, and the carved panels of oak leaves are done in rust brown fading into mustard yellow (fig. 3). Unfortunately, the furniture making at Byrdcliffe was not financially successful, as the pieces, mostly sold in New York City, proved too costly to produce profitably. In 1905 the woodworking shops were closed, and the artists and craftsmen concentrated on ceramics, weaving, and framemaking. The community, never financially self-sufficient and dependent upon Whitehead's inheritance for survival, closed soon afterward.

Some painted furniture in the arts and crafts style reflects traditions in America's colonial past, such as the oak dower chest made by Madeline Yale Wynne in Chicago. Wynne, a metalworker, woodworker, and painter, used several of her talents, in the early part of this century, to produce a series of bridal chests inspired by seventeenth- and eighteenth-century chests she had seen at the Historical Society in Deerfield, Massachusetts. Wynne's dower chests were generally made of darkly stained oak. They were carved with both abstract and figural decoration and had painted tops. The undersides of the lids were carved and painted with themes associated with marriage, such as the large

---

[5] Wendy Kaplan, "Spreading the Crafts: The Role of the Schools," in Wendy Kaplan, *"The Art That Is Life": The Arts and Crafts Movement in America, 1875–1920* (Boston: Museum of Fine Arts, 1987), pp. 312–14.

Fig. 3. Byrdcliffe Colony, linen press with panels, Zulma Steele and Edna Walker (designers), Woodstock, N.Y., ca. 1904. Oak, tulip-poplar, brass; H. 55″, W. 41″, D. 18¾″. (Mr. and Mrs. Mark Willcox.)

Fig. 4. Madeline Yale Wynn, dower chest, Chicago, 1900. From *House Beautiful* 11, no. 6 (May 1902): 366. (New York Public Library.)

white lilies against an azure mountain landscape on a chest Wynne made for the marriage of Bertha Bullock in 1900 (fig. 4). Wynne combined traditional American forms and decorative motifs from the colonial past with contemporary paintings of nature to create innovative pieces in an American arts and crafts style.

Another American artist who turned to furniture design was Will H. Bradley, best known for his book illustrations and posters in the arts and crafts style. In 1896 Bradley established the Wayside Press in Springfield, Massachusetts, an enterprise that included a periodical,

Bradley: His Book, as its focal point. He also proposed a school of design as well as studio and workshops for the production of pictures, books, tapestries, wallpapers, fabrics, and furniture. Most of Bradley's plans for Wayside Press were unfulfilled, although he continued to be interested in the improvement and beautification of the American home. From November 1901 until August 1902, Bradley prepared a series of designs for interiors for *Ladies' Home Journal.* The illustrations were introduced with the following: "Mr. Bradley will design practically everything shown in the pictures. It is not his hope that anyone will build a house completely as he designs it: he hopes rather to influence through individual suggestions—through pieces of furniture, draperies, fire accessories, wall-paper designs, all of which can be independently followed and detached from his entire scheme."[6] In his watercolor illustrations Bradley emphasized the cohesiveness of the interior and the total design. Each piece of furniture and each object was related to the individual room for which it was designed as well as to the house in general. To achieve this unity Bradley emphasized the structural and decorative elements of the furniture, walls, and beamed ceilings and repeated subdued warm earth tones of browns, umbers, greens, and yellows throughout the room.

Although none of Bradley's designs for individual pieces of furniture are known to have been produced, each watercolor shows the influence of both his English contemporaries and Frank Lloyd Wright in the use of spare architectural forms and simple decoration.[7] Bradley's furniture is characterized by a simple rectilinear construction, strongly delineated decoration, and light watercolor washes. A watercolor of a chest for a living room or hall, published in *Ladies' Home Journal* of March 1902, illustrates one of the pieces of incidental furniture intended as an alternate suggestion to those seen in Bradley's overall interior views (fig. 5). The design displays projecting vertical extensions similar to those found in the designs of Bradley's English contemporaries C. F. A. Voysey and M. H. Baillie-Scott. The lavender-washed bird motif in the celery green stained chest may have been inspired by

[6] On the Wayside Press, see Robert Judson Clark, ed., *The Arts and Crafts Movement in America, 1876–1916* (Princeton: Princeton University Press, 1972), p. 32. *Ladies' Home Journal* 18, no. 12 (November 1901): 7.
[7] Clark, *Arts and Crafts Movement in America,* p. 32.

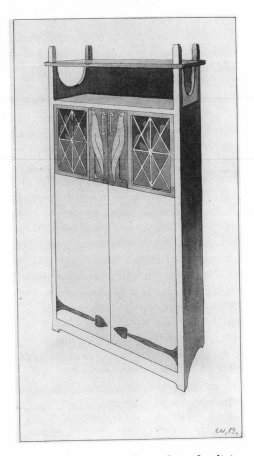

Fig. 5. Will H. Bradley, chest for living
room or hall, New York, 1901. Watercolor
and ink on paper; H. 8⅛″, W. 4⁷⁄₁₆″. From
Ladies' Home Journal (March 1902). (Metropolitan Museum of Art, gift of Fern Bradley Dufner.)

Voysey, although Bradley often used similar decoration in his illustrations from the late 1890s. The furniture designed by Bradley, but never executed, illustrates a trend in painted furniture to simpler, lighter, and less-decorated pieces than those of the 1880s and 1890s.

The most prolific and well known of the artists producing painted furniture and accessories at the turn of the century were Arthur F. Mathews and his wife, Lucia Kleinhans Mathews. Based in San Francisco, they were not only painters but also furniture designers, carvers, and civic reformers. They embodied the arts and crafts ideal of integrating all activities to create a better and more beautiful life. Although they were based in and drew inspiration from the California landscape and its indigenous colors and forms, they also evoked the heritage of the Mediterranean world, displaying an interest in classicism and craftsman ideals and producing paintings and furniture that manifested elements of California regionalism in the American arts and crafts movement.

Arthur was born in Wisconsin in 1860 and soon afterward moved with his family to Oakland, California, across the bay from San Francisco. He was trained as an architect although he later developed an interest in painting, which he pursued while studying in Paris and traveling through Europe. He eventually returned to California, where he first taught and later became the director of the California School of Design. It was at the school that he met Lucia Kleinhans, one of his students and ten years his junior; they were married in 1894 and settled in San Francisco. Throughout his life, Mathews received many commissions for decorative mural paintings for both private residences and commercial projects. His background in mural painting greatly influenced the furniture that he and his wife made, not only in the demonstration of decorative proficiency and thorough knowledge of architectural form but also in the friezelike bands of decoration and repetitive motifs. Their style of classical subjects and especially color had been greatly influenced by the French muralist Puvis de Chavannes, who also inspired other artists and craftsmen of the period including Stickley.[8]

---

[8] Harvey L. Jones, *Mathews: Masterpieces of the California Decorative Style* (Oakland, Calif.: Oakland Museum of Art, 1985), pp. 13–31. Stickley, "Thoughts Occasioned by an Anniversary," p. 54.

Following the San Francisco earthquake and fire of 1906, the Mathewses constructed a building that housed two painting studios—one for Arthur—and the facilities for magazine and book production as well as a furniture workshop and sales area. Arthur, with financial backing from John Zeile, oversaw the entire operation, including the journal *Philopolis*, which was published monthly and addressed issues of city planning as well as art. He also directed a small book-publishing house, Philopolis Press. The most complex of the many operations was the Furniture Shop, in production from 1906 until 1920, which manufactured furniture, frames, and decorative objects all in wood and all painted, both for domestic and commercial commissions. Arthur headed the shop and designed the bulk of its production, which at times required as many as fifty craftsmen. His assistant, Thomas A. McGlynn, also designed some of the pieces and attended to details in the execution of the designs. Lucia is thought to have collaborated on designs, supervised decorative carving and color choices, and decorated tabletop items herself such as jars and boxes.[9] The Furniture Shop's commissions ranged from small interiors to their largest project, the complete interior design and furnishing of the San Francisco Masonic Temple in 1913. Custom interiors were carried out down to the smallest details, including wood paneling, murals, easel paintings with custom frames, all the furniture, and specially designed fixtures and accessories. Everything was designed to be in perfect harmony.

Although the pieces manufactured by the Furniture Shop were expensive, they met the demand for high-quality decorations following the 1906 fire, and this partly explains the nature of the work put out by the firm. Its production can be divided into two fairly distinct categories: large suites of furniture designed to meet the requirements of various private and commercial clients and personalized pieces that were either given as gifts to friends or kept by the Mathewses. A carved and painted desk, which belongs in the latter category, exemplifies some of the major motifs, themes, and styles employed by the Furniture Shop (fig. 6). The form is quite simple, although there are some added carved elements, possibly not made by the workshop but purchased

[9]On various aspects of Arthur's work and business, see Jones, *Mathews*, pp. 24, 83–91.

Fig. 6. The Furniture Shop, desk, San Francisco, ca. 1912. Painted wood; H. 59″, W. 48″, D. 20″. (Oakland Museum of Art, gift of Concours d'Antiques, Art Guild.)

from outside suppliers.[10] The simple box shape is decorated on the exterior with a scene of figures in a pastoral landscape, surrounded by a carved and painted intertwined border of leaves and flowers. The figures are vaguely classical or Renaissance in dress and bearing; the coloring is bright, predominantly in reds, greens, and yellows, and modulated to create a harmony in both color and form. Nature seems to be the primary source of inspiration in terms of subject matter and color, and rather than literally depicting a classical subject, Arthur seems only to be interested in suggesting ties with classical themes. Rarely is there a definite subject in the couple's works. There are, rather, depictions of abstract concepts, much like the work of their contemporary in Scotland, Margaret Macdonald Mackintosh. The Mathewses derived much of their inspiration from the California flora, including coastal pines; cypress trees; fruit such as peaches, plums, apricots, oranges, and grapes; and flowers such as peonies and California poppies. The colors employed on the pieces decorated in oil-based paints, although yellowed from aging and varnish, also reflect the California landscape: vivid greens, yellows, and oranges, often combined with rich gilding.

The Furniture Shop also manufactured decorative accessories, such as candlesticks, covered jars, boxes, and picture frames. Again, the motifs on these pieces reflect an eclectic view of history in their mixing of periods. The covered jars, their forms possibly derived from ancient Chinese ceramic hill jars, were painted with continuous landscape scenes and figures around the body. Beneath the frieze of figures there is usually a narrow band of ornament encompassing small panels of California flora, such as cypress trees, and small landscapes. The lids of the jars are decorated with painted abstract patterns as well as somewhat crudely carved and painted figural scenes. As with the desk, the jars are painted in brilliant greens and reds. Other works produced by the shop include carved and painted frames; some were made specifically for certain paintings, often by Lucia, echoing the colors and designs depicted in the works of art that they adorned.

The painted furniture and other decorative arts produced by the Furniture Shop clearly illustrate regional differences in the arts and

---

[10] On the production of the Furniture Shop, see Jones, *Mathews*, p. 84. Kenneth R. Trapp, interview with author, Oakland, Calif., August 8, 1990.

crafts style in this country. Although some of the themes and subjects used on the pieces were inspired by classical imagery, many of the recurrent motifs as well as the coloring were taken from the California landscape.

A final group of painted furniture includes pieces with overall color or colored stains produced by manufacturers generally perceived as true arts and crafts designers who rejected color as a form of decoration. In the late 1890s David Wolcott Kendall, a designer and later the manager of the Phoenix Furniture Company in Grand Rapids, Michigan, developed a staining process that introduced colored finishes to oak. Suites of furniture were produced in a variety of colors, including several different brown stains as well as ones in canary yellow, copper red, green or "malachite," and a metallic black known as "Flemish." In an article for *Michigan Artisan* of February 1890 entitled "Modern Finishes," Kendall wrote:

Suppose you wanted to finish a room in yellow. Take a yellow or canary colored suite and in itself it would be a queer thing to put into a house. It is not expected that a whole house would be finished in that. In one room the wall paper could be in yellow tints or other light tones, and those with the yellow carpets and hangings to match, the walls hung with a few delicate water colors or etchings, with white frames and you have something nice, and not at all expensive considered in contrast with the ordinary furnishings of a room. Put in a pedestal with a white marble statuesque and see what the effect would be. Would it not be beautiful indeed?

The most popular tint invented by Kendall and imitated by his competitors, including Stickley, was the green, or malachite, stain. At an exhibition of furniture in Grand Rapids in 1916, Stickley displayed several suites of furniture stained in a variety of colors, including green, in a line called "Chromewald."[11] Although Kendall's enterprise seems to have been popular and profitable, the Chromewald line by Stickley supposedly met with little success.

[11] David Wolcott Kendall, "Modern Finishes," *Michigan Artisan* (February 1890): 4, quoted in Jane Perkins Claney and Robert Edwards, "Progressive Design in Grand Rapids," *Tiller* 2, no. 1 (September–October 1983): 43. On Kendall, see Claney and Edwards, "Progressive Design in Grand Rapids," pp. 33–56. Joseph J. Bavaro and Thomas L. Mossman, *The Furniture of Gustav Stickley: History, Technique, Projects* (New York: Prentice-Hall Press, 1982), p. 31.

The numerous examples of American painted furniture and decorative objects in the arts and crafts style illustrate different trends in form and subject matter. For the most part, the forms are extremely simple, often serving only as canvases for the painted decoration that adorns them, as in Burleigh's chest and the pieces by the Mathewses. Others, such as the Byrdcliffe linen press and the Bradley cabinet, more successfully integrate painted ornament and form in their restraint and conventionalization of motifs. In the more vigorously painted examples, the artists who painted the figures, landscapes, and flora were usually identified and celebrated artists as opposed to the anonymous craftsmen who produced the forms. Although there was a melding of the fine and decorative arts, there was still a distinction between the artist and craftsman in those pieces. In the more subdued examples, the artist and craftsman collaborated more closely to create a unified expression of the arts and crafts philosophy. The more brightly colored and figural examples are closely aligned to works created by their British forbearers, Morris, Webb, and Burges, among others, while the more abstract decoration seems more in keeping with forms by American designers including Stickley and Hubbard. All help to illustrate the importance of the role of color in creating a rich, harmonious, restful, and unified environment in the arts and crafts home. "If we look about us, we shall find everywhere an imperative demand for color, whether our search and meaning be restricted to the sensuous pleasure caused by the action of light upon the eye, or whether we accept the wider significance of color as an element of force, energy and abundant life."[12]

---

[12] Sargent, "Color: An Expression of Modern Life," p. 265.

"Near The Yates"
Craft, Machine, and Ideology in Arts and Crafts Syracuse, 1900–1910

Cleota Reed

In the first decade of the twentieth century, Syracuse, New York, emerged as one of the most important arts and crafts communities in the United States. Two people and their publications were the catalysts in this development: the china painter Adelaide Alsop Robineau (1865–1929) and her *Keramic Studio*, which began publication in 1899, and the furniture designer and manufacturer Gustav Stickley (1858–1942) and his *Craftsman*, which began in 1901. Two people do not constitute a community, however, nor did these two have a great deal in common. A third person linked them. She was Irene Sargent (1852–1932), a professor at Syracuse University, de facto managing editor and prolific contributor to *The Craftsman*, and friend and champion of Robineau. Associated with these three were others who, although not craftspersons or educators, supported the arts and crafts movement as a new and novel part of the ideology of American middle-class taste and proved important to its success in Syracuse.

The tendency to think of American arts and crafts movement communities as enclaves that were geographically or attitudinally re-

The author thanks Rebecca Lawton, curator of the Vassar College Art Gallery, who generously shared with her the results of the research that she conducted in preparation for the exhibition "The Arts and Crafts Movement in New York State," organized by Coy Ludwig for the Gallery Association of New York State in 1983.

Fig. 1. Yates Hotel, Archimedes Russell, architect, Syracuse, N.Y, ca. 1900. (Onondaga Historical Assoc., Syracuse, N.Y.)

moved from the bustle and complexities of urban life needs to be moderated in view of the Syracuse experience. Elsewhere in New York State, Byrdcliffe, Chautauqua, and the Roycroft community, each in its own way, sought a distinct and separate identity within its locale and a purer existence through a simpler life. In Syracuse, however, the movement flourished as an integral part of the city's commercial-cultural-political center. Its geographic nucleus was the Yates Hotel (fig. 1) in the very middle of downtown Syracuse, then a small city with a population of more than a hundred thousand.

The Yates was a Renaissance revival structure by Syracuse Hotel architect Archimedes Russell. It was built in 1892 to be the region's premier hotel.[1] The New York Central Railroad passenger line ran past it to the city's station a few blocks to the west. The Oswego Canal

[1] For Russell, see Eva Marie Hardin, *Archimedes Russell, Upstate Architect* (Syracuse, N.Y.: Syracuse University Press, 1980), pp. 66–69.

joined the Erie Canal one block to the north. City Hall was across the street. Banks were clustered nearby. Department stores, shops, theaters, and the city's outdoor markets were close at hand. Within a radius of four city blocks could be found most of the people and activities that between 1901 and 1904 gave the arts and crafts movement a critical mass in Syracuse.

To see how that mass, or mélange, was configured, we need to look at a public event of 1903 that awoke the greater community to the arts and crafts movement. This event was the arts and crafts exhibition sponsored by Stickley and his United Crafts enterprise. It was held from March 23 to April 4, one block east of the Yates Hotel in a handsome Queen Anne building of 1888, which was also the work of Russell (fig. 2). He had designed it as a residence and stables for a local worthy, D. Edgar Crouse. Stickley, who had come to Syracuse in 1899 to start a furniture manufacturing company, leased the Crouse Stables (as the entire building was called) in 1900 after its owner's death and used it for his showrooms and offices. He renamed the property the Craftsman Building and began *The Craftsman* there. In her study of Stickley, Mary Ann Smith rightly points out that "the local prominence of the Crouse Stables provided a certain status for Stickley's United Crafts or Craftsman enterprises."[2]

When Stickley launched *The Craftsman* in October 1901, Sargent was on board as a major contributor. It is not farfetched to say that if any one person besides Stickley was responsible for creating an arts and crafts fever in Syracuse, it was Sargent. A student of Charles Eliot Norton, an early acquaintance of Bernard Berenson, a skilled writer in six languages, a critic and an art historian, the widely traveled Sargent had originally joined the Syracuse University faculty in 1895 as a professor of Romance languages and by 1901 taught the history of art and architecture in the university's College of Fine Arts.

Sargent played a key role in bringing the magazine into being. She single-handedly wrote all of the features in the first two issues, setting forth the ideals of William Morris and John Ruskin and linking Stickley's fast-growing empire inexorably to the arts and crafts move-

---

[2] Mary Ann Smith, *Gustav Stickley: The Craftsman* (Syracuse, N.Y.: Syracuse University Press, 1983), p. 26.

Fig. 2. Craftsman Building, Archimedes Russell, architect, Syracuse, N.Y., 1887–88. (Onondaga Historical Assoc., Syracuse, N.Y.)

ment. Thereafter, other authors contributed, although she almost always wrote the lead article, setting a particular theme for the issue. From October 1901 to March 1902, she contributed twenty-six of thirty-three features. In all, she made eighty-four signed contributions to *The Craftsman* and probably a number of others, unsigned. She ended her association in April 1905, at approximately the same time that the Craftsman Building was sold and Stickley moved his offices to New York City.[3]

Sargent had major responsibilities for Stickley's 1903 exhibition. Stickley himself probably had little to do with the detailed planning and organization of the show, and he undoubtedly viewed it primarily as an advertising tool for his United Crafts venture. He was the major exhibitor; the showrooms, full of his home furnishing products, provided the exhibition's setting. At the time he had need to assert his leadership in the field. The early success of his furniture had spawned several competitors, including his own brothers, Leopold, John George, Charles, and Albert. Gustav thought he had the jump on them, and he intended to keep it.[4]

The chairman and primary organizer of the exhibition was Theodore Hanford Pond (1873–1933). This distinguished designer-craftsman had previously been involved in arts and crafts exhibitions in Boston in 1897 and Providence in 1899 and 1901. He sought to elevate the taste of the American public, and his vehicle was education. In 1902 the Rochester Mechanics Institute hired him to reorganize its curriculum much as he had already done in Providence at the Rhode Island School of Design. His aims were altruistic and democratic and reflected arts and crafts ideals. Sargent and Pond had in all probability jointly conceived the idea of the show a year earlier in 1902, when they had both attended a meeting of the Eastern Art Teachers' Associa-

[3]On Sargent, see Cleota Reed, "Irene Sargent: Rediscovering a Lost Legend," *Courier* 16 (Summer 1979): 3–13; and Cleota Reed, "Irene Sargent: A Comprehensive Bibliography of Her Published Writings," *Courier* 18 (Spring 1981): 9–25. Smith, *Stickley*, p. 149.

[4]A discussion of the Stickley brothers is beyond the scope of this paper, except to say that Leopold first worked for Gustav, then opened his own Onondaga Shops in nearby Fayetteville around 1901. John George apparently joined Leopold in 1904 when they incorporated as L. and J. G. Stickley. See Donald A. Davidoff, "The Work of L. and J. G. Stickley," *Arts and Crafts Quarterly* 3, no. 1 (1990): 6–9.

tion. They seem to have planned from the start to stage the exhibition in the two upstate cities in which they were active as art educators. After Syracuse the exhibition moved directly to Rochester.[5]

To assist in the selection of more than a thousand objects for display, Sargent and Pond invited others to join them as jurors. One was Frederick Stymetz Lamb (1863–1928), a stained glass artist from New York. Lamb had written for *The Craftsman* not only about stained glass but also about the beautification of American cities. Henry Turner Bailey (1865–1931) increased the ranks of art educators on the jury. This prominent designer-craftsman member of the Society of Arts and Crafts, Boston, was director of industrial art in the public schools of Massachusetts. Later in 1903 he became head of the Chautauqua School of Arts and Crafts in western New York. Closer to home, Sargent and Pond invited to the jury the Reverend Ezekiel Mundy (1833–1916), the distinguished head of the Syracuse Central Library.

Mundy was no stranger to the arts. In his youth he had learned the jewelry trade and "it was a matter of pride with him long afterwards that he understood the little intricacies of the goldsmith's art," a practice that he never abandoned, even after he became first a theologian and then a librarian. Syracuse University awarded him an honorary doctorate of literature in 1904. At the time of the arts and crafts exhibi-

---

[5] In her unpublished study of Pond, Rebecca Lawton proposes that their roles as art educators brought Pond and Sargent together. They both attended the April 1902 meeting of the Eastern Art Teachers' Association in New York City and *The Craftsman* later published at least two of the papers from this symposium, including one by Frederick Lamb: "The Beautifying of Our Cities," *The Craftsman* 2 (July 1902): 172–88. See also Coy L. Ludwig, *The Arts and Crafts Movement in New York State, 1890s–1920s* (Hamilton, N.Y.: Gallery Assoc. of New York State, 1983), p. 57. Another important contact for Stickley, resulting from the Rochester connection established through Pond, was his introduction to the Rochester architect Harvey Ellis. Ellis was chairman of the committee on arrangement for the Rochester venue of the exhibit, which ran from April 15 to 25, and he may have helped Pond with the Syracuse show as well. Immediately afterward, Ellis began designing for Stickley as well as contributing to *The Craftsman*. His obituary in the *Herald* (Syracuse, N.Y.) for January 6, 1904, says that "he had come to Syracuse some months earlier to be editor of the *Craftsman*," but Stickley's notice of his death in the February 1904 issue stated only that *The Craftsman* had lost a valued contributor to its department of architecture. Sargent's editorial duties continued unabated during Ellis's brief tenure. He died in January 1904. Stickley paid for his burial in an unmarked Syracuse cemetery plot. For Ellis, see Jean France, *A Rediscovery: Harvey Ellis, Architect* (Rochester, N.Y.: Memorial Art Gallery of the University of Rochester and Margaret Woodbury Strong Museum, 1973).

tion, Mundy was planning his new Carnegie Building, which would open in 1905. Erected two blocks south of the Yates Hotel, it included galleries for the new Syracuse Museum of Fine Arts, predecessor of the present-day Everson Museum of Art. In 1903 the museum had temporary housing in the Onondaga Savings Bank building, a block west of the Yates.[6]

The 1903 exhibition reflected both Sargent's well-articulated theoretical foundations for the movement and Pond's influence and connections. Its broad and enlightened scope featured "works by leading American arts and crafts designers, Native American weaving and basketry, school exhibits, and European examples." It went beyond many other exhibitions of the time in its emphasis on indigenous sources, the role of education, and the movement's international character. Sargent claimed that the exhibition was better housed than its predecessors elsewhere in the nation. It occupied three floors of the Craftsman Building in spacious, well-lit galleries. Sargent reported that a favorite display was the dining room arranged by the United Crafts (fig. 3), "in itself an education in all that pertains to form, color and refinement of decoration and detail. . . . The sideboard especially attracted the attention of visitors, and was judged to be one of the best pieces as yet built in the workshops of the United Crafts. It was long and low; massive, and yet refined in line; decorated only with wrought-iron fittings consisting of strap hinges and drawer-pulls." Stickley placed a similar sideboard in his home.[7]

Sargent, described as "one of the pioneers in the industrial art movement," opened the exhibition in Craftsman Hall to an invited group of 200 guests, including the press, the jurors, the committee of arrangements, the heads of departments from the workshops of United Crafts, and 30 patronesses, chosen as the best representatives of the

[6]Mundy file, Onondaga Historical Association, Syracuse, N.Y. See obituary in the *Herald* (Syracuse, N.Y.), June 8, 1916; and Dwight H. Bruce, ed., *The Empire State in Three Centuries* (New York: Century History Co., 1898), 3:216–18.
[7]On what was exhibited, see Irene Sargent, "A Recent Arts and Crafts Exhibition," *The Craftsman* 4 (May 1903): 69–83. Sargent's report on the exhibition informs us of the motives of the organizers—"To make the organization which conceived and executed it a center for furthering and fostering the decorative and industrial arts"—the content of Bailey's and her talks, and a detailed description of the exhibition. Ludwig, *Arts and Crafts*, p. 57.

Fig. 3. *Dining Room Furnished and Arranged by Gustav Stickley, Arts and Crafts Exhibition, Craftsman Building, Syracuse, N.Y.* From *The Craftsman* 4 (May 1903).

culture of Syracuse. The patronesses served as hostesses during the run of the exhibition, which was open to the public seven days a week from 10:00 A.M. to 10:00 P.M. The Syracuse press raved: "Nothing like it, experts say, has ever been shown in the United States," and "society bowed before the richness of the articles and stamped the exhibit with its approval."[8] In referring to "society" bowing, the press acknowledged the active association of Syracuse's cultural leadership with the show.

After Sargent's opening address, Bailey delivered a forceful and witty lecture in the cause of better domestic architecture and household art in the United States. "We have no fountains in America," Sargent quoted him as remarking gravely to his audience, "only statues that leak."[9]

[8] *Post Standard* (Syracuse, N.Y.), March 24, 1903.
[9] Sargent, "Recent Exhibition," p. 69.

Later, in a long review in the May 1903 issue of *The Craftsman*, Sargent cast the exhibition not only as an event of interest to people already engaged with the movement but as one that also had wider appeals and implications. She reported that "it brought together in repeated reunions the best representatives of local culture" and discussed the importance of exhibitions of the Syracuse kind to the design movement in general.[10] She, Pond, and Stickley meant the exhibition to appeal to the widest possible audience, including the city's civic and industrial leaders. They sought an inclusive movement rather than an exclusive one.

During the course of the exhibition, lecturers spoke on various aspects of the movement each evening. A tearoom, decorated in yellow, had been designed as part of the exhibition to attract "not only the hungry but the lover of that which is artistic." Lunch was served there daily on commercial restaurant china stamped with Stickley's United Crafts logo and made expressly for the occasion by Syracuse's Onondaga Pottery Company.[11]

Robineau showed examples of her recent work in the exhibition. Although well known as a china painter, her distinction at the time was primarily as editor-publisher of *Keramic Studio*, whose editorial offices were four blocks west of the Yates. She contributed seven vases, described by the *Post Standard* as "dainty pieces." Robineau gave her own report on the exhibition in the May 1903 issue of *Keramic Studio*, pointing out that the organizers of the exhibition had "sought to illustrate the new movement in the lesser arts; to show the progress which has been made, within a short period, toward that most desirable union in one person of the artist and the workman."[12]

More interesting, however, is the way in which she opened this issue with a pronouncement: "The Fourth Anniversary of the

[10] Sargent, "Recent Exhibition," p. 78.

[11] *Post Standard* (Syracuse, N.Y.), March 24, 1903. Customer service records, Syracuse China Corporation archives, lists a "Stickley order," dated March 11, 1903, for a yellow-green band, yellow-green fill-in badge, majestic green lines, one line inside band, one line on verge, light green band and dark green lines with two-color crest, on three sizes of plates, cups, bouillon cups, and saucers. The crest was Stickley's United Crafts *Als Ik Kan* logo. From 1913 to 1914, pinecones flanked the logo on an extensive dinner service as an underglaze decoration in brown (customer order 3497, Syracuse China Corporation archives, Syracuse, N.Y.). Some of the later Stickley ware was made by Lenox.

[12] *Keramic Studio* 5 (May 1903): x. *Post Standard* (Syracuse, N.Y.), March 24, 1903.

KERAMIC STUDIO finds the Keramic World at last joining the Arts and Crafts movement—but with so much caution and in such a serious spirit that we cannot but feel that the influence is to be permanent and not one of those passing fads so enthusiastically entered upon and so quickly dropped by fickle American fancy." This seems an unduly timid statement from Robineau, knowing, as we now do, of her remarkable, slightly later achievements as a porcelain artist. Nevertheless, the statement of public identification with the movement, following so closely on the heels of the Syracuse exhibition, is evidence enough that the show had a great impact on her. The following month, in the June 1903 issue, an unsigned article in *Keramic Studio* reviewed the works of the pottery exhibitors. It remarked, as Sargent had, on the setting and stated that "taken altogether it is doubtful if a more representative crafts exhibit has been made anywhere in the U.S. and certainly nowhere has such an exhibit been seen against so fitting a background as the one recently held at Syracuse, the Craftsman Building being finished throughout in the severely simple style of the crafts movement." The article concluded with a photograph of Robineau's entries in the show and justified her method of making them. She had cast them, reworking the shapes and the surfaces to give variety to each piece. The article pointed out (almost certainly quoting her) that "students are not to be discouraged from using the casting process by the advocates of 'all hand work,' who have gotten far enough into the crafts movement to become enthusiastic, but not far enough to recognize necessary limitations."[13]

Robineau had already been to Alfred University to study "the practical side of pottery" with Charles Binns at a 1902 summer session. She was now developing new glazes and learning to throw her own shapes on the potter's wheel.[14] Perhaps she meant her cautious statement about American ceramists joining the arts and crafts movement to ease her readers—who were late Victorian china painters—into the

[13] *Keramic Studio* 5 (May 1903): 1. "Pottery at the Arts and Crafts Exhibit, Craftsman Building, Syracuse," *Keramic Studio* 5 (June 1903): 36, 37–38.

[14] On Robineau, see Peg Weiss, ed., *Adelaide Alsop Robineau's Glory in Porcelain* (Syracuse, N.Y.: Syracuse University Press, 1981). In his essay for Weiss's book, Martin Eidelberg describes Robineau's transformation during this time from china painter to porcelain artist, attributing it largely to European influences, although a case can be made for other factors as well.

first stage of self-redefinition that she was herself undergoing. Her own work took a sudden leap at this point, catapulting her to fame a year later in the St. Louis World's Fair in 1904, and making her, without question, a major figure in the art pottery movement.

Sargent facilitated the growth of Robineau's reputation. As the major contributors to the two leading American magazines in the decorative arts, she and Robineau had much in common (although only Robineau was an artist), and they respected each other's publications. Sargent became Robineau's champion, publishing three major articles about her and her work between 1905 and 1929 in *Keystone*.[15] In 1905 Sargent had transferred her allegiance from *The Craftsman* to this magazine of the jeweler's trade almost immediately after Stickley moved his operations to New York City.

Robineau's work as a china decorator leaves no doubt about her affinity with the ideals of the movement before her association with Stickley and Sargent in Syracuse. She had been an advocate of modern decorative styles in her magazine since 1900, showing highly conventionalized art nouveau and arts and crafts motifs. Yet, like Stickley, her view of the place of machines in relation to the crafts was pragmatic. She saw that in the right circumstances the alliance of art with industry could be beneficial to designer, manufacturer, and consumer alike.

Although it has not previously been discussed in the literature about her, Robineau had already made such an alliance, and it deserves a close look. In February 1902, a year previous to the Syracuse arts and crafts exhibition, *Keramic Studio* had reported on an exhibition of the New York Society of Keramic Arts that had been held from December 9 to 11, 1901. Among the exhibitors was the Onondaga Pottery Company of Syracuse (later Syracuse China Corporation). It showed tableware with conventional decorations in underglaze and overglaze. In discussing these pieces, the article stated:

---

[15] Irene Sargent, "An American Maker of Hard Porcelain: Adelaide Alsop Robineau," *Keystone* 27 (June 1906): 921–24; Irene Sargent, "American Wonder in the Ceramic Field: A Sympathetic Appreciation of the Life-Work, Genius, and Notable Achievements of Mrs. Adelaide Robineau—An Inspiring Story of Effort and Triumph," *Keystone* 45 (January 1918): 65–69; Irene Sargent, "Clay in the Hands of the Potter," *Keystone* 57 (September 1929): 131–41.

Under the direction of Mrs. Robineau, the Pottery is making the experiment of introducing more artistic and original decorations on their printed ware. The effort is a commendable one, as a good deal of financial risk is involved in persuading the public to buy artistic designs, and in a big factory like the Onondaga Pottery where hundreds of girls are employed, the loss from work poorly done is greatly increased in introducing this class of design. Mr. [James] Pass, the manager of the Pottery is ambitious to raise the art standard of their porcelain, so that it will occupy a unique position in the American Pottery world and eventually abroad.[16]

The 1902 article illustrated sixteen dinner plates and mentioned the names of the designers but without specifically linking names with pieces. Two are known for certain to be Robineau's designs, however, and they will be considered shortly.

The Onondaga Pottery Company had been incorporated in 1871. Pass had worked there as a boy, when his father was the plant manager. After gaining experience in other major pottery centers, Pass returned to the company as a ceramic engineer in the mid 1880s and by 1902 had become its president. He closely oversaw all its operations and made important advances in engineering, production, and merchandising. By 1888 he had developed a revolutionary, commercially viable clay body that he called American china. His first designs were for Imperial Geddo ware, a line of delicate, exquisite, fancy shapes. He introduced his prototype fine dinnerware line at the new Yates Hotel in 1892. This line evolved into the Marmora shape. The pottery won a grand prize at the Chicago World's Columbian Exposition in 1893 with Imperial Geddo and Marmora. In 1896 Pass took a bold step by pioneering the manufacture of vitreous commercial china for the hotel industry. Onondaga Pottery Company became the nation's leading manufacturer of this product. (The company continued to produce fine china dinnerware until 1971 and is still, in 1995, a major producer of hotel ware.)[17]

Pass was a vital figure in Syracuse, socially and culturally as well as in industry. His diaries place him regularly at the theater and other arts events.[18] The initiative he took in using Robineau's patterns re-

---

[16] "New York Society of Keramic Arts," *Keramic Studio* 3 (February 1902): 219–21. Robineau's studio was frequently the meeting place of this society, but it is not stated where this exhibition took place. Weiss, *Glory in Porcelain*.

[17] History files, Syracuse China Corp. archives, Syracuse, N.Y.

[18] James Pass diaries, 1884–1908, Syracuse China Corp. archives, Syracuse, N.Y.

flected his sensitivity to the changes in design under way in America in the early years of the new century. It was a bold move in a highly competitive mass-market industry that catered to essentially conservative tastes to introduce products that departed from the norm to the extent that Robineau's designs did. Pass undoubtedly realized that *Keramic Studio*'s attention to his pottery's new products would add to their prestige and foster their acceptance. It would also enhance his efforts to encourage Binns, head of the department of clayworking at Alfred University at the time, to direct talented, progressive-minded graduates to the company. Pass was a remarkable man who, like Mundy, lent perceptive support to the arts and crafts movement in Syracuse without being an active member of it.

In March 1903, the month of the Syracuse arts and crafts exhibition, *Keramic Studio* published a photograph captioned "Onondaga Porcelain Plates Designed by Mrs. Robineau." These designs are different from those that had been illustrated the previous year. Until recently, no evidence existed that Robineau's designs were more than prototypes, but it is now certain that the pottery patented versions of two of her 1902 designs and produced them as underglaze decorations. The first of these, named Violet Border, was patented May 30, 1904. The second design, named both Moss Rose and Wild Rose Art Nouveau Border, was patented March 13, 1906. Robineau's decorations are graceful, stylized treatments of floral subjects and depart radically from the chaste, realistic Victorian floral designs the company was producing at the time. The outlines are filled with muted tones rather than bright colors, creating a modern, flat-patterned decorative border. Onondaga Pottery sold Robineau's designs as custom orders (rather than as stock patterns) to many clients well into the 1920s.[19]

Robineau designed her Moss Rose for the Yates Hotel, although it is not certain that the pattern was used there. Sometime in 1904 the

[19] *Keramic Studio* 4 (March 1903): 211. Patents, Syracuse China Corp. archives, Syracuse, N.Y. A third design by Robineau, Grape Border, was not patented but was produced for many years, beginning in 1907, and was quite popular. Several other designs were obviously influenced by Robineau and were a departure from the Victorian floral designs the pottery typically produced. Perhaps from her influence, Elmer Walter designed the lovely Chelsea pattern, which was patented at the same time as Violet Border. He also created a series of art nouveau designs called Modern Art series, which were very like decorations published in *Keramic Studio*.

Fig. 4. Tabard Room, Yates Hotel, Syracuse, N.Y., ca. 1940. (Onondaga Historical Assoc., Syracuse, N.Y.)

Yates opened its Tabard Room (fig. 4), a small tearoom-restaurant meant to be evocative of the famous late medieval inn of the same name that had survived in Southwark, London, until 1876. The room was accessible from both the street and the main lobby of the hotel. Its interior featured oak paneling, with English glass windows; a hammered-copper fireplace hood; and Stickley's Craftsman wall and ceiling lamps, chairs, and tables, suggesting that he most likely fitted the entire room. Robineau's Moss Rose pattern would have found an ideal setting in this room.[20]

[20]Customer service records, Syracuse China Corp. archives, Syracuse, N.Y. This entry, dated July 21, 1904, indicates that "Yates Hotel Border, New Art Nouveau #55805" was ordered from Dey Brothers, the local department store distributor. The entry gives instructions for applying gold decoration to fancy, footed salad bowls and gravy boats, probably on the Plymouth shape (the company's viably commercial fine china dinnerware shape). However, the order was not spelled out by shapes and sizes as other orders customarily were, which raises a question as to whether it could have been for a sample only. No pieces have been found to confirm the order. The July 1904 date of this order, however, offers a clue to the still-elusive date of the restaurant's opening.

Well before this, in February 1902, Stickley's house in Syracuse had been seriously damaged by fire. He had moved with his family into the Yates, and he resided there for several months while he rebuilt the interior of his home. During his time at the Yates he not only remodeled the interior of his house as a fine example of the Craftsman style but also oversaw Pond's and Sargent's planning for the arts and crafts exhibition envisioned for his Craftsman Building, a block away. During this time he may also have begun discussions on the design of the Tabard Room with the hotel's owner.[21]

It is interesting to note that shortly after the exhibition, Robineau began some construction projects of her own. In 1903 she built her studio on a hill overlooking the city. In 1904 she built adjacent to it an arts and crafts house designed with the help of her friend, the New York architect Catherine Budd. The interiors of Robineau's new home came from Stickley's line of custom-made Craftsman designs: paneling and moldings, lamps, bookcases, window seats, and stairways.[22] In their respective houses, she and Stickley became the true exponents of the "art that is life" in Syracuse.

The exhibition in 1903 at the Craftsman Building provided the foundation for arts and crafts enterprises that survived successfully in the Syracuse community for many years. The Benedict Art Studio produced lamps, fittings, and other decorative objects. L. and J. G. Stickley's Onondaga Shops thrived near Syracuse long after Gustav's Craftsman empire collapsed. In 1913 the Henry Keck Studio opened "near the Yates" and produced some of the finest stained glass in the country, closing in 1974. In 1908 Ward Wellington Ward, a gifted and prolific arts and crafts architect, began his practice in Syracuse, which continued until halted by his ill health in 1926.[23] Other architects also practiced in an arts and crafts spirit in the community, with the result that Syracuse, like many smaller cities across the country, has a wealth of surviving bungalow-, cottage-, Tudor-, mission-, and

[21] Peter Wiles (grandson of Gustav Stickley) told me in 1990 that his mother remembered "what fun it was to live at the Yates."

[22] I have been privileged to visit and photograph Robineau's house and thank present and past owners for their cooperation.

[23] See Cleota Reed, ed., *The Henry Keck Stained Glass Studio* (Syracuse, N.Y.: Syracuse University Press, 1983); Cleota Reed, *The Arts and Crafts Ideal: The Ward House: An Architect and His Craftsmen* (Syracuse, N.Y.: IDEA, 1978).

prairie-style houses reflecting the arts and crafts outlook of the first decades of the century.

Robineau closed her studio in 1921 and joined the College of Fine Arts faculty at Syracuse University, where she taught ceramic art until her death in 1929. Sargent, then nearing eighty, and still teaching at the university, paid final and eloquent tribute to her late friend and colleague in *Keystone*, describing Robineau as the first art potter of the United States.[24]

One may imagine Sargent, who resided at the Yates in her later years, dining alone in the Tabard Room, probably upon Moss Rose dinnerware, and musing upon the passing of Robineau while recalling her other acquaintances of long ago—Stickley, Pond, Mundy, Pass—and of the time, more than a quarter of a century earlier, when the exhibition that vitalized the arts and crafts movement in Syracuse opened "near the Yates."

[24] Sargent, "Clay in the Hands of the Potter," p. 131.

The Monastic Ideal in Rural Massachusetts

Edward Pearson Pressey and New Clairvaux

Jeannine Falino

"Democracy, individualism, voluntary cooperation, sentiment, a changed method of production of wares by handicraft, altruism, the simple life, a minimum of wage earning, a maximum of dependence upon the soil for a living; distribution of menial service and emancipation of the menial class, proportion between the mental, manual, and religious education." With these expansive words, the settlement of New Clairvaux was described by its founder, Unitarian minister Edward Pearson Pressey (fig. 1). The community was established in 1901 to combat what Pressey perceived as the eroding morals and corrupt standards of modern society. In naming New Clairvaux, he chose the twelfth-century spiritual and social example of Saint Bernard of Clairvaux as the religious foundation for his community.[1] Pressey secularized this spiritual base by including popular agrarian and labor re-

The author thanks the following individuals for guidance and insight in the preparation of this manuscript: Edward S. Cooke, Charles F. Montgomery Professor of Decorative Arts, Yale University; Sinclair Hitchings, keeper of prints, Boston Public Library; Greer Allen, Yale University printer, retired; Keith Morgan, Boston University.

[1] [Edward Pearson Pressey], "College Settlement in a Country Town, a Protestant Revival in Rural Massachusetts of the Monastic Ideal," *Boston Sunday Globe*, November 13, 1904. Saint Bernard (1090–1153) inspired monks of the Cistercian order in Clairvaux, France, to withdraw from the material world, take a vow of poverty, and engage in a variety of manual tasks, including farming.

Fig. 1. Edward Pearson Pressey and the New Clairvaux Village Shop, Egg Farm, Arts and Crafts Room, and Twin Maples Farm House, Montague, Mass. From [Edward Pearson Pressey], "College Settlement in a Country Town, Protestant Revival in Rural Massachusetts of the Monastic Ideal," *Boston Sunday Globe*, November 13, 1904. (Pusey Library, Harvard Library.)

form issues in his ideology. He advocated a return to the self-sufficient, preindustrial age in which the dignity of labor was revived and service to all men honored, to the greater glory of God.

Pressey chose to establish New Clairvaux in Montague, a quiet country town located in the western part of Massachusetts, east of Deerfield and the Connecticut River. Founded in colonial times, Montague lies in a region that was once known for its many farms and busy paper mills. By 1900, however, Montague had entered a period of decline characteristic of many rural New England villages that were afflicted by economic stagnation and significant losses in population.[2]

---

[2] Hal S. Barron, *Those Who Stayed Behind: Rural Society in Nineteenth-Century New England* (Cambridge, Eng.: Cambridge University Press, 1984).

In Montague and elsewhere, the traditional balance between city and country life that had existed in the early years of the Republic had been undermined by the slow decay of the agrarian infrastructure and corresponding growth of urban centers.

The changing state of rural and urban America was debated in the press beginning in the second half of the nineteenth century. Urban writers and social critics nostalgically lamented the abandonment of the countryside for the uncertain advantages of city life. Many expressed the concern that the diminishing rewards of country life accelerated out-migration, thereby endangering the delicate and vital balance between rural and urban culture. An allied concern for the erosion of country churches was led by ministers who felt that the excessive factionalization of rural ministries and dwindling congregations called for innovative approaches to their mission, including the professionalization of an emerging young clergy and the unification of weak and scattered denominations into cooperative congregations.[3]

These so-called country life and related rural church movements were led by urban intellectuals and reformers drawn from the academic or ministerial ranks of the urban middle class who aimed to revive and repopulate the agrarian base through a restructuring of rural institutions. In some cases, initiatives to repopulate the countryside worked hand in glove with reforming efforts on the behalf of poor city dwellers. Arcadian outposts were established by social reformers to reinvigorate both rural and urban dwellers, whether poor, immigrant, or educated middle class, with a combination of manual labor, fresh air, and intellectual pursuits. Participants were frequently introduced by the reformers to such traditional handcrafts as pottery, lacemaking, or cabinetmaking in the hope that the practice of these artisanal skills could offer alternatives to farm, factory, and office work.[4]

The association of a country setting with the traditional handcrafts was perhaps best carried out in England by C.R. Ashbee (1863–1942), who moved his Guild of Handicraft to the rural Cotswold village of Chipping Campden, where it flourished briefly from 1902 to 1908. In the United States, the New York mountain retreat of the Byrdcliffe Colony and the old mill site in suburban Philadelphia that became

[3] Barron, *Those Who Stayed Behind*, pp. 31–50.
[4] Associated Charities, A *Directory of the Charitable and Benificent Organizations of Boston* (Boston: Damrell and Upham, 1891).

Rose Valley were among the better-known, albeit short-lived refuges for members of the middle and upper classes but did not attract larger numbers of adherents. New Clairvaux was one of the most visionary and ultimately impractical groups of this type, which attempted to combine the philosophy and aesthetics of the arts and crafts movement with more radical agrarian, church, and labor reform theories.[5]

Pressey was born in 1869 to a poor farming family in Salem, New Hampshire, and graduated with valedictory honors from Pinkerton Academy at nearby Derry. Continuing his studies in 1891 at Harvard, Pressey eagerly absorbed current theories of social and agrarian reform, especially those advanced at a Harvard Socialist Club lecture by Morrison Swift. Swift had unsuccessfully appealed to the governor of Massachusetts to purchase neglected farms in the western part of the state as sites for disadvantaged city dwellers, including some who had previously deserted the countryside in search of urban progress and prosperity.[6]

Pressey's years of study at Harvard coincided with a flurry of social reforming activities by religious, cultural, and industrial leaders of the Boston area. Concerned about the living and working conditions of the city's poor, these reformers established dozens of charitable institutions and settlement houses in the metropolitan area. Many of the same prominent Bostonians also met socially at the Twentieth Century Club to discuss these troubling issues. Organized in 1893, the club was composed of members drawn from a variety of professions united in their desire for open discussions on matters of art and social concern. Members were addressed by some of the leading reformers of the day. Hull-House founder Jane Addams (1860–1935), British-born socialist

[5]Coy L. Ludwig, *The Arts and Crafts Movement in New York State, 1890s–1920s* (Hamilton, N.Y.: Gallery Assoc. of New York State, 1983), pp. 65–66; Eileen Boris, "Art and Labor: John Ruskin, William Morris, and the Craftsman Ideal in America, 1876–1915" (Ph.D. diss., Brown University, 1981), pp. 345–47. Jeannine Falino, "The Monastic Ideal in Rural Massachusetts: Edward Pearson Pressey and New Clairvaux" (Master's thesis, Boston University, 1984).

[6]On Pressey, see *Harvard Class of 1893, Fortieth Anniversary* (Norwood, Mass.: Plimpton Press, 1933), pp. 197–98; Margaret Rollins, *Carl Rollins at Montague, 1903–1908: A Talk by Margaret Rollins at a Meeting of the Columbiad Club, 10 December 1963* (New Haven: Yale University Press, Carl Purington Rollins Press, 1963), p. 4. On Pressey and socialist reform, see "Second Saint Bernard, The Reverend Edward Pearson Pressey and His New Clairvaux," *Boston Herald*, July 6, 1902. Alumni records, Pusey Library, Harvard University. Arthur Mann, *Yankee Reformers in the Urban Age* (Cambridge: Harvard University Press, Belknap Press, 1954), p. 155.

and Bennington museum curator John Spargo (1876–1966), Morrison Swift, and Russian anarchist Prince Peter Kropotkin (1842–1921) were invited speakers, as were New York photographer Jacob Riis (1849–1914) and British book craftsman T.J. Cobden-Sanderson (1840–1922). The club's local membership included Unitarian minister Edward Everett Hale (1822–1909); painter John Enneking (1841–1916); printer Louis Prang (1824–1909); Chicago journalist Henry Demarest Lloyd (1847–1903), then living on Mount Vernon Street in Boston; secretary and treasurer of the Society of Arts and Crafts, Frederick Allen Whiting (1873–1959); and scholar and social critic Vida Scudder.[7]

These social reformers hoped to empower the poor and immigrant urban population with education, trips to the surrounding countryside, and clean accommodations. The educational approach included manual training programs and the practice of handicrafts in the belief that the natural harmonies of labor, when introduced through schools and settlement houses, would spread within the lower classes and mitigate their economic distress through gainful employment. The Lend-a-Hand Society was one such charitable institution. Incorporated in 1891, it was inspired by a short story published in 1871 by founder Hale entitled *Ten Times One Is Ten*.[8]

Aware of these developments, Pressey was uncertain of how to best apply himself after his graduation in 1893 from Harvard Divinity School. He briefly taught night school at North Bennett Street Industrial School and South End Settlement House. Pressey then chafed in his role as a minister to what he perceived as the passive and complacent congregations of South Hope, Maine, and Derby, Connecticut. As he grasped the potential of the unused land he saw around him in

---

[7] Mina Carson, *Settlement Folk: Social Thought and the American Settlement Movement, 1885–1930* (Chicago: University of Chicago Press, 1990); James B. Gilbert, *Work without Salvation: America's Intellectuals and Industrial Alienation, 1880–1910* (Baltimore: Johns Hopkins University Press, 1977), pp. 110–17. *Survey of Twenty Years, 1894–1914* (Boston: Twentieth Century Club, 1914). Significantly, the book was printed by Rollins's Montague Press.

[8] Col. Frederic Ingham, *Ten Times One Is Ten: The Possible Reformation* (Boston: Roberts Brothers, 1871). Hale's inspiring tale is of ten previously unacquainted men who meet at the funeral of a mutual friend and decide to honor their deceased comrade by influencing the lives of ten others. The exponential possibilities of the story inspired the establishment of Lend-a-Hand societies around the country. Their motto was "Look up and not down / Look forward and not back / Look out and not in / Lend a hand!"

these country towns, Pressey began to see how the rural countryside could help alleviate the squalor of the city's poor. He became better acquainted with the Lend-a-Hand Society and together with Hale dreamed of a revitalized rural society composed of a relocated urban population similar to that envisioned by Swift. In their plans for this new, repopulated landscape, the disadvantaged and alienated urban worker could draw strength from a renewed contact with the earth and, through handicrafts, earn a respectable living far from the degrading influences of the city. Hale, who was nearing the end of a long life of public service, encouraged Pressey to provide the leadership for a rural community that could benefit from such an arrangement. Each minister contributed essays on the subject in Hale's publication, the *Lend-a-Hand Record*. Pressey's "Abandoned Farm Letters" extolled the virtues of country life. For his part, Hale wrote the "New Clairvaux Papers," which established the concept and name of Pressey's community.[9] Despite several years of appeal in the *Lend-a-Hand Record*, Hale was unable to garner support for an actual settlement but encouraged Pressey, his "second Saint Bernard," to form a group nonetheless.

By evoking the memory of a successful twelfth-century religious community, Pressey and Hale participated in the ongoing public fascination with the Middle Ages revived by A.W.N. Pugin (1812–52) and John Ruskin (1819–1900). The allure of medieval culture extended to such Roman Catholic saints as Bernard, Catherine of Siena, and Joan of Arc, whose intensity of faith offered comfort to modern, alienated Christians. Numerous books appeared during the 1890s on the lives of these and other Catholic saints, including one written in 1893 on the life of Bernard. Saint Bernard's directive that each monastery depend upon agriculture and husbandry for subsistence enabled the Cistercians to establish new colonies in western Europe on an unparalleled scale, a success undoubtedly well known to Pressey, who had studied the life of Saint Bernard while at Harvard.[10] The restless, urban search for a

---

[9] Alumni records, Pusey Library, Harvard University. On Pressey in Maine and Connecticut, see *Boston Herald*, July 6, 1902. Edward Pearson Pressey, *The Vision of New Clairvaux; or, Ethical Reconstruction through Combination of Agriculture and Handicraft, under Conditions Which Exercise Emotion, Sentiment, and Imagination, with Loyalty to a Supreme Ideal* (Boston: Sherman, French, 1909), pp. 92–95. The articles cited by Pressey, purportedly published in the *Lend-a-Hand Record*, cannot be located.

[10] T. J. Jackson Lears, *No Place of Grace: Antimodernism and the Transformation of American Culture, 1880–1920* (New York: Pantheon Books, 1981), pp. 150–53; Rich-

vital contact with earth, so much a part of the country life movement, found its religious parallel in Pressey's emulation of the Cistercian life.

In April 1900 Pressey wrote to Hale of his move from Derby to Rowe, Massachusetts, and his success in convincing new settlers to attend nearby public and religious schools and reclaim many of the abandoned properties in the area. He ran a Unitarian Sunday school and encouraged nature studies among the children through the Deerfield Valley Agricultural Society and Cornell University extension school, even as he found a wider audience for his ideas in lectures throughout New England. That Pressey's activities in Rowe constituted a prelude to New Clairvaux is known from the letter to Hale in which he sought the Boston minister's support for a new community that he intended to establish in Montague. Shortly thereafter, Pressey did move to Montague, where he began to preach in an abandoned church and tried without much success to establish a following for a school and community that was to be New Clairvaux. The prospect of failure may have induced Pressey to rapidly introduce a more nonsectarian, arts and crafts dimension to the venture. This shift in emphasis probably took place during a 1901 trip he made to upstate New York, where he saw Elbert Hubbard's bustling Roycrofters in East Aurora. On that same trip he also stopped in Buffalo to visit the Pan-American Exposition and viewed the art and crafts section designed by Louis Comfort Tiffany. Pressey began his work for New Clairvaux in earnest shortly after his return. To raise funds, he sought out speaking engagements to reform-minded religious and social groups and traveled as far west as Chicago, where Lloyd, a supporter of cooperative settlements, met with him. Within a year, Pressey had raised approximately $5,000 and attracted several settlers, enough to make a start.[11]

---

ard Salter Storrs, *Bernard of Clairvaux: The Times, the Man, and His Work* (New York: Scribner, 1892); Edward Pearson Pressey, "New Clairvaux: The Regeneration of a Town. How the 'Vision' Came, and What the Result Was—Growth of Ideal Communistic Family in the Connecticut River Hills. An Account of a College Settlement in a Decadent Massachusetts Village, from the Note Books of the Founder," *Boston Evening News*, January 30, 1904.

[11] Edward Pearson Pressey to Edward Everett Hale, April 6, 1900, Andover-Harvard Theological Library, Harvard University. Edward Pearson Pressey to Henry Demarest Lloyd, December 5, 1901. Pressey thanked Lloyd for his letter and promised him a copy of *Country Time and Tide*, the first copy of which had been printed four days earlier (reel 12, pp. 1225–26, Henry Demarest Papers, Division of Archives and Manuscripts, State Historical Society of Wisconsin, Madison). A second letter from Pressey to Lloyd, dated February 13, 1902, outlines Pressey's specific plans for New Clairvaux and the

The arts and crafts school and settlement established by Pressey at New Clairvaux were similar to others founded from the earliest days of the movement. Ruskin had extolled the virtues of manual labor in *The Stones of Venice*. In 1870 he had attempted to establish a revolutionary new community in Sheffield, England, called Saint George's Guild, whose agrarian base was to be supplemented with shoemaking. Like New Clairvaux, the network of Saint George's guilds that Ruskin envisioned did not prosper. Despite their failure, their founder inspired many societies, schools, and communities on both sides of the Atlantic, among which was New Clairvaux.[12]

At its peak from 1902 to 1906, the self-described "college settlement" at New Clairvaux was a rather loose arrangement of largely college-educated individuals that included six men (four of whom were ministers), several wives, students, and apprentices who shared common work areas but retained privately owned residences. Despite differences in theological training, each minister, like Pressey, sought alternatives to traditional religious paths. Unitarian Waldo Bromley Truesdell, a Harvard graduate of 1897, taught mathematics and science at Atlanta Baptist College, now Morehouse College, for a brief time before joining New Clairvaux. Truesdell purchased Twin Maples Farm in Montague, performed carpentry work for New Clairvaux, and contributed articles in the settlement publication entitled *Country Time and Tide* (fig. 2). Congregationalist George Willis Solley graduated from the School for Christian Workers in Hartford in 1889. After preaching at Congregational churches in Hampden and Deerfield, he became a Unitarian in 1896. He was appointed pastor of Christ Church (Unitarian) in Dorchester and in 1903 resigned to take up social settlement work at the Morgan Memorial in Boston. Solley was a member of the Twentieth Century Club from 1902 to 1909 and may have learned of New Clairvaux through fellow minister and member Hale or through Pressey's lecture to the group sometime before 1904. In 1904 Solley and his Irish-born wife, the former Sarah Dickson, who

expenses involved (reel 13, pp. 106–12, Henry Demarest Papers); Pressey, "New Clairvaux."

[12]Charles H. Kegel, "Ruskin's St. George's Guild in America," *American Quarterly* 9 (Winter 1957): 412–20. John Ruskin, *The Stones of Venice* (London: Smith, Elder, 1851).

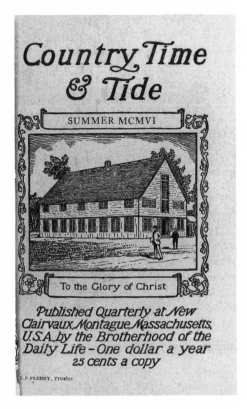

Fig. 2. New Clairvaux Village Shop. From
Country Time and Tide 8, no. 5 (Summer
1906), frontispiece. (Yale University.)

had been involved with textiles in the Dorchester Arts and Crafts Soci-
ety, moved to Montague, where they purchased Spring Farm. Another
member of New Clairvaux was Episcopalian minister George Nahum
Holcomb, who had graduated from Trinity College, the Divinity
School of the Protestant Episcopal church, and had been a special
student at Harvard Divinity School. He was preaching in Tyngsboro,
Massachusetts, when he joined the community in 1904. Layman
Charles Francis Kimball had been a member of the Christian Com-

monwealth Colony of Commonwealth, Georgia.[13] Kimball was the
major cabinetmaker of the group and with his wife and large family
ran the New Clairvaux egg farm. Carl Purington Rollins was a Harvard
student with printing experience who arrived in 1903 to operate the
New Clairvaux Press.

Beginning in January 1902, Pressey publicized his social experiment in *Country Time and Tide*, named after Ruskin's book *Time and
Tide*, a discourse on the "honesty of work and honesty of exchange" to
be found in an ideal community. Since no records from New Clairvaux
have survived, this periodical serves as the primary source of information on Pressey, his hopes for the community, and his perception of
its place in history. Pressey used the journal to attract new members
with articles on his growing community along with others about social
reform. Most issues included quotes by, or an article on, a particular
social theorist, the most popular among them being Ruskin, William
Morris, and Leo Tolstoy. Along with Saint Bernard, they became
known as the four "patron saints" of New Clairvaux. Together they
expressed the aesthetic, spirtual, labor, and land issues essential for the
"simple life" that Pressey sought for his community. The 1904 book
jointly authored by Pressey and Rollins, *The Arts and Crafts and the
Individual*, offered a succinct position statement on the community.
As coauthor, Rollins emerged as an important visionary for the group.
Pressey and Rollins patterned the settlement at Montague after Morris's
image of London as a pastoral "workshop in the field," which he described in *News from Nowhere* (1890), and according to the anarchist,

[13]On the "college settlement," see *Boston Sunday Globe*, November 13, 1904. On
Truesdell, see *Secretary's Report, Harvard Class of 1897, Third Report* (Cambridge:
Crimson Printing, 1907), p. 216; Benjamin Brawley, *History of Morehouse College* (At-
lanta: By the college, 1917), p. 93; W. B. Truesdell, "A Simple Life," *Country Time
and Tide* 4, no. 3 (July 1903): 73–75. George Willis Solley, *Thomas Solley and His
Descendants: The Story of a Hunt for an Ancestor* (Fitchburg, Mass.: Sentinal Printing
Co., 1911), pp. 165–66, 189. Twentieth Century Club membership directories, 1902–9,
Massachusetts Historical Society, Boston. Pressey lectured to the Twentieth Century
Club sometime before 1904, as the lecture, entitled "The Country and City Problem,"
was offered in a list of publications in *Country Time and Tide* 6, no. 3 (July 1904) and
no. 4 (August 1904). On the purchasing of Spring Farms, see Franklin County Deeds
482:360 (1904); 504:370 (1905); 522:88 (1908); 620:163 (1917), Greenfield, Mass. On
Holcomb, see clipping file, Pusey Library, Harvard University. On Kimball, see Donald
Drew Egbert and Stow Persons, eds., *Socialism and American Life*, 2 vols. (Princeton:
Princeton University Press, 1952), 1:264.

communal agrarian theories advanced by Russian reformers Leo
Tolstoy and Prince Peter Kropotkin. Aware of their American roots,
Pressey and Rollins were sustained by writings of Ralph Waldo Emer-
son, Henry David Thoreau, and Walt Whitman on the unique
American spirit that drew strength from the native soil. Pressey and
Rollins also attempted to establish the legitimacy of their venture by
linking it with related American models. Pressey emphasized New
Clairvaux's relationship to past and present utopian communities and
their leaders in articles on Shaker villages (1790–1817), Robert Owen's
New Harmony (1825), George Ripley's Brook Farm (1841), and Adin
Ballou's Hopedale Community (1842). He implied that like these
groups, New Clairvaux was participating in a movement of revolutionary proportions.[14]

Equally prevalent in *Country Time and Tide* were Pressey's articles
on such greater- and lesser-known figures of the arts and crafts movement as Gustav Stickley and Hubbard, whose Roycrofter community
had been visited by Pressey. Whiting contributed essays, and Pressey
publicized the community's relationship with the Deerfield Blue and
White Society, the Montague Society of Arts and Crafts, and other
organizations in the region.

Pressey's Country Town Training School for boys, later to be
named the New Clairvaux Plantation and Crafts School, was based
upon John Dewey's "learn by doing" theory of manual training. In the
same way that New Clairvaux can be viewed as a society in miniature,
Pressey's school followed Dewey's theory of the classroom as a still
smaller microcosm that introduced social and ethical values to children
through increasingly complex tasks. Surviving literature suggests that

---

[14]John Ruskin, *Time and Tide* (London: J. M. Dent and Sons, [1867]). A fire that
gutted the Pressey home in Montague presumably destroyed internal papers regarding
the community. The "patron saints" are discussed in *Boston Beacon*, September 10,
1904. On reforms, see Peter Kropotkin, *Fields, Factories, and Workshops* (Boston:
Houghton Mifflin, 1899). William Morris, *News from Nowhere; or, An Epic of Rest.
Being Some Chapters from a Utopian Romance by William Morris* (Boston: Roberts
Brothers, 1890). Articles on utopian societies that were published by Pressey include the
following: Napoleon Hoagland, "Adin Ballou: The Man Who Impressed Tolstoy," *Country Time and Tide* 3, no. 2 (August 1902); no. 3 (September 1902); George Holcomb,
"Robert Owen's New Harmony Experience," *Country Time and Tide* 6, no. 1 (May
1904): 1–3; Edward Pearson Pressey, "Religious and Social Vision of the Shakers,"
Country Time and Tide 7, no. 6 (April 1905): 165–66.

the children received their formal education in the local school system, supplemented by more than thirty courses at New Clairvaux. The curriculum included printing, gardening, forestry, domestic science, woodwork, and designing. It is probably no coincidence that these students provided a convenient pool of labor for the settlement in addition to being a potentially significant source of income for the community. Although Pressey claimed that a number of local children took part in the school, it seems that few attended. Even less evident were the city children considered to be most in need of an invigorating atmosphere. Perhaps to make up the shortfall, Pressey accepted at least two Puerto Rican students through the United States commissioner of education.[15]

The settlement of New Clairvaux reflected the contradictory nature of its time by expressing both progressive and reactionary ideals. In combining aspects of the country life movement and identifying New Clairvaux with other utopian and arts and crafts experiments, Pressey allied himself with social change. However, in his wistful yearnings for a bygone era, as first expressed by Ruskin and Morris, Pressey's choice of language betrayed his reactionary leanings. He gave the material substance of New Clairvaux a decidedly antimodernist cast when he described it as "a New England renaissance of the medieval abbey, with its agricultural industries, its manufactures, its arts of weaving, dying, brewing, bookmaking, its teachings, ministrations, example, and simple life."[16]

Pressey's Village Shop was the centerpiece of the New Clairvaux community, completed in February 1903. The structure and the activities that took place within it conformed to Pressey's ideal of his medieval abbey in New England (see fig. 2). The shop housed all crafts endeavors; seven of its eleven rooms were dedicated to woodworking, printing,

[15] For more on educational theories, see Gilbert, *Work without Salvation*, pp. 97–123. On the school, see advertisement, "A Country Town Training School," *Country Time and Tide* 1, no. 1 (January 1902); "Our Country Training School," *Country Time and Tide* 1, no. 5 (May 1902): 165–70; "The Junior Country Town of New Clairvaux," *Country Time and Tide* 1, no. 7 (July 1902): 1–6; "The New Clairvaux Training School Industries and Settlement," *Country Time and Tide* 3, no. 4 (February 1903): 122–31; *New Clairvaux Plantation and Crafts School*, 1904–5 (Montague, Mass.: New Clairvaux Press, 1904), brochure; *Turner Falls Reporter* (Massachusetts), February 25, 1903. Tuition initially was set at $125 but by 1904 was raised to $200 per year.

[16] *Country Time and Tide* 6, no. 3 (July 1904): 66.

basketry, dying, and weaving, while the remaining four were reserved for craftsmen and apprentices. These cozy, communal arrangements were overlaid with a less-publicized capitalist structure, for the Village Shop was incorporated by Pressey, who charged rent according to the amount of space occupied. The level of activity is difficult to ascertain in the absence of surviving objects, but the range of materials actually produced may be inferred from a 1903 advertisement for an exhibition and sale of crafts at the Park Street Church of Boston, where "furniture, rag rugs, embroidery, lace, raffia, palm baskets, leather work, and prints from the New Clairvaux shop" were on view.[17]

References to craftsmen's guilds and Ruskinian standards of workmanship appeared in an advertisement for furniture made at New Clairvaux in the very first issue of *Country Time and Tide* in January 1902. Tables with round and square tops were illustrated with battens having protruding pins and double-tenoned stretchers (fig. 3). These tables may be the same as those described in an adjoining advertisement: "A Perfect Library Table / Mr. Frank C. Cross of the / Cabinetmaker's Guild, will make you / a Five Foot table of old quartered oak / possessing the following qualities: - / HONEST WORK, / SOLID WOOD, (no glue, no iron) / INDIVIDUALITY, / ELEGANCE (without any gingerbread ornament) / an HEIR-LOOM / COMFORT, / BEAUTY, / ARCHITECTURE (in every detail of construction)." A "grandfather's clock . . . that generations unborn will talk about" was also offered in the same issue, but no furniture of any type has yet been discovered. In addition to Cross, who later produced hand looms, winders, and swifts for weaving, Kimball and, at a later date, Rollins were the furniture makers in Montague.[18]

The textile arts were primarily developed by Sarah Dickson Solley.

---

[17]On the Village Shop, see *Turner Falls Reporter (Massachusetts)*, February 25, 1903. *Boston Sunday Globe*, November 13, 1904; "Notice of Intent to Form a Corporation: The New Clairvaux Village Shop Association," reprinted in Gay Walker, ed., *The Works of Carl Purington Rollins* (New Haven: Yale University Library, 1982), cat. 85; *Country Time and Tide* 3, no. 3 (Midwinter 1903).

[18]*Country Time and Tide* 1, no. 2 (February 1902): 36. Both advertisements appear on the same page. See also *The Cabinet Work at New Clairvaux* (Montague, Mass.: New Clairvaux Press, 1907), brochure, which names Kimball and Rollins as the central figures in the cabinet shop. The text states that "metal fittings, woven fabrics, etc., used in connection with the work are made by members of the Montague Society of Arts and Crafts and local craftsmen."

Fig. 3. New Clairvaux tables. From *Country Time and Tide* 3, no. 1 (November 1902).

Perhaps the most intriguing member of New Clairvaux, Solley was the daughter of Rev. Benjamin Dickson, professor, resident fellow, and assistant librarian at Trinity College, Dublin. She recalled happy hours of her youth spent examining the illustrated medieval manuscripts at Trinity College library, which included the *Book of Kells*. Sarah Dickson Solley became known for her high-quality natural dyes and textiles, which she wove on looms made at New Clairvaux. She probably made or supervised the weaving of objects that can be seen in the sole surviving illustration of the textile room in the Village Shop (see fig. 1). Solley's previous success with textiles in the arts and crafts community may have emboldened her to part ways with New Clairvaux. By 1906 she used the name of Spring Farm Industries to market her own goods and those of local craftspeople who worked with her.[19]

The short, intense life characteristic of most utopian communities was also true for New Clairvaux. The publicity from several newpaper articles and the self-promotion of *Country Time and Tide* was not enough to attract settlers to Montague. Without the influx of new members, the community had begun to lose momentum as early as 1905, when Truesdell left to become submaster at Wilton Academy in Maine. In the same year, Holcomb became professor at Massachusetts Agricultural College (now the University of Massachusetts at Amherst) while maintaining his egg farm in Montague. Solley became pastor of the Church of the Unity in nearby Winchendon but returned periodically to run a boys camp at the school. Pressey's wife died in 1907, and he sold the Village Shop equipment to Rollins in 1909, including the press for *Country Time and Tide*. Hale, Pressey's mentor and the spiritual founder of the community, also died in the same year. Always more of an idealist than a pragmatist, Pressey was a poor manager of his many-faceted enterprise. His idealistic desire for self-sufficiency, not profitability, may have contributed to the departure of key members, each of whom owned his own land. Without an impetus to share any potential wealth and little evidence of new membership, the com-

---

[19] Solley, *Thomas Solley and His Descendants*, p. 189. "Young Woman Relates What She Saw and Heard at Montague, This State, Where College Men Have Established a New Utopia," *Boston Sunday Post*, June 12, 1904; Rollins, *Carl Rollins at Montague*, p. 12. Edward Pearson Pressey, "The Golden Chronicle," *American Cultivator* 17 (September 1904), Pressey Papers, Pusey Library, Harvard University. On Spring Farm Industries, see *Boston Beacon*, September 10, 1904.

munity slowly fragmented. Following a 1911 fire in his home, Pressey left Montague to attempt farming in Vermont. He finally settled in New York, where he became the Associated Press editor of the *Schenectady Gazette*. Pressey died in Schenectady in 1934, still convinced of his dreams.[20]

Despite the unlikely prospects for survival, settlement printer Rollins, New Clairvaux's most enduring craftsman and practitioner of the political principles behind the arts and crafts movement, was to transform the scattered remains of New Clairvaux into a new arts and crafts endeavor called the Dyke Mill, which lasted from 1909 to 1918.

Born in 1880 to a well-to-do West Newbury, Massachusetts, family, Rollins received his first printing press at the age of twelve, which he used to issue his own publication called *Stamp Journal*. He attended Harvard long enough to "read himself out of his inherited Republicanism into Socialism" and worked briefly for the *Georgetown Advocate*. From 1900 to 1903 he worked with the Heintzemann Press in Boston. Printer Carl Heintzemann produced many of the Boston journals devoted to the arts, including early issues of *Handicraft*, and attracted such notables in the Boston book arts movement as Bruce Rogers; Will Bradley; Henry Louis Johnson, who later published *The Printing Art*; and W. Addison Dwiggins.[21] It was through this group that Rollins met Whiting at the Society of Arts and Crafts; they became lifelong friends. It was undoubtedly these connections that brought Rollins to Montague in 1903 as printer for *Country Time and Tide*.

The work and writings of Morris made a deep impression upon Rollins. In 1903 Rollins published an article on Morris's typographic leadership for Johnston's premier issue of *The Printing Art*, and in 1905 he wrote enthusiastically to Whiting of his travels to Chipping Campden to see Ashbee, whose press and some workmen had been transferred from Morris's estate when the Kelmscott Press closed. Rollins concurred with Morris's socialist writings and believed them integral to an understanding of the arts and crafts movement. It was from this

---

[20] On Holcomb and the agricultural college, see *Turner Falls Reporter* (Massachusetts), September 20, 1905. The plantation school is discussed in *Turner Falls Reporter*, May 17, 1905. On the sale of equipment, see *Turner Falls Reporter*, December 2, 1907. Pressey's death is noted in *Turner Falls Reporter*, June 28, 1911.
[21] Rollins, *Carl Rollins at Montague*, p. 2. Nancy Finlay, *Artist of the Book in Boston, 1890–1910* (Cambridge: Harvard College Library, 1985), p. xiii; research files, Department of Prints and Drawings, Boston Public Library.

perspective that Rollins took issue with the endowment planned by the board of the Society of Arts and Crafts, Boston. He argued that "the arts and crafts movement was essentially an economic one," and that stocks and bonds were "securities . . . subtracted from the earnings of the people." An endowment, Rollins felt, would limit the society's potential to that of a mere promoter of an artistic revival rather than the instrument of social reform that was originally intended by its founders. His socialist leanings were perhaps most clear on the eve of the 1908 election, when he wrote, "I cannot doubt that the vision of Marx and Morris and [Eugene] Debs is a clear and right one."[22]

Despite Rollins's political stance, he was uninterested in leading a community or publishing a journal for the cause of socialism. Most of all, Rollins doubted his own ability to create a new Chipping Campden in Montague. In April 1909 he wrote that he could "see . . . opportunities quite as good as any Ashbee has had . . . the making of the Mill into a working commercial proposition standing on its own feet and becoming a source of income to me and the workers—and the alliance with the forces in the town—the Agricultural school, and the town in general—a great school and proving ground for the Arts and Crafts Movement, with a leader whom I could respect and follow—but to lead—I do not feel capable."[23]

In July 1909 Rollins decided, despite his misgivings, to establish the Dyke Mill in a former blacksmith forge and cabinetmaking shop in Montague. A craftsman first, Rollins focused on the demands of creating a functioning workshop and immediately moved in the press, looms, and woodworking equipment that he had purchased from Pressey. Like Pressey, Rollins incorporated the Dyke Mill. Given his socialist stance, this decision may have been imposed upon him by his financial supporters; it points out his concession to or dependence upon their capitalist views.[24]

[22] Rollins to Frederick Allen Whiting, May 30, 1905; Rollins to H. Langford Warren, June 16, 1907; Rollins to Edward Harmon Virgin, April 9, 1909, Rollins Papers, Arts of the Book Room, Sterling Library, Yale University. Rollins advertised himself as a lecturer "on the ethical significance of the arts and crafts movement" (*Handicraft* 4, no. 1 [April 1911], n.p.). Carl Purington Rollins, "Modern 'Special' Types," *Printing Art* 1, no. 1 (March 1903): 13–18.

[23] Rollins to Virgin, Rollins Papers.

[24] Letterhead from the Dyke Mill, dated July 7, 1909, lists Edward Harmon Virgin, president; Charles Ford Kimball, secretary; and Rollins as treasurer and manager. Virgin (Harvard 1899) had known Rollins from their Cambridge days and may have been a

In his new enterprise, Rollins printed advertising for such local craftspeople as the textile artist Julia Bascom (fig. 4); published handbills for local theatrical, musical, and socialist events; and began to print *Handicraft* when it was reissued in 1910. Aside from printing, Rollins organized cooperative groups to dye, weave, and make rugs and furniture. With the assistance of former New Clairvaux member Kimball, Rollins designed and made colonial revival and Mackintosh-inspired frames and carved signs (fig. 5).[25] He also produced bayberry candles and made thread, the latter mostly for the nearby Deerfield arts and crafts community.

Rollins's correspondence makes clear his obvious love for the Dyke Mill enterprise, yet he had little to show for his years of hard work. As a bachelor, Rollins seemed willing to endure financial hardship for a greater social good. However, in 1915 when he married and started a family, Rollins took on more pressing responsibilities that were better served by stable employment. In time he accepted the fact that Socialist ideals and subsistence wages were no longer enough to keep him in Montague. In 1920, to the mutual good fortune of Rollins and Yale University, he moved to New Haven, where he was appointed university printer in 1920. Until his death in 1960, he was the standard-bearer at Yale for handcraftsmanship in the realm of printing. Rollins inspired several generations of Yale undergraduates and left an understated and elegant mark on nearly all printed matter.[26]

Like the arts and crafts communities at Byrdcliffe and Rose Valley, New Clairvaux attracted only a small, educated population and failed to reach the disenfranchised workers that its founder claimed to understand. Pressey advertised New Clairvaux, its crafts, and school, yet it is doubtful whether word of the community reached the many settlement houses and working-class people in American cities.

---

financial backer of the venture. Rollins Papers, Arts of the Book Room, Sterling Library, Yale University.

[25] It was noted on the original cyanotype of plate 5 that "D. Murphy," probably Herman Dudley Murphy of Boston, gilded the frame that Rollins designed and made, indicating collaboration with one of Boston's best-known arts and crafts framemakers. I thank Louis H. Silverstein, curator of the Arts of the Book Collection, Yale University, for bringing this to my attention.

[26] Walker, *Works of Carl Purington Rollins*.

Fig. 4. Carl Purington Rollins, advertisement for *Mount Toby Colors*, the Dyke Mill, Montague, Mass., n.d. (Photo, Greer Allen.)

Fig. 5. Carl Purington Rollins and Charles Kimball, frame, the Dyke Mill, Montague, Mass., ca. 1909. (Photo, Arts of the Book Room, Sterling Library, Yale University.)

New Clairvaux differed in several significant ways from the arts and crafts communities at Roycroft, Rose Valley, Bryn Athyn, and Byrdcliffe. Unlike those settlements, New Clairvaux could not financially survive the early stages of its development, for it lacked the marketing strategies of Hubbard or the deep pockets of such benefactors as Ralph Whitehead of Byrdcliffe, Raymond Pitcairn of Bryn Athyn, and Edward Bok of Rose Valley. The lack of properly trained craftspeople also hindered the New Clairvaux settlement. Without the European craftsmen brought over by Rose Valley or the carefully selected artists at Byrdcliffe, the community experienced difficulty in establishing its reputation for well-made goods. Lack of funds, skills, and management made New Clairvaux one of the most vulnerable and impractical arts and crafts communities ever attempted. Based upon readings of *Country Time and Tide,* however, it probably held one of the most powerful visions of the future for the alienated middle and working classes of urban America.

Upon closing the doors of the Dyke Mill in January 1918, Rollins paid tribute to Pressey's efforts with the following: "New Clairvaux was a very tiny dot on the earth's surface and the sum total of its testimony infinitely less than that of its larger progenitors—the medieval abbeys, the Shaker settlements, the communistic communities. But in its small way it did stand for idealism in a world, as ever, needful to be reminded of the holiness of living an ideal life; and a proof of the difficulty of it."[27]

[27] Rollins, *Carl Rollins at Montague,* p. 17.

The Bryn Athyn Cathedral Project

Craft, Community, and Faith

Shelley K. Nickles

"How strange these manifestations of religion are," marveled English arts and craftsman C. R. Ashbee (1863–1942) upon visiting the Bryn Athyn community cathedral outside Philadelphia in 1931. And yet Ashbee considered the cathedral "very beautiful." He praised the craftsmanship and the guild system employed in building the structure and furnishings, which reflected the arts and crafts ideals of simplicity, handcraftsmanship, attention to materials, and the product of creative work. Ashbee's response of both admiration and bemusement reveals the complex relationship of the Bryn Athyn cathedral to the arts and crafts movement. The construction of the cathedral, begun in 1913 and dedicated in 1919, coincided with the flourishing of this movement in America. Scholars have since recognized the Bryn Athyn cathedral and furnishings as models of arts and crafts ideals of craftsmanship and

The author is grateful to Cheryl Robertson for help as adviser in completing her thesis for the Winterthur Program in Early American Culture, upon which this article is based. The assistance of Stephen Morley, director of Glencairn Museum, was invaluable in facilitating research at Bryn Athyn. Grateful acknowledgment is made to the Glencairn Museum for permission to quote from their materials and to Glencairn and the Academy of the New Church, Bryn Athyn, Pa., for permission to reproduce photographs.

styling.[1] The project's patron, Raymond Pitcairn, and the community by and for whom the cathedral was built have received far less attention, however, although their ideals and involvement determined the project's outcome. This omission fosters the mistaken impression that Bryn Athyn resembled self-styled American arts and crafts communities such as Roycroft or Byrdcliffe. In fact, Bryn Athyn was an insular religious community of high-church Swedenborgians that used craft as a means to a religious end. Bryn Athyn members disseminated their religious beliefs rather than pursuing any program for design or social reform.

The arts and crafts movement did, nevertheless, influence the project through the building's initial architect, Ralph Adams Cram (1863–1942), and certain designers who worked on the cathedral. Through an analysis of the Bryn Athyn cathedral project, focusing on the stained glass guild, this essay reveals how the acceptance of arts and crafts ideals was mediated by personal, community, and religious goals. Bryn Athyn illustrates how these ideals could be adopted but also transformed in their dissemination to individuals and groups who did not consciously participate in the movement.[2]

In the 1890s a group of "New Church" members founded the Bryn Athyn community. The belief that the vision-inspired writings of the Swedish theologian Emannuel Swedenborg (1688–1772) illuminate the true spiritual meaning of the old and new testaments distinguishes the New Church, officially called the Church of the New Jerusalem and commonly called Swedenborgian, from other Christian faiths. Conflicts over the implementation of Swedenborgian doctrine in New Church practice in the mid nineteenth century led to a splintering of the Church of the New Jerusalem into orthodox, conservative, and liberal factions. The forefathers of the Bryn Athyn community were

---

[1] Charles Robert Ashbee to Janet Ashbee, October 21, 1931, letter in the possession of Felicity Ashbee, London; permission to quote courtesy of Felicity Ashbee. Appreciation is also made to James E. Benjamin for directing me to this letter. On Bryn Athyn craftsmanship and styling, see especially Wendy Kaplan, *"The Art That Is Life": The Arts and Crafts Movement in America, 1875–1920* (Boston: Museum of Fine Arts, 1987), p. 315; Roger G. Kennedy, *American Churches* (New York: Stewart, Tabori, and Chang, 1982), p. 103; Tod M. Volpe and Beth Cathers, *Treasures of the American Arts and Crafts Movement* (New York: Harry N. Abrams, 1988), p. 187.

[2] For a more comprehensive discussion, see Shelley Kaplan, "The Bryn Athyn Cathedral Project, 1913–29: The Art and Craft of the Ecclesiastical Path" (Master's thesis, University of Delaware, 1990).

the orthodox, high-church group, known as the "General Church" of the New Jerusalem. This branch adopted an episcopal form of church government and a highly ritualized liturgy. The view that they should completely separate from the old church "both internally and externally" led to the resettlement, in 1897, of General Church members from Philadelphia to the suburb of Huntingdon Valley, Pennsylvania, where a number of congregation members already lived.[3]

General Church philanthropist John Pitcairn (1841–1916), founder of the Pittsburgh Plate Glass company, made possible this exodus by buying land for a New Church school and acreage that was subdivided into parcels for purchase by individual members of the congregation. The community renamed the area Bryn Athyn—Welsh for "hill of cohesion"—to reflect the homogenous community of New Church followers intent on pursuing their own "organized worship, organized social life, and organized education." To advance these goals, Pitcairn initiated the building of a new church with a substantial contribution to the building fund in 1908.[4] Pitcairn's son Raymond (1885–1966), an attorney in Philadelphia, assumed responsibility for the endeavor. Although the community's religious leaders played a role in the project, the cathedral bears the unmistakable influence of Raymond Pitcairn in its conception, style, and craft process. Pitcairn's interest in a medieval aesthetic, religious perspective, and community outlook together shaped the cathedral building.

In 1911 Bryn Athyn religious leader Bishop William F. Pendleton argued that the choice of a previous style, such as Renaissance or Gothic, for the church structure "was a matter of profound indifference

---

[3] Swedenborg's major works include: *The Arcana Coelestia, Divine Love and Wisdom, Divine Providence, Heaven and Hell, Apocalypse Explained, The Last Judgment, Conjugal Love,* and *The True Christian Religion.* On Swedenborg, see Sig Synnestvedt, *The Essential Swedenborg* (New York: Swedenborg Foundation, 1977). On the New Church and Bryn Athyn, see Marguerite Beck Block, *The New Church in the New World: A Study of Swedenborgianism in America* (New York: Octagon Books, 1960). R. B. Caldwell, Sr., "Distinctive Social Life," *New Church Life* 36 (March 1916): 137.

[4] Martin Pryke, "A Quest for Perfection: The Story of the Making of the Stained Glass Windows in the Bryn Athyn Cathedral and Glencairn," July 1989, typescript, stained glass file, Glencairn Museum, Bryn Athyn, Pa. (hereafter cited as GM), pp. 1–2. On the founding of Bryn Athyn, see Block, *New Church,* p. 260. On the building fund, see E. Bruce Glenn, *Bryn Athyn Cathedral: The Building of a Church* (Bryn Athyn, Pa.: Bryn Athyn Church of the New Jerusalem, 1971), p. 20.

Fig. 1. Raymond Pitcairn (*left*) and Ralph Adams Cram, Bryn Athyn Cathedral construction site, ca. 1914. (Photo, Glencairn Museum, Academy of the New Church, Bryn Athyn, Pa.)

because it imitates the expression of a different spiritual state than the one we look to." He articulated the possibility of "experimenting with something new." Although he did not list a particular preference, the bishop advocated hiring an architect who would adapt to community preferences rather than one who was an "avowed Gothicist."[5]

Pitcairn, however, advised employing Cram (of the Cram and Ferguson architectural firm), America's leading neo-Gothicist architect and a member of the Society of Arts and Crafts, Boston, to design Bryn Athyn's new house of worship (fig. 1). Cram planned the cathedral as a variation of an English church in the fifteenth-century perpendicular style, with the plan modified to accommodate General Church ritual. He also proposed a guild system, an idea that was fashionable among arts and crafts proponents on both sides of the Atlantic. By 1912 Pitcairn had

[5] Bishop William F. Pendleton, untitled document, April 1911, Bishop Pendleton file, GM.

gained approval from the church elders to hire Cram. From the architect's perspective, "all the conditions were phenomenally promising."
Cram believed that "there was a site of singular beauty, sympathetic cooperation, and apparently no limit set on expenditures. For basic inspiration, we had the spiritual and pictorial mysticism of Emanuel Swedenborg. I seemed to see here a chance to put into practice some of my
theories of a Medieval guild system, and the idea was cordially received."[6]
Indeed, three factors helped create a receptive environment for Cram's
arts and crafts ideals: Pitcairn's personal interest in the medieval, Bryn
Athyn's communalism, and Swedenborgian doctrine.

Pitcairn shared Cram's medieval aesthetic and his high-church
religious outlook. Evidence of Pitcairn's proclivity for medieval art can
be traced to his childhood and early education, when he compiled
scrapbooks of Gothic architecture. As he matured, Pitcairn began corresponding with contemporary medievalists such as William Goodyear
and Arthur Kingsley Porter. He also developed a library on the subject
of medieval architecture, still largely intact at Glencairn, his home.
To fellow congregation members who had questioned the use of an
old style for the New Church, Pitcairn argued that the New Church
should not demolish the old, but should maintain its positive attributes.
To the Bryn Athyn patron, the Gothic represented the glorious and
pure aspects of the old church before it was corrupted. Pitcairn also
believed that the Gothic cathedral was the appropriate plan for the
episcopal seat of high-church Swedenborgianism.[7]

In addition, Pitcairn cited two elements of Swedenborgian doctrine in justifying the craftsmanship and guild proposed by Cram for
the church building: the doctrine of correspondence and the doctrine
of use. Swedenborg's doctrine of correspondence showed that "everything in the world of nature is derived from a cause and correspondent
in the spiritual world"; hence, design and construction had potent symbolic associations for New Church adherents. A committee was formed
to ensure that Swedenborgian symbolism permeated the form and mo-

---

[6]On Pitcairn's hiring of Cram, see Pryke, "Quest for Perfection," p. 3. On the guild
idea, see Gustav Stickley, *The Craftsman* 1, no. 3 (December 1901). Ralph Adams Cram,
My Life in Architecture (1936; reprint, New York: Kraus Reprint Co., 1969), p. 248.

[7]Pitcairn's childhood was discussed by E. Bruce Glenn, interview with author, Bryn
Athyn, Pa., February 13, 1990. Raymond Pitcairn, "Christian Art and Architecture for
the New Church," *New Church Life* 40, no. 10 (October 1920): 611–24.

tifs of cathedral decoration. Since buildings and objects had a spiritual correspondence, construction methods and materials were also significant. Bishop Pendleton advocated the use of native materials as well as construction that was "thoroughly honest," a goal that coincidentally harmonized with arts and crafts construction ideals.[8]

The second element, Swedenborg's doctrine of use, consists of "service to his neighbor and thus to God, for it is in use and use alone that man can find his greatest happiness." While this doctrine is congruent with the arts and crafts idea of beauty in use and its emphasis on creative labor, Bryn Athyn workers perceived their craft in religious terms. Pitcairn claimed that the "soul" of building "should be the love of use, in the doing of which is found its joy and true reward."[9]

When Cram first suggested to Pitcairn in August 1913 that "all stained glass windows, hardware, and furniture be made at the Cathedral by a guild to be formed for the purpose," the community patron enthusiastically agreed. Pitcairn expressed hope that they could "accomplish in some degree the results which Mr. Cram" had intended, and he immediately began executing and embellishing Cram's suggestions. As the project developed, however, Pitcairn and Cram clashed over issues of implementation. Pitcairn felt that Cram did not offer enough direct guidance regarding the creation of a guild system; the patron's frustration was compounded by the infrequency of the architect's visits to the site. In addition, for the actual timber-and-masonry fabric of the building, Cram opted for the usual general or split contracts. Pitcairn charged, "In spite of many protestations of immense enthusiasm and interest in the unusual opportunity at Bryn Athyn, the firm of Cram and Ferguson, in point of fact, opposed some of the very departures from customary building methods, which were necessary." In contrast, Pitcairn sought to "eliminate every vestige of contract methods and machines," relying as much as possible on local materials handcrafted by artisans on-site.[10]

[8] Quoted in Raymond Pitcairn, "Bryn Athyn Church: The Manner of Its Building and a Defense Thereof Written in Reply to Ralph Adams Cram," typescript, ca. 1918, p. 9, GM. See also assorted documents, Willard Pendleton file, GM. Janet Doering, *The New Church: A Summary of Beliefs* (Bryn Athyn, Pa.: General Church Evangelization Committee, 1986), p. 7. On the committee, see documents in symbolism file, GM.

[9] Quoted in Glenn, *Bryn Athyn Cathedral*, p. 32. On "use," see Doering, *New Church*, p. 3.

[10] Pitcairn, "Bryn Athyn Church," p. 37. Pitcairn to Messrs. Cram, Goodhue, and Ferguson, September 11, 1913, John Pitcairn Archives, Cairnwood Library, Bryn Athyn, Pa. Pitcairn, "Bryn Athyn Church," pp. 39, 17.

Cram later defended his position in terms of professional responsibility and the supremacy of the architect. He praised the commitment to craftsmanship manifested at Bryn Athyn, but he argued that the enterprise degenerated into a "plebescite." In contrast to Cram's belief that in architecture "there must be a final and an unquestionable authority, and that authority must be the architect himself," Pitcairn and his artisans wanted to participate in design decisions, usurping Cram's control.[11] Ironically, the unique conditions of the Bryn Athyn project—community participation, religious dedication, a concern for quality, and the financial means to accomplish it—allowed Pitcairn to implement arts and crafts ideals more fully than the avowed arts and crafts proponent Cram, whose perspective as a professional architect impinged on the fulfillment of these ideals.

Continued misunderstandings between architect and patron led Pitcairn to request the firm's withdrawal from the project in 1917. Pitcairn, who had given up his law practice in 1914, replaced Cram as sole supervisor of the project although he continued to employ draftsmen who were still associated with Cram but who worked at the site. To compensate for his lack of architectural training, Pitcairn used full-scale models, a practice that had been advocated by the contemporary medievalist Porter. The resulting cathedral, dedicated on October 5, 1919, differed from Cram's scheme in height and in many specific design elements.[12] The church developed organically, with the additions of a council hall and a choir hall in the 1920s reflecting Pitcairn's growing interest in the Romanesque (fig. 2).

Despite Cram's early withdrawal from the endeavor, Pitcairn continued with the experimental guild and craft process initiated by the architect. Workshops and studios for all aspects of the building were erected around the cathedral, including model, carpentry, architectural, glass, and metal shops. A workforce of more than 110 men, comprised of Bryn Athyn community members and outsiders, was gathered for on-site labor. The financial expenditure was immense although the total cost of the cathedral is unknown.[13] The result of this commu-

[11] Ralph Adams Cram, "A Note on the Bryn Athyn Church," *American Architect* 113, no. 2214 (May 29, 1918): 712.
[12] Jane Hayward and Walter Cahn, *Radiance and Reflection: Medieval Art from the Raymond Pitcairn Collection* (New York: Metropolitan Museum of Art, 1982), p. 33. Glenn, *Bryn Athyn Cathedral*, pp. 49–53.
[13] Glenn interview.

Fig. 2. Bryn Athyn Cathedral, west view, Cram and Ferguson, architects, with modifications by Raymond Pitcairn, Bryn Athyn, Pa., dedicated 1919. (Photo, Glencairn Museum, Academy of the New Church, Bryn Athyn, Pa.)

nal labor is a tribute to craftsmanship revealed in all aspects of the building, from the teak doors to the Monel Metal grilles (fig. 3).

While each workshop on the Bryn Athyn site employed different artisans and produced various types of decorative or architectural embellishments, the stained glass project may be considered representative of the whole endeavor. An examination of the stained glass guild during its most dynamic years—from 1913 to 1928—reveals the way in which Bryn Athyn artisans achieved the goals of arts and crafts promoters such as Cram even as they pursued their own aesthetic, community, and religious agendas unconnected to that reform movement.[14]

In creating the stained glass guild, Cram had recommended artists associated with the movement, but Pitcairn based his hiring decisions

[14]Glenn interview. For a comprehensive discussion of the stained glass aspect of the endeavor, see Kaplan, "Bryn Athyn Cathedral Project," chap. 4 and apps. a, b.

Fig. 3. Parke Edwards, west door grille, Bryn Athyn Cathedral, ca. 1919. Monel Metal; H. 83″, W. 5′ 5½″. (Photo, Shelley K. Nickles.)

on his own aesthetic and communal ideas. For example, prominent stained glass artists Charles Connick and Herman Butler rejected Pitcairn's offers; they refused to leave their established positions in Boston and Rochester, respectively, to meet Pitcairn's residency requirement. Three other artists who did complete design work for Bryn Athyn in the early years of the project met with varied success. Artist Clement Heaton, a founding member of A. H. Mackmurdo's Century Guild in England, had been recommended by Cram. Pitcairn, however, vetoed the Cram-approved designs of Heaton—such as his *Woman Clothed with the Sun* watercolor design for the west window—because they reflected the freely interpreted medieval style typical of the arts and crafts movement (fig. 4). Pitcairn also found English New Church artist Conrad Howard's designs unsuitable. Howard had served as a background artist at the William Morris studios; his designs reflected Morris's creative use of the medieval. Although Howard worked for the Bryn Athyn stained glass project intermittently from 1913 to 1916, only one window placed in the cathedral can be definitively attributed to him. Lawrence Saint, who had worked with commercial stained glass designer Connick, maintained his employment at Bryn Athyn until 1928 because he was able to alter his style to fit Pitcairn's aesthetic. Although Saint was not a New Church member, his pious attitude helped him fit into the Bryn Athyn community.[15]

Ultimately, the artist who had the greatest impact on the stained glass project was Bryn Athyn community member Winfred Hyatt. His success must be attributed to the communal and religious bond he shared with Pitcairn, which gave him a willingness to conform to the patron's requirements and a desire to remain with the project through its completion. Hyatt began working on the project directly after finishing art school. His communal perspective inspired him to put aside his first love, painting, and devote his energies to the stained glass guild. In designing his *John Representing the New Testament* window, Hyatt adapted the medieval style in the two-dimensional approach and use of lead lines (fig. 5). Since Hyatt agreed to imitate the "old work" to Pitcairn's satisfaction, he designed the majority of the nearly 100 stained glass windows now in the cathedral. To realize a strict interpretation of the medieval style, Pitcairn sent Hyatt and other artists to Europe to copy designs and record old colors. Pitcairn also purchased a significant collection of medieval glass in 1921 so his artists could

[15] Connick and Butler are discussed in Raymond Pitcairn to Charles Connick, March 19, 1914, Charles Connick file, GM; Raymond Pitcairn to John Windrim, November 11, 1917, stained glass file, GM. On Heaton and Howard, see Clement Heaton and Conrad Howard/New Church Art files, GM. Stephen Morley, interview with author, Bryn Athyn, Pa., February 13, 1990. On Saint, see Raymond Pitcairn to Theodore Pitcairn, March 25, 1919, Lawrence Saint file, GM; Lawrence Saint, "The Romance of Stained Glass: A Story of His Experiences and Experiments" (1959) in Lawrence Saint file, GM. Robin Hathaway Keisman, "Working with Lawrence Saint: An Interview with John Hathaway," *Stained Glass* 78, no. 3 (Fall 1983): 239–40.

Fig. 4. Clement Heaton, design for west
window, Bryn Athyn Cathedral, 1913–14.
Watercolor; H. 22½″, W. 16″. (Glencairn
Museum, Academy of the New Church,
Bryn Athyn, Pa.)

Fig. 5. Winfred Hyatt, *John Representing the New Testament*, Bryn Athyn Cathedral, ca. 1932. Stained glass; H. 10′ 9½″, W. 3′ 5″. (Photo, Shelley K. Nickles.)

closely examine these study tools.[16] Unlike commercial firms, there were few deadlines at Bryn Athyn.

A commitment to community and a medievalist aesthetic also influenced Pitcairn's decisions regarding the glassmaking for the windows. Cram had suggested that Bryn Athyn experiment with medieval glass formulas to alter the quality of commercially available glass. Pitcairn implemented Cram's ideas by hiring an experienced glassmaker from Long Island, John Larsen, for this task. Cram had accepted Larsen's glass, but, like the Cram-approved window designs, it did not meet Pitcairn's requirements. Pitcairn urged Larsen to experiment further to recreate medieval "pot metal" glass—in which metallic-oxide pigment was mixed in the batch so that the color ran throughout the thickness of the glass. To further his goals, Pitcairn had examples of medieval glass analyzed by the family-owned Pittsburgh Plate Glass Company research labs. Through such scientific experimentation and perusal of manuscripts on medieval glassmaking, formulas for replicating pot-metal glass were developed. Pitcairn achieved success in his expressed desire to "come as close to the old technique, also color and texture of the 'real thing' as is possible." The glass produced in Larsen's factory for Bryn Athyn was described as a "fine imitation" of the medieval by an antiques dealer and was mistaken for medieval glass at a Sotheby's auction.[17]

When Pitcairn decided to incorporate this experimentation into the on-site guild system by creating a glassmaking factory at Bryn Athyn in 1922, he asked Larsen to train community member Ariel Gunther in the craft. Gunther, a recent graduate of the Bryn Athyn Academy,

[16]On Hyatt, see Martha Gyllenhaal et al., *New Light: Ten Artists Inspired by Emanuel Swedenborg* (Bryn Athyn, Pa.: Glencairn Museum, 1988), pp. 22–23; Raymond Pitcairn to Theodore Pitcairn, March 25, 1919; Ariel Gunther, interview with author, Bryn Athyn, Pa., February 13, 1990. For Pitcairn's collection, see Hayward and Cahn, *Radiance and Reflection.*

[17]On the medieval glass issue, see Raymond Pitcairn to George MacBeth, March 11, 1914, and George MacBeth to Raymond Pitcairn, March 13, 1914, George MacBeth file, GM. Cynthia Hyatt Walker, "Winfred Sumner Hyatt: In Retrospection," typescript, Winfred Hyatt file, p. 9, GM. Pittsburgh Plate Glass labs to Raymond Pitcairn, January 31, 1927, stained glass/Raymond Pitcairn correspondence file, GM. Raymond Pitcairn to John Larsen, November 2, 1920, John Larsen file, GM. Raymond Pitcairn to Henry Lawrence, August 23, 1915, Henry Lawrence file, GM. Lucien Demotte to Winfred Hyatt, May 7, 1921, and Raymond Pitcairn to Winfred Hyatt, February 21, 1921, Winfred Hyatt file, GM.

Fig. 6. Winfred Hyatt in Bryn Athyn studio, ca. 1930. (Photo, Glencairn Museum, Academy of the New Church, Bryn Athyn, Pa.)

devoted himself to the work until the factory closed in the 1950s.[18] From conception to fabrication—through the work of patron Pitcairn, designer Hyatt, and glassmaker Gunther—the project was a community enterprise. Bryn Athyn also became a rare example in the modern era of glass manufacture and stained glass window design and fabrication on the actual building site.

Although Bryn Athyn guild workers did not intend to serve as a model, the project was also exceptional in the extent to which it achieved the arts and crafts ideal of the medieval artist-craftsman who combined creative and manual labor. Despite increased specialization over time and varying degrees of expertise among artisans, Hyatt illustrates the flexibility in roles characteristic of the Bryn Athyn enterprise (fig. 6). Although primarily an artist, he contributed in numerous ways to the stained glass and the cathedral project as a whole. He offered

[18]Gunther's story is recounted in Ariel C. Gunther, *Opportunity, Challenge, and Privilege* (New York: Vantage, 1973).

suggestions regarding the cathedral design and the style of the interior furnishings. According to his record books, Hyatt selected glass and completed sketches, cartoons, painting, and cementing. While a symbolism committee suggested subject matter suitable for depiction in the cathedral windows, artists were free to initiate design ideas.[19]

The establishment of the glassmaking factory on-site allowed artists to learn technical details inaccessible in stained glass firms using commercially manufactured glass. Ironically, Heaton complained during his brief tenure at Bryn Athyn about having to play the role of both artist and craftsman, "The one set of ideas conflicts with the other so much that the two cannot exist together at once—I cannot design as an artist when I am thinking about tools and . . . chemicals!" In contrast, Howard appreciated his chance to help set up a kiln at Bryn Athyn, a technical task he had never been exposed to at the Morris studios. Indeed, designers and craftsmen had more flexibility at Bryn Athyn than at many arts and crafts enterprises.[20]

This examination of Bryn Athyn craft furthers our understanding of the scope and influence of the American arts and crafts movement by illustrating how these ideals were disseminated to individuals and groups who did not consciously participate in the movement but were also mediated by alternative value systems and goals. Clearly, the arts and crafts movement directly influenced the project through Cram and certain artisans associated with the agenda for social and design reform. The cathedral and its furnishings, the guild, and to a certain extent even the community itself, met craft reformers' goals. It is no surprise, then, that contemporary arts and crafts enthusiasts praised the Bryn Athyn cathedral project as a model of the movement's goals. As

[19] Glenn, *Bryn Athyn Cathedral*, pp. 51–52; Winfred Hyatt to Raymond Pitcairn, October 17, 1914, Winfred Hyatt file, GM; Copy of record book, 1917–18, Winfred Hyatt file, GM; Lawrence Saint to Raymond Pitcairn, July 30, 1917, Lawrence Saint file, GM.

[20] Clement Heaton to Raymond Pitcairn, July 27, 1914, Clement Heaton file, GM. Conrad Howard to Raymond Pitcairn, July 15, 1915, Conrad Howard/New Church Art file, GM. For the Tiffany firm, see Eileen Boris, *Art and Labor: Ruskin, Morris, and the Craftsman Ideal in America* (Philadelphia: Temple University Press, 1986). On William Morris, see A. Charles Sewter, *The Stained Glass of William Morris and His Circle*, 2 vols. (New Haven and London: Yale University Press, 1974), 1:18–20, 89. On Charles Connick, see Kaplan, "*Art That Is Life*," p. 144; Charles Connick, *Adventures in Light and Color* (New York: Random House, 1937), pp. 172–73.

one critic observed in 1921, "From far and wide the art pilgrims come to admire the stonecutting, the woodcarving, the wrought-metal work and, last but not least, the stained glass windows, all of which were fashioned in the spirit of patience and devotion that marked the handiwork of the artisan of the Middle Ages."[21]

Despite being upheld as a model of arts and crafts movement ideals, however, the decisions made by Pitcairn in the stained glass workshop offer a dynamic illustration of how Pitcairn and his community brethren transformed these ideals and gave them their own meaning, based on religious and communal perspectives. The heated disagreements between Cram and Pitcairn over the project's meaning and legacy further reveal the limitations of the arts and crafts movement influence. To Cram, Bryn Athyn itself seemed to be a realization of the fantastical medieval religious communities invented in his 1919 tract *Walled Towns*. The insularity and patriarchal organization of Cram's imagined society resembled the structure that already existed as Bryn Athyn. In Cram's utopian society, the guild system would be revived, and individual communal "congregations" would be organized around a unifying religion or philosophy.[22]

Despite superficial similarities with Cram's fictitious walled towns, however, Bryn Athyn did not model itself as a medieval community. Through craft, arts and crafts reformers like Cram attempted to create bonds that were preexisting at Bryn Athyn. As architectural historian Richard Guy Wilson has noted, a "medievally inspired communalism . . . helped provide a substructure" for Cram and the many other designers "who were motivated by religious convictions." Whereas Cram sought to revitalize religion through craft, Pitcairn desired to honor his community's existing faith with noble building methods. As Pitcairn's nephew Bruce Glenn asserted, the purpose was "to build soundly and well for the worship of God." In a final analysis of the project, Pitcairn reaffirmed religious intent over individual posterity in the history of craft revival: "If the church when finished may be a house worthy of the worship of Jesus Christ . . . the personality and

[21] In addition to Ashbee's praise, see Hazel H. Adler, *The New Interior: Modern Decoration for the Modern Home* (New York: Century Co., 1916), pp. 7, 279–86. *Philadelphia Public Ledger*, January 30, 1921.
[22] Ralph Adams Cram, *Walled Towns* (Boston: Marshall Jones Co., 1919), p. 44.

worldly thoughts of those who have aided in its building are better forgotten."[23] Bryn Athyn was foremost a religious community that, because of the unique vision of Pitcairn, was involved in craft.

In fact, Pitcairn believed that Cram, who widely publicized his guild experiment in the press prior to being discharged from the cathedral project, disseminated a false impression among outsiders of Bryn Athyn as a utopian craft community. Pitcairn argued that Cram had romanticized and "mythologized" Bryn Athyn's guild system; he insisted that Bryn Athyn was not attempting to recreate a medieval social experiment. Unlike arts and crafts devotees, Bryn Athyn members were not concerned with social or design reform dissemination. No evidence exists to indicate that Pitcairn had any interest in the writings of Morris or his American followers other than Cram. Pitcairn refused to allow his artists to accept outside commissions and did not sell Bryn Athyn glass or other products made there.[24] Ironically, the very insularity of the community prevented it from counteracting the image of an arts and crafts experimental community created by Cram in the press and perpetuated in subsequent literature.

The cathedral project did, nevertheless, leave a legacy of intertwined craft and religion. Inside the community, the influence of the arts and crafts movement on Bryn Athyn did not have an impact on its fundamental religious purpose; however, the time commitment and community labor required by the guild—and the craftsmanship that resulted—integrated craft into the community. Beginning in the late 1920s, Pitcairn made use of the architectural arts departments for the construction and decoration of his residence, Glencairn. He employed the same building principles as in the cathedral. The stained glass guild turned to designing and executing mosaics; some Bryn Athyn community members were directed into a lifetime of craft-related labor. After the closing of the Bryn Athyn glass workshop in the 1950s, when

[23] Richard Guy Wilson, "American Arts and Crafts Architecture: Radical Though Dedicated to the Cause Conservative," in Kaplan, "*Art That Is Life*," p. 113. On community motivation, see Glenn, *Bryn Athyn Cathedral*, p. 32. Pitcairn, "Bryn Athyn Church," p. 85.
[24] Pitcairn, "Bryn Athyn Church," p. 70. On Pitcairn's interests, see Glenn interview. On outside commissions, see Raymond Pitcairn to Rowley Murphy, June 22, 1922, Rowley Murphy file, GM; Raymond Pitcairn to Lawrence Saint, August 15, 1922, Lawrence Saint file, GM. Morley interview.

all remaining shops around the cathedral were razed, community
member Gunther began conducting tours of the cathedral and lecturing
on stained glass.

Despite the insular nature of Pitcairn's goals, the cathedral project
created a dialogue between the community and outsiders in two ways.
First, some artists who worked at Bryn Athyn went on to disseminate
the craft methods learned on the cathedral project in future commissions. Most notably, the exposure to many aspects of stained
glass window production gained by Saint at Bryn Athyn secured for
him a position leading the National Cathedral stained glass project,
which was modeled after Bryn Athyn's guild. Second, many non-
Swedenborgian artists and craftsmen came to Bryn Athyn to work on
the project. As one architectural draftsman brought in by Cram con-
fessed, the "work on the church is getting a tighter grip on my enthusiasm everyday, and Boston doesn't seem quite the same after having
lived in Arcadia." Bryn Athyn craft had an unintentional missionary
effect as well; several cathedral workers converted to the New Church.[25]
Certainly many gained an understanding of Swedenborgian belief and
Bryn Athyn community lifestyle, as have the thousands of arts and
crafts followers who have thronged to the Bryn Athyn cathedral over
the past century. Today the cathedral remains an ideal of craftsmanship
and creative labor and the material symbol of a community's faith.

[25] The draftsman was Donald Robb, quoted in Glenn, *Bryn Athyn Cathedral*, p.
49. Virginia Raguin, "Lawrence Saint and the North Rose of Washington Cathedral,"
Stained Glass 78, no. 3 (Fall 1983): 236. On conversions to the church, see Gunther
interview; O. Minard Smith, interview with author, Bryn Athyn, Pa., March 28, 1990.
See also Glenn, *Bryn Athyn Cathedral*, p. 104.

George W. Maher's
Planning and Architecture in
Kenilworth, Illinois
An Inquiry into the Ideology of
Arts and Crafts Design

Mary Corbin Sies

The state of recent scholarship on the American arts and crafts movement reminds me a little of life through the looking glass, where Alice and the Red Queen ran faster and faster only to find themselves back where they began. As scholars have undertaken more and more basic research on specific crafts, artists, workshops, or consumers, they have found that their ability to generalize meaningfully about the arts and crafts movement is little better than when they began. Indeed, the superb 1987 exhibition directed by Wendy Kaplan, "'The Art That Is Life': The Arts and Crafts Movement in America, 1875–1920," demonstrated visually that arts and crafts work does not constitute a single style. A plethora of recent studies has revealed that arts and crafts adherents derived from several distinct subgroups. Different constituen-

The research on which this article is based was made possible by generous support from the Horace H. Rackham School for Graduate Studies and the Alumnae Council of the University of Michigan and from the American Institute of Architects/American Institute of Architects Foundation.

cies of these artists and consumers infused the arts and crafts movement
with widely varying, even conflicting, ideologies.[1]

One of the few propositions to emerge uncontested from recent
scholarship is the observation that an ideology of reform lies at the
heart of the arts and crafts movement. That they can no longer generalize about the substance of that reform ideology has caused scholars
considerable consternation. In the United States, ideals of design reform and of social reform were not as consonant as they were in the
movement in Great Britain. Artifacts exhibiting progressive design principles were frequently associated with conservative social ideologies.
Some scholars, to their chagrin, have discovered a credibility gap between the rhetoric of the craftsman ideal and the actual production
processes of certain artifacts. A substantial part of investigators' confusion and disappointment can be attributed, however, to the assumptions
about arts and crafts ideology that they themselves have imposed on
their inquiries. The widely held notion that the arts and crafts "style"
was the immediate precursor to modernism, for example, has hampered
the free investigation of design ideology. Similarly, the belief that adherents of the craftsman ideal advocated an alternative culture that
would reunite art with labor has dominated most studies of arts and
crafts social ideology.[2]

Ideologies are never simply one-dimensional, nor should we think
of them as fixed values attached to a school or style of objects. We can

[1] The two benchmarks of arts and crafts scholarship are Robert Judson Clark, ed.,
The Arts and Crafts Movement in America, 1876–1916 (Princeton: Princeton University
Press, 1972) and Wendy Kaplan, *"The Art That Is Life": The Arts and Crafts Movement
in America, 1875–1920* (Boston: Museum of Fine Arts, 1987). See also Richard Guy
Wilson, "American Arts and Crafts Architecture: Radical though Dedicated to the Cause
Conservative," in Kaplan, *"Art That Is Life,"* p. 101; Catherine Lynn, "Reforming
America," *American Craft* 44 (June–July 1987): 42; Eileen Boris, *Art and Labor: Rus-
kin, Morris, and the Craftsman Ideal in America* (Philadelphia: Temple University Press,
1986); Robert Edwards, "The Art of Work," and Cheryl Robertson, "House and Home
in the Arts and Crafts Era: Reforms for Simpler Living," in Kaplan, *"Art That Is Life,"*
pp. 223–36, 336–57, respectively; Leslie Greene Bowman, *American Arts and Crafts:
Virtue in Design* (Los Angeles: Los Angeles County Museum of Art, 1990); Kenneth R.
Trapp, ed., *The Arts and Crafts Movement in California: Living the Good Life* (Oakland,
Calif.: Oakland Museum, 1993).
[2] Richard Stamm, "The Bradley and Hubbard Manufacturing Company and the
Merchandising of the Arts and Crafts Movement in America," in this collection; Wendy
Kaplan, commentary (Comments presented at the Winterthur Conference, Winterthur,
Del., October 18, 1990); Boris, *Art and Labor*, p. xi.

best define ideologies as belief systems constructed by particular human beings in response to a complicated set of historical circumstances; they are made of one group's schematic and sometimes multilayered images of social or aesthetic order.[3] Instead of accepting arts and crafts ideology as a given, scholars need to pursue research efforts that investigate it directly by analyzing artifacts to discover the meanings they held for their designers or organizations or consumers. We can best accomplish that task by developing interdisciplinary methods of analysis that focus on the connections between artifacts and contexts—that ask how specific people thought about and used arts and crafts artifacts and how, in turn, those artifacts embodied, reflected, or influenced ideas in a given place and time. If we truly seek to understand the substance of this style—an "art that is life"—then we must reconstruct what we can of the life so that we may grasp the full texture of meanings of the art.

The following case study of the built environment of the Chicago North Shore suburb of Kenilworth, Illinois, describes an investigation of the meanings of arts and crafts design. The specific focus is the suburban architecture and planning of Chicago architect George W. Maher in Kenilworth between 1891 and 1923. Because houses and, especially, entire planned communities are never the product of one artist's labor, this research included a study of the lives and circumstances of those who contributed to the making of Kenilworth's arts and crafts environment as well as an analysis of the buildings and landscape themselves. I argue that Kenilworthians embraced Maher's design work because it expressed so brilliantly their life circumstances and ideology; it, in the words of one critic, "ke[pt] pace with the thoughts and lives of the society to whom it ministere[d]."[4]

Many scholars have observed that arts and crafts architecture and home furnishings flourished across the nation in upper-middle-class suburbs like Kenilworth. Previous inquiries have taught us that the arts and crafts practiced or patronized in suburbia frequently exhibited that puzzling combination of progressive design principles paired with a

---

[3] On ideology, see Clifford Geertz, *The Interpretation of Cultures* (New York: Basic Books, 1973), pp. 193–233; Murray G. Murphey, "The Place of Beliefs in Modern Culture," in *New Directions in American Intellectual History*, ed. John Higham and Paul Conkin (Baltimore: Johns Hopkins University Press, 1979), pp. 151–65.

[4] Editorial, *Western Architect* 27 (March 1918): 25.

conservative social ideology. According to the standard summary, the arts and crafts design patronized in upper-middle-class suburbs was didactic, having as its aims the improvement of taste through simplicity in design and the promotion of "homely virtues" in the family. After simplicity, the most frequently articulated design principles were the wedding of the useful to the beautiful and originality—the conceptualization of artifacts as unique expressions of their designer, clients, and era. Other important design tenets included an emphasis on human-centered qualities like comfort and warmth, the use of indigenous materials for construction and inspiration, the honest expression of structure and function in both architecture and furnishings, and unity in design. While upper-middle-class consumers desired to rebeautify daily lives marred by industrialism, they were not particularly concerned with rebeautifying labor. The arts and crafts movement in the suburbs may have been a progressive cause artistically, but it was, as Frank Lloyd Wright termed it, a "cause conservative" socially.[5]

There is nothing ostensibly wrong with this general description; it just leaves many questions unanswered. How closely in their visual aspects and design principles did arts and crafts artifacts in actual suburbs resemble the standard? Who commissioned arts and crafts houses in exclusive suburbs, and what meanings did residents attach to their dwellings or furnishings? What was it about arts and crafts design that appealed to upper-middle-class suburbanites? Was it the artistry, philosophy, utility, reform message, or fashion? Why did a conservative clientele embrace an approach to architecture and interior design that evinced a progressive design philosophy? What was the content of their cause conservative, exactly? Despite much good work, scholars do not yet have much precise knowledge about the meanings people invested in many strains of arts and crafts design. This is particularly the case

[5] Eileen Boris, " 'Dreams of Brotherhood and Beauty': The Social Ideas of the Arts and Crafts Movement," in Kaplan, "*Art That Is Life*," pp. 208–22; Boris, *Art and Labor*, chap. 4; Peter Davey, *Arts and Crafts Architecture: The Search for Earthly Paradise* (London: Architectural Press, 1980); Wilson, "American Arts and Crafts Architecture" and Robertson, "House and Home" in Kaplan, "*Art That Is Life*"; Beverly Brandt, "Interiors" and "Architecture," in *Encyclopedia of Arts and Crafts: The International Arts Movement, 1850–1920*, ed. Patricia Bayer et al. (London: Quarto Publishing, 1989), pp. 19–50; Mary Ann Smith, *Gustav Stickley: The Craftsman* (Syracuse, N.Y.: Syracuse University Press, 1983).

for mainstream creators or consumers, who, like turn-of-the-century suburbanites, were not the radicals or luminaries of the movement or members of arts and crafts communities, strictly defined.

To investigate the meanings of Kenilworth's arts and crafts design, an ethnographic approach to history was employed, one based upon fieldwork that included both firsthand study of artifacts and the recovery of their historic contexts. The aim was reconstruction of the circumstances of community members caught in the historical acts, so to speak, of designing, commissioning, and using Kenilworth's built environment. Ethnographic approaches like this are sometimes called performance theories because the investigator focuses the research on the recovery and analysis of particular behavioral acts or performances. For the study of Kenilworth, three types of performances were recovered: those of the artifacts, those of the historical actors who came in contact with the buildings and landscape, and the relationship(s) between those acts. The research had three facets: information-gathering about the persons involved in Kenilworth's design or development; recovery of the history of the community itself; and fieldwork to document each building, determine its original appearance and uses, and inspect each extant structure firsthand. The research enabled me to reconstruct, analyze, and interpret those performances associated with the suburb's built environment, thus providing a window on the principles and ideology of Kenilworth's arts and crafts design.[6]

The meanings embodied in a given built environment tend to be specific to their context. Historians seeking a thorough understanding of buildings or neighborhood planning need to explore the full range of factors influencing their design—some artistic and formal; others social, technological, or cultural; and a few local and idiosyncratic. This consideration begins with an examination of the historical setting for some of Maher's most intriguing arts and crafts design work, in Kenilworth. In 1891 Chicago businessman Joseph Sears, with the assistance of a company formed to help finance and manage development, founded his new suburb on approximately one square mile of lakeshore property seventeen miles north of the Chicago Loop. Kenilworth was

[6] Mary Corbin Sies, "Toward a Performance Theory of the Suburban Ideal, 1877–1917," in *Perspectives in Vernacular Architecture*, IV, ed. Thomas Carter and Bernard Herman (Columbia: University of Missouri Press, 1991), pp. 197–207.

not an arts and crafts community dedicated to the production of hand-crafted items or to the working out of alternatives to the labor practices of industrial capitalism. It was a planned, exclusive residential suburb designed and developed by and for members of the new stratum of urban upper-middle-class society that came into being after the Civil War. From its inception the suburb was planned by Sears and viewed by many of the original residents as a model—a controlled experiment in the design of a cultured, neighborly, healthful, and family-centered suburban mode of living.[7]

The historical actors who contributed to the shaping of Kenil-worth's original environment and character formed a remarkably homo-geneous community. They included Sears, his friends and professional associates who made up the Kenilworth Company, the suburb's archi-tects and builders, and its first generation of residents. As members of the new, urban, upper middle class, the majority of Kenilworthians were employed or married to persons who were employed in one of three occupational categories. Nearly half were salaried employees in the new business bureaucracies (47 percent in 1900 and 46 percent in 1910); 14 percent (13 percent in 1910) were professionals in law, engineering, medicine, or architecture; and another 14 percent (11 percent in 1910) were culture producers, persons holding occupations like teacher, artist, museum administrator, or advertiser. Most men and women heading households in Kenilworth were native-born Protestant Americans (76 percent in 1900 and 80 percent in 1910), and the mem-bers of every household but one came from families of northern Euro-pean ancestry. Kenilworthians performed similar roles in society. They were the managers of business, consumption, education, and philan-thropy and the dispensers of professional or, in the case of most women, volunteer services aimed at improving the quality of life. As such, they were entrenched in the urban industrial establishment that more radical arts and crafts advocates repudiated.[8]

[7] *Kenilworth: First Fifty Years* (Kenilworth, Ill.: By the village, 1947); Colleen Browne Kilner, *Joseph Sears and His Kenilworth* (Kenilworth, Ill.: Kenilworth Historical Society, 1969); Mary Corbin Sies, "American Country House Architecture in Context" (Ph.D. diss., University of Michigan, 1987), chap. 7; Michael H. Ebner, *Creating Chicago's North Shore* (Chicago: University of Chicago Press, 1988); Barbara Ehrenreich and John Ehrenreich, "The Professional-Managerial Class," *Radical America* 11, no. 1 (1977): 7–31.
[8] Alfred D. Chandler, Jr., *The Visible Hand: The Managerial Revolution in Ameri-can Business* (Cambridge: Harvard University Press, Belknap Press, 1977), pp. 3, 8;

In addition to similarities in occupation and background, these new suburbanites were subject in common to the pressures and stimuli of lives lived in a city pulsing with change. Chicago at the turn of the century presented an unsettling spectacle of opportunity and debacle, opulence and filth, of antagonistic forces that seemed ready to rend civilized society at any moment. Despite their relocation to the suburban periphery, Kenilworthians were tied firmly to the city by ambition, occupation, and inclination. Like their counterparts in burgeoning cities nationwide, they met the challenges of metropolitan living in ways befitting their upper-middle-class roles and social standing. Professional training and cultivation of business values fostered among these residents a common creed of social responsibility and service and a "can-do" attitude toward urban problems as well as opportunities. Membership in the same churches, country clubs, civic organizations, and cultural institutions reinforced their tendency to respond to shared experiences in similar ways. In addition, residents were linked by their buying patterns—by their consumption of increasingly standardized reading matter and their purchases of consumer durables that were associated with preordained images of social status and fulfillment.

Kenilworthians' mutual interests and common experiences led them to perceive their world and to make sense of it in relatively similar ways. Members of the founding generation forged a belief system that both reflected and mediated the cultural strain of the circumstances of their daily lives. Belief systems enable human beings to bring order and stability to their experiences in a given society; they provide a means for defining our place in our environment so that we can act purposefully within it. The belief system of Kenilworth's founders performed this role by striking an uneasy but efficacious balance between the traditional values of previous generations and the new values of the

Ehrenreich and Ehrenreich, "The Professional-Managerial Class," pp. 12–14. Manuscript population schedules, Village of Kenilworth, New Trier Township, Cook County, Ill., 12th and 13th U.S. Federal population censuses (1900 and 1910), National Archives, Washington, D.C. The remaining 24 percent of Kenilworthians listing occupations in the 1900 census are as follows: 4 percent were owners of manufacturing enterprises (and should be considered members of the upper class), 10 percent held working-class jobs, 5 percent were widows or retired persons, and 5 percent had occupations unknown. In 1910, 6 percent were manufacturers, 11 percent had working-class jobs, and 13 percent lived on their "own incomes" or had occupations unknown. Persons employed in service for private families were excluded from the calculations.

urban marketplace. These suburbanites believed firmly in the same tenets of hard work, Christian ethics, and domestic virtues that had served their parents and grandparents. To the founding generation, the home, the family, and community life were the key repositories for these traditional values. Sears's primary motive in establishing Kenilworth, according to his daughter, Dorothy, was the creation of an entire community where his and other men's children could obtain better opportunities for their moral, physical, and intellectual development. At the same time, however, residents cultivated more worldly qualities like rationality, cleverness, and opportunism, which promised advancement in the urban world of business. In their occupational lives, goodness was measured by efficiency and success by appearance; a man's standing was more likely to be decided on the basis of wealth and career achievement than character.[9]

Most Kenilworthians proclaimed their allegiance to both traditional and bureaucratic values without indicating that they perceived any inherent contradictions between them. Their belief system influenced profoundly the form of the environment they created to give formal expression to their standing in the metropolis and to bring order to their daily lives. Like their counterparts in other planned, exclusive suburbs of the same era, members of this community believed that the environment played a powerful and, perhaps, decisive role in shaping moral character and influencing human behavior. From their earliest discussions, Sears and the friends and business associates who joined in the suburb's creation planned Kenilworth as an ideal residential environment that would balance and accommodate many competing demands: family, community, status, individuality, nature and urbanity, Christian virtue and business acumen.

The founding generation had, however, another powerful reason for carefully engineering their suburban experiment; this was their commitment to positive environmental reform. They believed that a properly designed community of homes tailored precisely to their needs could provide citizens of any class or ethnic background with the means to achieve a wholesome and productive modern life. During the 1890s

[9]On belief systems, see Geertz, *Interpretation of Cultures*, p. 220; and Murphey, "Place of Beliefs," p. 154. See also Kilner, *Joseph Sears and His Kenilworth*, p. 119; Sies, "American Country House Architecture," chap. 7; *Kenilworth: First Fifty Years*.

and through 1910 or so, Kenilworth attracted many residents with wide-ranging interests in intellectual, artistic, and scientific matters. These were idealistic persons who became involved in a variety of charity, social housekeeping, and environmental reform causes. The new sub-urbanites had experienced the degraded housing conditions of urban neighborhoods firsthand; they understood the dangers that sanitation problems, crowding, and the inability to control social and physical surroundings posed for raising families. Sears and his wife, Helen, for example, lost an infant daughter and a nephew to the diptheria epi-demic that raced through Chicago in the summer of 1882. Many mem-bers of the new urban upper middle class embraced environmental reform causes from the rather self-important sense of social steward-ship that they derived from the service ethic at the rhetorical heart of their professional or managerial training. Regardless of the source of their reform ideals, Kenilworthians set out quite self-consciously to design a model residential community that would organize their own lives and inspire positive environmental reform in the lives of others.[10]

In creating their suburban design experiment, Kenilworthians worked out design programs for the model suburb and the model subur-ban home that, together, constituted a formula for the modern Ameri-can residential environment. Historians have named this formula the suburban ideal. Distilled to its essence, the suburban ideal asserted that the most proper form of American shelter was the single-family home with a garden and plenty of open space situated in a locally controlled, homogeneous community. To its turn-of-the-century consumers, how-ever, the suburban ideal was more than a housing formula. It was a set of cultural resources for managing life in a stress-filled, rapidly changing society—a powerful strategy for a newly fashioned American way of living. The suburban ideal amounted to an ideology generated by a homogeneous class of urban Americans, and it received its most

---

[10] Paul Boyer defines "positive environmental reform" as techniques for "remolding the city's physical environment as a means of elevating its moral tone" (Paul Boyer, *Urban Masses and Moral Order in America, 1820–1920* [Cambridge: Harvard University Press, 1978]). Sies, "American Country House Architecture," chap. 7; Kilner, *Joseph Sears and His Kenilworth*, chaps. 28, 33, p. 103; Ehrenreich and Ehrenreich, "The Professional-Managerial Class," pp. 20–21.

articulate expression in the built environments created in upper-middle-class planned, exclusive suburbs like Kenilworth.[11]

Maher (1864–1926) was a successful and respected Chicago architect whose practice consisted of suburban houses, community planning, educational structures, and small commercial buildings for mostly upper-middle-class clients in the Chicago suburbs and elsewhere in the nation. By social background, professional expertise, architectural philosophy, and personal inclination, Maher was ideally suited to give formal expression to Kenilworth's suburban ideal. He was not the official architect for the Kenilworth Company, but his association with the suburb goes back to 1891, when he completed his first two commissions there. In 1893 Maher built a home for himself in Kenilworth and settled down, marrying artist Elizabeth Brooks, who gave birth to a son, Philip, a year later. Thus Maher began an intimate and fruitful relationship with the community. During the next thirty years, he became involved with nearly every phase of the suburb's development, designing thirty-eight houses, the suburb's schools, a church annex, the assembly hall, the golf clubhouse, and Kenilworth's 1923 master plan as well as overseeing the acquisition and landscaping of parkland. Both as a professional man and as a neighbor, Maher possessed a genuine understanding of Kenilworthians' life circumstances, their values, their social ambitions, and their social ideals. That knowledge was the special quality that made his work organic; it made Kenilworth's landscape one of the most articulate and evocative expressions of the suburban ideal anywhere in the nation.[12]

[11] Geertz, *Interpretation of Cultures*, pp. 219–20; Carol Aronovici, "Housing and the Housing Problem," *Annals of the American Academy* 51, no. 1 (January 1914): 1–7. See also Kenneth T. Jackson, *Crabgrass Frontier: The Suburbanization of the United States* (New York: Oxford University Press, 1985); Robert Fishman, *Bourgeois Utopias* (New York: Basic Books, 1987); Margaret Marsh, *Suburban Lives* (New Brunswick, N.J.: Rutgers University Press, 1990); Sies, "American Country House Architecture."

[12] The standard source on Maher is H. Allen Brooks, *The Prairie School: Frank Lloyd Wright and His Midwestern Contemporaries* (New York: W. W. Norton, 1972). See also J. William Rudd, "George W. Maher: Architect of the Prairie School," *Prairie School Review* 1, no. 1 (1964): 5–11; J. William Rudd, "George W. Maher—Architect" (Master's thesis, Northwestern University, 1964); Gary Hollander, "Rockledge: A Summer House Designed by George W. Maher," *Tiller* 1 (July–August 1983): 10–16; Edward S. Cooke, Jr., "George Washington Maher," in Kaplan, *"Art That Is Life,"* pp. 396–97.

Maher was born in Mill Creek, West Virginia. He received all of his architectural training on the job, first with the Chicago firm of Bauer and Hill and then, around 1880, as a draftsman in the office of J.L. Silsbee, where he absorbed and developed the ideas that would anchor his architectural philosophy. During his career, which spanned the years 1888, when he opened his own office, to 1923, Maher was associated with the new progressive school of Chicago architects. He was never a member of "The Eighteen," the inner circle surrounding Frank Lloyd Wright, but he shared their admiration for the work of Louis H. Sullivan and their quest to create an organic architecture that derived from purely local conditions. By 1895 Maher had achieved a distinctive personal style in his work, and for the next two decades he enjoyed a busy, successful, and financially remunerative practice. His designs were widely exhibited and published in both American and European professional journals, and he was elected a fellow of the American Institute of Architects in 1916.[13]

Maher was a leading figure among Chicago architects calling for an organic architecture. Although not listed among the founding members of the Chicago Arts and Crafts Society, he applied in his own work many of the design principles that we associate with an arts and crafts approach. He also shared the movement's advocacy of reform, arguing in a series of speeches and published papers that an honest and sincere architecture could inspire and elevate the American citizenry. In designing the model suburb, he noted that "the underlying principle is in the assisting of one another and all, towards a higher conception of life." Maher broke rank with the most radical arts and crafts advocates, however, in defining reform as an activity to be directed by professionals. He affirmed the new urban professional's responsibility to become involved in social stewardship: "He [the architect] should consider himself fortunate in living in a growing community, where as a citizen [he can] exert his influence and skill in the . . . fashioning of future improvements . . .—this is a privilege we professional men should grasp, aiming to work unselfishly for the common good." In articulating the professional's duty to assume a leadership role in municipal betterment activities, Maher's views were in accord with those of his

[13] Rudd, "George W. Maher," pp. 5, 7, 10. On "The Eighteen," see Brooks, *Prairie School*, pp. 28–31.

neighbors. On no account would they sanction a reform effort that compromised their prerogatives as professionals.[14]

Maher believed that only an organic architecture could improve the human condition. In Kenilworth he strove "fearlessly" to "interpret in his work the needs and ideals of his fellows and his generation." To design an organic architecture, he argued, the architect needed to "dig deep into the currents of life around us, feel the pulse of the times and then actually execute the ideals of the present hour." How did the architect discover the pulse of his times? Maher presumed that every community had a viewpoint, or motif, as he called it, a set of closely held convictions that he likened to a "folk language—ordinary but constant." The architect's duty was to identify and to express that motif; by doing so simply, directly, and harmoniously, the designer could create an art that would ennoble and perhaps enlarge "our own native motives." In his "motif and rhythm" theory, Maher endeavored, in typical progressive fashion, to develop a systematic and efficient formula to guide the architect in this task. Here, then, was an architect and an architectural philosophy perfectly matched to the task of giving physical form to a design program tailored precisely to its clients' lives and needs. The key to understanding the appeal of Maher's arts and crafts design work in Kenilworth lies in the success and consistency with which he accomplished just that.[15]

We can reconstruct Maher's efforts to bring Kenilworth's suburban ideal to expression by analyzing the suburb's design programs for the ideal suburban community and the model suburban home, with special emphasis on Maher's contributions to them. The recovery of these design programs is based on a thorough study of Kenilworth's planning and of all 135 of the houses built between the suburb's founding and 1917. The research included the documentation of each artifact's original appearance and a formal analysis of its design. Consultation with a variety of written and other primary sources brought to light additional information about the behaviors associated with each building or land-

[14]George W. Maher, "An Architect's Responsibility to His Community," *Western Architect* 35 (1922): 8–9.

[15]George W. Maher, "Progress," *Inland Architect and News Record* 35, no. 5 (June 1900): 35. George W. Maher, "The Western Spirit," *Inland Architect and News Record* 47, no. 3 (April 1906): 38. George W. Maher, "The Viewpoint," *Inland Architect and News Record* 37, no. 4 (May 1901): 26.

scape feature: how it was used, what role it played in the life of the community, and how it was thought of or described or depicted by particular residents. From this body of evidence a set of principles emerged that I believe shaped the design programs that came by gradual consensus to govern the planning and architecture in the suburb between 1891 and 1917. The two programs reveal directly just what was getting said through the founding generation's creation and use of Kenilworth's built environment.

Kenilworthians' needs, ambitions, and values are manifested clearly in the six principles of the design program governing the form for their ideal residential community. The first principle was the desire for order; it was achieved through comprehensive planning of the suburb's design and development. By the time Kenilworth's first residents had settled in their homes, the suburb possessed a finished look and an astounding quality of infrastructure. Members of the Kenilworth Company had underwritten the suburb's professional design, the installation of technically up-to-date services, and had developed procedures to manage marketing, sales, and growth. All of the initial planning was completed by Franklin P. Burnham, a director of the company, one of the first residents, and the company's official architect. After Burnham moved to Pasadena in 1899, Maher promoted additional landscape embellishments and took an active role in all of the suburb's planning decisions.[16]

From 1920 to 1923, when Kenilworth decided to annex the acreage on its western border, Maher drew up an ambitious comprehensive plan for its development. Besides platting most of the new territory for residences in the manner of the original, his scheme called for elaborate improvements along the railroad right-of-way that would have made Kenilworth the showpiece of the North Shore. The comprehensiveness of both Maher's plan, which was only partially realized after his retirement, and Burnham's initial design reveal the community's passion for order and disinclination to leave the development of any environmental

---

[16] Sies, "American Country House Architecture," pp. 381–404; Kilner, *Joseph Sears and His Kenilworth*, pp. 144–45, 147–48; *Kenilworth: First Fifty Years*, pp. 4–5; "Improvements at Kenilworth," *Economist* 3 (April 12, 1890): 450; "Real Estate," *Economist* 4 (October 4, 1890): 535; "Avoca Addition to Kenilworth," *Economist* 6 (October 3, 1891): 579.

feature to chance. Neighbors from other North Shore suburbs sometimes attributed the artistry of Kenilworth's environment to its residents'
preoccupation with appearance, which the outsiders believed derived
mostly from a heightened concern with status. Kenilworthians certainly
promoted their community's social position, but this alone cannot account for the comprehensiveness of their environmental engineering.
The founding generation envisioned a moral community that would
restore the human comfort, stability, shared values, and social cohesiveness that had eluded them in the city, and they considered the
systematic application of rational principles to the planning of their
suburb the surest means of realizing their vision.[17]

The felicitous character of Kenilworth's environment could not
have been achieved without the extensive application of technology—
the second factor in the design program—to the improvement of the
site. Members of the Kenilworth Company were especially concerned
with delivering clean water and the best waste disposal technology available so that they could provide the clean and safe environment that
residents desired. The installation of these and the impressive array of
other urban conveniences was supervised by Burnham. Maher's chief
contribution to the suburb's technological improvements derived from
his arts and crafts design philosophy. He insisted that practical measures
be made aesthetically pleasing. A good example is the work that he
completed to help contain the Skokie, a ditch prone to flooding that
farmers had dug across the village site to drain marshy areas into Lake
Michigan. Maher finished his engineering of the Skokie by designing
picturesque stone bridges over the waterway where it coursed under the
roadbeds, transforming a mundane utility into an attractive landscape
feature.[18]

Like their counterparts in other planned, exclusive suburbs, Kenilworthians believed in the benefits of living in close daily contact with
their natural surroundings. Thus nature, the third tenet of the design
program, contributed to the shaping of Kenilworth in symbiotic part-

---

[17] George W. Maher, Greater Village Plan of 1922, "Annexation of Golf Property
Controversy" file, Kenilworth Historical Society, Kenilworth, Ill. (hereafter cited as
KHS); Ebner, *Creating Chicago's North Shore*, pp. 64–68, 227–30.

[18] Kilner, *Joseph Sears and His Kenilworth*, pp. 144, 215; *Kenilworth: First Fifty
Years*, pp. 4, 17; *Architecture in Kenilworth*, brochure [ca. 1975], KHS.

nership with technology. Throughout his residency, Maher was the leading spokesman for the natural embellishment of the suburb; he argued that every built feature should be integrated or harmonized with the natural environment. His campaign succeeded in 1899 when he talked Sears into granting the North Shore Railroad franchise along the Kenilworth right-of-way and using the proceeds to purchase and develop parkland. Maher commenced his landscape planning with the beautification of the railroad entrance to the suburb, a job he considered simply another instance of rendering a practical function in an artistic manner. On the land acquired with the franchise fee he screened the tracks with plantings, placed a fountain in the central square, and, in the parkland flanking the fountain, designed elaborate curbs with built-in stone seats and monumental urns that were filled with greenery. During the 1890s Maher and others promoted tree planting to convert the major streets into parkways. As the driving spirit of the Kenilworth Park Board, Maher was the central promoter of park and playground acquisition and improvement in the community.[19]

It is difficult to say whether Kenilworthians placed greater emphasis on the values of family or community—the fourth and fifth elements of their suburban design program. "The early citizens developed their organizations and institutions to foster the spirit of home surroundings that made the village especially attractive to those whose first interest was their children."[20] Members of the founding generation agreed that a model suburb must provide a safe environment for children and first-rate facilities for their educations. But Kenilworth also provided children and adults with an abundant community life and a quality of associations suitable to most residents' social aspirations. Maher helped to shape these efforts by designing nearly every building in Kenilworth that contributed to the enrichment of family or community life. For many of these commissions, as was the case with his landscape planning, he donated his professional services.

Together with the parks and playgrounds, the most important fam-

[19]Violet Wyld (George Maher's niece), interview with author, Kenilworth, Ill., May 21, 1983. Maher, "An Architect's Responsibility to his Community"; *Kenilworth: First Fifty Years*, pp. 29–32; Kilner, *Joseph Sears and His Kenilworth*, p. 208.
[20]*Kenilworth: First Fifty Years*, p. 1.

Fig. 1. George W. Maher, Joseph Sears Public School, Kenilworth, Ill., 1912. From *Western Architect* 20 (March 1914): 175. (University of Michigan Art and Architecture Library.)

ily institutions in Kenilworth were its excellent schools. Maher designed the buildings for most of these, including the Rugby School for Boys and the first public school, but one of his finest educational commissions was the Joseph Sears Public School, completed in 1912 (fig. 1). The school clearly displayed Maher's loyalty to arts and crafts principles; indeed, the building exemplified William Morris's advice: "Have nothing in your [building] that you do not know to be useful or believe to be beautiful." The plan was immensely practical, featuring passive solar elements and great flexibility. Within the classrooms, Maher combined technology and artistry to furnish an atmosphere of safety, comfort, and beauty for the community's schoolchildren. Each room was lighted "by means of the saw-tooth skylight construction on the roof arranged for north light," which prevented shadows and sunspots. The heating and ventilating system used humidified forced air and was state-of-the-art, eliminating classroom radiators, which Maher felt were unsightly and potentially dangerous. In finishing the interior, Maher used soft colors and custom-made weathered-oak furniture in graded sizes. All features of the kindergarten, including the placement of windows, were scaled to suit the school's littlest users. On the exterior, the Sears school exhibited the clean, modern, horizontal lines associated with prairie school architecture, an effect accentuated by the narrow parapet

Fig. 2. George W. Maher, Village Hall, Kenilworth, Ill., 1907. From *Inland Architect and News Record* 50, no. 3 (October 1907). (University of Michigan Art and Architecture Library.)

running the length of the building to encase the design of the sky-lights.[21]

Kenilworth's early social life consisted of a varied and highly organized round of clubs, parties, sporting activities, and special evenings, the last often held to showcase the community's abundant musical talent. Many of these gatherings were sponsored by a few key community institutions, and Maher contributed buildings for three of these. He designed the Kenilworth Village Hall, built in 1907; the gymnasium and guildroom addition to the nondenominational Kenilworth Union Church, built in 1909; and the golf clubhouse on the suburb's west side, built in 1917. Of these, the most important, both in terms of its place in community life and its architectural merit, was the village hall (fig. 2). Although it housed Kenilworth's two premier social clubs—the Kenilworth Club and the Neighbors, the women's club—the village hall served as a community center built by and for all of the suburb's

[21]"A Democrat in Architecture," *Western Architect* 20 (March 1914): 27–28.

citizens. The building campaign, for example, was a community-wide cooperative effort spearheaded by the Neighbors, who collected monies from donations, fund-raisers, and the sale of subscriptions to almost every family in the village.[22]

Maher's design for the village hall accommodated the many theatricals, civic assemblies, evening lectures, club meetings, and holiday celebrations held there in a simple and direct fashion. The open plan featured an assembly hall with stage and dressing rooms in the large space to the left of an off-center entry. Maher placed the library/clubroom and a kitchen to the right and lavatories in a short rear wing on perpendicular axis with the entry. In its straightforward satisfaction of the necessities of the commission, the village hall embodied the ideal in arts and crafts architecture; it was an unpretentious building, free of any imposed historical style, whose design derived from its surroundings and the needs of the community that commissioned it. In composition, the hall was a prairie-style building—a long, low, single-story horizontal mass capped by a low-pitched hipped roof with wide, overhanging eaves and shingles laid in horizontal courses. To balance the horizontality of the composition, Maher gave the openings a vertical treatment, creating a rhythm of floor-to-ceiling windows alternating with paired windows of more standard height down the length of the facade. In keeping with arts and crafts principles, Maher did not allow any applied ornamentation to interrupt the simplicity of exterior expression. Instead, he harmonized the building with its natural surroundings by adorning every other window with a planter and recessing the main entry to accommodate a mature elm tree that he refused to remove from the site.[23]

Kenilworthians understood that if they were to preserve the special character of their suburb, they would have to devise effective means for maintaining control over its growth, development, and personnel. Local control was the final article in their design program for the ideal residential environment. They achieved it by constructing an intricate network of strategies—public and private, official and unofficial—that were enforced and reinforced by the extraordinary consensus among

---

[22] *Kenilworth: First Fifty Years*, pp. 56–59; "Kenilworth Assembly Hall" file, KHS.

[23] An excellent summary of arts and crafts principles as applied to architecture can be found in Davey, *Arts and Crafts Architecture*, chap. 2.

residents regarding the suburb's proper course of development. Maher made two simple but vital contributions to the community's ability to maintain itself. First, he persuaded his neighbors that planning and land-use control were essential for the protection of their physical environment. He played a leading role in establishing two institutions—the Park Board and the voluntary Kenilworth Improvement Association—that were charged with overseeing land use and maintaining the suburb's parks and landscaping. Second, Maher's design achievements imparted to Kenilworth a strong physical identity, which continues to mark the suburb as a place apart. In particular, the visual distinctiveness of his buildings and the landscape architecture that he created to demarcate the suburb's three principal entrances signaled to both outsider and resident alike that they were entering a special preserve. [24]

The strong consensus among Kenilworthians concerning the suburban ideal extended to the form of their dwellings as well. Residents sought suburban homes whose design would express and accommodate their character and circumstances of daily living in a practical and beautiful manner. An analysis of Kenilworth's first 135 houses revealed that a program of at least seven principles governed their design. The first of these was efficiency—that is, the efficient organization and expression of domestic functions. Maher achieved efficiency in his houses by applying the basic arts and crafts tenets of simplicity, utility, and structural rationalism. This meant planning the home from the inside out to fulfill every requirement for daily living without indulgence or wasted space. "True art," he said, "must follow necessity; it must always be useful." [25]

Compared to the Victorian standard, Maher's residences exhibited a radically simplified floor plan. Regardless of size or arrangement, his first-floor plans contained only those spaces that the local consensus suggested were essential to suburban living: vestibule or hall, living room, dining room, porch, kitchen, butler's and serving pantries, and rear vestibule or mudroom (figs. 3, 5, 6). Comfort and utility guided Maher's choices for interior finish and furnishings. He favored large,

---

[24] *Kenilworth: First Fifty Years,* pp. 11, 30–33.
[25] Sies, "American Country House Architecture," pp. 404–26; Maher, "The Viewpoint," p. 39; George W. Maher, "Truth in Design," *Inland Architect and News Record* 35, no. 1 (February 1900): 4.

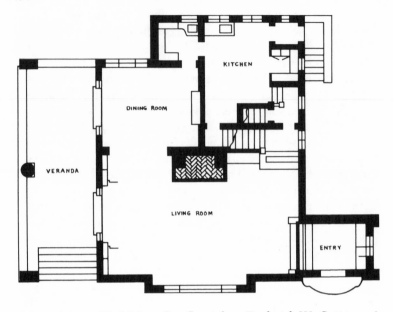

Fig. 3. George W. Maher, first-floor plan, Frederick W. Sutton residence, Kenilworth, Ill., 1908. (Anne B. Keating.)

old-fashioned fireplaces, built-in items like nooks with settees, heavy oak beams, and low ceilings to convey a sense of privacy, security, and ease. For the exteriors of his houses, Maher advocated simple and familiar forms—those most appropriate for expressing the domestic purposes of the building. He said that a dwelling should "leave the impression of quietness of home rather than a dazed impression of grandeur." Like the W. L. Serrel residence (1907), most of Maher's houses featured simple lines of composition that honestly represented the interior arrangement (see figs. 5, 6). The architectural interest of his residences derived typically from three sources: massing; an emphasis on obviously domestic features like porches, chimneys, and decorative glass windows; and the occasional staccato note of an unusually shaped window or entry. The overall effect was one of simplicity, modesty, domestic informality, and decorative restraint.[26]

[26] George W. Maher, "Originality in American Architecture," *Inland Architect and News Record* 10, no. 3 (October 1887): 34.

A Residence at Kenilworth, Illinois

George W. Maher, Architect, Chicago

THIS design certainly does not leave the beholder calm; it is distinctly disturbing, so piquant is its character. It has a flavor of Chinese, Scandinavian, and Gothic; and in its situation among great trees and shrubs, it makes a picture from every point of view. There is nothing of the strong and heavy horizontal lines which one usually associates with Mr. Maher's work; on the contrary, the peaks and valleys of the roof, the network of the shingles and diamond panes, the branchlike design of the piazza arches, all give a fanciful airy design which reminds one somewhat of a Swiss chalet, and yet it is unlike it. The first-floor plan shows great openness; the second story shows a unique owner's chamber. Both this house and that on page 52 have hardwood finish in the lower story, hot-water heating, and open plumbing. Their cost ranges from $5,000 to $8,000.

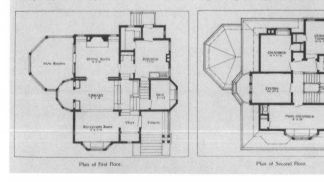

Plan of First Floor.   Plan of Second Floor.

Fig. 4. George W. Maher, first- and second-floor plans and exterior, George W. Maher residence, Kenilworth, Ill., 1893. From *Architectural Review* 14 (March 1907): 53. (University of Florida Architecture and Fine Arts Library.)

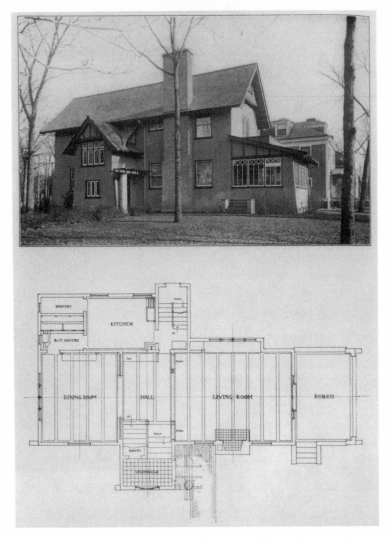

Fig. 5. George W. Maher, plan and exterior, W. L. Serrel residence,
Kenilworth, Ill., 1907. From *American Architect and Building News*
94, no. 1703 (August 1908). (University of Florida Architecture and
Fine Arts Library.)

Residence of Mr. Charles Roe, Kenilworth, Illinois

George W. Maher, Architect, Chicago

ABOUT fifteen miles north of the center of Chicago is Kenilworth, on the shore of Lake Michigan. It is a suburb of Chicago, and a spot of quiet and rest, doubly homelike after the tumult of the great city. This homelike quality is a treasure which was sought after in the design of this house, mainly through simplicity of plan and elevation. The result is not architecture of any particular school, but rather a rational growth of design from ideas advanced by the occupants-elect of the house. The first floor is designed to open up comfortably in order to present the largest size with a small area, to give a homelike appearance, and to avoid a cramped effect.

The living-room is a joy forever, with its fireplace in the center of the long side of the room. This is the right portion for a fireplace in a long room, for both practical and artistic reasons.

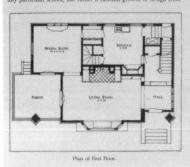

Plan of First Floor.

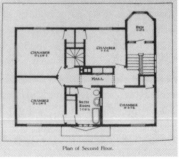

Plan of Second Floor.

Fig. 6. George W. Maher, first- and second-floor plans and exterior, Charles Roe residence, Kenilworth, Ill., ca. 1907. From *Architectural Review* 14 (March 1907): 52. (University of Florida Architecture and Fine Arts Library.)

Technology was an important element in the program for the model home, just as it was in the program for the model suburb. Kenilworthians' primary interest in domestic technology centered upon regulation and control of the home's interior. The goal was to obtain a comfortable and therapeutic environment that would inspire the inhabitants to cultivate healthy habits of hygiene and housekeeping. Maher's dwellings were equipped with "all the modern conveniences": furnaces, gas and electrical fixtures, one or two well-ventilated bathrooms that featured the de rigueur open plumbing, and rationally planned service areas supplied with every convenience needed to facilitate household cleanliness (see kitchen arrangements in figs. 3, 4, 5, 6). Maher was fascinated by technology. He both exhibited and encouraged in his clients an attitude of embracing technology as a symbol of progress and an indication of one's ability to keep in step with the times. He was frequently on the lookout for new domestic gadgets or appliances to introduce; hence, his houses often included extras like hot water heating, electric bells, speaking tubes, and outdoor electrical fixtures.[27]

Nature figured just as prominently as technology in Kenilworth's domestic design program. Indoor/outdoor living was an integral part of the community's suburban lifestyle. For example, Maher's own dwelling offered a dazzling array of opportunities for opening up to the fresh air (see fig. 4). On the first floor there was a front porch, a generous sunroom, a tiny conservatory in the bay of the library, and built-in seats under casement windows in the front room and den. On the second floor he included window seats in two of the bedrooms and a balcony adjoining his wife's studio. Although Kenilworth, with the exception of the lakefront, did not offer dramatic natural beauty, Maher endeavored to harmonize his houses with the surrounding landscape. Sometimes this required substantial planting. Throughout the village, neighbors took great pride in cultivating tree and flower specimens, keeping their window boxes filled with greenery, and sharing the products of their vegetable gardens.[28]

[27] See, for example, "George Maher," *Inland Architect and News Record* 32, no. 2 (September 1898): 20; or "George Maher," *Inland Architect and News Record* 27, no. 2 (March 1896): 19.
[28] Untitled photograph of George Maher residence, 424 Warwick in *Kenilworth—the Model Suburban Home*, pamphlet [ca. 1904], KHS.

Residents' homes embodied a careful balance among the values of family, individuality, and community; these formed the fourth, fifth, and sixth articles in their design program. To foster familial unity, Maher routinely provided one central democratic household living space instead of the multiple first-floor rooms of parlor, morning room, library, and drawing room that were found in the Victorian city residence. In the suburban living room, all family members could gather in the evening to share the day's experiences (see figs. 3, 5, 6). Maher believed that a properly designed home should provide both psychological and practical service. Nearly all of his living rooms featured a prominent hearth at their center for warmth and conviviality and comfortable furniture capable of accommodating both adults' and children's activities. The living room of the C.M. Roe residence, for example, featured an inviting fireplace and inglenook (see fig. 6) in front of which the Roes placed a lighted worktable where family members would read, write letters, or play games within the circle of warmth emanating from the fire. Opposite the fireplace, a comfortable chair placed within the bow of the bay window provided a sheltered space for semiprivate contemplation. In the front corner, a piano stood ready to host the musical evenings that the family enjoyed together or in the company of their neighbors. The Roe living room typified Maher's domestic interiors in conveying an atmosphere of warmth, informality, hospitality, and repose.[29]

Like his neighbors, Maher believed that "our democracy exalts the individual," and he sought ways to encourage individuality through domestic design. He accomplished this in Kenilworth by planning houses to fit each family's needs and by treating each design as an entirely different proposition. When the architect exercised his utmost skill and sensitivity to create a composition that expressed his understanding of the client's needs and character, the result, in Maher's view, was art itself.[30]

Maher tried to create a unique floor plan for each residence that he designed in the suburb. His own dwelling exemplifies a wholly

[29] Maher, "Originality in American Architecture," p. 34; an interior photograph is found in George W. Maher, "Residence for C. M. Roe, Kenilworth, Illinois," *Inland Architect and News Record* 46, no. 5 (December 1905).
[30] Maher, "Western Spirit," pp. 39–40.

individualized residence that, at the same time, possesses all the basic elements of Kenilworth's design program (see fig. 4). Because his home sheltered the lives of three artists—his wife, Elizabeth; her father, Alden Brooks; and himself—Maher organized his floor plan to furnish as many private and working spaces as possible. In addition to private bedrooms for his son and father-in-law and a large, unusually shaped master bedroom, Maher provided two secluded work spaces: the second-story painting studio, used primarily by Elizabeth and Alden, and a modest first-floor den, tucked to the side of the staircase, for himself. In his first-floor plan, Maher furnished an ingenious assortment of semiprivate nooks and crannies—including a hall seat, a window seat, the conservatory alcove adjoining the library, and the sunroom—while maintaining the open planning that he preferred. The exterior of his residence possessed visual distinction and was unlike any of the homes Maher designed for his neighbors. Since all three of the adult occupants were passionate lovers of nature, Maher set the dwelling in a frame of foliage and cultivated much of the yard to appear as if it had grown up wild.[31]

Kenilworthians frequently entertained one another in their homes, a pattern reflected in the design of the houses and in the sixth principle of the suburb's design program, community. Maher's large living rooms and open floor plans were spacious and flexible enough to perform the dual function of sheltering family activities and the numerous informal social occasions of Kenilworth society. In addition to musical evenings, residents regularly hosted club meetings, amateur theatricals, card parties, intellectual "salons," and, of course, dinner parties. Maher designed his houses to be hospitable in several ways. Those first floors that were axially planned provided hosts and guests alike with the sensation, if not the reality, of spaciousness (see figs. 4, 5). In all of his Kenilworth commissions, Maher dispensed with the defensive room arrangements of city houses created to shield the family from strangers. From the vestibule, neighbors stepped into a hall or the living room itself from which they could easily see into the primary family living spaces (see figs. 3, 4, 5, 6). Given the intimate and open nature of social relations in the planned, exclusive suburb, families did not need

[31] "A Residence at Kenilworth, Illinois," *Architectural Review* 14 (March 1907): 53.

to worry about protecting themselves against visits from socially undesirable neighbors.[32]

Most of Kenilworth's residents, following Sears, regarded their suburb as a world apart, a community made special by its unique physical and social environment. An important part of the suburb's special character derived from Kenilworthians' efforts to cultivate beauty in the design of the home, the culminating principle in their design program. Maher was consistent in his application of this basic arts and crafts tenet to his own work. He wrote that "it is in the home that the heart of the nation is most responsive and therefore naturally subject to the most advancement. It is here that the architect receives his highest inspiration and finds the greatest motive power for beautification."[33] Like many arts and crafts adherents, Maher believed that art in the form of a beautified environment could inspire in his clients idealism and spirituality.

Maher strove for beauty by designing houses that exhibited originality, harmony with nature, and aesthetic unity. In his motif and rhythm theory, he contrived a means for combining all three approaches so that every aspect of his houses—composition, interior design, landscaping, furnishing, and ornament—would constitute a simple artistic whole. For each dwelling he chose a motif, such as a geometric or foliate symbol that he felt captured the circumstances of his clients' lives, around which he coordinated the composition and details of his design. In his own dwelling, the diamond shape was the guiding motif, prominently established in the window beside the entry porch (see fig. 4). Maher went on to approximate the shape in the composition of the stylized roof with its sharp points and flared eaves and to repeat it across the exterior in the diamond-patterned shingles and windowpanes. On the interior he established the motif in the patterned brickwork of the mantel and repeated it throughout the house in the windows and glass doors of built-in cabinets and bookcases.[34]

A more mature application of the theory can be found in the Roe residence, designed in 1905 (see fig. 6). There Maher established the broad ogee arch as his guiding motif, displayed most prominently in

---

[32] Kilner, *Joseph Sears and His Kenilworth*, pp. 223–28, 240–42.
[33] Maher, "Western Spirit," p. 39.
[34] George W. Maher, "Art Democracy," *Western Architect* 15 (March 1910): 30.

the openings of the porch and front entry and in the shape of the small conservatory. He embellished the motif with a floral pattern and worked it into the decorative glass of the large living-room window and repeated it in a more stylized version in the leaded-glass second-story windows. On the interior he established the motif in a large ogee arch containing the living-room mantel. The motif then echoed throughout the dwelling in a very stylized fashion, as in the shape of the benches for the inglenook and in the windows of every room. The decorative effect of the motif and rhythm theory was simple, distinctive, and appears to have been both aesthetically and psychologically pleasing to residents.[35]

Perhaps the most astonishing finding from the field analysis of Kenilworth's landscape and of the first 135 houses was the coherence of the suburb's planning and architecture, despite its emergence in response to dozens of separate transactions among Kenilworth Company officials, new residents, and the architects and builders who won commissions there. As they built the new suburb, all parties forged a community-wide consensus of how it should look and what values it should promote and embody. The principles at the heart of Kenilworth's two design programs make clear that Maher's houses, public buildings, and the suburb's elm-lined parkways meant more to the early residents than acceptable shelter and a posh address. Kenilworth's built environment was an essential part of the founding generation's everyday lives; it reflected, embodied, and transmitted important communal meanings.

But what were those meanings? What ideology did Maher's arts and crafts houses and landscape planning articulate for their consumers? Neither of the design programs governing the suburb's built environment provides evidence that Kenilworthians self-consciously embraced the Craftsman ideal or an arts and crafts social ideology. Several principles of the program for the ideal residential community, in fact— order, technology, and local control—violated the character usually associated with an arts and crafts philosophy. So, too, did residents' exploitation of physical and social engineering to create the "natural" surroundings and appropriate atmosphere they desired for their homes. Even Maher's motif and rhythm theory, which at first glance appears

[35] Maher, "Residence for C. M. Roe," interior photograph.

to be a means for enacting unity in design, departs from the arts and crafts spirit in a substantial way. In essence, the theory constituted a modern professional's effort to devise a scientific, rational system to manage a consistent design challenge.

The ideology articulated in Kenilworth's landscape was, instead, that of the suburban ideal of an exclusive group of upper-middle-class Chicagoans. Maher's planning, his arts and crafts houses, and his landscape architecture embodied his and his neighbors' formulas for mediating the challenges and circumstances of their daily lives. Kenilworth's built environment, in other words, constituted for those who designed and used it a figurative means of making sense out of a complex social reality that they, in fact, could neither control nor entirely understand. We can never delineate with certainty all the layers of meaning that Kenilworth's landscape harbored for its turn-of-the-century residents, but we can reconstruct the broadest outlines of its public meanings. For Kenilworthians, the suburban ideal seemed to accomplish two pressing purposes: the creation of a formal environment that precisely accommodated their own circumstances of daily living and the design of a model environment that promised to bring order and improvement to the lives of other urban dwellers.[36]

If the suburban ideal, and not the Craftsman ideal, supplied the ideological meaning for Kenilworth's environment, what role did the arts and crafts movement play there? Why did Maher and the neighbors for whom he built houses embrace arts and crafts principles of design? The simple answer is that Kenilworthians found them to be a suitable vehicle for expressing their ideology. To understand why, we must continue to sort through the layers of meaning that residents invested in their built environment. The bridge that connected their conservative social ideology with the progressive aesthetic ideology of the arts and crafts movement was their mutual emphasis on design reform. Kenilworthians found the instrumental aesthetics of the arts and crafts philosophy appealing because it reinforced their own belief in the effectiveness of positive environmental reform. Although residents shared the arts and crafts mission of rebeautifying domestic artifacts, they differed dramatically on the ultimate purposes design reform would serve.

---

[36] Geertz, *Interpretation of Cultures*, pp. 210–11.

Kenilworthians adapted the arts and crafts movement to their own cause conservative, the affirmation of their new suburban lifestyle and the creation of ideal suburbs, a healthier homelife, and more productive citizens through strategies of positive environmental reform.

We can view the manner in which Kenilworthians adapted the arts and crafts idiom to express their own ideology in Maher's planning, architecture, and design philosophy. Maher and his clients borrowed outright the tenets of simplicity, utility, structural rationalism, aesthetic unity, and the cultivation of beauty, which promised to bring order into their households and enhance their own lives. Other values like handcraftsmanship and the reform of wage labor, which ran counter to their belief system, they simply left alone. More revealing was the transposing of meaning that occurred as Maher incorporated certain arts and crafts principles that were socialist in origin into his own ideology and philosophy of design. His understanding of originality or what he termed the "organic quality of design" provides a good illustration. Maher took to heart the assumption that great art derives from the lives of ordinary people and must be judged by its satisfaction of genuine social needs. His planning and architecture in Kenilworth succeeded precisely because of its organic quality. It satisfied the needs and expressed the lifeways of his upper-middle-class neighbors brilliantly; in Maher's words, his houses "paint[ed] . . . a living portrait, giving full expression to what he saw." But Maher's understanding of originality departed substantially from that of more radical arts and crafts adherents. In giving an organic quality of expression to the suburban ideal, he served the self-interest of a narrow and privileged stratum of society and exercised his professional prerogative to determine what his clients needed and how those needs might best be met. Maher's commitment to arts and crafts principles was sincere, but his interpretation of them was tied to his social position and the historical circumstances of his own place and time.[37]

Maher wrote that a living architecture "must express motifs kindred to the life around it . . . and must be a part of the mind of the community."[38] Judged by those criteria, the environment that he shaped in Kenilworth was very much alive; Maher's planning and archi-

---

[37] Maher, "Western Spirit," p. 41.
[38] Maher, "Truth in Design," p. 4.

tecture simply gave common sense expression to Kenilworthians' suburban ideal. The ideology that Maher shared with his neighbors, made manifest in the programs for model suburb and model suburban home, balanced masterfully the mix of competing needs and values and pressures that constituted the historical circumstances of his and his clients' lives. For its suburban creators and consumers, Kenilworth's built environment worked; it made sense to them on their terms. To historians studying Kenilworth eighty years later, however, Maher's design work seems full of ideological and political incongruities. From our demanding critical perspective, an idealist's sincere experiment with an aesthetic principle can begin to look like the shallow or even cynical co-option of a cherished political ideal. The logic of Maher's use of the arts and crafts idiom to enliven his suburban architecture only becomes evident when we untangle the meanings his work held for those who originally interacted with it. Additional studies using similar methods and focusing on other artifacts may help us eventually come to terms with the puzzling and complicated substance of American arts and crafts design.

Midwest to California
The Planned Arts and Crafts Community

Karen J. Weitze

In 1902 Edward Gardner Lewis initiated efforts toward his first planned community. Platted across from the grounds for the future Louisiana Purchase International Exposition at the outskirts of St. Louis, the Olmstedian residence park of University Heights hosted a publishing empire and an internationally recognized art pottery, becoming the seat for the American Woman's League. An arts and crafts community, subsequently incorporated as University City, Lewis's town sought the middle landscape between civilization and nature, reflecting the progressivism of the era. Leo Marx identified and named the literary middle landscape in 1964. For physical places, the term implies a man-made, man-enhanced setting, "as attractive for what it excludes as for what it contains." Lewis developed University City during a ten-year period and in 1912 took his ideas to California for a second attempt at a model town—Atascadero. The middle landscape is typically separated from preexisting populations by water (as on an island) or by wasteland (often a desert). At the century's turn, St. Louis sat at the West's eastern edge, focusing the dreams of Lewis Pacificward. A singular destiny of the Far West was to develop as America's middle landscape, with California as its keynote. Many accounts of the West described the terrain from Denver to the Pacific Coast as an empty desert encountered before a lush island. For the arts and crafts community, the West offered more than the opportunities of geographic isolation. Socialism, experimentation, and the women's movement thrived there, particularly in coastal

Substance of Style

California and Washington. Together, University City and Atascadero offer a paradigm for the American arts and crafts full-scale planned place. Fittingly, Lewis created his mildly Socialist, utopian communities through the mainstream of the women's movement, through the thousands of American clubwomen who "held the middle ground."[1]

University City and Atascadero reflected the immediately preceding age of utopian fiction. Between 1886 and 1896 more than 100 such novels were published in America. These tales popularized ideas of communal property and trade unions, universal suffrage and education. Edward Bellamy's *Looking Backward*, written in 1887 and depicting Socialist Boston in the year 2000, sold more than one million copies in the United States and England during the 1890s. Women's groups offered Bellamy's book through their publications; in the 1930s *Looking Backward* was still ranked as the second most influential book written since 1885. Following Bellamy was William Dean Howells with *Traveller from Altruria*, *Letters of an Altrurian Traveller*, and *Through the Eye of the Needle*, serialized in 1892–94, partially published in 1894, and appearing as a trilogy in 1907. Altruria, an island of "recycled Jeffersonianism . . . a literary border country that lies between the nineteenth-century city and the eighteenth-century country," corroborated the reality of the response to both University City and Atascadero.[2]

A particularly keen example of the utopian genre, evocative of the University City-Atascadero paradigm, is Joaquin Miller's *The Building of the City Beautiful* of 1894. Miller, a California poet, opened his novel with Matthew 19:24: "It is easier for a camel to go through the eye of a needle, than for a rich man to enter the kingdom of God." The passage captured both intellectual and working-class sentiments of the day. Post–Civil War business magnates abused new-era machinery and their fellow man; between 1880 and 1900, 38,303 labor strikes

[1] Leo Marx, *The Machine in the Garden: Technology and the Pastoral Ideal in America* (New York: Oxford University Press, 1964), pp. 65, 138; Robert W. Winter, "The Arroyo Culture," *California Design, 1910* (Salt Lake City, Utah: Peregrine Smith Books, 1989), pp. 9–29; Annette K. Baxter, in *The Clubwoman as Feminist: True Womanhood Redefined, 1868–1914*, ed. Karen J. Blair (New York and London: Holmes and Meier Publishing, 1980), p. xiv.

[2] Jean Pfaelzer, *The Utopian Novel in America, 1886–1896: The Politics of Form* (Pittsburgh: University of Pittsburgh Press, 1984), pp. 3, 48, 51, 63; William Dean Howells, *The Altrurian Romances* (1907; reprint, Bloomington and London: Indiana University Press, 1968), pp. xi–xii.

occurred in the United States. Miller's City Beautiful in the Oakland Hills portrayed a Socialist middle landscape with characteristics later also found in Lewis's Atascadero. In Miller's cooperative society, noisome sweatshops were banned; everyone worked a partial day; the stunning natural site was both isolated and enhanced through irrigated agriculture; vegetarians dined communally; enlightened health care was provided; and a single church unified religions. Form-giving features in the fictional Oakland Hills utopia also defined Atascadero: the city had a showcase central core, while "far out and around at the foot of the mountains ran a [train] track of glass . . . sparkling fountains and pleasant porches" accented wooded lanes.[3]

Miller, like nearly all individuals responding to the arts and crafts movement, mentioned both John Ruskin and William Morris. Miller's suggestions for a City Beautiful were agrarian and futuristic: "We have conserved all that was good in the Indian's life, and discarded that which was outgrown." His aesthetic for public buildings was, like that of the majority of utopian writers, astylistically classical, with an implicitly more vernacular outlying residential component. Miller's City Beautiful is not the White City of the Columbian Exposition in Chicago the year before: instead, it is a holistic, conceptual City Beautiful absorbing the assumptions of the arts and crafts House Beautiful. Its middle landscape embodied the moral tenet "have nothing in your house [community] that is not useful or beautiful."[4] Lewis, too, talked of the City Beautiful, briefly publishing a journal focused on the arts and crafts, *Beautiful Homes*. His realization came through University City and Atascadero.

The states that became the strongest supporters of Lewis were those that were most active in the Socialist movement. In 1912, 118,000 members belonged to the Socialist party; 1,200 public officials held positions of standing, and more than 300 journals and newspapers were

---

[3] Joaquin Miller, *The Building of the City Beautiful* (Chicago: Stone and Kimball, 1894), pp. 1, 112–13, 124, 125, 130, 147, 151, 163, 173, 184; Pfaelzer, *Utopian Novel*, p. 27. See also, Alexander Craig, *Ionia: Land of Wise Men and Fair Women* (Chicago: E. A. Weeks Co., 1898) and C. W. Wooldridge, *Perfecting the Earth: A Piece of Possible History* (Cleveland: Utopian Publishing Co., 1902).

[4] Miller, *Building the City Beautiful*, p. 165. Kevin H. F. O'Brien, " 'The House Beautiful': A Reconstruction of Oscar Wilde's American Lecture," *Victorian Studies* 17, no. 4 (June 1974): 403.

published. The Socialist party was the first political party to give women an equal vote, and many, many women were concerned about their legal inability to participate in government. Rheta Childe Dorr's *What Eight Million Women Want* sold a half-million copies in 1910. In 1913 St. Louis Socialist interests published the *National Rip Saw* with 150,000 circulation, while in Girard, Kansas, *Appeal to Reason* reached 761,747. These were the two top Socialist publications in the nation; both were founded early, in 1904 and 1895, respectively, with Kate O'Hare editing the former after 1912 and running as vice president on the Socialist ticket in 1920. As suffragist efforts grew, Lewis wrote prolifically in his own publications on equality and the vote. The vote preoccupied his American Woman's League and subsequent American Woman's Republic, and through the large number of women's clubs tied together through the General Federation of Women's Clubs, he tapped an eager audience willing to aid in the building of the arts and crafts City Beautiful.[5]

At the heart of Lewis's first community near St. Louis lay ambitions for a publishing network that would take advantage of the low postal rates established in the mid 1880s and the marketing possibilities opened through rural free delivery in 1897. The number of women's magazines, featuring domestic arts and women's topics, increased dramatically in the late nineteenth century. Lewis, a man of many schemes before his venture in the Midwest, bought the St. Louis–based magazine *Winner*, and, in 1902, changed its name and focus. The new *Woman's Magazine* sought the rapidly growing rural domestic audience. Its downtown St. Louis publishing plant outgrown, the enterprise needed new facilities; University City was first a site chosen for the Woman's Magazine Building, an octagonal eight-story tower that dominated the immediate skyline, with its adjacent, lower-profile Press Room Building. Lewis shepherded the completion of construction for visibility by attendees of the 1904 neighboring world's fair. From 1902 to 1904, too, Lewis expanded his empire to include *Woman's Farm Journal*, basing it in University City as well.[6] The idea for a full-scale community surrounding his publishing center came next.

[5] James Weinstein, *The Decline of Socialism in America, 1912–1925* (New York and London: Monthly Review Press, 1967), pp. 1, 16, 17, 23–26, 44, 48–49, 53–59, 85, 92, 96. Blair, *Clubwoman*, pp. 95, 111, 113.
[6] Sidney Morse, *The Siege of University City: The Dreyfus Case of America* (University City, Mo.: University City Publishing Co., 1912), p. 59; Department of Planning,

Camp Lewis of 1904, a tent city that Lewis erected for his magazine readers as a reasonably priced motel to encourage their visiting the Louisiana Purchase International Exposition, may have inspired the University City landscape siting and community planning. Within walking distance of the fair, Camp Lewis made rural people feel at home. Lewis met his readers, with pre-mailed identification badges, at the train station. Camp Lewis evoked the middle landscape. "St. Louis, itself, lies below the eastern horizon in a pale haze of smoke. Westward, the outlook is to the prairies of Missouri. West, North and South stretches a wide rolling level, for hundreds of miles." Between 200 and 400 tents defined Camp Lewis. "Every tent had raised floors and electric lights. . . . About each tent was a lawn of well-kept grass and flower beds." Camp Lewis provided baths; nursery, recreation, hospital, and communal dining tents; barber shops; and reading rooms, interconnected by boardwalks. The cost for the summer city was $25,000. Approximately 80,000 people stayed at Lewis's accommodations.[7]

Immediately after the fair, Lewis undertook an eighty-five-acre residence park. University Heights featured ten blocks with ten university-named streets, showcasing curving vistas, deeply set-back houses, granitoid sidewalks, electroliers, and street-lining maples, elms, sycamores, and Carolina poplars. Dwellers underwent the equivalent of a design review process for construction materials and house style. Lewis's residence company handled the upkeep for streets, gutters, sidewalks, water mains, and street trees. The community had garbage and ash collection, snow removal, and landscape service. Houses on the public-encountered streets were to cost a minimum of $6,000 by deed clause, scaling down to $1,500 at the rear of the park. Lewis required that residents be Caucasian, reflective of St. Louis's generally southern heritage. In 1906 the whole of Lewis's developing community incorporated as University City (fig. 1).[8]

City of University City, *Historic Preservation Completion Report* (July 1, 1973–June 30, 1974); Nini Harris, *Legacy of Lions* (University City, Mo.: University City Historical Society, 1981), pp. 41–54.
[7]Morse, *Siege of University City*, pp. 240–42, 271, 275; Harris, *Legacy of Lions*, pp. 56–57.
[8]University Heights Realty and Development Company, *University Heights, St. Louis, Missouri* (St. Louis, 1906); *University Heights: A Restricted, Private Residence Park* [broadside] (University City, Mo.: Lewis Publishing Co., ca. 1906); *University Heights: A Residence Park in a City of Homes* (University City, Mo.: Lewis Publishing Co., 1910).

Fig. 1. University City, Mo., 1932. From *Post-Dispatch* (St. Louis). (Photo, University City Public Library.)

As his ideal community took form, Lewis continued to expand his publishing enterprises, adding *Woman's National Daily* in late 1906 and *Beautiful Homes* in 1908. Lewis attracted the attention of major publishers almost immediately. During the gala year of 1904 the Lewises were photographed with William Randolph and Phoebe Hearst on the steps of the Woman's Magazine Building. *Beautiful Homes* featured Lewis's community-planning ideals, attracting its readers with its tonal cover designs of house and country and urging the art committees of the Federation of Women's Clubs to contact the "thousands of intelligent women eager to learn and to act." The magazine's editorial staff included a woman architect, Mary Hale Lafon. By January 1909 *Beautiful Homes* featured an article by Mabel Urmy Seares entitled "The Bungalow Habit." During its second and final year of publication, Seares contributed more articles, as did another Pasadena writer and architectural photographer, Helen Lukens Gaut. The magazine praised "plain food," "bare floors," and "comfortable chairs," discussing and illustrating California bungalows and bringing the crafts aesthetic to many women who might not otherwise have been exposed to it.[9]

Each issue of *Beautiful Homes* featured a section on a particular facet of the arts and crafts movement: lace making, rugs, baskets, metalwork, stenciling, pottery, and furniture. But it was the architecture that most reflected the Lewis idea of planned place. *Bungalowcraft* of Los Angeles and *Keith's on Home Building* of Minneapolis both sponsored frequent advertisements in Lewis's magazine. Repeatedly, too, articles appeared on the machine-produced concrete dwelling. These prefabricated structures fostered the futuristic-pastoral middle landscape, Lewis's personal ideal. Paralleling the inclusion of articles by Seares and Lukens Gaut, *Beautiful Homes* particularly showcased the work of women architects, especially those from California. In January 1910 Julia Morgan's Turner house was illustrated; in May of that same year a home designed by Mrs. Sherman Glasscock in Pasadena for John Herd was featured.[10]

The Lewis publishing enterprise depended upon volume and inexpensive mailings for newspapers and magazines. A second-class postal entry allowed a one-cent-per-pound rate. Lewis was quite aware of both Sears and Montgomery Ward, whose composite mail-order business cleared $50 million in 1903 alone. His Press Building featured modern, efficient machinery. The original one-story structure was 100 feet wide by 275 feet long. Of simple beaux arts classicism on its exterior, the building's interior looked to the future. Along one side were a row of nine oversized presses, reflected opposite by eight folding and binding machines. The west end furthered the mass production through cutting and trimming equipment. "In the middle of the building, seven railroad mail cars stood in line waiting to receive the 200 tons of magazines that were mailed out to all sections of the country each month."[11]

[9]Morse, *Siege of University City*, p. 279. *Beautiful Homes* (hereafter cited as *BH*) 1, no. 1 (October 1908): 2–3, 20, 24. Mabel Urmy Seares, "The Bungalow Habit," *BH* 1, no. 4 (January 1909): 14–15.

[10]*BH* 2, no. 3 (June 1909): 27; Helen Lukens Gaut, "Four Inexpensive California Bungalows," *BH* 4, no. 5 (September 1910): 10; "Some Typical California Homes," *BH* 3, no. 3 (January 1910): 15; *BH* 4, no. 1 (May 1910): 4–5.

[11]Morse, *Siege of University City*, pp. 29, 299; Dept. of Planning, *Preservation Completion Report*, continuation sheet 7.

Not all of Lewis's postal enterprises were successful. As early as 1904 he incorporated the Woman's Magazine Postal Bank and Trust Company, an institution that evolved into the People's United States Bank. Intended to establish a rural postal banking system, headquartered in University City, the postal bank was ahead of its time. Regional centers were planned for New York, Chicago, St. Louis, New Orleans, and San Francisco, with established banks cooperating in each city. Bank of California was the partner bank for the West. Lewis erected a severe reinforced concrete Egyptian revival temple for the headquarters in University City. Underwritten by the savings of many rural magazine subscribers, the bank was outwardly utopian. Yet, the banking industry and the postal system both refused to accept the heavy investment of the People's United States Bank monies in Lewis's own enterprises. By the time of its dedication in 1906, the bank headquarters had been reassigned as the publishing plant for *Woman's National Daily*.[12]

Upon incorporating University City, Lewis embarked upon another key component of his unfolding middle landscape, the American Woman's League. In 1907 he announced the league through his publications. A club itself, and a conduit for existing women's clubs, the league became popular during the suffragist doldrums following Susan B. Anthony's death in 1906, peaking in 1912 coincident with the plateau of influence achieved by the Socialist party of America. The league maintained contact with the General Federation of Women's Clubs, paralleling their concerns with child labor laws, housing, education, public libraries, civic beautification, and nature conservancy. Lewis further proclaimed women's needs for financial self-sufficiency. As was true with every Lewis enterprise, the league also had its purely business aspect. It acted as a magazine subscription agency and as such was valuable. Membership sought was one million women, with a planned endowment of $26,000,000.[13]

The league owned the Lewis Publishing Company—producing *Woman's Magazine*, *Woman's Farm Journal*, *Woman's National Daily/Weekly*, *Beautiful Homes*, and *Palette and Bench*—and the Lewis real estate—chiefly the University City residence park unsold

[12] Morse, *Siege of University City*, pp. 299–310; Harris, *Legacy of Lions*, p. 61.

[13] On self-sufficiency, see Harris, *Legacy of Lions*, pp. 71–84. Club reports appear throughout *Woman's National Daily* and *Woman's National Weekly* (hereafter cited as WND and WNW). Morse, *Siege of University City*, p. 60.

property—with plans for ownership of the postal bank. Lewis also set up another, distinctive money-making arm of the league, the Chapter House program. American clubwomen were typically without permanent places to meet, rotating assemblage in individual homes. Appealing to farm communities of 500 to 1,000 people, the league offered to build permanent clubhouses in return for a quota of sold magazine subscriptions. Lewis organized a network of nearly 100 magazines, including his own publications combined with a large group of magazines assembled from "class A" publishers brought into the enterprise. The network had a vibrant arts and crafts tone. At least ten journals discussed agriculture; another six, health. Others covered crafts, architecture, and art, inclusive of *American City, House Beautiful,* and *International Studio.* From California came *Pacific Monthly, Orchard and Farm,* and *Sunset.*[14]

League education activities were crucial for Lewis's emerging utopian townscape. Through the widely dispersed clubs and chapter houses, and through the centralized Peoples University in University City, education became multifaceted and motivational. In mid 1910 the league had more than 1,200 chapters, with membership varying from several dozen women in rural communities to more than 1,000 in Los Angeles. At least 30,000 women actively participated in the league nationwide. Clubs sponsored weekly instructive lectures on cooking, preserving, dressmaking, embroidery, physical culture, arts and crafts, travel, science, and education. The league encouraged all of a town's clubs, even if unaffiliated with Lewis's organization, to meet in the league clubhouse. From University City a circulating library sent phonograph records out to chapters weekly, with each chapter then forwarding its shipment to another chapter and receiving a similarly forwarded shipment in turn. A woman could check out records directly from University City through the mails. By 1909 Lewis added films to the circulating library, accompanied by printed lectures on world travel. The league equipped clubhouses with record players and moving picture machinery.[15]

Another arm of the league, the National Woman's Exchange, set

[14] Morse, *Siege of University City,* pp. 593, 755; E. G. Lewis, "The Month's Review," *BH* 3, no. 2 (November–December 1909): 30.

[15] *BH* 1, no. 5 (February 1909): 2; *BH* 2, no. 3 (June 1909): 2; Lewis, "Month's Review," p. 30.

up a branch showroom in each chapter clubhouse, displaying "the products of the league's schools and members in sculpture, printing, pottery, bookbinding, embroidery, and the arts and crafts, as well as the more homely products." "The woman who can [make] an exquisite piece of embroidery . . . can, through the Exchange, place [it] on sale [at a good price]." As a distribution system for the "more homely products," the exchange was commonly known as the "jam plan."[16] The salesrooms of the exchange expanded upon the displays of the arts and crafts societies and even upon those of certain urban department stores. Major arts and crafts exhibits had immediately foreshadowed Lewis's middle landscape, with the arts and crafts exhibition at Syracuse, New York, in 1903, and with that at the world's fair in St. Louis in 1904.

Most ambitious in the league's educational program was its Peoples University in University City. The school was to offer courses ranging from simplified business to dressmaking, bookbinding, and art. For the most part, coursework was by correspondence. Of the planned multibuilding campus, only the Art Academy of 1909 saw construction. Designed by the St. Louis firm of Eames and Young, the academy complemented the beaux arts Woman's Magazine Building and the Press Room Building. Planned, and partially realized not at University City but at Atascadero, were a forecourt and a central avenue with circular plaza with a monumental shaft and fountain. As envisioned, the academy was to have been divided into the applied arts and crafts and the formal arts of drawing, painting, and ceramics.[17] A single art school evolved, with sculpture, drawing and painting, pottery, and textiles.

Hungarian sculptor George Julian Zolnay directed the academy. Zolnay had come to the United States as director of the art department for the Louisiana Purchase International Exposition. As a graduate of the Imperial Academy of Fine Arts, Vienna, and the Royal Academy of Bucharest, Zolnay adapted well to St. Louis and remained after the

[16]*BH* 1, no. 5 (February 1909): 2; "The Woman's National Exchange," *WND* 7, no. 9 (March 5, 1909): 10.

[17]On planning, see Harris, *Legacy of Lions*, pp. 71–84; Dept. of Planning, *Preservation Completion Report*; "University City Art Notes," *Palette and Bench* (hereafter cited as *PB*) 2, no. 7 (April 1910): 170. "University of the League," *BH* 2, no. 5 (August 1909): back cover.

closing of the fair, becoming involved in the St. Louis Artists' Guild. In collaboration with Eames and Young, Zolnay designed the lion entrance gates for University City in 1909 and was soon appointed to head the league's academy. Under his directorship, Ralph Chesley Ott, muralist for the Woman's Magazine Building, headed drawing and painting. W. Laird Turner handled textiles. Soon, however, the academy focused almost entirely on ceramics. Both Lewis and his wife, Mabel, were amateur potters. In 1903 they had uncovered a vein of kaolin on their property. The Lewises experimented with their own kiln, guided by Taxtile Doat's *Grand Feu Ceramics*, serially published in translation through *Keramic Studio* beginning that same year. Lewis invited Doat to visit University City in mid 1909, subsequently offering him the opportunity of establishing an art pottery at the academy. Doat returned in December with his two assistants, Eugene Labarrière and Emile Diffloth. Doat sent his equipment, prepared clay, and a number of ceramic pieces from France to University City. *Woman's National Daily* featured a photograph of the moving van, shipped complete, being pulled by six horses as it arrived on January 13, 1910.[18]

Lewis, with Doat, attracted other potters of considerable talent. Even before the year's close Lewis announced that Adelaide Alsop Robineau would be working with Doat at University City, returning to her home in Syracuse during summers and conducting a league summer school there. Robineau, along with her husband, Samuel, brought the spirit of the arts and crafts Syracuse circle, centered on Gustav Stickley, to University City. Parallel with Lewis, the Robineaus published journals, including *Keramic Studio* and *Palette and Bench*, and organized subscriptions to other arts and crafts magazines for their readers. Their subscription pool featured Stickley's *Craftsman* and *International Studio*. Samuel Robineau translated Doat's *Grand Feu Ceramics*. As a part of the Robineau involvement in the league, their *Palette and Bench* shifted publication directly to Lewis.[19]

Also among the potters drawn to University City was Frederick Hurten Rhead. Emigrating from England in 1902 and working for

[18] Dept. of Planning, *Preservation Completion Report*, continuation sheet 10; Harris, *Legacy of Lions*, p. 76; *BH* 2, no. 3 (June 1909): 2; *WND* 10, no. 65 (January 15, 1910): 13.

[19] E.G. Lewis, "Mrs. Robineau and Her Pottery," *BH* 3, no. 2 (November–December 1909): 14; *PB* 1, no. 2 (September 1909): advertisement.

Fig. 2. Faculty of the Art Academy, Peoples University, University City, Mo., 1910. *Left to right:* Frederick H. Rhead, Samuel Robineau, Edward Gardner Lewis, Adelaide Alsop Robineau, Mabel Lewis, Eugene Labarrière, George Julian Zolnay, Emile Diffloth, Taxile Doat. The middleground platter was the first object fired at the academy. (Photo, University City Public Library.)

several potteries including Weller and Roseville through 1908, Rhead joined the academy simultaneously with the Robineaus. He became the academy's primary teacher of ceramics, with the Robineaus and Doat crafting pottery and tiles for exhibition and sale (figs. 2, 3). Diffloth was the chemist for glazes; Labarrière was the thrower and moldmaker. Kathryn E. Cherry, of St. Louis, completed the pottery staff, teaching china painting with assistant Jesse Bard and attracting more correspondence students than any other academy artist. Rhead wrote the academy's textbook, *Studio Pottery*, in 1910; assisting him at the academy were Edward Dahlquist and Frank J. Fuhrmann. University City Pottery, represented by fifty-five pieces made by Adelaide Robineau, took the grand prize at the Esposizione Internazionale d'Industria e de Lavoro in Turin, Italy, in 1911, in competition with Europe's finest potteries. League honor students, a status achieved through corre-

Fig. 3. Frederick H. Rhead, in his office at the Art Academy, Peoples University, University City, Mo., 1910. (Photo, University City Public Library.)

spondence work, spent a year in residence at the academy and then guided other correspondence students in the league chapter clubhouses and created memorial art work for their hometowns.[20]

As planning, construction, and hiring went forward for the academy of the Peoples University, so also did planning, construction, and expansion occur for the league chapter clubhouses. Lewis introduced the chapter house, as six standardized variants of a bungalow, between January and March 1909 in *Beautiful Homes*. The cost ranged from a

[20]"University Art Notes," *PB* 2, no. 6 (March 1910): 134; *PB* 2, no. 11 (August 1910): 298; *PB* 3, no. 1 (October 1910): 30. "Porcelains," *PB* 2, no. 6 (March 1910): 141–44; Frederick H. Rhead, "How to Build a Piece of Pottery," *PB* 2, no. 8 (May 1910): 215–18; and *PB* 2, no. 10 (July 1910): 271–72; *PB* 2, no. 9 (June 1910): advertisement. Frederick H. Rhead, *Studio Pottery* (St. Louis: Peoples University Press, 1910); Paul Evans, *Art Pottery of the United States* (2d ed.; New York: Feingold and Lewis Publishing, 1987), pp. 243–49, 286–91; Harris, *Legacy of Lions*, p. 79. On league honor students, see "University City Art Notes," p. 134; Dept. of Planning, *Preservation Completion Report*, continuation sheets 9–10.

projected $1,200 to $10,000. When first announced, the clubhouses were to be of reinforced concrete construction, allowing for uniform site erection. Lewis's vision of the middle landscape was consistently futuristic, with an emphasis on the machine. He again and again showcased concrete construction, making a point of Thomas Edison's experiments in prefabrication. Stylistic detailing for the league bungalows most often focused on the prairie school. Original clubhouse architects, Helfensteller, Hirsch, and Watson of St. Louis, supplied the drawings; the league awarded local contractors the actual commissions. As built, clubhouses were typically wood frame, stucco-on-wood frame, and brick, with materials chosen by the contractors. Contextual setting for the clubhouses was uniformly that of preexisting middle-class residential neighborhoods, with the American Woman's League bungalow visually just another house on the block. Lewis always shifted his capital from one going venture to another, undermining his own plans for uninterrupted, streamlined schedules. Basic designs—exterior and interior—as well as the funding remained centralized in University City; followthrough was customized town by town.[21]

Lewis rallied women across the United States to earn their community's chapter house; the efforts he demanded were exhaustive. He tied funds to the size of the town in which the clubhouse would be built, only partially to the actual cost of construction, asking that women sell $1.00 per inhabitant in subscriptions, annually, in a multi-year effort. The league and the network of publishers split the first-year proceeds; thereafter, the league's half of the monies began to pay for the chapter houses while the publishers retained their percentage. For small, rural towns, Lewis's greatest audience, the women needed to involve their whole community, with multiple magazine sales per household. A typical subscription ran $2.00 to $4.00 a year. Again, Lewis's concept and local league chapters' realities differed somewhat. Predictably, clubhouses went to construction slowly, but a number did so in the first year. The fund-raising mechanism, however imperfectly applied, made success a near impossibility for Los Angeles, with its population of 130,000 in 1910. Not surprisingly, Los Angeles acquired

[21] *BH* 1, no. 4 (January 1909): 2; *BH* 1, nos. 5–6 (February–March 1909): illustrated plans. "News of the American Woman's League," *WND* 10, no. 59 (January 8, 1910): 14.

Fig. 4. Helfensteller, Hirsch, and Watson, chapter house of the American Woman's League, Edwardsville, Ill., 1909. Dedication gathering for the class 2 bungalow. (Photo, Edward G. Lewis albums, University City Public Library.)

its league chapter house uniquely, without league subscription sales and without using one of the Lewis standardized clubhouse designs.[22]

Host towns donated the lots for the league clubhouses. The Art Academy of the Peoples University, for the chapter house task under the direction of Ott, made interior design and furniture choices. Aesthetics were uniformly arts and crafts, with Stickley-like mission furniture selected. Dedicated in July 1909, the league's first chapter house was that for Edwardsville, Illinois, within twenty miles of St. Louis (figs. 4, 5). Edwardsville neighbored Leclaire, the enlightened model town founded for the N.O. Nelson Manufacturing Company of St. Louis. Nelson's community pioneered profit sharing, affirmative ac-

[22]Lewis, "Month's Review," p. 30.

Fig. 5. Helfensteller, Hirsch, and Watson, chapter house of the American Woman's League, Edwardsville, Ill., 1909. (Photo, Edward G. Lewis albums, University City Public Library.)

tion, company-supported education, and a healthful residential and workplace atmosphere. Edwardsville's chapter house was a class 2 structure, essentially the simplest class 1 bungalow ($1,200) with an added salesroom for the National Woman's Exchange program. The second completed clubhouse opened in Peck, Idaho, for the Big Canyon chapter. Peck typified league chapter house–sponsoring communities, characteristically very small and rural. Also in 1909 the league sponsored a building at the Alaska-Yukon-Pacific Exposition in Seattle, as did the General Federation of Women's Clubs. A class 2 clubhouse, that for the world's fair exhibited scale models of the class 1–6 clubhouses and for University City itself.[23]

[23] On the chapter house, see *BH* 2, no. 5 (August 1909): 2; "League Chapter House of Class 2 at Edwardsville, Ill.," *WND* 8, no. 62 (March 19, 1909): 5 [with photograph]; "Some Local Chapter Houses Already Finished and Occupied," *WND* 11, no. 30 (April

Construction notices in Lewis's magazines indicate that thirty-seven clubhouses were actually built across the United States from 1909 to 1912. The figure represents approximately 1,200 league chapters. Most chapters simply did not achieve a clubhouse and continued to meet in clubmembers' homes. Of the thirty-seven clubhouses, twenty-one were of the class 1 bungalow type; these were uniformly found in rural, small towns. Of the remaining sixteen clubhouses, nine were of the class 2 expanded bungalow category, with four of the class 3 type and two of the class 4 type, and Los Angeles a special case. Geographically, concentrations of league chapter houses are apparent: Illinois sponsored nine; Missouri, five; Texas, Montana, and California, three each; Idaho, Kansas, Iowa, New York, and Florida, two each; and Washington, Wisconsin, Kentucky, and Georgia, one each.[24]

All of the states represented, with the exception of Kentucky and Georgia, participated heavily in the Socialist movement during 1910–20. All sponsoring states, with the exception of Georgia, Florida, and Missouri, had achieved partial voting rights at the state level by early 1912. California, Washington, and Idaho had established full-state voting rights for women by this date. Most of Lewis's success lay in states with both strong Socialist party participation and partial suffrage. A core area circumscribed Missouri, Illinois, Kansas, and Texas, with Populist strength in all but Illinois, and with Christian Socialist strength there. Only Georgia presents itself as an anomaly. In reality, its clubhouse sponsors can be interpreted as tied to Florida's political climate. The paradoxical environment was that of Missouri, a strong Socialist state, with no women's rights—a deeply unstable foundation for Lewis's utopia.[25]

Lewis's enterprises became overextended. Complex litigation centered on accusations of fraud, particularly mail fraud, haunted Lewis

2, 1910): 9 [with photographs of six clubhouses]; John S. Garner, "Leclaire, Illinois: A Model Company Town (1890–1934)," *Journal of the Society of Architectural Historians* 30, no. 3 (October 1971): 219–27. On expositions, see "A Matter of Inspiration," *WND* 8, no. 57 (May 13, 1909): 11; *BH* 2, no. 6 (September 1909): 2; "Women to Have Buildings at Fair," *WND* 7, no. 49 (January 7, 1909): 9; *BH* 2, no. 4 (July 1909): 2.
[24]"News of the American Woman's League," *WND* 13, no. 26 (December 30, 1910): 4; *WNW* 14, no. 35 (March 2, 1912): 4–5.
[25]Weinstein, *Decline of Socialism*, pp. 16–25, 94–102, 116–18; "Suffrage Map of the United States," *WNW* 14, no. 49 (April 6, 1912): 3.

from 1902 until a final federal court sentencing in 1928. In November 1910 Lewis was forced to consolidate his publication efforts. He sold *Palette and Bench* to a buyer in New York; *Beautiful Homes* was suspended, as were *Woman's Magazine* and *Woman's Farm Journal*. In March 1911 *Woman's National Daily* became *Woman's National Weekly*. Socialist publishers of this period faced much the same situation as Lewis. By mid 1918 most had been forced out of business, with urban survival only for "those not dependent upon the mails for distribution." In May 1911 University City enterprises went into receivership. A second indictment followed in February 1912, with receivership status maintained except for the league and the academy. Lewis made a strong effort to save his pottery works and his political structure, both key to his arts and crafts community planning. During the disruption of mid 1911, the Robineaus returned to Syracuse, while Rhead went to work at the Fairfax Sanitarium, north of San Francisco, to start Arequipa Pottery. Lewis restructured the academy, under Doat, as the University City Porcelain Works.[26]

Like Rhead, Lewis looked to California during the upheaval. He had been involved there through the California Vineyards Company since about 1905. League chapters organized in several small farming towns as early as mid 1909, with two chapter houses built at Corning, in the Sacramento Valley, and at Compton, just southeast of Los Angeles in the orange groves, in 1910. Near San Francisco, chapters formed in Santa Rosa, San Jose, and Oakland, with Oakland sponsoring a junior chapter for young women in addition to two adult chapters, the Golden State chapter and the Brooklyn Township chapter. The Oakland-Berkeley area was a vibrant Socialist enclave, with Rev. J. Stitt Wilson the Socialist mayor of Berkeley in 1911 and with the state's oldest, and second largest, Socialist newspaper, *The World*, published in Oakland during the same years. Los Angeles ultimately offered Lewis an even more supportive environment, with its Socialist newspaper, *California Social Democrat*, the largest in the state, founded in 1911 and reaching an audience of nearly 12,000 by 1913. The Los Angeles league chapter won sponsorship of its clubhouse from the *Herald*, one

---

[26] Morse, *Siege of University City*, pp. 738, 745–46, 768; *PB* 3, no. 4 (November 1910); *PB*, n.s., 1, no. 1 (December 1910); *WNW* 13, no. 89 (March 25, 1911); *BH* 4, no. 6 (November 1910); Weinstein, *Decline of Socialism*, p. 93.

of the city's major newspapers. Over 1,000 women, led by internationally recognized suffragist leader and Christian Socialist Caroline Severance, attended the dedication of the two-story, Craftsman bungalow
with shingling and cobblestone detail. Severance became California's
first registered woman voter in 1911. In 1910 the league held meetings
in Hemet, Orange, Pasadena, and Pomona, east and south of Los
Angeles, and in Santa Barbara, 100 miles to the north.[27]

Politically, then, California offered Lewis support. In another action of 1911, Lewis founded the American Woman's Republic. Emphasizing self-government by and for women, in a form parallel in its
particulars to the United States government, the group met in mid
1912 in University City. The convocation called for political secession
for a number of women's colonies, still headquartered in University
City, but physically dispersed, with an infrastructure beyond league
clubhouses. California was to provide the site for the first colony. The
Lewises traveled throughout California gathering support; Rhead lectured on their behalf at Stanford, the University of California, and at
Mills College. By December 1912 the California colony was planned
for the southern part of the state, with second and third colonies discussed for Florida and the Gulf Coast.[28] The American Woman's Republic sought the vote actively.

Lewis planned Atascadero, sited on 23,000 acres between Santa
Barbara and Monterey, as an agricultural colony. He adapted his community to a tree-filled location, which he then enhanced through landscaping, curvilinear streets, beaux arts core, parks, outlying orchards,
and experimental farmland (fig. 6). The western middle landscape reflected the mild climate, promoting the indoor-outdoor life. Most of
the houses were modest bungalows, ranging from $2,000 to $2,500 in

[27]*WND* 10, no. 65 (January 15, 1910): 14; *WND* 10, no. 71 (January 22, 1910):
14; *WND* 11, no. 2 (February 28, 1910): 3; *WND* 10, no. 96 (February 21, 1910): 7;
WND 11, no. 14 (March 14, 1910): 3; *WND* 11, no. 19 (March 21, 1910): 3; *WND*
12, no. 39 (September 17, 1910): 6; *WND* 13, no. 17 (December 19, 1910): 4; Morse,
Siege of University City, pp. 72–75; Weinstein, *Decline of Socialism*, pp. 94, 116.

[28]"Letter from Mr. Lewis Telling of the Campaign," *WNW* 13, no. 100 (June 24,
1911): 4; "The California Colony," *WNW* 15, no. 77 (December 21, 1912): 4; "Last
Day for the Colony Option," *WNW* 15, no. 81 (January 18, 1913): 5–6; "The Woman's
Republic," *WNW* 15, no. 92 (April 5, 1913): 3. Frederick H. Rhead to Taxile Doat,
Arequipa Sanitarium, Fairfax, Calif., October 15, 1911 (University City Public Library
Collections).

Fig. 6. Planned Civic Center, Atascadero, Calif., 1914. Watercolor rendering from *Atascadero Colony Bulletin* 5 (October 1914). (University City Public Library.)

cost, with a few more elaborate dwellings built. Lewis hired San Francisco's Bliss and Faville to design the community. The domed central-cross, brick-faced reinforced concrete administration building was under construction in mid 1914 but was not completed until 1918. The printery, completed in 1916, was Atascadero's second public building in use. Again Lewis intended to build a publishing empire. *Atascadero News* was in production in early 1916, with *Illustrated Review* following in 1917. By 1918 Lewis also issued *Back to the Land* and further orchestrated supplements for the San Francisco *Chronicle* and the Los Angeles *Times*. Even before the printery was operational, Lewis had been publishing *Atascadero Colony Bulletin* from University City, since 1913. Doat designed and executed ceramic heraldic plaques for Atascadero's public buildings.[29]

Other key features for the community core included the Atascadero Inn, designed to have the dining room overlooking the plaza, with all rooms on the upper floor provided with sleeping porches; an opera

[29] Karen J. Weitze, "Utopian Place Making: The Built Environment in Arts and Crafts California," in *The Arts and Crafts Movement in California: Living the Good Life,* ed. Kenneth R. Trapp (New York: Abbeville Press, 1993), pp. 84–87.

house, planned to have lecture and club rooms as well as opera facilities; and a department store, approached from a series of terraces rising from extensive gardens. Europe's entry into World War I and the immediate changes following in the economy of the United States severely affected Lewis's abilities to get his new California town built. The opera house existed in design only, while the hotel and department store were combined as a single structure, redesigned by St. Louis architect John J. Roth. Lewis was successful in the construction of a federated church in 1917 and the Cloisters, the colony's beachside hotel, in 1919. A hospital, lumber mill, and several industrial buildings completed the town. Lewis included a pro-rated portion of civic buildings and improvements costs in the price of a residential lot, with part of the department store profits reverting to each landowner in the colony. As at University City, a college was integral to Lewis's planning. At Atascadero, however, the necessity of a grammar school superseded a continuation of a Peoples University scheme. The grammar school opened in 1914. Bliss and Faville additionally designed a permanent-residence apartment building, with health care facilities for its elderly occupants, but this structure also remained unbuilt. In 1913 Rhead moved to nearby Santa Barbara; in August of the same year Doat visited Atascadero, with plans to reestablish an art porcelain manufactory after the war. Doat's permanent return to France in 1915 cut short plans to exhibit University City pottery at that year's San Francisco world's fair and implicitly ended plans for the Atascadero art pottery works as well. University City pottery did arrive in Atascadero, some remaining there today.[30]

Lewis's visions for the American Woman's Republic colony at Atascadero were again dressed as a futuristic, utopian landscape. Lewis connected a gleaming central core; bungalows in the hills; a separate, productive, yet healthful industrial section; farms; and another Peoples University by a trackless electric trolley. He intended colony products to be sent by rail to University City, and, once again, distributed by the mails. Atascadero was planned as a kind of model town exhibit for travelers between the Panama Pacific International Exposition in San Francisco in 1915 and the Panama California Exposition in San Diego

[30]"Three Cars on the Way," *Atascadero News,* July 15, 1916.

in 1915–16; as the Southern Pacific train passed the outskirts of Atascadero at its east, nightly, the town was to be awash in electric lighting.
World War I, coupled with Lewis's persistent troubles with the federal
government, caused the collapse of his political empire. The league
and the American Woman's Republic disintegrated, partly encouraged
through the general acceptance of progressivism following Woodrow
Wilson's election in 1912 and certainly made final by the achievement
of the woman's federal vote in 1920. Atascadero settled as a back-to-the-
land community, attracting mostly retired, older couples seeking a life
modeled after Bolton Hall's *Three Acres and Liberty* and *A Little Land
and a Living*, first published in 1907 and 1908, and subsequently
widely circulated.[31]

Lewis's arts and crafts middle landscape focused on the characteristics present in the University City-to-Atascadero development. The utopian, model community attributes in both the Midwest and California
included a carefully selected natural site; intensive man-made landscaping with deliberate adaptation to the site and attention to climate; a
formalized civic plan with attention to streets, street furniture, introduced plantings, parks, vistas, viewsheds, interrelated public building
design and spatial arrangement, and a highlighted Olmstedian residential component; a powerful patron; a distinct group of community
members; and, most significant, an influential literati heavily immersed
in the arts. The women's movement, printed publications, self-
conscious discussion of community goals, and specific regard for the
crafted arts, particularly pottery, were other constants. The arts and
crafts full-scale civic endeavor is distinct from the religious utopia, the
industrial town, the agricultural colony, the Garden City, and the
picturesque suburb as an early twentieth-century planned place and
offers another view of the complexities of turn-of-the-century American
life. Although definite characteristics were held in common, the arts
and crafts town, too, existed apart from the arts and crafts artisan-
craftsman colony of this same period, such as Elbert Hubbard's Roycroft at East Aurora, New York, Rose Valley outside Philadelphia, and

---

[31] "A Vision of the Future," WNW 15, no. 87 (March 1, 1913): 4; "Another Very
Interesting Letter from California," WNW 15, no. 90 (March 22, 1913): 4; Bolton Hall,
Three Acres and Liberty (New York: Macmillan Co., 1907); Bolton Hall, *A Little Land
and a Living* (New York: Arcadia Press, 1908).

the California enclaves established in the Berkeley-Oakland hills and
the Pasadena Arroyo Seco. The arts and crafts town achieved a physical
form beyond that previously sought by clustered idealists, combining
art and politics and shifting a traditional view of religion toward a
nature-based futurism.